WINE
FOR
NORMAL
PEOPLE

A Guide for Real People Who Like Wine,

BUT NOT THE SNOBBERY THAT GOES WITH IT

Elizabeth
SCHNEIDER

Certified Sommelier, Certified Specialist
of Wine, MBA, Normal Wine Person

CHRONICLE BOOKS
SAN FRANCISCO

Library of Congress Cataloging-in-Publication Data available.

ISBN 978-1-4521-7134-0

Manufactured in China.

Design by Kelley Galbreath.
Maps and Illustrations by Crystal Cox.

10 9 8 7 6 5 4

Airbnb is a registered trademark of Airbnb, Inc.; B-52 is a registered trademark of
The Boeing Company; Band-Aid is a registered trademark of Johnson & Johnson
Corporation; Beastie Boys is a registered trademark of Beastie Boys Michael
Diamond, Adam Horowitz and Adam Yauch; Coke is a registered trademark of
The Coca-Cola Company; Cornell University is a registered trademark of Cornell
University Educational Corporation; Court of Master Sommeliers is a registered
trademark of Court of Master Sommeliers, American Chapter Nonprofit Mutual
Benefit Corporation; Finding Dory is a registered trademark of Disney Enterprises,
Inc.; Goldschlager is a registered trademark of Sazerac Brands, LLC; Google is a
registered trademark of Google LLC; Hobbits and Lord of the Rings are a registered
trademark of The Saul Zaentz Company; Jell-O is a registered trademark of
Kraft Foods Group Brands LLC; Kahlúa is a registered trademark of The Absolut
Company; Mad Libs is a registered trademark of Penguin Random House LLC;
Magic 8 Ball is a registered trademark of Mattel, Inc.; Merriam-Webster is a
registered trademark of Merriam-Webster, Incorporated; Nissan is a registered
trademark of Nissan Jidosha Kabushiki Kaisha TA Nissan Motor Co., Ltd.; Noxzema
is a registered trademark of Alberto-Culver USA, Inc.; Nutella is a registered
trademark of Ferrero S.P.A.; Peanuts by Schulz is a registered trademark of Peanuts
Worldwide LLC; Popov is a registered trademark of Sazerac Brands, LLC; QR
code is a registered trademark of Denso Wave Incorporated; Smurfs is a registered
trademark of Studio Peyo S.A. Company; Sotheby's is a registered trademark of
SPTC, Inc.; Sprite is a registered trademark of The Coca-Cola Company; Star Wars
is a registered trademark of Lucasfilm Ltd. LLC; Tour de France is a registered
trademark of Societe Du Tour De France; Toyota is a registered trademark of
Toyota Jidosha Kabushiki Kaisha; Twinkies is a registered trademark of Hostess
Brands, LLC; University of North Carolina is a registered trademark of University
of North Carolina at Chapel Hill, The Educational Institution; US Weekly is a
registered trademark of AMI Celebrity Publications, LLC; Where's Waldo is a
registered trademark of DreamWorks Distribution Limited; Wine Spectator is a
registered trademark of M. Shanken Communications, Inc.; Winebow is a registered
trademark of The Winebow Group, LLC.

Chronicle books and gifts are available at special quantity discounts to cor-
porations, professional associations, literacy programs, and other organi-
zations. For details and discount information, please contact our premiums
department at corporatesales@chroniclebooks.com or at 1-800-759-0190.

Chronicle Books LLC
680 Second Street
San Francisco, California 94107
www.chroniclebooks.com

Dedication

TO M.C. ICE AND ALL THE PODCAST LISTENERS (MY WINE TRIBE)
WITHOUT WHOM *WINE FOR NORMAL PEOPLE* WOULD NEVER EXIST.
AND TO MY LITTLE SHINING STARS, ARIANA AND VIVIAN.

CONTENTS

CONTENTS CONT.

5

Old World Regions • 94

6

New World Regions • 234

EVERY

YOU NEED

ABOUT

in Two

THING
TO KNOW
WINE

Pages

started working at a big hulking winery fresh out of business school.

In my first week on the job in sunny California, I was talking to a few people about Italian wines I liked and I mentioned Dolcetto as a favorite. That's when he pounced! My snotty, arrogant new boss was Johnny-on-the-spot, and as he was heading toward the printer he not-so-casually stopped and said, "OK, if it's your favorite, tell me this: Is Dolcetto a grape or a region?" I was caught off guard.

Using my basic wine knowledge (again, mostly with the experience of lifting the glass from table to mouth, but with some wine classes, too), I tried to deduce the answer. I knew that the wine was Italian and most wines from Italy were named by region, so I took an educated guess. I said it was a region.

His welcome-to-your-new-job, helpful response? "It's a grape. I guess you don't know as much about wine as I thought you did, Miss Wine Lover. Better hit the books."

I stayed there for about four years and I've been in the industry for another ten so I've learned that these lavish displays of schmuck-ery are everywhere in wine. The only thing you can do is walk away from these wine peacocks without losing it on them, and maintain your dignity by realizing that you are NOT a moron, you're just on a normal-person learning curve. Wine is one of the few subjects I know of in which many people in the industry discourage you from learning yet put you down for not knowing stuff.

The best analogy for our journey into wine is learning a foreign language: You're not fluent on day one, and part of the fun of study is that you can always learn more! Further, immersion is the only way to truly know the subject. In wine, basics like wine vocabulary, geography, naming conventions, and pronunciations can get you on your way to fluency. So that's what I aim to give you in this book: the basics, plus more if you want to take your knowledge further. Use the book how you want and know that my aim is to make the sections easy to understand, exciting to explore, and a little quirky and funny because there's no reason to be boring and lame when writing about something that's for pure pleasure!

To help contextualize vocabulary, region, or customs, you'll see question-and-answer boxes throughout the book. These are questions I've received countless times from normal people who listen to the *Wine for Normal People* podcast and attend my classes and events, and from my husband, M.C. Ice, who is a normal wine person and co-podcaster, and whose name you will see throughout the book. I've inserted the questions where they're most needed, in the hope that I can preempt confusion around certain issues by calling them out. I won't get them all, so you can always find me online and I'll answer whatever I didn't get here (and use it in the second printing, so thank you in advance!).

Note: While we'll be exploring wine worldwide, for simplicity, dollar amounts given in this book refer to US dollars.

of fermented grapes. And our first vocabulary term.

NORMAL WINE PERSON: This is someone who likes wine, likes drinking wine, and likes learning about wine but doesn't like people talking down to him or her or participating in one-upmanship of knowing this arcane fact and that random producer. On the other extreme, he or she doesn't want wine to be totally demystified because who wants the subject so dumbed down that it's no longer challenging or interesting? If this is you, you're a normal wine person (regardless of your weirdness in other areas of your life, which you don't have to share).

Wine Is a Game of Geography and Vocabulary

And now, to conclude the introduction, I'm going to wave my magic wand and reveal to you the secret to learning wine. Once I tell you this, you may not need the hundreds of other pages I've slaved over but I'll take that risk.

If you need no further detail once you read the answer, drop the book and watch some bad TV. If you want more, let's start with the basics on wine words and get into wine, for normal people.

So what's the real secret to understanding wine? It's all in the vocabulary and the geography. If you have a handle on these two things, you'll be at one with the world

1

LET'
IT ON T
A REAL A
t
TASTIN
TALKIN

S GET

IE TABLE

PPROACH

G AND

G WINE

t's a modern-day miracle that I continued drinking wine after my first interactions with it. In my early twenties I had absolutely no idea there was a lexicon behind fermented grapes that I was required to know to communicate with wine people. I ridiculously thought you could just drink the stuff and read a little to learn about it. The hubris!

I was quickly schooled when my sister and I went to wine tastings or to wine shops around Boston and tried to talk to the staff; each interaction became an exercise in humiliation. As I walked out of any given wine store with sweaty palms, a flushed face, and god-knows-what in the bottle, I also left with my self-esteem tucked away somewhere in the Cabernet aisle. And since I didn't know what exactly Cabernet was (grape? region? blend?), it was likely my confidence would sit next to dark, big-shouldered bottles for eternity.

I don't joke when I tell you that people would say entire sentences where I understood every individual word, but had no idea what the words meant once strung together. Stuff like the following:

The Chardonnay is expertly balanced. It's got nervy acidity and mineral components that offset the oaky, lightly astringent, but fuller-bodied textures. This is one to lay down—Old World wines have great ageability.

Yikes.

It took years before I heard something like that and got the gist of what people were talking about. Maybe that's where you are now and why you're reading this book; you're questioning why this inexplicable language exists, while trying to get a handle on what it all means.

If it helps at all, here's the truth: Wine has its own lingo. It's annoying. It's

frustrating. Wine people use words that we know in regular life in completely different contexts. Catching up on this insider world is like walking into the middle of a movie—you're going to need to get up to speed to watch along with everyone else, but it's really hard to ask for a quick recap from someone in the silence of the theater. No one wants to take the time to explain the plot to you. I've been there: From the minute I got iced out of conversations about wine with people who knew more than I did, I wished this jargon would go away.

I still sort of wish people would be transparent when describing wine. And when I was a brand marketer, I wished people would use plain English instead of talking about "core competencies" and "impactful messaging" and "bandwidth." But I've come to terms with the vocab by drawing on my time in high tech. Maybe I can make this parallel and give you peace of mind, too.

I've realized that there is something to be said for words that are specific to certain industries, and although at first glance it seems stupid, some words are distinct and useful in describing wine.

But that doesn't resolve the main issue with wine words: The terms are ill defined and overused. So, in this chapter, I start with the premise that if we can get definitions on the table and truly unpack what these words mean in plain English, then

LET'S GET THIS PARTY STARTED

If you're going to taste—as opposed to chug—wine, you're going to need some equipment.

GLASSWARE: Make sure your glass is clear and has a stem. Heat from your hand warms the wine, changing the flavors in the glass. You may not like me saying this, but stemless glasses are no good for our purposes.

WHITE SURFACE AND GOOD LIGHTING: A piece of paper, a napkin, a tablecloth, really anything white, and a place with bright enough light are *musts*. You need to be able to look at the wine, and you need a white surface to do that. In my classes and tastings, I always say if you pay good money to go to a wine tasting somewhere and the organizers have black tablecloths and black napkins, get a refund. Total rookie move. If you don't want the refund, at least get someone to give you a white napkin. I'll explain why this is so important in a minute, but trust me, you need it.

DON'T OVERFILL, NO EXTRANEOUS SMELLS: You need swirling room. Filling the glass one-third or less for serious tasting (and one-half or less for drinking where you're paying less attention to this process) presents the best odds for getting what you need out of the wine without spilling it everywhere. And stay away from yummy kitchen smells, scented candles, or perfume—you need a place to taste without competing smells.

we can get through a lot of BS in wine. I know that you already know the standard terms and you're probably schooled in how to taste wine, but we're taking things a step further now and delving deeper. In my mind, wine lexicon is so fundamental to understanding wine that vocabulary must be a legit chapter and it has to be our start. It can't be tucked in the back of a book and written in a clinical manner. "Wine speak" is the first chapter because it's a foundation for what follows.

I've tried to make it interesting, and to pick the words that wine people use all the time but maybe don't fully understand. My hope is that you connect with my descriptions, that you remember them, and that you use them in the right way, so they start to have meaning. Hey, *in vino veritas* starts with us, right? So here's a normal look at the lexicon of wine tasting and other important wine terms.

THE BASICS OF TASTING TALK

Let's start with something you definitely know about: tasting wine.

This process involves a lot of ceremony, but once you get it down, you'll see that it doesn't involve a lot of creativity. Still, there are tons of terms to know and that's what we'll tackle here. All wine people, more or less, stick with the following tasting process.

SEE: Look at the wine. Notice the color and any special (or gross) characteristics.
SWIRL: Aerate the wine by swirling it around in the glass.

SNIFF: Put your nose in the glass and smell the beautiful (hopefully not icky) things you are about to taste.

SIP: Take a sip and swish it around your mouth. Notice the flavors and textures of the wine.

SIZE UP: Enjoy the fruits of the laborious process. Decide if you like what's in the glass.

Got it? I think we're done here. Now I can crack a bottle of Syrah and call it a day.

OK, OK, I'm not going to leave it there. That defeats my goal of being more helpful than other wine people you've encountered. That said, I *am* going to leave the nuanced mechanics of tasting to those folks and instead explain the three most important steps of tasting and the most significant terms that go with them: sight, smell, and taste. This should help you appreciate wine more and feel comfortable that you have good judgment about what you've tasted. That way, if you go to a wine tasting or decide to have one with your cat on a Tuesday night, you'll know how to pinpoint what you like in a wine and convey that to someone who may be in a position to help get you a wine you like (a wine shop person or server, for example).

THE THREE STEPS OF TASTING AND THE JARGON THAT GOES WITH THEM

Step #1: Sight Words

Look at the wine . . . because you should always look at something before it goes in your mouth.

I'm amazed at how many people get a glass of wine in a restaurant or at a friend's house, lift it to their mouth, and sip without looking inside the glass. Would you ever stick food in your mouth without glancing at it? I wouldn't. Wine is a product of nature and of chemical reactions. Things can go awry in the winemaking process and even more in transport and storage. So before you get fancy and start analyzing if it's ruby-garnet or gold-rimmed platinum, let's get serious: To prevent a disgusting experience, look at the wine in the glass.

Clarity Words and UFOs (Unidentified Floating Objects)

You look into your glass and something is amiss. How would you describe it? Here are some common tip-offs that your wine is skunked.

CLOUDY: This may not be a flaw if the wine is unfiltered, but you should proceed with caution and spend some extra time sniffing before you sip. If something is wrong, don't drink it!

SEPARATED OR WATERY: The wine is a red color on the bottom with a thick layer of clear on top, or some variation of this. This separation is likely caused by temperature control issues in storage or transport. Expect a bad wine.

FOAMING: Unless it's sparkling wine, bacteria has been here and the wine is probably spoiled.

BROWN: If it's brown and it's a younger wine, most likely heat or bacteria has affected this bottle. Down the sink!

CRYSTALS FLOATING AT THE BOTTOM: In whites, this isn't a flaw, but you need a filter. These are tartrate crystals (pieces of tartaric acid bonded together), and they're salty, hard, and gross to drink. Get 'em out of the glass by using a mesh filter or even a small spoon to dig them out.

LARGE PIECES OF CORK OR SEDIMENT: Get those floaters out! Don't drink this until you get a filter.

Pretty Color Words and Their Utility Beyond Snobbery

If you want to gather intel on a wine, you need to see its true color. But when I tell most people to pick up a glass of wine and look at it, you know what most, if not all, do? They hold the glass up to the light. When you do that, you see the light . . . and the ceiling, the wall, and the details of the light fixture. That's distracting, and it's going to prevent you from seeing the color of the wine. Instead, get that glass on an unadulterated white surface where it can show you its story. If you hold the glass at a 45° angle on a white surface, you'll see

Q+A

Why would I need to look at the color to learn about the wine? As far as I can tell that is a near-useless skill. I already know it's red, white, or rosé.

OK, hear me out. Color can give you clues about what you're about to pop in your mouth—yet another reason to look at your wine. But you're right, to make this skill useful, you need to know how to interpret what you see, so now let's figure out what this info is telling us. Rather than do this in general terms, we'll consider an example and discuss what the wine is telling us.

variations as the color fans out along the side of the glass.

Hue, as with everything in wine description, is subjective. Check out the box on page 20 for some ideas of how to describe color.

Example: A Golden, Brassy White Wine

I pour you a glass of a yellow-gold wine. When you give it a swirl, the legs are thick and gloppy as they run down the sides of the glass (longer explanation later, but legs are the rivulets of liquid that drip after the wine has settled in the glass from swirling it around).

Without smelling or drinking the wine, you already have clues about what to expect. For instance, there are only a few things

BASIC WINE COLOR DESCRIPTIONS

WHITE	RED	ROSÉ
Clear	Brown	Pink
Light/Pale	Ruby	Salmon
Greenish	Garnet	Copper
Straw/hay colored	Brick red	Orange
Yellow	Crimson/blood red	Light red
Golden/brassy	Orange	
Amber	Purple/black	

that make a white wine this dark: Certain grape varieties like Viognier and Gewürz-traminer have more pigmented skins when ripened to full potential. If the skins sit with the wine for a while before fermentation, this can make the wine golden.

In addition, these grapes were probably grown in a warm climate. Think of this: If you grow an orange in a cool climate and one in a warm climate, which will be bright orange in color, ripe, and fruity? The one grown in a warm climate. The one from the cool climate may have some unripe green or yellow spots and, when cut open, won't be juicy. The same goes for grapes. Darkly colored grapes can only exist when they've basked in the sun and had time to develop pigment in their skins. In cooler climates with shorter growing seasons, there is neither the time nor the intensity of sunshine to get grapes that ripe, so they'll have a lighter color.

Ripeness can give us some clues about color, but other factors are even more significant in turning the wine golden.

OAK: After hanging around in an oak barrel for a while, the wine gathers oak tannin (I'll get to what this is in a second if you're not sure), which darkens it to a signature gold color.

SUR LIE AGING: Dark color can mean yeast corpses may have darkened the door. Wine aged on its *lies* (yeast that dies after fermentation is complete; more on that later) can also be darker, but it's not usually a dark yellow color, just a deeper shade of straw or hay.

SUGAR: Sweet wines are frequently darker because grapes used for these wines are a little shriveled. The grapes are picked later, water in the grapes evaporates, and the skin and its pigments are a bigger part of the wine, so the transfer of color from the skin is more prominent in sweet wines than in dry ones, where skin contact is limited.

AGE: Like dark age spots on white skin, age darkens white wine. A darker white wine could be old. Older white wines slowly move toward an amber color.

If you know the golden, brassy wine isn't old and isn't sweet, then it's probably going to be either oaky or fruity, or both. And thick legs will tell you alcohol is major, so expect a bigger, fuller-feeling wine in your mouth, and maybe some burn up your nose on the sniff. Just by looking—without putting your mouth to the glass—you already know what you're in for. Not bad, huh?

Step #2: Smell Words

Sniffing is the single most important step in wine tasting and description. Consequently, it's the area where most wine people speak BS.

But it's important to get this right: Consider that some experts estimate that about 90 percent of what we call taste or flavor is actually smell. While textures can make or break a wine, aromas are fundamental to your enjoyment of it.

Basic Smell Words

They're basic, but just so we're in lock step, let's define these procedural words.

AROMAS: The smells in wine that come from fruit. This term is usually associated with wines from a vintage within the last five years or so because younger wines smell more like fruit than older wines.

BOUQUET: The smells that develop with time in a bottle or that come from wine-making—nuts, spices, and creaminess fall into this category. As wines age, they pick up some other smells, which are usually

Q + A

Damn! Is this how wine people seem to know so much about a wine before drinking it?

Yup. You can flip these rules to draw conclusions and they'll be spot-on. Pale whites (and lighter reds) usually indicate high acid wines and lower alcohol—less ripeness means acidity isn't baked out by the sun and sugars don't reach a level where the juice ferments to high alcohol levels. If the wine is nearly opaque with thick legs, it's going to be from a warm climate (think of the very orange orange from a warm area), with lots of fruit flavor and a strong punch of alcohol. Are there exceptions? Yes, but these guidelines should help form some idea of what you're in for.

great but definitely differ from what originally came from a vine.

NOSE: The smell of a wine, its aromas, its bouquet, and everything else that you sense with your nose.

SWIRLING: I bring this up to remind you that you can't do this in a wussy fashion. Please don't just swish the wine up the sides a little and call it a day. Since you heeded my earlier procedural note and didn't fill the glass up all the way (page 17), you aren't going to spill the wine. So get some wrist action going for 10 to 15 seconds. Let the air integrate with the wine before you stick your nose in the glass. That splashing around will activate the smell compounds in the wine—the esters and the aldehydes, for the dorks among you—to let the wine show you its

best aromas. Even if you put it in a decanter and let it sit for hours, a little jaunt around the glass will help reactivate any smells that may be lying dormant. *Do it.*

DOGGY SNIFFS: (This is a *Wine for Normal People* technical term.) You may need to think on this for a second. How does a dog sniff the ground? If you don't know, next time you see a pup, check her out. I watch my Welsh terrier Ellie all the time. She puts her nose to the ground and takes short little sniffy-doggy inhales. You know what she doesn't do? Inhale like she was sniffing a Thanksgiving turkey. Wine sniffing is not inhale-like-it's-your-last-breath sniffing. This is a delicate inhale so you can gather information without overwhelming your smell receptors/olfactory bulb/brain.

If you don't fatigue your nose, you can go back in for another sniff and get more information from the wine. If you sniff it like you're an aardvark near an ant colony, you're going to kill your nose receptors, just like when you go past a perfume counter in a store and can't smell anything except the nastiness they just squirted on you.

Q+A

My nose isn't sensitive. I never get it right when people describe wine to me. In fact, I can't describe it at all because I'm just not smelling what they get in the glass.

I don't accept this. Here's how smell works: Take a whiff of something and if it's scented it will bond with a receptor in your nose. That receptor sends a message upstream to your olfactory bulb, which processes the smell and sends it to your brain. Your brain IDs the smell and decides if it's something you know and like.

Humans don't have that many smell receptors—only about 5 million. By comparison, dogs have somewhere between 220 and 300 million receptors and special anatomy for sniffing stuff out. They're the real experts. Still, humans are pretty adept at naming and distinguishing smells. Through training, humans can name up to 10,000 scents. Some new evidence suggests that if we actually pay attention, humans may be able to distinguish between 1 trillion smells! So you can do this!

Meaningful Descriptions of Wine Smells and Flavors

One of the big sticking points for most people is the "name up to 10,000 scents." We don't always have the words for what we smell, and that can make us shut down when we're thinking about wine because it's overwhelming. I think it helps to add context to descriptions, and that's what the rest of this section aims to do, along with actually sharing a list of words that people commonly use to describe wine so you're in the know. When we're done, you should be better able to articulate what you smell in a glass. When we've nailed that, we'll take a tangent and get serious about how to fill in gaps in your tasting vocabulary so the words become meaningful and useful for you.

Let's Start with Bad, Bad Smells

Between earth, man, and van (or boat or train or plane), there are countless ways a wine can go off the tracks. I'm only going to hit on the big ones here, but if you come across another one, be confident that the stink is not in your head.

OFF: A catchall tasting description for nasty-tasting things in a wine. If something tastes bad in a wine and it's not just bad winemaking or poorly grown fruit, it's off. Use this word if you don't want to get more specific on the variety of bad—it's a safe umbrella term.

CORKED: This should technically go in the "winemaking" vocab, but given that it's something you experience as smell or flavor, it makes more sense here. For the dorks among you, a wine is corked when chemicals called TCA (2,4,6-trichloroanisole) or TBA (2,4,6-tribromoanisole) inhabit the liquid. The wine will taste/smell like a wet basement, moldy paper, or a dirty wet dog (just for the record, Ellie smells great when she's wet; this is for other dogs). Sometimes it smells like old potpourri or moldy, dried flowers.

You can't usually detect TCA/TBA from smelling the cork; you need to smell the wine to see if it's OK. This is a main reason waitstaff pour you a sample in a restaurant. Humans are really sensitive to TCA/TBA, so when they're present it doesn't take much digging to find. Trust yourself. If it's bad, bring it back to the wine shop or send it back in a restaurant. Since anywhere from 0.25 percent to 5 percent of bottles have cork taint, don't second-guess yourself. Chances are, you're right.

As a nerdy aside, you may be surprised to know that although it occurs more often in bottles that have a cork closure, cork taint can happen with a synthetic cork or screw cap, too. TCA/TBA can lurk around in barrels, on untreated wooden pallets that hold boxes of wine getting ready to ship out, and on winery walls and floors, just waiting to do its destructive dance on any nearby wine.

OXIDIZED: When too much oxygen gets into a wine, it can taste like vinegar or rusted metal. It's a sour/bitter sensation that makes

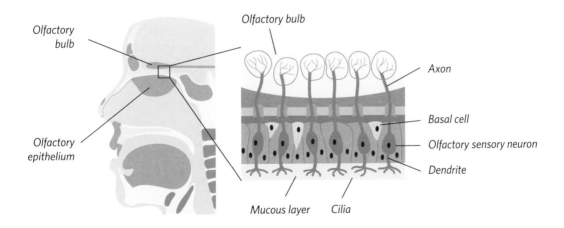

Olfactory bulb

Olfactory bulb

Olfactory epithelium

Axon

Basal cell

Olfactory sensory neuron

Dendrite

Mucous layer   Cilia

your jaw clench a little and tastes like a rusty spoon or bad salad dressing. Sometimes a wine can *look* oxidized, so you'll get a clue before you smell and sip—it will be an amber color if it's a white wine or a bricky brown if it's a red. If it's oxidized, pour it down the sink; it's a lost cause.

MICROBIAL SPOILAGE OR VOLATILE ACIDITY: Spoilage happens when nasty wine bacteria ruins the wine. Acetic acid bacteria (spread by fruit flies) is found on grape skins. These bacteria can build during the fermentation process, with yeast pitching in to make the flavor even worse. Every wine has some volatile acidity, but if it's too strong, the wine smells like vinegar, nail polish remover, or nasty chemicals. Volatile acidity can actually "blow off" after a little decanting, and some people think it adds interesting flavors to a wine, but that's only when the levels are low. If you're noticing a pungent, vile vinegar note when you smell the wine, ditch this bottle before you sip it. Otherwise, try the decanting trick, and if it works, drink away.

SULFUR COMPOUNDS: These can manifest in a few ways. Scents like rotten eggs, garlic, or rubber are there to stay (hydrogen sulfide) so pour out the glass or order a new one. Burnt match (sulfur dioxide used as a preservative in wine) will usually disappear after a few minutes if you let it sit or you swirl the wine in the glass a few times.

WINE THAT SMELLS LIKE IT'S BEEN COOKED: Wine shouldn't smell cooked or like hot jam. If it does, it's been exposed to heat. Sometimes you can detect a problem if there are stains up the cork (if the wine is red) or if the cork is slightly pushed out of the bottle. Wine people call this cooked quality "maderized" since the Portuguese wine, Madeira, is deliberately cooked to get a special flavor (see the Portugal section on page 210 to learn more). In a regular wine, however, it's completely unacceptable.

Wine's Awesome Smells

Before I lay all this out, I'll remind you again that no one's "smell experience" is the same. Each of us has different DNA and different experiences that lead to our recognizing certain smells and calling them what we think they are. What I think is lemon, you may be sure is lime. Some terms are obvious; some need explanation. Rest assured, I'm including ones you know and ones that may be obscure for the sake of thoroughness, not because I think you have no idea what an apple is.

In my mind, there are four basic categories to think about when you're smelling wine: fruity stuff, herbs and spices, outdoor smells, and additions from the winemaker.

Fruity Stuff

FRUITY FLAVORS: Many wines (but not all) smell like fruit. Grapes are a fruit so that makes sense. What doesn't make sense is that most wines don't smell like grapes. We'll talk about this in the "How Wine Gets Its Flavor" chapter (page 60), but just as a preview, compounds in certain types of grapes make them smell similar to things you know and love—raspberries, blackberries, apples, green peppers. If a wine is from the New World (anywhere but Europe), there's a high probability it's going to smell like fruit.

But how do you know if what you're smelling is cherry vs. strawberry, as many wine descriptors state? Or plum vs. blackberry? With time and experience, you'll be able to determine small differences between fruits. If you can't, a great shortcut is to determine categories.

- Is it dark fruit (blackberry, plums)?
- Is it berrylike (strawberry, raspberry)?
- Is it citrusy (lemon, grapefruit)?

Just getting in the ballpark will help you begin to describe the wine or understand other people's descriptions of these smells.

Herbs and Spices

GREEN/HERBACEOUS: Think of freshly cut herbs such as thyme, basil, oregano, or tarragon—or freshly mowed grass—and you'll understand this green sensation. Green pepper is a common flavor in Cabernet Franc, Cabernet Sauvignon, and Sauvignon Blanc. It's the chemical methoxypyrazine that gives green pepper its distinctive smell, and it's also present in these grapes (so it makes sense they'd smell similarly).

SPICY: Some wines have a prickly sensation; when you sniff them they make your nose twitch, and when you taste them they make your tongue tingle. Some smell like black pepper (Zinfandel, Syrah) or white pepper (Grüner Veltliner). Some have spice aromas like cardamom (think chai tea) or cumin (Gewürztraminer comes to mind). Others that have been in oak for a while smell like cinnamon, cloves, or nutmeg. Wine people will make a distinction between baking spices and pepper or other types of spices. Hit your spice rack and smell the contents of the containers if you're unfamiliar with these scents. You'll find them often in your glass.

Outdoor Smells

EARTHY: To understand earthiness, you're going to have to play in the dirt. I don't care if you live in New York, Toronto, London, or Hong Kong—you can get your hands on a potted plant or go to a garden or nursery and snag some soil to smell. If you want to "get" earthiness, you gotta smell different

earthy things. Look for potting soil to understand dark earth notes, dried dirt for that dusty sensation, and crushed gravel for mineral notes (which I'll detail in a second). If you encounter "earth" in a garden shop or in nature, put it in a plastic bag and bring some home. Next time you have a Bordeaux or a Tempranillo, pull out the potting soil or dried, dusty earth, respectively, and sniff it. Then you'll know what earthiness is in wine. It's one of the easier terms to figure out once you have the tools at your disposal.

MINERAL: Have you ever been near a waterfall? The water is crashing down around you and you smell a distinct, metallic note. If that doesn't conjure up a notion of what "mineral" smells like for you, imagine you're sitting on a rock at a park on a hot day. The rock has a certain smell as it heats up in the sun. If you spill some water on it, you can smell it even more. That's mineral.

I'll warn you: Mineral/minerally/minerality is a broad descriptor. It includes stuff like waterfalls, streams, chalk dust, hot rocks, slate, and any other lighter earthy smell that isn't dust, potting soil, and "dark earth" smells. I find that of all smells in wines, the mineral category is the most spot-on. When you pay attention, you'll smell an uncanny similarity to rocks, chalk, etc., in a glass, so look for it, especially in European whites.

BARNYARD/GAMY: "Barnyard" and "gamy" are slightly different terms, but are usually used in tandem. I know, they both sound like nothing you'd ever want in a wine. But combined with other components, they can be interesting and delicious. With good fruit and spice flavor, and kickin' acidity, a Pinot Noir from Burgundy that's a little goat-y is ridiculously tasty.

Wines that taste like a barnyard—think chickens running around, a touch of manure, hay, animal sweat, saddles—have a strong "sense of place." You know they aren't too many steps away from the land (and have less influence from the winemaker).

I can't do this smell justice with words. That earthy stank is something you have to catalog the next time you're near a farm so you can ID it in a Burgundy or a Bordeaux. Hit up Google for a petting zoo near you.

Gamy is a wild meat flavor that you sometimes find in a wine like Syrah or Mourvèdre. It tastes meaty (sometimes even like bacon) but also earthy. If you're not into eating wild game (rabbit, venison, pheasant), you can think about the smell of cooking meat and combine that with the smell underneath a shrub. And if you don't know what that smells like, climb under the privet hedge and take a whiff.

Generally "barnyard" and "gamy" are acquired tastes. I don't know many people who love these flavors right off the bat. Some winemakers argue that they're flaws, but given that the wines displaying these flavors are generally from highly esteemed areas, I'd say it's a style and sometimes a good one at that.

FLORAL: Because of certain chemical compounds in grapes (like esters and terpenes) wines can smell like flowers. Whites often smell like gardenia, jasmine, lily, and orange blossoms. Depending on the producer and region where they are grown, you'll likely find some or all of these notes in Riesling, Viognier, Muscat, or Torrontes. Reds can smell like roses, violets, or even lavender. Nebbiolo is known for its distinctive rose notes; Merlot, Cabernet Sauvignon, Malbec, Gamay, and Sangiovese can have violet aromas; and Syrah and Grenache can smell like lavender. If you like these lovely outdoor aromas, you'll love finding them in the glass. If not, at least now you have a good list of which wines to avoid.

PETROL/GASOLINE: This may sound gross, but petrol is part and parcel of wines that are from *some place* as opposed to wines that could be from *any place*. Riesling, especially, when it's been in a bottle for a few years, develops a chemical compound that creates a petrol/gasoline quality. It's not harmful; no one dumped gas in your wine. It's actually caused by a chemical compound (1,1,6-trimethyl-1,2-dihydronaphthalene or TDN) that's created during the aging process as acids change in the bottle. Wines made from ripe or late harvest grapes that grow on slate soils in vineyards with good light exposure, and are from regions that don't practice irrigation (basically the definition of top German Riesling regions), are more likely to show petrol notes. If you like Riesling and you like it a bit aged, get used to that smell. It's part of the grape's pedigree.

Additions from the Winemaker

VANILLA/CARAMEL/BUTTERSCOTCH/SMOKE FLAVORS: Where do they come from? If you taste vanilla, burnt sugar/caramel, dill, coconut, cloves, cinnamon, nutmeg, or even smoke, you're tasting the effects of oak aging. Some winemakers consider oak to be their "spice rack" and use it to add flavor to the wines (more of a New World philosophy). Others prefer to use oak for its other benefits, like color and tannin stabilization. Depending on the barrel (wood type matters, which we'll get into in great depth in Chapter 3) and how much

it's toasted, you'll get varying amounts of oak influence in your wine. No matter what, I can promise you that the flavors mentioned here are not characteristics of grapes, so if you taste them, oak was used!

BUTTERY/CREAMY: Malolactic fermentation is a secondary fermentation that converts tart malic acid (think green apple) present in the grapes to soft lactic acid (creamy round sensation). It happens in most reds and some whites and can happen spontaneously or be encouraged by winemakers with the addition of bacteria. Wines that are high in acid often benefit from this process because they taste creamy and soft after MLF, as this process is often called for short (you'll also hear ML or malo).

The problem with malolactic fermentation is that it has to be controlled, and when it's not, you get wines that may be excessively buttery or creamy. Have you ever tasted a Chardonnay and swear you just licked butter? A chemical by-product called diacetyl produced during malolactic fermentation yields those nutty, caramel, butter, and cream flavors. A touch of it is fine—it can help round out a wine and lead to a tastier, longer-lasting finish, which is a great thing, especially in reds. But too much is nasty—especially in Chardonnay. It all depends on your personal taste.

"Malolactic fermentation" is an important term to know. If you don't like that buttery, creamy flavor or texture, look for wines like Chablis from Burgundy or German Riesling, where most of the Chardonnay doesn't undergo full MLF.

GET IN THE RING AND TRAIN THAT NOSE!

In my writing and gabbing, I'm as guilty of chucking out weird descriptions as anyone in the wine industry. Granted, they aren't as "out there" as some wine critics' descriptions (Syrah described as "meat blood" and Viognier as "buddleia"), but regardless of who says it, the descriptions for wine can leave you scratching your head or, worse, feeling bad about yourself.

Although some people are legitimately limited by their smell apparati (very few of us) and after age sixty our sense of smell declines, the overwhelming majority of us are just not training hard enough and forcing ourselves to work to recognize smells. If you look at drinking wine as an Olympic sport (it really should be, no?) and train for it constantly, you will find that you'll recognize things you never could before.

C'mon Rocky. Let's cue up "Eye of the Tiger" from 1982 and get you in training mode because that's how you're going to start recognizing this stuff.

To get started in identifying important smells and flavors in wine, check out the Wine Tasting Sheet (page 332), which has detailed vocabulary that I use in my classes. Keep them in front of you when you're tasting wine, and those terms on the tip of your brain will miraculously materialize when you see them on paper!

TO START YOUR TRAINING, DO THESE TYPES OF THINGS:

- Actually smell your coffee before you drink it.
- Smell an apple before you bite into it.
- Sniff the lemon wedge after you squeeze it in your iced tea (and smell the tea while you're at it).
- Smell the cut grass of a freshly mowed lawn, or the roses in your garden, or the forest when you take a hike.
- Crack open everything in your spice rack and smell it all!

By becoming more in tune with what you smell, your brain will take note and create memories that you can more easily retrieve when you smell them in wine. At first you may want to have spices, teas, fruit, or dirt nearby to compare and pinpoint smells, but with time you won't need them. Eventually you'll gain a level of comfort with familiar smells, and describing them will become second nature.

Step #3: Taste Words

Now let's move to tasting, but with purpose. When you taste with purpose, you'll pay attention to how the wine feels in your mouth. Like all things wine, it's not as easy as it seems. Unless it's a simple, boring wine, the wine will change in your mouth in a matter of seconds. There are three basic phases wine people talk about when tasting: the attack, the mid-palate, and the finish.

THE ATTACK: Sounds unappetizing, right? (It's from a French term, but I hate it for its violence.) The attack is the first impression you have when the wine enters your mouth: the initial smells and flavors, the texture, the acidity, and the tannin (page 32). You'll note these immediately and have an opinion. That opinion may change, but this is your first reaction.

THE MID-PALATE: After holding the wine in your mouth for a second, right before you swallow, the wine may change. The flavors and sensations may intensify as the wine gets closer to your nasal receptors and they send clearer aromas to your brain for identification. If the wine sucks, the aromas and flavors may disappear before you swallow. People sometimes refer to that as a "hole." Like "there's a hole in the mid-palate." If the wine is good, you may get more interesting and subtle flavors you didn't pick up at first.

THE FINISH: These are the lasting flavors and sensations in your mouth after you swallow the wine.

PALATE: A general term for the overall impression of how a wine feels and tastes in your mouth. People may say things like "it smells really fruity, but on the palate it's more like rocks and herbs and it's mouthwatering."

Now the question is: How do you get an impression of the wine in each phase? To do that, you have to slow down your tasting. Here's how.

- Take a small sip of wine—enough so it can roll around your mouth.

- Hold it in your mouth and suck in air (only if you're home or you'll be banned from social events for making nasty wine noises).
- Roll it around in your mouth again to coat your cheeks and tongue.
- Wait a sec before swallowing.

Try it and see if you can identify the three phases of the wine. It may take time, but with practice you'll be sipping and describing the attack, the mid-palate, and the finish like a champ.

HOW TO GET RETRO NASAL AROMAS

After you taste the wine, you can get "retro nasal" smells by keeping your mouth closed, and then pushing air out of your nose steadily and forcefully. That will sometimes show you extra flavors or things to think about after the wine leaves your mouth.

Your Mouth: Its Limitations and Its Most Important Jobs

Your tongue and mouth are texture detectors. Although nowhere near as nuanced as smell, texture leads to your overall preference for the wine, so your mouth plays an important role, too. Remember, TEXTURE + AROMA = FLAVOR. It all needs to work together.

Your tongue and taste buds do several things. They sense salty, sweet, bitter, sour, umami (savory, like mushrooms or miso), and fat in anything you put in your mouth. Along with sensors in your cheeks, they can also detect structural stuff in the wine like weight or alcohol content, creaminess (from malolactic fermentation), mouth drying (from tannin), and mouthwatering (from acidity) sensations.

Your mouth will react, sometimes strongly, to certain elements in the wine depending on your genetic sensitivity and experiences with certain foods. Tart sensations from acidity really bother some people. Some love sugar and crave sweet wines. It's very personal! The feeling of the wine in your mouth is the (wine word) MOUTHFEEL.

For help with vocabulary on texture and finish (you can use the smell descriptors for flavor as well), look at the Wine Tasting Sheet (page 332) for descriptions that may be useful.

Structure Words

Although the word "structure" sounds either really snotty or like a men's clothing store from the '90s that carried an alarming amount of mustard-colored button-downs, we'll leave those and say that structure is the interplay between key components in wine and how they balance each other. The best way to explain structure is to get out of wine for a second and move to painting. For a painter to create a picture, he needs something to paint on. For many artists, that thing is a blank canvas.

What makes a canvas? Four pieces of wood, the glue and staples that hold them together, and the cloth stretched tight and secured over the wood. But what if something went awry in the canvas-making process and the wood pieces didn't quite line up right when put together? When the canvas is stretched, the whole thing is off balance, and the picture painted on this surface is going to be slanted to one side or in some way uneven. That skew will put you off no matter how beautiful the painter's creation. Wine's structure is similar.

Let's think about what makes a wine well constructed. It's not flavor; instead it's stuff like acid, tannin, alcohol, and sugar (or lack thereof). These are what make wine *wine* and not grape juice. In our painting analogy, these are the main slats of wood over which canvas is stretched. The aromas and flavors like fruit, dirt, spice, and whatever else you taste or smell are like da Vinci's *Mona Lisa* or Munch's *The Scream*: The artists' vision is in the color, form, and style on that canvas. Some people like Picasso, some prefer da Vinci, but without a canvas that's made right, we'd just have a floppy piece of fabric that can't be displayed.

So it goes with wine: no structure = no wine. Bad structure = bad wine that no amount of flavor/finesse/pretty packaging can save. Hence structure is one of the fundamental things wine critics like to talk about. Now you know what it is.

But we have to go further. There are four main "structure" components of a wine: acid, tannin, alcohol, and sugar. Let's hit on each and talk about how to detect them and distinguish them from each other.

Mouthwatering, Jaw-Clenching Acid

If you've taken a psychology class, you've read about experiments on humans' conditioned reactions to acidity. If not, let me do a quick experiment with you so you can see how acidity affects us in food and wine.

Take a second to imagine yourself cutting open a ripe, yellow lemon. Imagine the smell and then imagine putting it in your mouth. Is your mouth watering?

Probably. We're so sensitive to acid that just the thought of it evokes that sensation.

Now stick some Chilean Sauvignon Blanc in your mouth and see what happens. It's the same sensation. That is acidity. It's in reds and whites. You may sense other flavors and sensations (like mouth-puckering tannins in reds), but if you focus on the area under your tongue and it's watering, the wine has acid. Acidity is intrinsic to a grape. It gives Sauvignon Blanc, Chenin Blanc, Riesling, and Albariño refreshing textures. When it's not overpowering, acid gives the fruit a lift—a bright, juicy sensation. Some grapes are more acidic than others by nature, and some acidity has to do with ripeness levels. Cooler climates produce more acidic wines; hotter ones tend to make less acidic wines (see Wine Styles, Climate, and Wearing a Jacket on page 85).

And with that, we come to the wine speak terms for acid. Because god forbid they made it easy, this industry requires that we have a bunch of other words that also indicate acid in different strengths and levels of goodness.

AUSTERE: The term is not entirely positive, and I associate it with acidic wines, but it can be used to describe tannic ones, too. It's like a stern teacher—no smiles, lots of discipline, tough love. This is not a wine to drink when you've got a cut in your mouth or a canker sore. An austere wine is lean—a little excessive in the acid category and not much fruit to balance that baby out and make it well-rounded and delicious.

TART: This is even worse than austere. Think of unripe fruit. A tart wine is slightly painful to drink. Some people describe it as sour, since it makes your mouth contort in the same way as sour food. Most likely a tart wine was made from grapes that weren't quite ripe and had no other character (like minerals, earth, etc.) to balance the acid. The upshot: If you like the wine, use "acidic," not "tart," to describe it.

NERVY/RACY/CRISP: These describe the positive side of acid. People use "nervy," "crisp," or "racy" when they love the wine's acidity and think it's a good yin to

the yang of fruit or earth flavors. I personally hate these terms because I feel like they were incorporated into wine speak by people who wanted more flourish in wine language (lots of critics are journalists turned wine writers). Love them or hate them, the words are used constantly so you need to know them.

Tannins

By far the most unexplained term in wine is "tannin." It's a factor most common in red wines but it can be in whites too, when they've been aged in oak or have sat with their skins before fermentation. Here are a couple of ways to think about the sensation.

- You eat arugula with no dressing. You realize you've become a rabbit and you will eat anything to get a new flavor in your mouth that doesn't make it pucker.
- You go to the dentist. They put that white suction straw thing in your mouth. They leave it in a little too long. The inside of your mouth feels like it's chapped.

That bitterness is an important evolutionary thing for humans—usually poisonous, nasty stuff is bitter and you can feel it on the back of your tongue. Your body is saying, "Yo, I've warned you. Swallow at your own peril." Tannins in wine can fall into that warning, but unlike poisonous stuff in nature, these are safe to drink.

Tannins are in the skins, seeds, and stems of grapes. They balance acidity and fruit flavor to give the wine dimension. They help reds maintain color, prevent spoilage, and are a natural preservative that helps wine age. Because they

DORK OUT ON TANNING & LEATHER

Tanning is a process in which plant extracts are used to harden leather from soft animal skins. The plant extracts toughen the hide because they link up with proteins and change the constitution of the skin to something you can use to make bags, boots, and jackets.

Similarly, tannins link with protein in our saliva, changing our mouth's constitution momentarily and creating a kind of oral desert. Tannins are in other stuff, too: coffee, tea, walnuts, and unsweetened dark chocolate, to name a few. They create similar sensations in your mouth, so watch out for them the next time you eat or drink this stuff to really "get" what tannin is.

like to link up with protein and fat, red wines with tannin are usually great with protein-rich food—everything feels softer and velvety when combined. They stick around and lengthen the finish ("finish," again, being the final flavors in your mouth after you take a sip of wine).

Some grapes are more tannic than others: Tannat, Cabernet Sauvignon, Nebbiolo, and Syrah are the most tannic in the world. Tannins come from oak, too, especially if the oak is new. Oak tannins are rough and dry the heck out of your mouth; they can feel harsher than grape tannins in a wine.

The word "tannin" has more synonyms than "acid." Outside of wine professionals, I rarely hear people describe a wine as "tannic." More likely, I hear the terms here—along with some others you can figure out once you get the gist of the concept.

Good Tannin Words

When you hear the following, it usually means the describer has a favorable impression of the wine.

CHEWY: Aptly, this means you feel like you're chewing on the wine. A chewy wine will leave a dry feeling in your mouth for a while and cause you to smack your lips. When someone says a wine is "chewy," it usually has strong tannins and high alcohol. The alcohol makes the tannin seem softer or sweeter and lessens the drying impact. Once you experience it, you'll know what it means and remember it.

FINE TANNINS OR FINE-GRAINED TANNIN: These are terms you'll hear wine snobs dole out like advice from Lucy at the Peanuts' lemonade stand. It is a compliment to the wine. It means the tannins are balanced with the acidity and fruit, and they are lush and silky, rather than bitter, green, course, or harsh (see the following section for details on these).

SOFT/ROUND/VELVETY: A round wine has soft tannins, often so subtle that you can barely detect them. It feels like a liquid ball rolling around your mouth. "Soft" can also mean the tannins are mature, but in this case you'll often also see the words "silky" or "velvety," which somehow class up soft or round to mean the wine is fabulous. In the sexist world of wine descriptors, these are sometimes called "feminine" wines.

POWERFUL/ROBUST/FIRM: Powerful wines will dry out your mouth but have a punch of flavor, and other textures like acid and alcohol to balance them. A robust or powerful wine often has high alcohol and a variety of flavors that take over your mouth. Again, to use the sexist term, these are "masculine" wines.

Negative, Judgmental Tannin Words

When you hear these words, it usually means the describer thinks something is amiss with the wine.

ASTRINGENT: Every time I hear "astringent," I think of Noxzema face-cleaning cream. Noxzema is harsh, a little burning, and when I used it as a teen it left my skin feeling like I just got slapped on the cheek.

Q+A

Why do I like some wines with tannins and hate others?

Because some tannins are bitter and gross, and others are softer and rounder feeling! Which one you get depends on the viticulture and wine-making practices of the producer, which we'll learn more about in Chapter 3 (page 60). For now, what you need to know is what people mean when they describe the wine as "tannic" or when they use other words that pussyfoot around or embellish the word "tannic" so you are clear about what's in the bottle.

In wine, astringency is that slapped sensation—but in your mouth. The feeling is prickly, harsh, and dry.

"Astringent" is usually used when the tannins are overboard and not balanced. This is the "resolvable" kind of tannin—astringency probably will get better with time. That's different from "green tannin" or "harsh tannin," which generally means the winemaker picked too early or pressed the grapes too long and too hard, extracting nasty flavors, and hence the wine is likely never going to improve.

BITTER: Although OK in moderation, in excess it means the winegrower did a bad job of taming the tannins in the grapes by picking too early or growing in an area without adequate sun for the grape type. It can also mean that the winemaker let the skins soak for too long in the juice. This likely won't improve with age.

TIGHT/CLOSED: This means that the wine is being stingy with offering any flavor apart from mean, lean dryness. The upside: Often with time in a decanter or wine glass, the juice will change for the better and open. The power of oxygen to improve flavors and textures in wine is impressive. The wine may also be in desperate need of a meditation retreat—aging in a cool, dark cellar, which will allow those tannins to chill out and become a more acceptable guest at your table. It's often just the wine going through a phase—you could try the same bottle in six months and the experience would be completely different. Still, I gotta say that "tight" and "closed" are not glowing reviews in wine.

YOUNG: Sadly, this is user error: It's when we open a bottle before its prime. Some young wines are brash with harsh astringency and needed age for tannins to soften, but if you've opened it, it won't get that time to soften. It's always a bummer when you open a bottle too soon, but it happens to all of us at some point.

Alcohol: It's What Makes Wine Wine

You may not drink any other adult beverage apart from wine, but if you've ever had the glorious experience of downing a shot (I have this feeling that if you're reading this book, you probably have dabbled), you know what alcohol tastes like. If not, allow me to explain, as, sadly, I'm a retired pro. (I blame that darn northeastern liberal arts university. In that small town we had little to do but drink Popov vodka and Goldschlager.)

Alcohol is warm, and it burns the back of your throat and your esophagus as it goes down. That warmth is why it's so good on a cold night or after a long, bad day.

So when you have a wine that seems to make your mouth or your esophagus burn, *shazam!* You've identified a wine that's high in alcohol and one that's out of balance, too! Lucky you (I say sarcastically).

All the components of structure matter, but without alcohol, wine would be just weird grape juice. Going back to the picture frame analogy, alcohol is often the piece of the frame that throws off a wine's symmetry. Lately there's been a trend toward lower alcohol wines, but for me it's not about the level of alcohol as much as it is about the balance between alcohol and the other stuff in the wine; we need to keep all factors in perspective.

Alcohol has to do with grapes ripening in the vineyard. This is a true art and science. For instance, sometimes in waiting for the tannins and acid to soften in the grapes on the vine, viticulturists wind up "baking" the grapes in the sun and achieving extraordinarily high levels of sugar in the wine, which convert to high levels of alcohol during fermentation. It takes skill, experience, and sometimes dumb luck to pick the grapes at a point where everything balances out once the wine is made. If you get it right, the alcohol plays nice with everything. If you get it wrong . . . burn baby burn!

Terms to Describe Alcohol

BODY: "Body" can be used to describe wines of all alcohol contents. A light-bodied wine, for instance, is usually one with a low alcohol level. It's not very mouth filling— it feels light and acidic. A medium-bodied wine feels like it has something going on; it sticks around your mouth a little, but it's not overwhelming. It's like an appropriate houseguest: It leaves while it's still pleasant to have around. A full-bodied wine is big and heavy, and sticks around. Sometimes that's great, unless the wine doesn't taste good and then it's really, really bad.

Q+A

I've heard people talk about alcohol levels, but what is high alcohol? Is that something I can figure out?

In most countries around the world, producers and importers are required to list the alcohol content on the label. The information can be minuscule and in a light font, but it's always on the bottle somewhere. Start paying attention to this. It makes a huge difference in flavor and in food pairing. Scales vary, but this is my opinion, based on way too much primary research.

Low alcohol: Anything below 11.5% alcohol by volume (ABV)
Medium alcohol: 11.5%–below 13.5%
High alcohol: 13.5% and up

OILY: This is a term that could be related to a lot of different things: malolactic fermentation, glycerol (a natural by-product of fermentation), or alcohol. There are wines like the whites of Alsace, France (Pinot Gris, Gewurztraminer, and Riesling, especially), that have a texture similar to olive oil. Viscous, a little weighty, and soft feeling in your mouth, these wines are luscious and substantial. My husband, M.C. Ice, hates the sensation—he thinks it's slimy. I love it. No accounting for taste.

HOT: Per my earlier comment on the shot, if a sip of wine warms your mouth, your throat, or your esophagus, it's high in alcohol (unless you are extremely sensitive to alcohol and all alcohol does that to you), or hot. I find this to be a negative trait. To me, hot = off balance, and it tells me that alcohol is dominating other components in the wine.

BIG: Although this can sometimes refer to lots of flavor and tannin combined with high alcohol, most times a wine is "big" if it is mouth coating and mouth filling. Since acid makes your mouth water, tannin dries it out, and sugar is a different beast altogether, the sensation that usually makes a wine feel rich and full is the warm, soft feeling of high alcohol. Blockbuster, fruity wines are made from (over)ripe grapes that usually result in higher alcohol. If you hear someone describe a wine as "big," you can look on the bottle and usually find an alcohol level in excess of 14 percent; high in my book.

LEGS/TEARS: If you swirl a glass of wine, you're going to see a clear liquid rim form above the wine where you swirled. Then you'll see small columns of clear or sometimes slightly red-tinted (in red wines) liquid drip down the sides of the glass. Those are "legs" or "tears."

Alcohol has a lower surface tension than water. Water drips down the side of the glass first, and then the alcohol follows. The higher the alcohol content, the more prominent the legs. This is my party trick—I'm an expert of sorts when it comes to guessing the alcohol content of a wine without seeing the percentage on the bottle. I can tell just by the legs. Try it and I bet you'll at least be able to guess if the wine is low, medium, or high alcohol after a while. And if you really want to impress your friends, tell them that surface tension thing is called the Marangoni effect, after Italian physicist Carlo Marangoni, who observed it.

Sugar: With People, All Sweetness Is Good; with Wine, Not So Much

Now to the final support of our four-sided painting: sugar. Most wines aren't sweet, but dryness, or the absence of sweetness, is an important structural component, too. Detecting sweetness in a wine seems like a no-brainer, but it's harder to sense than you think. Our mouths can sense sugar, but we often get confused about what is sweet and what is fruity. It's important for us to get this right, though, because if you ask for a sweet wine when you wanted a dry, fruity one, you will be disappointed by the sugary drink you get. It's also important because cheap wines use sugar to disguise a poor job in the vineyard, and detecting sugar in a wine may tell you something about the dubious quality of that wine. Here's the good news: Like bitterness in tannins, sweet is something our mouths actually can sense. Use the box on the facing page to figure it out.

Wines can be sweet for a few reasons. In nondessert wines, sugars that don't ferment are called residual sugars. Sometimes the yeast doesn't eat all the sugar in the wine, leaving it a bit sweet. Some winemakers add sugar back into the wine (usually in the form of unfermented grape juice) to give the wine a bit of sweetness; this is common in German Riesling, for instance, where sugar is needed to balance the screaming acid. And in some dessert wines, winemakers actually stop the fermentation while there is still sugar in the wine; they can add grape-based alcohol so the yeast die on the spot and stop frothing it up. More on that in the next chapter.

Sugar Words

CLOYING: Yuck. When a sweet wine has no acid to balance out the sugar, it's cloying. You get a mouthful of sweet stickiness and then nothing to lighten it up or clean out your mouth. It's like flat Coke. The best sweet wines have acid to take the edge off the sugar and aren't cloying.

DRY: The opposite of sweet. The driest wines only contain unfermentable sugars. There's a catch though: Even if it has a bit of sugar in it, a wine will seem drier if it has high tannin or acid. If it's got high alcohol, it may seem sweet even though it has no sugar. Ah, biology, why must you play these nasty tricks on us? I know it sounds complicated, but with time you'll discern what's what!

OFF DRY: This should be called "a tad sweet" or "not so dry." It's misleading because this wine is slightly to moderately sweet. If you have an aversion to sweet wines, make sure you look out for this before you buy Riesling, Gewürztraminer, or Chenin Blanc, especially. As a side note,

SUGAR, FRUIT, OR ALCOHOL?

Do you want to know if a wine is really sweet or just seems like it? Your tongue is your best ally. Do the sugar test. Here's what to do.

- Hold your nose.
- While holding your nose, stick the tip of your tongue into the wine.
- If you can sense a sugar tingle on your tongue, the wine is sweet. If not, the wine is dry, meaning it has no sugar.
- Release your nose. If you still think the wine smells sweet, rest assured that it's your brain/ nose playing tricks on you by free-associating scents you perceive as sweet (ripe fruit, stuff with cinnamon, vanilla, or nutmeg) with the things you're smelling in the wine. If you need an example, think about vanilla extract. It smells so sweet and delicious but tastes horrible.

even if you don't like off-dry wines to sip, these are the best pairings with spicy food. Get one for your Indian, Thai, or Chinese meal, and you'll be a believer.

Structure Words of Lack and Perfection

Acid, tannin, alcohol, and sugar and their requisite euphemisms are the big dogs of structure, but a few other structure words are important to know.

BALANCE: Although we've discussed the structural frame, which implies balance, we haven't defined the sensation. Balance is wine nirvana. A balanced wine has interesting but not overwhelming flavor, and tannins, acid, and alcohol (and maybe sugar) that each play their role but are happy to be part of an ensemble cast. With no single component hogging the stage, balanced wines feel good in your mouth, and are interesting because you have to analyze them to figure out what's so damn tasty about them (the fruit flavors? the mouth-cleaning acid? or everything all together?). They can be the best sippers because they're so complete on their own.

COMPLEXITY: A wine that has a lot going on in a number of arenas—layers of flavors that keep revealing themselves with sniffs and sips and different elements of structure that give it a lot of dimension—is complex. My rule of thumb: If you need a lot of words to describe it, the wine is complex. Many wines are simple, meaning you can say a wine tastes like apples and butter (like for a Chardonnay) but that's just about it. A complex wine may have notes of apple and butter, but also lime, pineapple, white flowers, minerals, and sharp acidity.

EXTRACTED: The best way to describe this is through an analogy I read in an issue of *Wine Spectator*: "Extract is to wine as jam is to fruit." Jam is boiled-down, sugary, intense fruit. Extract is the level of concentrated flavor and texture in the wine. If someone says a wine is highly extracted, imagine a cooked-down fruit that has little water left so it's all fruit flavor. Extracted wine has rich flavor that comes from ripe grapes or from certain winemaking techniques.

JAMMY: If the fruit hung too long on the vine and tastes sweet and jellylike, it's jammy. It may have so much fruit that it overpowers other interesting flavors like earth or structural components like tannin or acid. I love a jammy Zinfandel, but when I get a wine that tastes like gelatin, it's a loser for me (at that point just add grain alcohol to grape jelly and have a Jell-O shot, no?).

FLABBY: This is a gross word even outside wine speak. The first time I heard it, I thought it was a stupid wine word, but after tasting a wine that was just like warm fruit juice, I got it. Flabby wines are like Jabba the Hutt from the Star Wars series: amorphous, nasty blobs. They usually come from warm or hot climates that are better for growing soy than grapes. In these climates, the flavor and structure get baked out. There's nothing there except ripe fruit flavor and high alcohol. Blech.

INSIPID: If you hear this, run for the hills. An insipid wine is flavorless plonk. This can be a result of bad grapes—garbage in, garbage out—or bad winemaking, or a combo of it all. "Insipid" is the ultimate wine insult.

Other Tasting Terms

TYPICITY: This is the Anglicized version of the French *typicité* or the Italian *tipicità*. It describes whether or not the wine conforms to the way most wines from the region or area taste or are expected to taste. It's kind of like buying the same brand of tissue each time. If, one time, the tissue was more like a napkin than a tissue, you'd be mad.

You'll hear "typicity" with regard to European wines because of their vineyard classification systems (page 89). If a wine doesn't meet the typicité requirements for an Appellation d'Origine Protégée wine in France, for instance, then it doesn't taste like it's from Bordeaux/Alsace/Rhône/etc., and it may not get approval from the local wine board to put the appellation on the bottle. It may be declassified to a less prestigious classification. Typicity requirements are great for us as wine shoppers because the regulations mean that we can expect, within reason, the wines to have a reliable flavor profile.

CLASSIC: If a wine is made in a classic style, it's designed to stay true to the winemaking methods, grapes, and flavors that are traditionally associated with a place and have been for centuries (in Europe) or decades (everywhere else). You may also hear this word with regard to vintage. Since there is variation from year to year, a classic vintage is a year that is typical of the weather of the area, and hence the grapes can make a wine that has classic flavors. If you want to taste a wine that is typical of a region (with typicity!), ask for a classic style.

The preceding Q + A is why I don't subscribe to the "drink what you like" philosophy. We're creatures of habit, and if you do that, you'll stay with the same stuff you always drink. If you don't push yourself, you'll never appreciate why certain wines are so great. As written by Paulo Coelho in my favorite book, *The Alchemist*: "If you think adventure is dangerous, try routine; it is lethal." I think it applies to wine so perfectly.

The bad news: You have to push through some unpleasant taste experiences and explore. You'll drink some things you'll never like. But if you're a beer or coffee drinker, chances are you didn't like them when you first tasted them either. Keep trying different producers and vintages, with and without food, with different company. Give stuff a try when you have an opportunity, even if you hated it in the past. Try to articulate what it is that you don't like about the wine and then see if that still bothers you the next time you try something from that region or grape. If it does, try it again in a year—you may find your ideas have changed.

Q+A

Right now I don't like Bordeaux or Loire wines, and I'm not that big on anything outside California. Am I destined to never understand or like the wines experts rave about?

No! Your taste for flavors and for attributes in wine will change over time. Your senses of smell and taste change, too, and you acquire a liking for new flavors with time, exposure, and experience. What you taste one year and hate, you may revisit two years later and love.

Exercises to Test Your Moxie

Now you've learned the terms and process of tasting, so let's take your skills for a trial run. Buy an acidic wine (try a Sauvignon Blanc, Chablis, or dry Riesling), a tannic wine (Cabernet Sauvignon, Syrah, or Nebbiolo), one with 14 percent alcohol or more, and a sweet wine at any price point.

Try to use the words we've learned to describe the wine.

HOW TO USE WINE SPEAK
WITH AN EXAMPLE WINE

WINE-SPEAK WORD	MY WINE
ACIDIC (mouthwatering, tart, austere)	Even though it was really tannic, I felt a good amount of acidity. It was refreshing and kept the wine from being heavy.
TANNIC (mouth drying, robust, round, astringent, young, tight, bitter)	Very tannic. The wine may be a little young because it's a current vintage and it was very astringent.
ALCOHOLIC (hot, full-bodied, legs, big)	The alcohol was in balance. It had a medium body.
SUGAR (cloying, dry, off dry)	Dry wine.
EARTHY, MINERALLY, BARNYARD, GAMY, GREEN	I like the earthy, potting soil aromas. It tasted a little like a green pepper too, which I liked.
SPICY, SMOKY, GASOLINE	Some black pepper but not that spicy.
TEXTURE, JAMMY, OILY, FINISH	Really mouth drying from the tannin. Lots of fruit flavor after I swallowed. It was jammy. Long finish.
NORMAL DESCRIPTIONS that you'd use on your own	The nose was like tobacco and fruit, but it tasted like ripe blackberries, plums, and dark cherries. Mostly ripe fruit.
OFF? Was the wine bad and can't be evaluated?	Totally fine.

For example, identify what acidity tastes like in a wine. Figure out if it's a quality you like or don't like. If you don't like it, describe it as tart. If you like the acidity, describe it as racy (or just acidic). Do that for the wines with other attributes.

Now the most important questions: Did you like the wine? What did you like about it?

With this info, you can use the things you liked or didn't like in the wine to communicate with sommeliers and wine shop folks. If you start doing this regularly, you'll be an expert at describing wine in wine-speak and you'll start to order or take home great wine almost every time. You can make a chart like the one on the facing page.

The Wrap-Up

This chapter has lots of detail, but the gist is that wine is about both having a sensory experience and sharing that experience. To do that you have to communicate what you taste and what you like. Learning, tasting, and talking should help you convey what you want when shopping for wine or ordering it in a restaurant, which is the ultimate goal.

The final thought I'll leave you with is this: If you go through the steps of wine evaluation, you may notice that a wine has great balance, and certain typical flavors and textures even if it's not for you. This doesn't mean it's bad or poorly made—just that you don't like it. This is an important distinction and a good reason to master the process of tasting and talking wine.

2

A Q

NOT-SO

TOUR O

WINE GE

uick

-TECHIE

F HOW

TS MADE

For most of us, winemaking is really boring unless you have a chance to see it in action. I don't want to make this chapter technical and boring, so I'm going to give you a really quick step by step on how wine gets made, call out the factors that give wine flavor, and then raise some questions about why knowing about some of this stuff matters.

VINEYARD WORDS EXPLAINED

Bottom line: Wine is farming. Before we dive into the quickie tour of how to make wine, I have to tell you that, in wine, the factor that matters most in winemaking is the vineyard. If you don't start with incredible raw material, you've already lost the opportunity to make great wine. I want to get some essential terms and concepts about the vineyard down in this chapter, because it is the heart of wine and winemaking. Let's start with an understanding of what "vineyard" means.

VINEYARD: This is the actual land where grapes grow. Some wineries have "vineyard" in their names, but that doesn't necessarily mean they grow grapes; they may not have a winery or even a physical presence. They may use someone else's facilities to make wine, and they may buy fruit from a bunch of different vineyards. Confused yet? I was when I started in the business. It's odd for sure.

This is opposed to a WINERY (domaine, house, château, weingut) that is an entity that makes wine. It's not necessarily a place that grows grapes. A winery could buy all its grapes from winegrowers, but make the wines and market them under a specific name.

Here's another weird thing: Some wineries are fake—they don't even make the wine; they just put their name on the bottles. That's often the province of big hulking wineries who have DBA/Doing Business As names. They may make a bunch of wines under the same roof but bottle them under different names. Look at any wine that comes in a 1.5 liter bottle, and that's often the case.

TERROIR (TEHR-WHAH): The most important concept in wine, terroir is a French word that has no precise translation in English. It includes some concrete things and some more philosophical concepts. On the concrete side, terroir is the land of the vineyard. It's the elevation, slope, soils, subsoils (which lie deep in the ground), water drainage, sun exposure, access or proximity to water, and climate. These are the things farmers or *vignerons* (winemakers/growers—normally the same person—in France) worry about. Terroir also includes the idea that every piece of land is unique and has characteristics that no other piece of land in the world has. It's the special sauce that gives each vineyard the ability to produce grapes of a certain flavor that is not replicable.

The idea of terroir is a little cerebral, but after you taste wines that are expressive of the place where they're grown, you'll understand that only that piece of land could make wines with that taste (for good or for bad). In some regions, like Burgundy, for example, the geological history of the area has been so volatile that plots of land as little as 100 feet (30 meters) apart can produce completely different wines. That's terroir.

VITIS VINIFERA (VIH-TIS VAHY-NIF-ER-UH): The Latin name for the European vine species, these are the grapes we know and love—Cabernet Sauvignon, Chardonnay, Merlot, Pinot Noir, etc. Grapes from these species taste very different from other species of *Vitis* that you may see in North America, for instance, *Vitis labrusca* (Concord/grape juice grapes), *Vitis riparia*, or hybrids of these or others with *vinifera*.

Planting *Vitis vinifera* outside its native home proved impossible for centuries. These types of grapes are sensitive to cold and especially to diseases and bugs native to other parts of the world. Of special note is the horrible sap-sucking root bug called PHYLLOXERA (FIH-LOX-ER-AH). This nasty, quickly reproducing bug punctures the vines' roots, which react by swelling up and forming growths. The growths prevent the roots from taking in nutrients from the ground. Without nutrients, the vines die quickly. The bug can move to new regions on people's clothes and shoes and on farming equipment, or can be introduced on plants that come from another growing region.

Globalization in the mid-1800s brought this bug from the United States to France, and all hell broke loose. Vineyards all over Europe lost countless acres, and some native vinifera grapes became extinct. Until a Texan discovered that North American grapevines were resistant to phylloxera and grafting vinifera onto American roots would allow the vines to maintain their character and survive, the "wine blight" decimated more than 70 percent of vineyards in France.

Today, most vines, except in a few areas around the world (Chile, Tasmania in Australia, and parts of the Okanagan Valley in Canada, notably), are grafted onto American roots. It's a good solution and allows *Vitis vinifera* to thrive in areas where it never would have survived before.

VARIETAL: This is a fancy word for kind of grape, or grape variety. It's industry jargon and is used if someone is talking about Chardonnay, Cabernet Sauvignon, Sauvignon Blanc, or any wine that isn't a blend.

CLONES: Like Dolly the sheep or fancy flowers, vines are cloned to replicate certain characteristics. Winemakers can choose clones that control vine vigor or increase disease resistance, and select those clones that will work best for their sites. In the Old World, this is less of an issue—they're using native vines that nature gave them. For example, in Burgundy, you grow the Pommard clone of Pinot Noir in and around Pommard and the Dijon clone in and around Dijon. But in the New World, there is more choice about what to grow since you get to select the "mother vine" from which to get the identical clipping. This is a nuanced, detailed thing, but I bring it up because I've encountered more than a few snotty wine people who love to spout off info about clones.

My advice: Don't worry about knowing the specifics, because it matters less to flavor than they'd have you believe. I raise the issue so you have a general idea of what people are talking about when they bring up clones in wine.

SOIL: You know what soil is. But you need to know that different soils create dramatically different flavors, and some grapes do fabulously well on certain soils and less well on others. Grapes are a contrarian crop; they produce the best flavors when they struggle to grow. The best soil types have good drainage—allowing water to flow off the roots, but leaving enough to give the vines what they need to survive. There are thousands of soil types; see the following Soil Types chart for some you may hear about.

DIURNALS OR DIURNAL TEMPERATURE SHIFTS: Let's put on our meteorologist hats for a second and talk about temperatures. Diurnals are the difference between the high and low temperatures that occur within a day. Why does this matter for grapes? If you grow fruit in an environment where it's hot during the day and not that much cooler at night, the fruit never really stops ripening even when the sun is down. That means the fruit ripens faster, gaining high sugars and low acidity, since heat "bakes out" acid. If you have dramatic diurnals, as top wine regions do, the grapes can get enough sun during the daytime to ripen and develop fruit flavor and sugars (which turn to alcohol), but at night, they can hoard acidity. That means the final wine will have an excellent balance of fruit, alcohol, and acid to keep it fresh. When wine people talk about big diurnals, your ears should perk up—it likely means the wine will have a nice balance, which is awesome for us.

VINTAGE: You may know that "vintage" is the year on the bottle. I'm adding it because a lot of people don't make the necessary association with weather. That's what vintage indicates. Every vintage has a story to tell. Some are great; some suck. It's all up to Mother Nature.

Next time someone gets uppity about vintage with you, just know they are talking about the dudes getting blown down in hurricanes on beaches or buried in snow while reporting weather conditions.

If you want to start following vintage, pay attention to the wine sites that report on hail, frost, sun, and rain throughout the growing season (April through October in the Northern Hemisphere, September through March or April in the Southern Hemisphere). You'd be surprised at how good and bad years will stand out in your head.

SOIL TYPES

Limestone	Loam	Schist
Granite	Sand	Slate
Clay	Shale	Gravel
Chalk	Volcanic	Alluvial

Remember that weather differs from CLIMATE, which refers to long-term weather patterns over a period of thirty years or so, and what the region typifies in terms of average temperature, rainfall, sunlight, and other factors.

FARMING WORDS EXPLAINED

There are so many farming terms that you'll hear in wine if you get into it deeper. First and foremost, you'll hear winegrowers refer to grapes as berries. I'll do it, too. Grapes are classified as berries, so that one makes sense.

People may talk about green harvesting—when workers remove "green" or unripe grapes from a vine to lower the yield of grapes and concentrate flavor in the remaining grapes.

They may discuss plowing in pomace, or the remains of grapes after they are pressed, to enrich soil. The list goes on, but there are a few major things you will hear regularly.

HAND HARVEST: When grapes are ready to make wine, they've got to come off the vine. There are lots of ways to make this happen. One is by a machine that travels up and down the rows of the vineyards and shakes the vines to remove the grapes. Low-budget wines are almost always mechanically harvested. Also, in places with labor shortages, like Australia, growers often don't have a choice but to mechanically harvest grapes. Mechanical harvesting isn't terrible for grapes, but in an ideal world, it's best to cut them off by hand because then the grapes don't pop or break,

so you get pure raw materials in the wine (for example, no excessive tannin from the juice kickin' it with bitter stems). Wineries will often boast that their grapes are hand harvested, and now you know why.

ORGANIC: Organic farming is about keeping soil healthy and controlling vineyard issues by using naturally occurring stuff to fight off maladies. For example, winegrowers use compost instead of chemical fertilizer, and introduce natural predators into the vineyard to eat pests that eat grapes (spiders to eat bad bugs, hawks to eat rodents). Farmers use sprays made from ingredients that occur in nature. It's back-to-basics farming. In the United States, there are three ways a wine can be labeled if it's organically farmed:

- *100% Organic* has the US Department of Agriculture (USDA) seal. This wine can contain only naturally occurring sulfites (or sulfur dioxide, an antimicrobial substance) in less than 100 parts per million (ppm).
- *Organic* has a USDA seal indicating the wine consists of 95 percent organically grown ingredients (the other 5 percent must not be available organically). The wine has the same sulfite requirements as 100% organic.
- *Made with Organic Grapes* or *Made with Organic Ingredients* means the wine contains at least 70 percent organic ingredients. It can have artificial sulfites added, but it may not contain more than 100 ppm. It does not have the USDA organic seal.

The labeling is hotly contested mostly because the USDA has decided that the use of sulfites (which are organic and occur naturally in wine as a by-product of fermentation) to preserve wine prevents the wine from being organic. It's a problem because wines without sulfites are generally unstable; they get funky faster since sulfites help prevent spoilage. Frankly, it's a strange law because the wine industry is the only one I know of that can't call its product organic, even when it's made with 100 percent organic grapes.

BIODYNAMIC: Developed in the 1920s by an Austrian dude named Rudolf Steiner, biodynamics is a philosophy that views a farm/vineyard as a single living organism. Farmers don't use synthetic chemicals, and they view the land as a closed nutrient system, using homeopathic teas, composting, natural predator-prey relationships, cover crops, and animals that live on the estate to keep a vineyard balanced. Farmers who practice biodynamics do certain rituals, make special herbal preparations, and pay attention to the tides, phases of the moon, planets, and seasons to decide when to do things like thin the canopy of the vine, use those natural teas, and harvest.

By talking with biodynamic practitioners, I've learned that some crazy-seeming stuff can be explained logically. For example, growers will put "preparations" in a cow horn and bury it. Sounds oddball but if you fill a cow horn, which is on the smallish side, with manure and herbs and then bury it for six months or so, you get decomposed matter that is a great fertilizer for vines. You dig up the horn and steep the preparation, like a tea, in water and then spray it on the vine roots. This stimulates root growth and creates healthy vines. The specific herbs are better for the roots than chemical preparations and are good for soil health.

Biodynamic farmers follow the phases of the moon because sap from plants flows up and makes grapes more flavorful

Phases of the moon, tides? WHAAAAT?

I know biodynamic farming sounds kind of out there. But the important thing to note is that it's about making a farm self-sustaining and bringing it into balance with nature after it's been messed up by human intervention. To do this, growers only use stuff found in nature.

on days when the gravitational pull of the moon is stronger. Accordingly, those are the days growers should harvest the grapes to make the best-tasting wine. Makes sense, no?

FROM THE VINEYARD TO THE WINERY

How do you turn berries that grow on a vine into Bacchus's Beautiful Bounty? (I know you love alliteration, too—just admit it.) Since people have been doing it for thousands of years, way before the technology we have today was a glimmer in someone's brain, you can guess that it can be done fairly easily. You take grapes, then let yeast pig out on the sugar in the juice and turn it into alcohol. You maybe get out the chunks of grape and seeds, and voilà! Drink away.

Oh, but you want to make *good* wine? That requires another set of skills. Let's review how that should be done.

Making Awesome White Wine

1. Plant grapes that make sense for the region where you're growing them. Look at the climate, the elevation of the vineyard, the soil type, the drainage, and the sun exposure (a.k.a. terroir). Match the grape types to the site and trellis the vines (hang them up on wires) as necessary to increase sun exposure on the berries. Hope that Mother Nature doesn't screw you by showering your vineyard with hail, rain, frost, snow, or whatever else during flowering and into grape development, which is the process that will ultimately lead to good, healthy berries.

2. If all goes well, berries will form from the flowers. Again, hope that Mother Nature is cooperative and doesn't brew up a heat wave or hailstorm so your berries can stay healthy while they grow. Cut the leaves to control the shade levels on the grapes to ensure they get the amount of sun (in cool climates) or shade (in hot climates) they need to mature.

3. Decide how you want to control the uncontrollable: pests, fungus, bacteria, birds, deer, whatever. You may spray chemicals or other stuff on the grapes to kill bugs, mold, and mildew, which can be organic or straight poison. As consumers, we have very little idea of what goes on in vineyards, and there aren't rules currently regarding disclosure, so too bad for us.

4. Pick the grapes when the sugar/ripeness levels seem right. Most wineries use a combination of experience and devices to measure sugars and ripeness. When the berries seem to be in their ideal state—the color, the acidity, the tannin, and the fruit or earth flavors are delicious—pick 'em. Do it by hand or by a machine, but get the grapes off before they become overripe!

5. Try not to ruin the fruit on the way to the winery—don't let the grapes get crushed or split. If they break, the stalks, stems, and seeds may impart a lot of bitterness to the juice, and you don't want that.

6. Destem the grapes to get out the mini branches that will make the wine taste bitter and gross.

7. Gently press the grapes using a bladder press or your feet.

8. Or if you want more flavor and tannin or lower acidity, crush the grapes and allow a little time for the juice to hang out with the skins and seeds. This is usually for more aromatic

Q+A

Hold it. I read somewhere that you can make white wine out of red grapes. How is that possible if you're letting the juice hang out with the red-colored skins?

Great question. Yes, you can make white wine out of red grapes. The goal in this case is to do a light press, and then get the juice away from the skins as quickly as possible because once color gets in, there's no getting it out! It makes for a very pure-flavored wine, or for a really nasty one if the juice inside those grapes is not balanced and tasty. Most Champagne is a blend of Chardonnay, a white grape, and Pinot Noir and Pinot Meunier, two red grapes. Also, Pinot Gris/Pinot Grigio is grayish purple, but the wine is white.

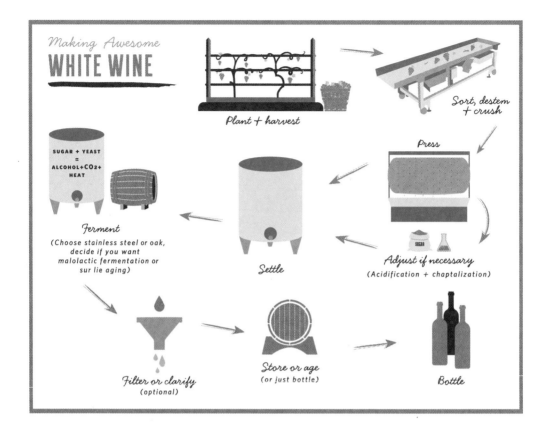

Making Awesome WHITE WINE

Plant + harvest

Sort, destem + crush

Press

SUGAR + YEAST = ALCOHOL+CO2+ HEAT

Ferment
(Choose stainless steel or oak, decide if you want malolactic fermentation or sur lie aging)

Settle

Adjust if necessary
(Acidification + chaptalization)

Filter or clarify
(optional)

Store or age
(or just bottle)

Bottle

---

grapes; you avoid this when you're looking to make bright, refreshing, pure-fruit-tasting wine.

9. Let the juice sit for a bit so any big particles in the wine settle to the bottom of the tank. Add sulfur dioxide to prevent bacteria from spoiling it.

10. Pump the juice into a cement, fiberglass, or stainless steel tank or a wood barrel.

11. Acidify or chaptalize. Let me explain.

ACIDIFICATION: If the region has a hot climate or experienced hot weather, it's possible the acid level is too low for the wine to be balanced. Winemakers in these regions are often permitted to add tartaric, malic, or citric acid to improve the balance, color, and flavor of the wine. (I'm putting it here because it's often done before step 12, but it can also be done after fermentation.)

CHAPTALIZATION: In cool climates, in which grapes sometimes don't gather enough sugar/ripeness to get a decent alcohol level, a winemaker can add table sugar (sucrose), beet sugar, cane sugar, or grape concentrate prior to fermentation to give the yeast a little more to work with. This increases the alcohol level and makes the wine feel fuller and richer in your mouth.

12. Let the juice ferment. Add yeast or let yeast from the vineyard do its thing. (It's less common to allow natural yeast fermentation in white winemaking because it's easier to mess up the delicate flavors of white wines. Winemakers often choose safer cultivated yeast.) Either way, the yeast eat sugar in the juice and turn it into alcohol and carbon dioxide, and the alcohol they produce kills them.

13. Allow or inhibit the secondary, or malolactic, fermentation to obtain creaminess and softness. (If you add sulfur dioxide or chill the wine to a certain temperature, the bacteria for the process can't work.) As a refresher from Chapter 1: Malolactic fermentation softens the tough green-apple-like malic acid into softer lactic acid, which is great in fuller wines and undesirable in fresh, zippy ones. If malolactic fermentation didn't happen on its own and you wanted it to, add some bacteria to make it happen.

14. Now it's wine! Leave it in the barrel or vat in which it fermented on top of the dead yeast cells (see *Sur Lie Aging*, page 20) to get nutty, yeasty flavors and a fuller texture, or take it off the yeast (rack it) and squirt it with sulfur dioxide to prevent spoilage.

15. If you want, barrel age it (decide on barrel size, oak type, toast, and length of time you want to store it—tons more on this in Chapter 3).

16. If you want, clean it up so it looks pretty (totally unnecessary, just for aesthetics). Here are the options for cleanup.

> COLD STABILIZATION: Chill the wine to a cold temperature to get out proteins and tartrate crystals, which are harmless but which many people don't like to look at or end up filtering out.

> FINE THE WINE: Use egg whites, gelatin, clay, or fish bladders (called isinglass—that's right, many wines are *not* vegan) to make the wine less hazy or to get rid of unwanted tannin.

> FILTER THE WINE: Run it through something with small holes that takes out big particulate matter (yeast, bacteria, grape leftovers). It can strip flavor but reduces the chances of spoilage and of sediment, so it's a tough call.

17. Bottle the wine. Choose bottle type (usually based on traditional bottles used from the region of origin—Cabernet goes in the "Bordeaux Bottle," Chardonnay in the "Burgundy Bottle"); color; and closure (screw cap vs. cork vs. fake cork). Make a sexy label and age the wine in the bottle or ship it.

And there you go. With seventeen easy steps, you can do it in your kitchen, right? Home winemaking kit here you come! You're now ready for rosé.

Making Irresistible Rosé Wine

1 THROUGH 6. If you're going to make pink wine, follow the steps in the white winemaking section, but use red grapes.

7. After bringing the red grapes into the winery, gently press the grapes to obtain the desired color and flavor. Or, less commonly, allow them to sit in a vat until their own weight crushes the skins and juice flows out the bottom of the vat (called a *saignée*, or bleeding, because you're bleeding off a little flavor and color from red grapes). By either method, the wine gets fresh, bright red fruit and herb flavors instead of some of the darker fruit and spice notes you get if you press and macerate red grapes, which we'll get into with red winemaking.

8. After the press or saignée, the wine is made just like a white, so go back to steps 9 THROUGH 17.

Rosés come in a range of colors and flavors depending on the grapes used and the amounts of pigment and flavor that come out during the saignée or the press. You can probably guess that it's difficult to make a generalization about the flavors of all rosés, but the only common themes are a pinkish color and fresh acidity. Also, if the bottle says "rosé" and not "blush," you'll be drinking a dry wine.

Q+A

What exactly is rosé? Is it just red and white wine mixed together?

Except in Champagne, where mixing red wine with white for pink bubbly is perfectly acceptable, quality rosé winemaking has its own methods. Rosé is made like a white wine, with a little bit of color entering the picture before fermentation. With the exception of White Zinfandel, most rosé these days is dry, not sweet.

Making Ridiculously Good Red Wine

Red winemaking is more complex than making white or rosé. It doesn't mean that it's easy to make good white or rosé, but there are many more balls in the air with red. On the flip side, there are also many more opportunities to "correct" a red if something goes bad. Whites and rosés are much less flexible so you have to work hard to get great grapes off the vines or you'll be left with plonk!

1 THROUGH 5. These steps in red winemaking are the same as for whites, except for reds the process of VERAISON, or the point at which grapes obtain their dark pigment, is pivotal. If Mother Nature throws a curveball during veraison, the grower may need to cut more fruit off the vine during pruning so the remaining grapes get concentrated ripeness. With fewer grapes, each one can achieve enough flavor, tannin, and color to make a good-looking and good-tasting red in your glass.

6. This is where red diverges from white. Now you destem the grapes and gently crush them to create MUST—a soup of some whole grapes, skins, juice, and seeds—which gives reds color, tannin, body, and richness.

7. Decide if you want to let the stuff hang out and macerate in oak (to add flavor and texture), stainless steel, cement, fiberglass, or an amphora (these Grecian urns are making a comeback!).

8. If you're in the New World, you may cold soak, or chill, the fermenting must for lighter pigmented grapes to allow for color and flavor to come through without alcohol and tannin extraction, which happens during the higher temperature of fermentation.

   If you are an Old World producer, you probably don't do this because you're OK with the wine looking lighter in color.

9. Chaptalize or acidify, if necessary.

10. Decide on the temperature at which you want to ferment if you're using a stainless steel, temperature-controlled tank (pretty common these days)—hotter temps mean more color and tannin and a quicker ferment; cooler temps lead to a fresher, fruitier, brighter wine. Yeast make heat, so monitor the

temperature throughout the fermentation to make sure it doesn't overheat.

11. Add yeast or let yeast from the vineyard munch sugar and create alcohol, fermenting the juice.

12. Get those damn skins into the juice to give the wine color, tannin, and flavor! Carbon dioxide is a by-product of fermentation, and that makes the heavy grape skins and seeds float to the top of the tank. To get color and flavor out of them, you need to pump the juice over them, punch them down into the juice, and generally submerge them to get every last bit out of them.

13. Now it's wine. Take it off the yeast and the crushed-up skins and seeds (rack it). Press the skins to get off any remaining juice (it will be concentrated stuff but it's a reserve to blend in, just in case you need more tannin or flavor later), and put the wine into a clean tank/barrel/amphora/cement egg. Squirt it with sulfur dioxide to prevent spoilage, if you are into that.

14. If malolactic fermentation didn't happen on its own, add bacteria to make it

Q+A

I get the steel tank that imparts no flavor and the barrel that imparts oak flavor to the wine. But what's the deal with amphora or cement eggs?

In their quest to make their fruit shine, winemakers have rediscovered vessels from ancient Greece and Rome. Both amphora and cement eggs (they really *are* shaped like eggs) allow the fruit to shine, make the wine fresher and smoother in your mouth, and let little bits of oxygen circulate and help the wine develop interesting secondary flavors without introducing new flavors like oak does. As winemakers learn more about these vessels, we could get even better wine!

happen so your red is more palatable (most reds go through the process).

15. If you want, barrel age the wine (decide on barrel size, oak type, toast, and length of time you want to age it).

16. Pick one or more options for cleanup (or none) listed in step 16 for white wine: cold stabilization, fining, filtering.

17. Bottle the wine—choose bottle type, color, label, and closure (screw cap vs. cork vs. fake cork), and age it in bottle or ship it.

Cranking Out Bubblies and Fortifieds

These wines are easy to love but hard to make. I'll explain bubblies and fortified wines within the region sections (Champagne, Oporto, Jerez, Germany, and Roussillon; see the Index [page 340] to find those sections within the book) when I've piqued your interest in how people make those specific wines, but here's a preview.

First, there are three ways to make sparklers.

Sparkling Method #1: Traditional or Champagne Method

To make sparkling wine like the Champenoise, you make white wine and then bottle the wine with a mixture of yeast and sugar to create a second fermentation in the bottle in which it is sold.

Yeast create carbon dioxide in addition to alcohol (see step 12 in the red wine-making section). That gas gets trapped in the bottle and combines with the wine, making it fizzy and bubbly.

The problem is that the wine is also cloudy. Remember that after yeast eat sugar, the alcohol they produce kills them.

As described in Sur Lie Aging (page 20), it turns out that dead yeast actually create bready, full, nutty flavors, so it pays to keep those dead cells around for a while in a wine like Champagne. But when you're done, you need them out so the wine isn't dirty looking. The bottles are shaken and slowly turned to get the dead yeast into the neck of the glass, close to the mouth of the bottle. Then winemakers just freeze the neck and mouth of the bottle to make a yeasty wine ice plug that pops out upon opening without losing too much wine. This is called DISGORGEMENT.

The wine lost from popping the top is replaced with a wine and sugar mixture, called DOSAGE, that determines how sweet or dry the final product is.

Champagne Method, Méthode Champenoise, Méthode Traditionnelle: If you see these words on the bottle, you'll know that the wine was made in the same way as Champagne. It is always stated on the label of Cava, many American sparkling wines, Crémant from France, and many English and South African sparklers. Look out for it!

Sparkling Method #2: Tank Method

In this method (also called Charmat or Cuve Close), you make white wine, but instead of the second fermentation taking place in the bottle, it's done in a big stainless steel tank, and then the wine is bulk filtered and bottled under pressure. This is a great method, especially when the goal is to preserve the grape's fruitiness and freshness, which could be overwhelmed by the bready flavor of the dead yeast (examples of wines made by Charmat are Sekt from Germany, made of Riesling, and Prosecco from Italy).

Sparkling Method #3: Carbonation

Buying a sparkling wine for $5? It was probably carbonated. Yup, just like soda. Producers use really cheap white wine as a base and then add bubbles. Not great, in my opinion, and you can get better still wine for that price, but it's your call.

Making Sweet and Fortified Wines

Look at Port in the Portugal section (page 210), Sherry in the Spain section (page 224), Languedoc-Roussillon in the France section (page 146), and the Germany section (page 175) for more detail, but as a gross simplification, here are the three main methods of making sweet and fortified wine.

Method #1: Fortify During Fermentation

Fortification, or adding alcohol/brandy to a fermenting wine, kills the yeast and leaves behind whatever sugar it didn't have time to eat.

For this method, you do all the steps you would for red winemaking until fermentation. Then you stop the fermentation by killing yeast with the addition of lots of alcohol. This method is used most notably in Port and with Vins Doux Naturels in the south of France. With Port, the alcohol level is usually no more than 8 percent before fortification, and for Vins Doux Naturels, it's about 10 percent. For each wine type, the flavor differences come from the grapes used and from the aging regimens—Port, especially, shows great differences in flavor based on aging method.

Q + A

Seriously, does anyone drink Sherry besides old ladies? What about sweet wines other than Port? Who drinks this stuff?

I drink Sherry (I'm not that old) and you should, too. It's excellent before dinner as an aperitif with nuts and cheeses, and the sweet Sherries couldn't be better on ice cream. Don't knock the sweet wines either. Remember that before the 19th century, sweet wines were the most sought-after type of wine. There's a reason: They're awesome, especially with dessert or blue cheese!

Method #2: Fortify After Fermentation

For Sherry, alcohol is added after fermentation is complete. So the wine is made like a normal white wine and then alcohol gets added in. That means there is no sugar left in the wine, and therefore Sherry and Sherry-style wines can be bone-dry. Any sweetness in these wines is added later. Flavor differences come from the quality and type of grapes and then from a system of fractional blending (old and new wines are blended in small proportions to get the desired style), with nuances differing based on the style the producer wants.

Method #3: Late Harvest and Botrytized Wine

What is botrytized wine? You may have heard of Sauternes from Bordeaux, famous

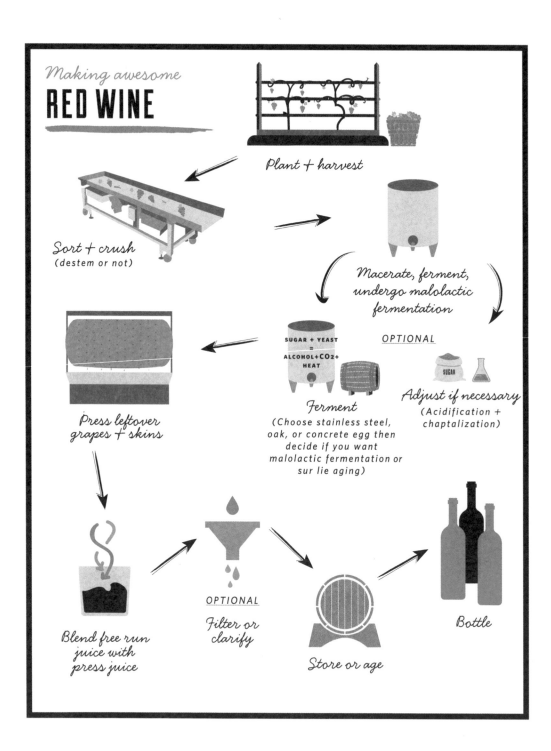

Making awesome
RED WINE

Plant + harvest

Sort + crush
(destem or not)

Macerate, ferment,
undergo malolactic
fermentation

OPTIONAL

SUGAR + YEAST
=
ALCOHOL+CO2+
HEAT

Ferment
(Choose stainless steel,
oak, or concrete egg then
decide if you want
malolactic fermentation or
sur lie aging)

Adjust if necessary
(Acidification +
chaptalization)

Press leftover
grapes + skins

Blend free run
juice with
press juice

OPTIONAL
Filter or
clarify

Store or age

Bottle

sweet Rieslings from Germany and Austria, or Tokaji from Hungary (if not, we cover them in the region sections [pages 116, 177, and 230], so you can learn more there). Although they use different grapes, they share a common bond: The white grapes for these wines are attacked by a nasty fungus called BOTRYTIS (bo-TRY-tis), which has been renamed "noble rot" in many languages to make it seem less disgusting.

Botrytis happens when humid conditions are followed by a cool spell (common in these areas). Instead of making the grape unusable and rotten, the fungus concentrates sugars and flavors and leaves the acidity of the grape intact. The white wines produced are sweet without being overly sugary and unbalanced—the acidity puts the concentrated sugar and the honeyed, bready, tropical flavors in check, and the wine is pure goodness without being overwhelming.

This is different from LATE HARVEST, which means you let the grapes hang on the vine until they are nearly raisined but not rotted. This ensures concentrated sugars, but without those unique botrytis-induced flavors.

To get late harvest wines or those that are botrytis-affected, you wait and check on the vineyard until the sugars are concentrated or botrytis has formed. It may take a few trips through the vineyard rows to get the grapes in the state you want them, since ripening isn't always uniform and botrytis formation can be sporadic: Often one bunch has it and a neighboring one doesn't.

Another option is to make your own raisins! Take very ripe grapes and dry them on straw mats or in ventilated boxes to concentrate flavor and sugar.

With late harvest/botrytized wines, you then make the wine like a regular white

Q+A

I gotta ask. How the hell did someone figure out that wine could be made from grapes with heinous fungus on it?

Well, the history is nebulous, and there is no lore surrounding the specific person who made the discovery. According to one story, late harvest wines were "discovered" when there was a breakdown in communication of when to harvest at Schloss Johannisberg in the Rheingau of Germany, but the story doesn't say anything about botrytis specifically. It's so ugly and looks poisonous, but I imagine that a few centuries ago some dude had his harvest ruined by botrytis and thought to himself, "No one will know if I make wine out of this crap. I'll sell it anyway." In his quest to make a buck, he stumbled upon liquid gold. So kudos to that dude, whoever he was.

wine depending on the style desired. Yeast generally can't turn all the sugar into alcohol before killing themselves, so these rich, sweet bottles often have low alcohol and plenty of sugar.

The Real Role of the Winemaker

Was that explanation of winemaking completely general? Yup. This was to give you a rough idea of how the sausage gets made.

It's accurate, more or less, but it's not the real story of the wine in your glass.

Yes, all wine starts in the vineyard. Where else would it start? Mars? It's an agricultural product. But ultimately there is a person behind every wine, and what that person or that group of people decides to do or not do *really* creates the wine.

The one and only thing I want you to take away from this chapter is that although grapes have their own characteristics, the decisions of the vigneron or winemaker are what make a wine. Good judgment and a good understanding of a vineyard and options available in a winery will yield good wine. Bad judgment, well, you get my drift.

In the Vineyard

There shouldn't be that much that someone can do in a vineyard to affect the taste of grapes, right? Stick vines in the ground and let 'em grow. Au contraire. The decisions in the vineyard may be the most significant ones that affect the taste of a wine.

It starts with planting decisions. Are you matching the grape to the site with the best soil, sun exposure, and drainage? Or would you prefer just to plant based on climate—certain grapes do well in cool climates so you plant them there? Or do you do a combination of both? Choosing a site based on climate, which is common in the New World, will get you ripe grapes, but you may lose the sense of place. That may be fine if you're using those grapes to blend with other, more flavorful grapes. Or it may yield crap wine.

Cutting away leaves that may shade the grapes from getting sun ("managing the canopy") and limiting the amount of grapes per vine are strategies to increase flavor and may be a great idea. Or if you trim the leaves too much and there's a heat wave, your grapes may be prone to sunburn. The result: baked or raisined-tasting grapes.

What about picking decision? Take a grape like Zinfandel. If you pick on the earlier end of ripeness, you get moderate alcohol, and strawberry, raspberry, and herbal notes from the grape. You get some acidity and tannin. Pick late, and prune, plum, and stewed strawberry flavors are the order of the day, along with high, high alcohol (more than 15 percent) and sometimes harsh tannin. With Chardonnay, if you pick too late, the acid precipitously drops and then you have a flabby, fruity, structureless mess.

My point: You get a completely different style of wine depending on when you got into the vineyard to pick the grapes.

I could go on and on—pesticide choices, irrigation practices, clone selection, cover crops, and more. The vinegrower's choices strongly affect the outcome of the wine.

Q+A

What the hell, Schneider? What about natural wine? Or noninterventionist wine? Or the lady I met at a small vineyard who says she just lets the grapes express themselves and then bottles the stuff?

Well, I'll counter by saying that those wine types result from the decisions of people. Inaction is a decision that leads to very different results than active winemaking.

In the Winery

This situation is often more pronounced when you consider the hundreds of decisions that winemakers make to impact the flavor of a wine. It could be things like when to use sulfur to prevent spoilage, how long to macerate grapes in a grape soup, what techniques to use to extract color and tannin from red grapes, and whether or not to acidify/chaptalize/filter/use additives. We know that things like yeast, malolactic fermentation (page 27), and oak are game changers for a wine. The permutations are endless, and a winemaker makes each decision based on experience, tradition, and sometimes spur-of-the-moment thinking.

I could raise many more issues. To filter the wine or not? To cold stabilize it or let it lie? But those are topics for another book. My point is not to detail the process of winemaking as much as it is to tell you the importance of asking questions and figuring out what the answers to those questions tell you about the wine in your glass.

The Wrap-Up

Ultimately winemaking is about two relationships: man and nature, and man and machine (what's in the winery). It's a highly intellectual process if taken seriously and not formulaically (the large wineries have recipes that they follow year after year, which is why their stuff always tastes the same, regardless of vintage). Our job as wine lovers is to figure out not the *how* or the technical details, unless that interests you, but more the *why*. You connect with certain wines because of the decisions a winemaker made in the vineyard or in the winery. If you have a better idea of what a producer did with a wine you like, you'll be in a great position to

A UNIQUE RELATIONSHIP

———

In Europe, the winery decisions are especially complex, since so many companies are neither growers, nor winemakers, but *négociants* (neh-go-SYAN).

Particularly important in France, especially in Burgundy, these merchant houses are like wineries, but different. A négociant buys grapes or wine from smaller growers within an area, creates a final blend, and markets and sells it under its own name. This business practice is vital in places where the producers are so small that they couldn't make enough wine to get to market. It's not easy to do this well—you have to have vision about what will blend well from grapes you didn't grow or wine you didn't make, so négociants have to have skill. If you see *négociant-éleveur* (neh-go-SYAN eh-leh-VUR), this means the négociant blended and aged the wine, so expect something a bit more complex in the bottle. Another wrinkle to consider when thinking of decisions in the winery.

understand more about your preferences. This will help you find other producers who are doing the same thing. And that should satisfy any wine lover's goal: Get more great stuff to drink.

3

HOW GETS ITS AND YOU SHO

WINE
FLAVOR
WHY
SHOULD CARE

he title of this chapter seems so basic that it may appear ridiculous I'm even addressing it. The answer is grapes and winemaking, right? Sort of. But there's a lot more to it than that: There's a set of factors that are seldom explained, so I want to resolve them here and now.

I'll offer myself as the patsy. When I first started drinking wine, I thought that Chardonnay tasted like apples and Pinot Noir tasted like raspberries and Sauvignon Blanc tasted like grapefruit, for instance, because the winemakers put fruit juice with apples, raspberries, and grapefruit into the wine, giving it that extra hit of interesting flavor.

It wasn't the sharpest analysis. But in my defense, I was young when I started drinking wine in earnest (meaning not out of a jug, mixed with Sprite in my dorm room). I'll also justify my naïveté by pointing out that to a normal, logical person who is new to drinking the good stuff, it doesn't really make sense that grapes, in fermented form, should taste like anything except grapes. I mean, hard apple cider doesn't taste like grapes; it tastes like apples, right?

What I was missing, and what no one explained to me for a long time (like six months or more until I admitted to my sister, my partner in wine dorkery, that I was confused), is that although it's made from grape juice, wine has flavors that are, for lack of a better word, un-grapey. As I discussed in Chapter 1, widely identifiable, distinct factors in certain wines are like other things we've tasted or smelled: flowers, apples, tobacco, coffee, and butter, to name a few. But where do these un-grapey flavors come from? It's hard to tell. The situation is not helped by the anointed wine authorities

who give us random wine descriptions but never tell us where flavors originate. You're mostly on your own in trying to figure out what components in a wine make you like it or hate it. Is it because you like the way the grape tastes? Is it because you like where the grapes were grown? Is it because you like oak flavor? How will you know the answers to these questions unless you're able to figure out what derives from where?

The goal of this chapter is to help you break this down so you can get a better idea of what you actually like or dislike in a wine. Consider that if you hate a wine, your hate focus may be the result of something other than the grape. If it turns out it's the grape itself, by all means, nix the wine from the list. But, if you figure out that you don't like the place where it's grown or the winemaking methods used, you've got to try other renditions from different places or from different producers. You can't miss out on great wine because you cut off all Chardonnay or Merlot after drinking one or two nasty examples.

As we go through this chapter, please do me a favor: Think up a grape or wine style that you think you dislike. Apply what I'm saying to this grape, and when we're done, you may have a change of heart and take a second look. You'll have to let me know.

So now, *get your Sherlock trench on, think like Benedict Cumberbatch, and let's reveal some wine truth.*

SIX FACTORS THAT MAKE WINE TASTE THE WAY IT DOES

Lots of factors contribute to taste. But whereas you can dismiss a food because you think it's skunky (for instance, cabbage in any form is completely unacceptable for me), it's not so easy with wine. You need to learn how to break down the wine to its flavor components and, equally important, you have to know how to articulate what you taste. Understanding origins of flavors and textures better can get you another few steps closer to a holistic view of what's in your glass.

Factor #1: Location, Location, Location

You can't make great wine from a bad site or from the wrong pairing of grape and site. That's why, when I described winemaking in Chapter 2, I started in the vineyard, not in the winery. It is the basis for everything in wine. So let's dig into how that affects flavor now.

Bananas and Latitude

The best way to start explaining this is to talk about bananas. Yup, those yellow things that have nothing to do with wine (go with me on this please).

Here's the question: Where do bananas grow?

Time's up. They grow in tropical climates where it's hot and humid, and there's decent rainfall. I have yet to see a banana tree grow wild in Boston, Toronto, or London, and

Q+A

The Wall of Wine in the shop is a nightmare—it stresses me out every time I go in. What's the difference between the fifty different Cabernet Sauvignons? Why does it matter that one is from Sonoma and another is from Napa?

My husband/podcast cohost M.C. Ice's day job is real estate. I'm going to take a page from his book. Much of wine quality and flavor is a result of location, location, location. Where the grapes grow makes all the difference in flavor. Also, the philosophy of the winemaker is often driven by place, so you have to learn the style/tradition of each place to know what to expect in a bottle.

even in warmer places like Florida or Southern Italy they're not a major crop. Why? Because those places aren't in the tropics. The conditions aren't right for bananas.

Wine grapes are the same. They can only grow in a latitude band in the Northern Hemisphere and in the same band in the Southern Hemisphere—from latitude 30° to 50°. The closer you get to 30° (closer to the equator, so it's hot), the more likely you are to end up with fruity, jammy, ripe grapes, often with low acidity. The grapes bake in the sun, and frequently little flavor is left when they're picked. The closer you get to 50°, the more likely it is that the grapes may

in Chapter 1 that includes all the things in the vineyard that make that piece of land unlike any other on earth.

If you look at a vineyard, there are tons of things that influence it—latitude, slope, sun exposure, access to water, altitude, and the variety of soils in which grapes grow, along with the traditions of winemaking in the region. These factors, along with technical stuff like the ability to drain water off the roots, how deep the roots go, and how hard the vines struggle to get the nutrients they need, change the way grapes taste. Some grapes are perfectly suited to certain terroirs; others aren't. Winemakers and viticulturists (grape farmers) are constantly looking for a perfect balance. Plant well and you've got a great wine. Plant the wrong thing in the wrong place and your wine will be awful.

A Note on Terroir Haters

To me, the idea of terroir seems like basic agriculture, but I should tell you that its effect on flavor is not undisputed. When I was trained in California by the big hulking winery where I got my start, a wine educator told me that there was no scientific evidence that soil or location changes the flavor of grapes/wine. I had a hard time believing this so I read articles about the difficulty in determining links between soil and flavor. Turns out, science doesn't have an answer for us. Technically he was right.

I'm a friend of science, but it doesn't explain everything in wine grape growing. You don't need to be a geologist to know that place matters in grape growing—you just have to drink a few wines from certain parts of the world to recognize that the same grape growing in different vineyards with different soils, slope, and sun exposure (i.e., terroir) tastes different. Any normal person can taste certain earthy,

not get ripe every year and the acidity of the wine may remind you of sucking on a lemon or biting into unripe fruit. For reference, the northwestern US-Canadian border in Washington state is at around 49°, and the wine regions of the former East Germany are at 51°. These far northern and southern (in the Southern Hemisphere) places are usually the homes of white wines—reds can't gather color or flavor in these chilly areas, and most winemakers have figured this out. (If they haven't figured it out and you've tried those wines, your mouth has likely figured it out for you. Yick.)

Terroir Is Everything

Now that you get why latitude matters in grape flavor, let's discuss how it ties to the French concept of terroir—not my adorable dog (who is a Welsh terrier), but the untranslatable French concept we defined minerally, dusty, soil-y, chalky, farmlike characters in particular wines once he or she learns to recognize them. And if you go to winegrowing areas with certain soil types and smell or taste the rocks or dirt in the vineyard (yeah, it's gross, but this is your key to being a true wine nerd), you'll notice that the wine has flavors and aromas like that soil. Scientific explanation or no, observation proves this for me, at least.

Exercises in Terroir

If you want to really understand how terroir shows up in wine, here are some great examples. Try these wines and get back to me. I make no guarantee you'll like the character of these wines, but I'm sure you'll taste what I'm describing!

CHALK or mountain stream in Sancerre (Loire Valley Sauvignon Blanc) or Chablis (Burgundy Chardonnay), both from France

SLATE (spicy, like a waterfall) and gasoline/petrol taste in Riesling from Mosel, Germany

GRAVEL AND/OR POTTING SOIL in wines from Bordeaux's Left Bank (fancy way to say the west side of the river, but that's all detailed in the Bordeaux section, page 107)

You Care Because . . .

If you currently doubt that place matters, you'll be a convert after you experiment with these wines. If you don't like the taste of earth/dirt/rocks in wine, you'll know to steer clear of wines that have this as a major feature. If you like it, now you know what that flavor tastes like and which places display it best. Either way, this is fundamental in your understanding of wine—terroir is a major flavor factor.

Factor #2: All Grapes Are Not Created Equal

You're used to going to the grocery store and buying green or red/purple grapes. They come in those giant plastic bags, and they all look and taste pretty much the same. They also taste *nothing like wine.* With good reason—these are not wine grapes. Although they are still *Vitis vinifera*, most are a subspecies of grape called Sultana that is sweet, juicy, seedless, and easy to pop in your mouth. (But not in your dog's. Grapes and raisins can be lethal for dogs, so keep your pup away from them and from the wine rack while you're at it.)

Q+A

The grapes I buy to eat don't taste like flowers or raspberries or strawberries. Why are wine grapes different?

For the same reason it's cool to own a dog, but a disaster to own a wolf. Different subspecies make a difference.

Grapes for wine production are more complex than those you get in the plastic bags because they're a different, more flavorful subspecies (wolf vs. dog). When you pluck ripe wine grapes off the vine, they should taste kind of like the wines they make, which is usually un-grapey if we use table grapes as a reference for grape flavor. They also have seeds, which can add texture and tannin to the grape juice, giving them a bitterness you won't find in table grapes.

There are a few categories of flavors intrinsic to grapes. Within these broad categories are more specific descriptions that wine dorks use (you can find many of these in Chapter 1), but let's dig at the root of the question of fruit vs. other stuff.

We can't leave grapes without talking about our buddy, discussed obsessively in Chapter 1: structure. Structure components vary enormously depending on the grape type. Take tannin. Its bitter, astringent nature is a big reason some people don't care for reds like Cabernet Sauvignon, Nebbiolo (the main grape in Barolo from Italy), and some Syrah. These grapes are tannic—their thick skins can cause a bitter sensation that make the wines seem drier and sometimes more tart. Similarly, high-acid grapes like Riesling, Chenin Blanc, Sauvignon Blanc, Pinot Noir, and Sangiovese can make a wine appear drier and sharper despite abundant fruit aromas and flavors. Grapes like Grenache/Garnacha, Gewürztraminer, and Zinfandel tend to be naturally higher in sugars, so these wines may appear to be sweeter due to more abundant alcohol.

Q+A

Grapes are fruit, so I get why they smell or taste fruity. But how is it possible that wine grapes taste like spice or flowers or other fruit?

Sugar, acid, and other chemical compounds in the grape produce similar aromas and flavors found in other fruit. That's why Malbec smells and tastes like plums, Chardonnay is like green apples, and Merlot sometimes tastes like blueberries. The same concept applies for floral smells. Riesling sometimes smells like white jasmine, and Nebbiolo can smell like roses. Green pepper notes in Cabernet Sauvignon are from the compound methoxypyrazine inherited from its parents, Cabernet Franc and Sauvignon Blanc. Other common notes are white pepper in Grüner Veltliner, and Indian spices in Gewürztraminer (a.k.a. the "spiced Traminer" grape). These notes occur naturally in grapes.

You Care Because . . .

If you love the honeysuckle smell and taste of a Viognier, then you like that grape. If you come across one you don't like, it's not the grape's fault. Blame the winemaker or the grower who cultivated the grape. If you hate the smell and flavor of strawberries, you may want to take Grenache off the list (lots of rosés are made from Grenache, or Garnacha, as it's called in its native Spain). Although it may be variations on a theme, Grenache usually smacks of strawberry. If you dislike tannin, you may need to get more accustomed to the sensation in a Nebbiolo-based wine or have it with food to soften the grape's nature.

The interplay between structure and aroma sometimes varies based on growing region, but certain grapes just have characteristics that we need to learn because they are the building blocks of wine. Because the flavor of a grape is often disguised by other factors (oak [page 71] and yeast [page 69]), we have to take the time to learn what nature serves up before man takes over. To help with that, see the chart

REDS

GRAPE	SMELL/TASTE DESCRIPTORS
CABERNET FRANC	*Fruit:* Black and red cherry, red berry, blackcurrant *Other:* Violet, earth, green pepper, tea leaves, black pepper *Textures:* Smooth texture with medium acid and strong tannin
CABERNET SAUVIGNON	*Fruit:* Blackcurrant, black fruit, green bell pepper *Other:* Violet, roses, mint, earth, green herb *Textures:* Full-bodied, tannic and acidic, can be high in alcohol
GAMAY	*Fruit:* Red berry, red cherry, cranberry, blackberry *Other:* Dark flowers, balsam, black pepper, mineral, licorice *Textures:* Low tannin with good acid and medium alcohol
GRENACHE/ GARNACHA	*Fruit:* Red berries, black cherry; in old vine versions: olive, fig *Other:* Earthy, herbal, black pepper *Textures:* Low tannin, medium acid but high alcohol
MERLOT	*Fruit:* Blueberry, blackcurrant, black fruit, red cherry, fig, prunes *Other:* Game, mint, herbs, truffle, licorice *Textures:* Medium acid, medium tannin, lush; can be too smooth
MOURVÈDRE/ MONASTRELL/ MATARÓ	*Fruit:* Black fruit, prunes, strawberry *Other:* Fresh herbs, earth, barnyard, grilled meat, mint, truffle *Textures:* Generally high in tannin and in alcohol
NEBBIOLO	*Fruit:* Red and sour cherry, blackberry, dried dark fruit *Other:* Roses, violets, herbs, black pepper, tar/pavement, earth *Textures:* High tannins and high acidity
PINOT NOIR	*Fruit:* Red berries, sour cherry, rhubarb, red currant, blackberry *Other:* Minerals, dried herbs, truffles, mushrooms, forest floor, violets, roses, beets *Textures:* Usually acidic with moderate tannin and alcohol
SANGIOVESE	*Fruit:* Sour and red cherry, orange peel, ripe tomato or black fruit *Other:* Violet, green herbs, black tea, dried dirt, potting soil *Textures:* High acid and tannin, medium to high alcohol
SYRAH/ SHIRAZ	*Fruit:* Plum, blackcurrant, raspberry, blackberry *Other:* Black pepper, herbs, lavender, olives, earth, black tea *Textures:* Firm tannin and acid in cool climates; low acid, soft tannins in warm climates
TEMPRANILLO	*Fruit:* Strawberry, blackberry, black cherry, prune, fig *Other:* Dusty earth, tobacco, savory herb, spice *Textures:* Low acid, soft tannins
ZINFANDEL	*Fruit:* Ripe black plum, prune, raisins, blackberry, red berry *Other:* Black pepper, violets, mint, berry briar (woodsy, wild) *Textures:* Low tannin, medium acid, creamy; can feel hot

WHITES

GRAPE	SMELL/TASTE DESCRIPTORS
ALBARIÑO	*Fruit:* Grapefruit, apple, pear, peach, lemon zest, apricot *Other:* Jasmine flowers, minerals, saline/salt water or brine, yeast *Textures:* Acidic, crisp, dry, sometimes creamy, light, bright
CHARDONNAY	*Fruit:* Green apple, lemon, lime in cool climates; tropical fruit flavors, sweet citrus notes, red apple, pear in warm climates *Other:* Minerals, floral, spicy *Textures:* Full, soft, low acid, savory, rich in warm climates; high acid, austere, biting, crisp in cool climates
CHENIN BLANC	*Fruit:* Green apple, citrus; red apple, pear, peach, in warm climates *Other:* Minerals, fresh green herbs, ginger, almonds, honey *Textures:* Acidic, full, sometimes sweet
GEWÜRZ-TRAMINER	*Fruit:* Lychee, pineapple, guava, peach, orange, lemon peel *Other:* Rose petals, white flowers, Earl Grey tea, honeysuckle, cardamom (like chai tea), Indian spices in Alsace *Textures:* High alcohol with just enough acid to keep balance
GRÜNER VELTLINER	*Fruit:* Lime, lemon, pineapple, guava, apple, pear *Other:* White pepper, arugula, green herbs, white flowers *Textures:* Slightly bitter, acidic, dry, creamy, medium-bodied
MUSCAT/ MOSCATO	*Fruit:* Grapes (yes, grapes!), orange zest, tangerine, ripe peach *Other:* Bouquet of white flowers, roses, honey, musk spice *Textures:* Crisp acidity but full; can be viscous if sweet
PINOT BLANC	*Fruit:* Green apple, lemon, lime *Other:* White pepper, spice, almonds, minerals, chalk *Textures:* Medium- to full-bodied with noticeable acidity
PINOT GRIGIO/ PINOT GRIS	*Fruit:* Pear, apple, lime, peach, nectarine, lemon, melon *Other:* Minerals, almonds, honey, honeysuckle, white flowers *Textures:* From dry to sweet, tart to full-bodied and creamy
RIESLING	*Fruit:* Peach, pear, red apple, citrus, lychee, sometimes blackcurrant *Other:* Minerals, slate, white flowers, herbs, honey, petrol *Textures:* Ranges from dry to sweet, with high acid; can be viscous
SAUVIGNON BLANC	*Fruit:* Tropical fruit, jalapeño chile, melon, fig, in warm climates; citrus, green apple, green pepper, in cool climates *Other:* Grass, herbs, hay, smoke, minerals, honey, gardenias *Textures:* Full with high acidity, in warm climates; high acid, medium to light bodied, in cool climates
VIOGNIER	*Fruit:* Peach, honeydew melon, tangerine, baked apple, baked pear *Other:* Lemon cookie, honey, white flowers, sour cream, fresh linens *Textures:* Low acidity, high alcohol

on pages 67–68 of some popular grapes and what they generally taste like. There are ranges even within grapes because of terroir and because of different clones that taste slightly different. Still, there is a broad resemblance across grape type.

Factor #3: Yeast

You can't have wine without yeast. But what is rarely discussed is that yeast is important in determining the end flavors in a bottle. Let's talk about the unicellular organisms that make wine possible.

The Vineyard vs. the Packet

Yeast lives on grape skins, leaves, and stems in the vineyard. Some winemakers just pick grapes, crush them up, and leave them in a vat (called **NATURAL YEAST FERMENTATION**). If everything goes right, the wine ferments, changing the grape sugar into alcohol, as the ambient yeasts eat sugar in the grape juice. This is risky business: Natural yeast is a little wild and crazy. You can't control the flavors it produces, so you say a Hail Mary and hope it does right by the grapes you worked so hard to grow. With luck, you'll get good-tasting rustic notes (think dirt, earth, farmyard), rosy, floral ones, and even fruity notes. Without luck, your wine could taste like goat poop or not ferment fully and be sweet and funky.

Your other option: Add yeast cultivated in a lab. Here, you'll get predictable results—so predictable that you can use yeast strains to influence flavor. Maybe you want more varietal character, maybe more earthiness, maybe even new flavors that are present in only mild concentrations in the grape. *All your Champagne dreams and caviar wishes can come true by adding packets of cultivated yeast!*

Q+A

I know that yeast makes fermentation happen, but isn't that just functional? What does it have to do with wine's flavor?

Much more than you think! A winemaker's choice of yeast can determine whether a wine tastes fruity, floral, or even minerally. It's the hidden, secret weapon. There are companies that cultivate certain yeast to accentuate flavors in a wine, and some winemakers use it to create flavor that was barely present to start with.

There's nothing wrong with using cultivated yeast. In fact, this yeast is preferred: The wine industry is a business, and if you're in it to make money (or even just to sell enough wine to make it until the next harvest), "inoculated" or lab-cultivated yeast is the way to go. Although natural yeast is still on the grape skins and stems when they're brought into the winery, the "cultured" yeast crack the whip, making the process faster, more efficient, and consistent. Apart from those "designer" strains that augment flavor, there are "workhorse" strains of yeast—they ferment and leave little additional flavor. Many top winemakers use these. Either way, when you use cultivated yeast there is no room for different or off flavors. You'll get what you need and want from lab yeast—a completed fermentation!

Winemakers have many opinions on yeast, but regardless of how you get the yeast into the grape juice, the process of fermentation is the same. This process is frothy and frantic, with a sad ending: After their feeding frenzy, the organisms die. Their gorging kills them, suicide machines that they are!

But it's not always the end of their influence on flavor.

The Postmortem Power of Yeast

As we discussed in Chapters 1 and 2, yeast also has a postmortem function in the flavor of wine: As the dead yeast break up through stirring (*bâtonnage*) or sur lie aging, they release enzymes that make the wine nutty and bready.

You Care Because . . .

Yeast can affect whether or not you like a wine. Natural yeast fermentations can sometimes create weird earthy flavors that may not be "clean" enough for your taste. If you sense a bready, nutty character, it could be from the yeast used or from sur lie aging. This is usually positive, and may be a flavor you love in a white, so keep your eyes peeled for it. Yeast is another thing that contributes to your like or dislike of a wine's flavor, and yeast treatment is usually touted on a winery's website in a discussion of how the wine was made. Details on whether the wine has gone through sur lie aging are worth googling if it's something you are curious about.

Factor #4: Creamy, Dreamy Malolactic Fermentation

We've discussed malolactic fermentation (page 27) a few times because it is a major contributor to flavor. Malolactic fermentation can transform the wine's texture from sharp and tart to smooth and soft. Case in point: Many California Chardonnay winemakers rely on malolactic fermentation, and you can taste the creaminess in their wines, sometimes above all else. At certain temperatures or by using sulfur or specific yeasts, a winemaker can inhibit MLF, which often occurs spontaneously in a tank. With white wines like Riesling, Pinot Grigio, and Chablis (unoaked Chardonnay), a winemaker will scramble to prevent MLF so she gets pronounced acidity and varietal character in the finished wine.

For a big, fat, oaky Chardonnay, MLF is essential. Those winemakers deliberately bump up diacetyl, the chemical that gives butter its flavor (and fake butter, too—it's used in microwave popcorn). They do this by a bunch of different techniques, including using yeast strains that promote diacetyl production, lowering the temperature of the fermentation, and encouraging excess production of lactic acid bacteria. In excess, this is considered by most wine pros as a flaw. By the producers and consumers of certain Chardonnays, it's considered fabulous.

You Care Because . . .

If you love creamy, buttery whites, you now know the process that produces them and can seek them out. If you don't love them, now you know malolactic fermentation is an enemy of your palate and you can seek wines that haven't been through it or have only been through it partially. Plenty of whites don't go through malolactic fermentation, including some Chardonnay. If you are an ABC-er (Anything But Chardonnay) and you seek out these non-malo wines, you may open up a whole new world of white wine for yourself and discover a new love for the grape you once maligned.

Factor #5: Oak and Its Love Affair with Wine

I love listening to wine snobs talk about oak. I especially love when they say things like:

Our wine is unique in that 63.74 percent of our Cabernet was aged in French oak from a forest that is said to have housed the original Smurfs—Papa Smurf's ancestors. And 28.92 percent was aged in Slovakian oak, which was hand selected by descendants of Hansel and Gretel. The remainder is Merlot. That was aged in American oak, cut from the same tree as George Washington's wooden teeth.

Although I could do without the pontification, there's no doubt that wood plays a big part in winemaking. There's a science and an art to oak, and its use or abuse is up to the winemaker.

Philosophies on Oak

There are two main reasons why winemakers use oak, and it's important to consider each.

THE BEST WINES IN THE WORLD DON'T USE OAK FOR FLAVOR: They use it to stabilize color and tannins and to aid in natural filtration of a wine since, as the wine hangs out in the barrel, nasty post-fermentation particles (dead yeast, leftover grape stuff) settle to the bottom where they can be removed from the wine. With time, oak can also make a wine feel smoother, fuller, and taste more complex because of the chemical reactions between wood and liquid.

Winemakers also use oak barrels because they provide a good environment for oxygen to react with the wine: A small amount of air seeping into barrels can allow the wine to change slowly and mildly without it turning to vinegar or becoming spoiled in other heinous ways.

MANY NOT-SO-GREAT WINEMAKERS USE OAK AS A FLAVORING COMPONENT: If their grapes aren't perfect, winemakers may want to goose up the flavor. If you do certain things to oak (we'll get into it in a second), it can produce new flavors. Since liquid takes on the flavor of its captor (like when you put water in a brand-new water bottle and it tastes plasticky), this process can happen easily.

Traditionally, Old World winemakers use oak as aging and clarifying vessels, accepting the light "other" flavors as bonuses. New World winemakers traditionally have used oak as a flavoring tool. And they've gone hog wild. Many do everything in their power to manipulate the oak and give their juice just the right nonwine flavors.

Palates have changed over the years and people are less into oaky flavor these days, but as a rule, you'll still find oak to be a bigger factor in New World wines than in those of Europe.

Flavors and Aromas from Oak

Now you know why and how oak can be used. As a general rule, you're tasting oak if you taste or smell the following elements.

SWEET OR BAKING FLAVORS	Vanilla, caramel, toffee, chocolate, cinnamon, nutmeg, allspice, clove, coconut
COFFEE FLAVORS	Mocha, espresso
HEAVY FLAVORS	Cigar box, cedar, oak, leather, smoke
OTHER STUFF	Dill, cut wood from a hardware store

Oak flavors are important to pinpoint; if you dislike the flavors oak imparts, you may mistakenly attribute the offensive taste to the grape, and strike it from your list—a bad idea all around.

Like wine grapes, oak used for barrels is a specially selected species, not the tree in your backyard or local park. People have been using oak for about 2,000 years (and making wine for more than 6,000), so there's been time for experimentation and winemakers know which species work well with wine and which don't. People originally used oak for wine storage because it's easy to bend and make into barrels—easier than palm trees, for example, which folks used in Mesopotamia without much luck (yup, I did just drop the Cradle of Civilization on you). Then people figured out that oak was more porous and actually had characteristics that made wine taste better, so they kept using it. Although some use chestnut (the Italians love it), acacia, or other types of wood, oak is standard in most of the wine world.

There are a few things that contribute to flavor when it comes to oak. No need to memorize them, but it can be helpful to have a vague idea of what they are so when a non-normal wine person mentions them, you know why they are boasting.

LOCATION, LOCATION, LOCATION (AGAIN): There are ideal forests for oak barrels. France, the United States, and eastern Europe contain the top-notch woods. The best trees grow in cooler climates, where they develop slowly and yield a tight-knit grain. In France, Troncais, Allier, Nevers, and Vosges are cooler weather places; Limousin is warmer. If you visit a winery, you may see some or all these forest names stamped on a barrel.

Most French oak imparts limited flavor to wine, creating mellow vanilla, cinnamon, tobacco, and smoke flavors. Wider-grained American white oak from places like Missouri, Ohio, Virginia, and Oregon is strongly flavored, resulting in heavy baking spice, clove, vanilla bean, coconut, and dill flavors.

Q+A

How do you get those savory flavors from a tree? I've been to a hardware store/a park/seen a tree before. I don't know any trees that smell like the stuff you describe. How is it possible a tree makes wine taste like that?

Not only is it possible—it is real! But I agree it's fascinating that someone discovered that doing certain things to an oak tree could yield flavors similar to stuff we eat. (By the way, you may also be asking yourself, "With all those savory flavors, should I start snacking on oak?" Um, nope.)

Raw materials make a big difference in flavor, but sometimes it's a money issue: French barrels are more than double the price of American ones!

Making a Barrel—Chainsaw Massacre, Seasoning, and Human Toasters

What you do to the poor tree after you chop it down majorly affects the wine. Three main things are critical.

IS THE OAK SPLIT OR SAWN? Think about sawing a 2 x 4—it smells a lot different than wood that's split with an ax (think firewood). If you split oak by hand with an ax, it falls with the grain of the wood. You'll get softer scents than if you use a chainsaw, which breaks up the natural grain and creates stronger aromas. Splitting generally produces a better result for barrels, but from an environmental perspective it's a terribly wasteful process because the best coopers only use the straightest grain, which is about 4 percent of the tree. To get the diameter needed for enough barrel staves, trees grow for a hundred years, and each only produces two to four barrels—a lot of effort for little yield.

IS THE OAK "SEASONED" OR DRIED IN AN OVEN? If you've ever seen a tree split open in a forest (you may abhor nature, so I'm not making assumptions), you might recall that it's not dry inside. When you cut open a tree, it's damp. You can't make a barrel out of wet wood so you've got to dry it.

You have two choices: You can leave it outside to let the elements dry it out, also called seasoning, or you can dry it by sticking it in an oven. The first way takes three to five years and can mean that you get unpredictable results because flavors in the wood may change when exposed to weather. This can also lead to softer textures in the wine since the harsh aromas of the wood have mellowed out over time. The second way is quicker, cheaper, and predictable, but once the wood dries, it is what it is. There's no chance for interesting flavors to develop. French oak is usually seasoned; American oak is often kiln dried.

HOW IS THE WOOD TOASTED? Think about brunch. You order toast. You expect the toast to be warm and to have a slight burnt flavor. You may like it just a little golden or you may like it charred. Either way, there's a definite flavor that the toaster lends to bread.

You can think of a wood plank or stave as a giant piece of bread. Depending on customer (winery) preference, the human toasters char the wood to order. From light to heavy, how the cooper burns the wood over an open flame makes a huge difference in how the wine tastes—just like your toast at brunch. Because it's something they have control over, wine people often refer to barrels as the winemakers' spice rack. It's a good analogy, especially since, similar to adding too much spice in cooking, it's quite possible to burn the barrels to the point that they steal the show from the wine.

You Care Because . . .

Oak is an essential determinant in wine's flavor. If you can't separate oak from grape flavors, you could miss out on amazing wine. In the hands of another producer, growing in a different place, and using a different kind of oak barrel, you could love the grape/wine type. If you can keep a vague idea of the flavors from oak in mind, you may be able to separate what you think is the unpleasant taste of oak from the good stuff and move past a bias against certain grapes/wine types.

A CAVEAT ON BARREL ORIGIN

Because I've been asked this a bunch of times: Know that when people say they use French oak, it doesn't mean the barrel is constructed in France. It is ridiculously expensive to ship big, bulky finished barrels overseas, so instead most coopers (barrel makers) or wineries select the wood they want from the forest, season it (page 73), and ship it to cooperages (barrel-making facilities) closer to the wine-making region. For instance, Napa has a couple of big French cooperages that construct the barrels from wood shipped from overseas.

NEW VS. PRE-OWNED: Just as with cars, there are advantages and disadvantages to new vs. used barrels. Brand-spanking new barrels burst with flavor (think new car smell). They'll be more cinnamon-y, coconut-y, clovelike, etc. If a winemaker wants to use oak as a flavor component, choosing new barrels is the way to go. If he or she is just looking for a touch of flavor, or for the properties of oak to stabilize tannin and color, barrels that have been used once or twice will have less of an effect on the taste of the wine. Top winemakers usually opt for a portion of each to get good balance, but especially with tannic, fruity wines, the flavor and structure of a wine are powerful enough to handle 100 percent new oak and still be balanced.

SIZE MATTERS—BARRIQUES, BARRELS, AND CASKS: This is a surface area thing, so get your mind out of the gutter. In a small barrel (like the kind you cut in half and use as a planter when it's retired), more of the liquid is touching the sides of the barrel so the oak flavors will mingle with more of the wine and you'll taste more of the influence of wood. This is called a *barrique,* or barrel. Because it's something you may hear often, here's a size difference: Bordeaux barrels are 225 liters (59 gallons), Burgundy holds 228 liters (60 gallons), and larger vessels like butts and casks hold double that or more. In a big cask, the oak isn't in contact with as much of the wine, so the wood flavors are more diffuse.

You also care because now when snoots start talking about this stuff, you can just imagine a lumberjack in a red plaid shirt and know that's what barrels are all about.

Factor #6: Age in Certain Wines Affects Flavor

What Makes a Good Ager

Wines with high acidity, lots of tannin, and moderate alcohol are great candidates for aging. Vintage, region, and winemaking affect a wine's ability to age, but for the most part, reds like Cabernet Sauvignon, Nebbiolo, Syrah, and red blends from top vineyards are great for longer-term aging (ten-plus years). Whites with high acidity and tons of aromas—Chenin Blanc and Riesling especially—are top candidates, too. Sweet wines, high-end Champagnes, and vintage Ports will last decades. Most other stuff is better younger, and that's most of what we drink, which is why I'm adding age as a last factor that affects flavor.

People are constantly seeking to drink a wine at its PEAK—the often elusive point when the wine tastes best. The problem is that no one has a concrete idea when this is, despite the fact that they make many speculative pronouncements. The stuff is locked in a bottle. Except if you have a gadget that lets you take out a little wine without oxygen ruining the rest, you can't taste it to know if it's at its best until you open it. To make matters more confusing, wine is probably at its best for a few years, so there's a range of time for the peak. Then there's the issue that what you think is a peak, I may think is either too soon or too late!

Old Wine—What Will You See and Taste?

We do know some stuff about age and its effect on wine. First, wine is alive! It's constantly binding together in new ways and changing even in an environment with little oxygen; this is called reductive aging.

You'll see and taste those effects. Like graying hair, red wines will get lighter with time, and like age spots on skin, whites get darker with time. Tannins will be mellower, and fruit flavors will change into stuff like earth, mineral, tobacco, and leather. The wine may seem less acidic as other stuff changes in the bottle—new aromas form, affecting the perception of acidity, even though the actual amount of acid never changes. The finish may appear longer. With good storage conditions (no vibration; no light or heat affecting the wine; cool, humid environment) and a little luck, you'll get a great-tasting wine after it hangs around in a bottle for a few years or decades.

My advice: Don't wait too long to drink that special bottle, because after the peak passes, the jig's up. If you wait too long, as most people do, the fruit disappears and you get acidity with no flavor. It's disgusting. Don't lose track of drinking windows if you're into aging. *Wine is for drinking, so get to it—better to err on the early side than the late side when holding wine.*

Q+A

How long should I age a bottle of wine? Doesn't all wine improve with age?

Wine isn't like Twinkies. It has a shelf life. I wish I could tell you there's a magic formula to figure out how long you can age a wine, but there isn't. The key about age is that not all wines are made to age—less than 5 percent of wines can stand more than five years in the bottle from the vintage date—and that's great. It means there's something ready to drink all the time, excellent for thirsty people like us. Still, age can affect the way a wine tastes if it's a wine that does get better with time. Wine keeps on a-changing even in an environment with little oxygen (reductive aging). Tannins mellow and fruit flavors change, and with good storage conditions and the right wine, you'll get a phenomenal tasting experience when you open it after a few years or decades.

WHO ARE YOU CALLING DUMB?

"Dumb" is actually a real wine term! And it isn't good. During the aging cycle, wine can get to a phase where it loses flavor, texture, and anything interesting that makes you want to drink it. In Bordeaux it's called *age ingrat*, "difficult age," and it's like the wine's adolescence. The wine isn't spoiled; it's just nothing. Is there anything you can do to fix the wine once it's open? Sadly, no. No one has a magic key for figuring out when a wine is dumb; it's just bad luck most of the time. If you have another bottle and hold on to it for a little longer, the wine may bloom into a beautiful glass of fabulous. The moral: Aging wine is risky, and we don't always get what we expect from it.

You Care Because . . .

In your life as a wine lover, you will meet with something that requires age or has been aged. It's important you know what to expect if you have an older wine, and a framework to judge whether or not age has been kind to the wine, or whether it just looks, smells, and tastes old and tired!

The Flavor Decision Tree

Now you know how to break apart a wine into different flavors. Here's a decision tree to bring it home. I don't want to be a Negative Nellie, but since it's easier to decide

what you *don't* like in a wine, we'll put it in those terms.

- If you hate oak in a wine, try either unoaked versions or ones from different areas that may use different types of oak.
- If you hate earthy wines, try ones from different places—New World wines tend to be less earthy. Stay away from known "dirty" wines like Cabernet Franc, Burgundy, or Italian reds, and the wines of Bordeaux, which tend to reflect the land more than other bottles.
- If you hate creamy wines, look for those that haven't gone through malolactic fermentation.
- If you don't like wines that taste like vegetables, stay away from Sauvignon Blanc, Cabernet Sauvignon, and Cabernet Franc, or others that are described as "herbal" or "grassy."
- If you don't like tannin, try versions that are less tannic. Keep in mind that Cabernet Sauvignon, Syrah, Nebbiolo, and some Merlot are super tannic and you'll rarely find versions devoid of tannin. In other words, don't hold out hope that you may get something you like next time if you despise tannin. That said, wines from warmer places will have less of the mouth-drying sensation.
- If you've tried a ton of different versions of the same grape from different places, I'll give it to you—you hate the grape, so *fugedaboudit*. It's time to move on.

The Wrap-Up

We've entered an era where we are increasingly conscious of what we put in our bodies and where it comes from. Wine is not so very different from food in this regard. The

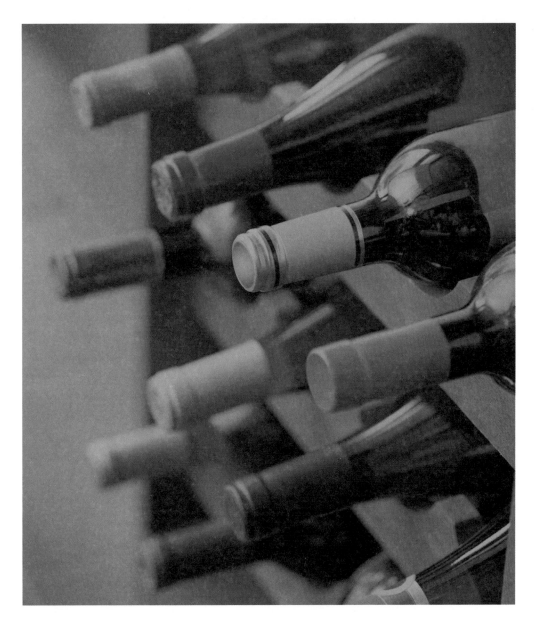

differences between winegrowing, wine-making, and wine flavor depend heavily on the factors discussed in this chapter. Knowing them and knowing the questions to ask about them will take you so far in learning about wines and regions, and about your own preferences. When you put the knowledge from this chapter into practice, you'll find yourself better able to reach the ultimate wine goal: understanding what's in the glass so you can drink fabulously well all the time.

4

WI

GEOGR

and

TWO

WO

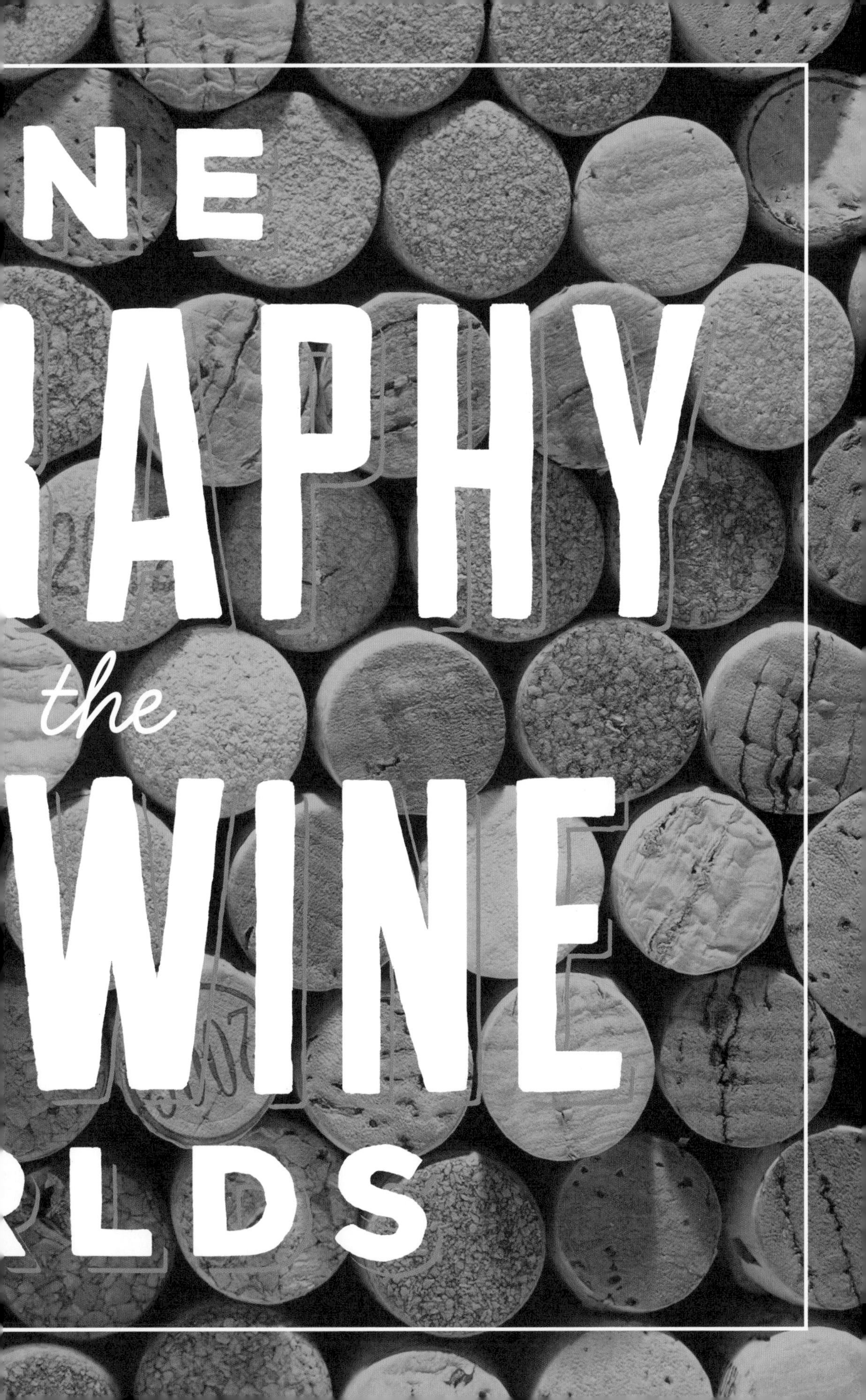
NE
RAPHY
the
WINE
RLDS

n the first three chapters we addressed vocabulary. Now it's time for geography—the other key to understanding wine. Before we get into the nuance, you should know that there's a rhyme and reason to where grapes grow in the Northern and Southern Hemispheres. We've discussed why it's important in Chapter 3 (page 60), so as a quick review here's a cool geography tip that should help you figure out why wine regions are where they are: If you fold the globe in half along the equator, the parts of Europe and North America that grow grapes overlay the same parts in the Southern Hemisphere that also grow grapes—latitude is latitude. From about 30° to 50° north or south latitude, you're in business for cultivating wine grapes.

A Wine World Divided . . .
OLD WORLD AND NEW WORLD

Although there's a fairly fixed latitude where grapes can grow, within that there's a ton of variation. And actually there is another big split in the wine world that's fundamental. This is where it gets tricky because it's more philosophical than land based.

In wine, you may hear people talk about "Old World" or "New World." With these descriptions, you'd think we were living in the days of Magellan. I'm pretty sure we're in the 21st century, yet the wine world still uses the distinctions they used more than 500 years ago. Such a backward industry in so many ways.

Since we probably can't start a revolution to change that, we need to figure out what the heck people mean when they say Old World or New World, because they're loaded terms.

From a geographical perspective, Old World is Europe and parts of the Middle East. Why "old"? Because it's where wine and wine culture began. Old World producers follow the basic philosophy that making wines must reflect the land, or terroir. When it comes to wine, the Old World has quite a résumé.

The traditions and customs surrounding winegrowing—including the species of grapes used (*Vitis vinifera*)—and winemaking developed in Europe and the Middle East. Winemakers there have a ton of experience and have set the precedent of wine styles, aging vessels (oak or amphora), and suitable locations for top-quality wines.

New World is an everything-but-the-kitchen-sink term. It's everywhere else that grows grapes that's not Europe or the

Middle East. All the major places in the winegrowing New World were colonies of some European country—South America, North America, Australia, New Zealand, and South Africa each have ties to Old World wine traditions.

From the 1600s to the 1800s, European colonizers brought grapes to these "new" lands as an essential crop and figured out how to grow them in different climates and soils. Many of these folks were planting grapes for sacramental wine: Booze in the name of religion has a big legacy. But wine culture spread beyond religious purpose, and countries like the United States (fourth in world wine production) and Argentina (fifth in world wine production) are now huge consumers and producers of wine.

Apart from the legacy and location of the regions, some other things are different in each place: how they name wines, how the wine tastes, and each place's philosophies on technology to name a few. Although there's been cross-pollination of ideas in the wine world, these divisions still exist for the most part and probably will continue.

A Wine by Any Other Name Is the Same?

Old World vs. New World and Place vs. Grape

To pause for a second, this is where lots of people abandon ship in the wine aisle, passing quickly over the European wines for something more user-friendly. Let's prevent you from doing that.

Here's the deal: Old World producers *generally* name wines by place (there are some big exceptions, including the Dolcetto I mentioned in the story about my jerky ex-boss in the introduction to this book). This means you have to know what grows in that place to know what's in the bottle *and* know what style of wine is made in that place. It matters and is worth knowing, so that's covered in the next chapters.

New World producers always name wines by the grape or tell you explicitly if the wine is a blend (and often what's in that blend).

What this all boils down to is that the grapes you know and love are masquerading as place names on the bottles you may or may not be able to read. I won't bore you with an exhaustive list, but in the chart there are some good examples of different names for the same wine.

Q+A

Why do French, German, and Italian labels look like hieroglyphics to me? What is all that information on there and what's important?

The labels look foreign because they are, in fact, in foreign languages. If you don't speak those languages, the labels are going to be confusing to you, much the same as if someone asked you to read anything that's not in your native tongue. Plus there's often not a grape name on them, which, if you're used to buying New World wines, could be confusing.

WHITES

OLD WORLD	V.	NEW WORLD
Chablis, White Burgundy, Pouilly Fuissé, Mâcon	↔	Chardonnay
Sancerre, Pouilly Fumé, Bordeaux Blanc (although this is a blend with Semillon and Muscadelle)	↔	Sauvignon Blanc
Condrieu	↔	Viognier
Vouvray, Savennières	↔	Chenin Blanc

REDS

OLD WORLD	V.	NEW WORLD
Bordeaux	↔	Some combination of Cabernet Sauvignon, Merlot, Cabernet Franc, Petit Verdot, Malbec, Carménère
Red Burgundy	↔	Pinot Noir
Cote Rôtie, Hermitage, St-Joseph, Cornas, Crozes-Hermitage	↔	Syrah or Syrah blend
Côte-du-Rhône	↔	A blend of different grapes (23 are allowed and there is a white version, too), mostly Grenache, Syrah, and Mourvèdre
Chianti, Brunello di Montalcino	↔	Sangiovese blend
Barolo, Barbaresco	↔	Nebbiolo
Rioja	↔	Tempranillo blend

Q+A

Why is there such a difference in naming conventions for the same stuff? Why aren't California Chardonnays called Russian River or Monterey, or red Burgundies called Pinot Noir?

Most wine people today will tell you it's because the wines of Europe are terroir driven (there's that word again that refers to the land and the specific conditions of the vineyard that make it unlike any other place) and that the New World plants grapes anywhere and everywhere, with less regard for place. But there's a little more to it than that.

A Historical Dork-Out on Old World Naming

It's well documented that Romans spread viticulture (wine-grape growing) all over Europe, and that part of what made spreading the practice easier was that there were lots of native grapes all over that darn continent—what we know today as France, Germany, Spain, and Portugal all had solid raw materials. As the Romans made wine in certain places and brought it back to the Mother Ship, they followed the ancient Greek tradition of noting the place from which it came, not the grapes from which it was made. (It was too hard to keep track of all the native foliage at that point. I mean, they were making wine, but their main job was to pillage and conquer so we can assume cataloging grapes was a lower-level priority.)

These early imbibers would probably come home and say something like (*disclosure: This is a historical reenactment, not direct quotes*):

MARCUS LUCIUS: *Hey Antonius, great day in the forum! Just saw a gladiator get eaten by a lion. Very cool. So, I was up north pillaging and when we were done I picked up this vino. It's pretty great. You want some?*

ANTONIUS AUGUSTUS: *Definitely. Gimme a swig. What is it?*

MARCUS LUCIUS: *It's Sancerre.**

ANTONIUS AUGUSTUS (*post swig*): *That's good, dude. I've had Sancerre.* It's that place that has white soil, no? I think I passed it when we were going east from pillaging Vouvray. Have you had that stuff? Unreal.*

MARCUS LUCIUS: *Yeah, I dig it.*

The Greeks started and the Romans continued the whole "name by place" business, but it was taken to a new extreme by the monks, the ultimate wine nerds (abstaining from lots of other fun stuff can mean you concentrate intensively on the one allowable fun subject). They studied individual vineyards and small plots of land in Germany and France and kept detailed records. These guys were all about how the place in which grapes grew influenced their flavor.

---

*NOTE: *I'm fully aware that these aren't the Latin names for these places, but you get the point.*

These Old World traditions live on. Think of it this way: It's basically like signposts when you're traveling in a foreign country. When you're a tourist in Florence and you see a sign for the Duomo, you know what that means and what you'll find (assuming you did research on the architecture in Florence beforehand). When you're a "tourist" in a wine shop, you see a Chablis and you know what that means, too (a highly acidic, unoaky Chardonnay from northern Burgundy).

There's no reason to get stressed out about European wines or to pass them over. Think about these wines as opportunities to learn something cool about a place where wine is made (and another place to put on the agenda for travel).

New World Naming

The New World got serious about the wine game in the 1800s, and strangely followed the naming of the Old World for a long time. I say strangely because instead of calling stuff by local names they called wines by their European names (e.g., Pinot Noir was called red Burgundy, Chardonnay was called Chablis, etc.) until Europeans went from being peeved by this to being irate and dealing through national governments to ensure their place names weren't "demeaned."

I get it. If the Australian government decided that Sydney should be named New York City because it was kind of similar, New Yorkers would be furious (I'm a native New Yorker and I know I'd be ticked). There's only one New York, and only one Bordeaux and Rioja and Rhône, so grape names should be used instead.

As far as I can tell, grape names became standard in the New World not out of

respect for "sense of place," but for other reasons. The grapes were planted in too many places in the New World for them to be called specific names (in the early days not much was done to match the land to the grape). Also, winemakers liked the precision of making one-grape-dominant wines as opposed to blending, as is common in Europe. They were making wines after the Industrial Revolution so they had the technology to help them. The one-grape model took hold all over the New World. Place was less important than what you could showcase from the grapes and from winemaking.

This has all changed significantly in recent years—with New World winemakers showing more interest in the land than in winemaking techniques, and Old World winemakers using technology—but the naming conventions hold.

Grape and Place Pronunciations

Now we've got the reasons stuff is named the way it is, but then there's the issue of how to pronounce it. As a normal wine person, you already know how to say a lot of grape names and wine names. However, I do think some grapes, and especially some places, need clarification. If you already know this stuff, skip over this section, please. If you want more information on grapes or regions, look in the region sections.

Dirt, Rain, and Technology: Wine Styles Around the World

Didn't think when you started learning about wine that you'd be pulling out all

GRAPE	PRONUNCIATION
Albariño	Al-bah-REE-nyo
Cabernet Sauvignon	Cab-ehr-NEIGH SOH-veen-yon
Chardonnay	Shard-oh-NAY
Chenin Blanc	SHEN-in Blon
Gewürztraminer	Gah-VURTZ-tra-mean-ah
Grüner Veltliner	GROO-nah Felt-LEAN-ah
Merlot	Mare-LO
Pinot Grigio/Gris	PEE-no GREE-Zho/Gree (Not "grease," as a wine sales guy outside Chicago I was working with once called it. Urgh.)
Pinot Noir	PEE-no Nwah
Riesling	REEZ-ling
Sangiovese	San-jo-VEH-zeh
Sauvignon Blanc	SOH-veen-yon BLON
Shiraz	Shuh-RAZZ
Syrah	Sir-AHH
Tempranillo	Temp-rah-NEE-oh
Viognier	Vee-ohn-YAY
Zinfandel	ZIN-fun-dell

PLACE	PRONUNCIATION
Alsace	AL-zahz
Beaujolais	Bo-zho-LAY
Bordeaux	Boar-DOUGH
Brunello	Brew-NELL-oh
Côtes du Rhône	Coat doo Roan
Loire	LWAHr (soft "r")
Mosel	MO-zle
Rioja	Ree-OH-ha

the stuff you learned in earth science, did you? I never did. But the fact of the matter is that if you want to *really* know wine, I mean *really* know it and not just spout crap about it at a party, you've got to think about land and climate.

Sexy? No. Where all wine starts? Yup.

Wine Styles, Climate, and Wearing a Jacket

We've talked a few times about fruit and cold climates. The summary is that fruit doesn't grow that well in cold climates. You need sun and warmth to ripen stuff, so Siberia, for instance, is not raising big crops of lush, ripe fruit. If, per chance, you can get grapes to grow in a cooler climate, they generally are not so juicy or sweet. Some years, when it's especially cold, the fruit may not even get ripe. Some years it may get really ripe. On average, though, the fruit will probably have acidity that will make your mouth water, and it may be a little bitter, but it will never be super sweet or dripping with delicious juice that gets all over your hands so you have to eat it over the sink.

Relating that to wine, if you think about the locations of some of the places that grow grapes, you can understand that unless global warming really takes off, they aren't capable of making wines that taste like lush, dripping fruit.

Following is a very general list of some places where you may need a jacket when you travel (hence, the style of wine is crisper, more acidic, and earthier and less fruity).

On the flip side, some places are much closer to the equator. These areas often have more fertile soil and usually don't grow just wine grapes, but other delicious stuff (almonds, olives, lemons, avocados).

*(a.k.a. wine regions with a
lower average temperature
during the growing season)*

Germany

Champagne

Parts of the Loire Valley in France

Chablis in Burgundy and the
Côte d'Or (where all the uber-
expensive wines come from)

Mountains of Italy in
the Northeast

Much of Austria

New Zealand's South Island

New York State/Finger Lakes

Niagara Peninsula in Canada

*(a.k.a. wine regions with a
higher average temperature
during the growing season)*

Parts of California—much of
Paso Robles, the Central Valley
(where jug wine comes from),
Lodi, Amador, some of Napa
and Sonoma

Southern Italy

Greece

Most of the Central
Valley of Chile

Most regions of Argentina

Many parts of South Africa

Most parts of Australia

Southern Spain

Southern France/the Rhône,
Provence, Languedoc-Roussillon

Israel and Lebanon

Here, you definitely don't need a jacket in the daytime and may need sunscreen. (Grapes can get sunburned, so this is a good way to think about style. If you need sunscreen, the grapes probably are at risk of scorching, too.) The wines from these regions are fruity, ripe, and lush, and usually have less tannin and acid.

I hope that gives you a picture of how the world shakes out in terms of style. Are there anomalies and pockets in certain areas that are cooler or warmer? Yes. But this is a good rule of thumb to get you thinking about climate and style.

Nature vs. Nurture

Old World winemakers have been making wine for generations—before refrigeration and stainless steel tanks and mass marketing took hold of this industry. Given that, they tend to rely more on what the land gives them than on what they can do with the grapes once they're in the winery. If you were a farmer in the 1600s, that's what you'd do, and then you'd teach your progeny to do the same, and they'd teach theirs, and so on. You get the point. Technology is adopted less quickly in the Old World because the winemakers are already in a groove.

In general, New World winemakers love shiny toys. They create and like technology and are more comfortable with it. Since there is less wine tradition in the New World, it is all about creating new and more efficient ways of doing things.

And can we smartphone-toting, plasma screen–loving, computer obsessives blame them? It's so cultural—the new places kind of "grew up" with technology, so wine people in the New World went with the flow and innovated. As a result, they have a focus on using technology to assist them in the winemaking process. It's a legacy and it's great for all of us who love wine, but it bears mentioning that this runs a bit counter to the "earth first" and "use what your mama gave you" (by mama I mean Mother Nature, of course) leanings of the Old World.

You may be wondering what technologies these New World winemakers use, so here are examples (detailed in Chapter 3).

OAK AGING TO GIVE GRAPES FLAVOR: This is generally done more in the New World, where many winemakers call barrels "the spice rack."

MOTIVATING MALOLACTIC FERMENTATION: This gives a buttery flavor and creamy texture to a wine. Although Old World wines go through malolactic fermentation, Old World winemakers often start the process later (after the yeast has killed itself by converting all the sugar to alcohol), creating less of a buttery sensation.

Q+A

Why do I care about people using technology or not? What does that have to do with wine flavor or winemaking? Seems a little "in the weeds."

Because you can taste the difference in the wines. Technology and winemaker choices about how to use it can make all the difference in changing a wine's flavor. This can be good, or it can mean the wine really sucks as a result. Since you are the ultimate arbiter of taste, you can take a position on this based on your palate.

USING STABILIZATION AND FILTRATION: This produces a "cleaner" wine before bottling. Although some would argue the point, the common New World practices of cold or heat stabilizing a wine (see page 51) and fining/filtering a wine can strip away flavor and tannin, which can make a wine last longer and be more complex.

USING LAB-CULTIVATED YEAST: Rather than relying on yeast that naturally lives on grape skins to ferment, using hand-selected yeast allows fermentation to finish, so you get clean flavors that don't have anything weird or earthy to them. The downside: Flavor is less "interesting" (then again that can be a good thing, too, if the interesting flavor is "skunky").

Vintage: Get Thee to Weather.com

Vintage, which is an indication of weather in a given year, has a close relationship to place. For instance, you may live in a place where the weather is fairly consistent. For you, it's a rare year where strange things happen, and storms and unlikely weather events get meteorologists geeked up for their crowning moment of glory where they get hours of airtime talking about lightning, wind, and rain.

Or you may live in a place where weather dictates your life. For example, when I lived in Boston, whipping cold wind, freezing temps, snow, and rain (for nine months of the year) meant that some years we barely went outside for months at a time and in other years we were overjoyed that, even though it was minus 14°F (minus 25.5°C) with the wind chill, we could brave the streets without snowshoes. Weather ran our lives.

So what does this have to do with grapes and vintage? In places in active weather zones, their growing seasons (spring and summer) each year are wild cards. You never know if you'll have horrible wind that could rip the clusters off the vine as the grapes are forming and reduce your harvest, or if you'll have torrential rains that will bruise the grapes as they are ripening, or if you'll have a heat wave that could mean your grapes get annihilated by the sun.

On a continent that is very far north and surrounded by seas to the north, south, and west, and mountains that form their own weather systems, Europe is bound to have tumultuous weather annually. That means sometimes you'll hit the jackpot and your crop will be amazing, but sometimes it will suck and only the best winemakers will be able to make lemonade from those unsightly lemons. If you've ever vacationed in Europe, you know that often whatever you packed is inevitably the wrong thing for precisely these reasons: Welcome to the Old World.

Elsewhere in the winemaking world, there is weather but it's not quite as volatile. We've addressed California, but let's hit a few more places. Argentina's wine regions, located very high in the mountains, are dry and escape much of the rain and bad weather they would experience if closer to the coast. Australia is plagued by drought, so winegrowers don't have to worry much about rain. A lot of their growing season is controlled by irrigation systems. Chile and South Africa have more variation but are still pretty consistent with weather. There are erratic regions like Virginia, Oregon, and the Finger Lakes of New York in the United States, but the main growing regions in the New World tend to have more stable weather.

We can generalize, but no two years are the same for agriculture, no matter where you are. You may love a wine one year, only to find that it is horrible the next. Could it be that the winemaker changed the blend or degraded the quality? (A lot of big wineries do this two to three years after launch on their lower-range products, BTW.) Sure, but for established brands, it's usually about weather.

Before you buy anything, you should pay attention to that number on the bottle and do a little poking around (I like Decanter's vintage charts), especially if that wine is from the Old World or a weather-prone New World region.

So that's why people get dorky when it comes to vintage. It matters, and it matters a lot to the flavor and quality of the wine.

Classification Systems

Before we get into the wine regions around the world, you need to know one more important thing: All wines in well-established winemaking countries are part of classification systems. Some are simple, and some are complicated, but most are useful because they designate something on the bottle that tells us what to expect inside it. Once you start looking for these designations, it will help you be a better wine shopper, so it's worth your time to puzzle over this for a second.

After what I've just laid out in terms of how each "world" has its own philosophy regarding wine, it should be no surprise that the divide between New World and Old World classification systems is wide and deep. Most New World countries have a vague and general appellation system, and Old World countries are detailed almost to a fault.

Q+A

What the heck is an appellation?

An appellation is a legally defined geographical area where grapes are grown. You're going to hear this word a lot in the wine world. Equate it with place and you're good to go. Countries use the names and regulate them to give us more information about where the wine is from and to protect the region's name so others don't try to use it to make their wine seem like something it's not (for instance, sparkling wine can't be Champagne unless it's from that area of France).

New World Systems

The New World doesn't give a lot of information on the bottle. For example, sometimes appellations are nested within each other (subappellations), but you won't see the larger region on the bottle—that's something you'll have to learn on your own. All you'll see is a place name that specifies that the grapes were all or mostly grown in a specific area. There are no restrictions on how the wine should taste, on yields from the harvest, or on winemaking techniques required. All the appellation tells you in the New World is that a majority of grapes for that wine were grown in that specific area. The winemakers can do as they please.

This makes place name meaningless unless you can figure out what each of the appellations is telling you. With New World wines, I find that the smaller the area, the more predictable the wine flavor. So for a huge appellation like "California," there's no way to know what you'll get in the bottle, since grapes can come from anywhere in a state that makes 90 percent of the wine in the United States. However, if you see Santa Maria Valley from Santa Barbara County, you'll most likely get a high-acid yet fruity wine.

I've listed the appellation systems of the New World on pages 90–91. Because there's variation, I also detailed what's required of the vintner to place certain details on the bottle.

Old World Systems

Europe is a whole other bag of beans. Wine traditions obviously stretch back further in the Old World than in the New World, so classifications reflect these traditions, specifically those of France, the first country to formalize a modern, government-run classification system in the mid-1930s. Another factor in the Old World is that the major wine-producing nations in Europe are members of the European Union, which under its Common Agricultural Policy regulates vineyards and wine production. (Big difference from the United States: Europe's agriculture arm deals with wine regions, while the US tax arm deals with wine regions. Whose is probably more accurate?)

tip

Usually more specific appellations yield more specific wine types.

Under EU law, winemaking and vineyard practices, wine classification, and labeling are fairly standardized, although the pan-European system makes room for each nation's quirks by allowing them to adapt the previous practices of their own

NEW WORLD CLASSIFICATIONS

COUNTRY	CLASSIFICATION SYSTEM	LABEL REGULATIONS
ARGENTINA	**Geographical Indication (GI)** Loose system of subareas or designation of origin or DOC (few of these)	**85% of the grape** must be in the bottle to put a grape on it (no other regulation specified).
AUSTRALIA	**Geographical Indication System** Three levels (in order from biggest to smallest): • **Zone** (large area or a state like South Australia, also Super Zone like Southeast Australia, which includes nearly all regions outside Western Australia) • **Region** (e.g., Eden Valley) • **Subregion** (e.g., High Eden)	• **85% of what is stated on the label** in terms of region, grape, and vintage needs to be in the bottle. • **If two grapes are listed,** the first name has to make up a bigger portion of the blend. Both combined have to be at least 85%.
CANADA	**Vintners Quality Alliance (VQA)** Specifies origin, vintage, and varietal rules. Not regulated by the Canadian government but by members and a board in British Columbia (BC) and Ontario.	• **100% of the grapes** must be from the province. • **95% of the grapes** must be from the region. • **85% of the grapes must be from the vintage** and grape listed. • **In BC,** only *vinifera* grapes can be used for VQA.
CHILE	**Denomination of Origin System** Three levels (in order from biggest to smallest): • **Regions** (e.g., Valle Central) • **Subregions** (e.g., Rapel Valley) • **Appellations** (e.g., Colchagua)	• **Only 75%** of what is stated on the label in terms of region, grape, and vintage needs to be in the bottle.

systems. The goal of the unified system is to improve quality, reduce supply of crappy wine (by reducing yields through regulation and providing incentives for better growing), keep labels as simple as possible, and protect the place names from being used outside the regions.

Revised in 2011, the European system includes two levels: Protected Geographical Indication (PGI), a simple category that includes table wine and the more restrictive "country wine," and Protected Designation of Origin (PDO), which the EU defines as products "produced, processed, and prepared in a given geographical area, using recognized know-how."

More on the Protected Geographical Indication

Table wine is basic stuff. It's the base tier of wine, but it doesn't mean it's plonk (although it can be!). It's just not from any specific, called-out area, and it has no restrictions on farming, winemaking, blending, grapes—anything. It's wine from anywhere in the country—"Vin de France" or "Vino" in Italy for example—and the

NEW WORLD CLASSIFICATIONS (CONT)

COUNTRY	CLASSIFICATION SYSTEM	LABEL REGULATIONS
NEW ZEALAND	**Geographical Indication System** Simple in New Zealand. For practical purposes you'll see a region like Marlborough or Central Otago. There are no subregions yet.	• **85%** of what is stated on the label in terms of region, grape, and vintage needs to be in the bottle. • **If two grapes are listed,** the first name has to make up a bigger portion of the blend. Both combined have to be at least 85%.
SOUTH AFRICA	**Wine of Origin System** • **Regions** (e.g., Coastal Region) • **Districts** (e.g., Stellenbosch) • **Wards** (e.g., Simonsberg-Stellenbosch)	• **100%** must be from the place stated. • **At least 85%** of the wine must be from the vintage stated. • **85%** of the wine must be from the grape stated.
UNITED STATES	**American Viticultural Area (AVA)** Regulated by the Tax and Trade Bureau (which has little interest in agriculture, as you can tell by the name). AVAs are determined by: • Wineries that petition • Political boundaries (around a state or a town) • Historical use of the name of an area ("Napa Valley" has been called that for a long time.) • Similar geographical features (Carneros straddles Napa and Sonoma Counties but has a consistent climate across boundaries.)	• **85%** of grapes have to come from the AVA. • **Or 75%**, if the AVA is a county or state name, with some exceptions (wine that says California must have 100% California grapes; wine that says Washington must have 95% Washington grapes). • **75%** of the wine must be from the grape stated. • **95%** of the wine must be from the vintage stated.

label can specify producer, grape variety, vintage, and country of origin but not much else. This is what most people drink with their lunch in Europe. It is called vin, vino, vinho, wein, wine, or something similar. You may see a country name attached like "Vin de France" or "Deutscher Wein."

The slightly higher level of PGI wine specifies a large region with loose regulations on yield, alcohol, and other winemaking practices. These wines are supposed to be typical of the region, but that "typicity" has wiggle room because this level was created to let producers make nontraditional blends (see the discussion of Super Tuscan wine in the Italy section, page 202) and label their wines with grape names to compete with New World wines. Although they are all the same initialism (PGI, or IGP, depending on the language), the "country wine" level has different names in different countries.

- **France:** Indication Géographique Protégée (IGP) or Vin de Pays (VDP)
- **Italy:** Indicazione Geografica Protetta (IGP) or Indicazione Geografica Tipica (IGT)
- **Spain:** Indicación Geográfica Protegida (IGP) or Vino de la Tierra (VT)
- **Portugal:** Indicação Geográfica Protegida (IGP) or Vinho Regional (VR)
- **Germany and Austria:** Landwein
- **Greece:** Traditional Appellation or Country Wine
- **United Kingdom (not part of the EU):** Regional Wine

More on the Protected Designation of Origin Wines

These restricted origin wines are based off the French system of Appellation d'Origine Protégée (AOP), which has strict rules about grape varieties, blends, farming and vineyard practices, and winemaking methods. The wines are governed by local wine authorities and control boards. Each wine must be tasted by the board for "typicity"—the wine has to taste like it came from the place, regardless of quality.

These PDOs vary in size from massive regions to an acre or smaller. They are only a guarantee of origin and winemaking practices. (Although inside sources tell me that unethical winemakers apparently cheat like devils on this and fudge yields, vintages, and blends constantly, so take it for what it's worth. As I'll say time and again in the region sections, producer counts!) Similar to the New World, the smaller the appellation, the more distinctive or typical the wine, so a wine from the vineyard of La Tâche in Burgundy is more unique, predictable, and expensive than a general Burgundy wine.

The PDOs have two levels in most countries and different names (see right).

Although the requirements vary by appellation and country, PDOs require 100 percent of the grapes to come from the appellation stated and 85 percent of the grapes to come from the vintage or variety, if listed. Each country has nuances within the categories I list, but these broader categories are on the labels of every European PDO wine, so you can look for the category often as a seal on top of the bottle (Austria, Italy) or on the label (France, Germany, Portugal, Spain).

Confusing enough? Yes, but now you have a guideline when you see these terms on the bottle. For now, just concentrate on what is more restrictive and what is less restrictive. As I mentioned with the New World, often the smaller the area, the more consistent the wines. For instance, all wines

OLD WORLD CLASSIFICATIONS

COUNTRY	LESS RESTRICTIVE PDO CLASSIFICATION	MORE RESTRICTIVE PDO CLASSIFICATION
FRANCE	N/A	**AOP** (Appellation d'Origine Protégée) or AOC (Appellation d'Origine Contrôlée)
ITALY	**DOC** (Denominazione di Origine Controllata) **DOP** (Denominazione di Origine Protetta)	**DOCG** (Denominazione di Origine Controllata e Garantita)
SPAIN	**DO** (Denominación de Origen)	**DOCa** (Denominación de Origen Calificada)
PORTUGAL	**IPR** (Indicação de Proveniência Regulamentada)	**DOC** (Denominacão de Origem Controlada)
GERMANY	**QbA** (Qualitätswein bestimmter Anbaugebiete)	**Prädikatswein** (formerly known as QmP or Qualitätswein mit Prädikat; more detail on this in the German section)
AUSTRIA	**Qualitätswein**	**Prädikatswein including DAC** (Districtus Austriae Controllatus)

from Barolo in the Piedmont of Italy should share some common characteristics if the producers are playing by the rules.

The Wrap-Up

Now you're up to speed on the divided worlds. Let's move on to some fun stuff— the regions and what great wines you can discover from them.

5

OL
WO
REG

n the intro to this book, I tell you the magic secret to knowing wine: It's all about vocabulary and geography. So if vocabulary is the heart of the wine world, geography is its soul and the Old World is the "old soul" of it. In the previous chapter, I explained what the Old and New World are and the differences between them. What follows in this section are the details on the most important regions in European wine.

Have I included every last region where grapes grow in Europe? Nope. But all the important stuff is here along with info on what the wines taste like and why they're interesting. There are some regions I feature that you may not see in other wine books. I want to share them with you because these regions make tasty wine that are worth hunting down.

And two pieces of housekeeping on Old World . . .

1. As an important general note as you are buying and trying Old World, remember that because of the cooler climate in most areas of Europe vs. parts of the New World, the wines of the Old World will often be higher in acidity, lower in alcohol, and have flavors other than fruit as their primary characters. They tend to be stunning with food and, honestly, sometimes kind of bad without it!

2. If I were you, I'd probably dip in and dip out of the regions as my interest dictated. If I had my way, you'd read the intro sections of the countries before you get into the details on the specific regions (like read about Italy and then get into Tuscany), but it's your book and your wine journey so choose your own adventure, to steal a phrase from my favorite childhood books.

Western Europe
AUSTRIA

I don't know where most of my family is from—some part of Germany, Russia, or Poland that used to be full of Jews—but I do know that some of my maternal grandfather's family was from Austria, so it gives me a certain loyalty to the place. Maybe that's just an excuse for why I love the wines, but I'm going with it.

Austrian wine may not have the mass "brand" that its neighbors Italy and Germany have, but making wine is no new venture for Austrians. The Romans started making wine here about 3,000 years ago. Recently archaeologists found grape seeds in urns dating to about 700 B.C. from vineyards along the Danube River. The place has serious wine cred.

Although it may seem like a fringe player these days, after World War I Austria was the world's third-largest wine producer. Was it good wine? No! It was bulk junk exported to Germany and other countries that couldn't grow large volumes of grapes because of their own sketchy weather conditions. But I think it's important to let you know that Austria has been a big player and could be again, although I doubt that will happen given a small issue the country faced in the '80s.

I hate having to mention this, because I don't want you to get the wrong idea and avoid wine from this country, but Austria had a big ol' wine scandal in the mid-1980s. It was then that a large, unethical producer added a chemical found in antifreeze to fatten up the body of its wines (turns out that diethylene glycol really fills in the holes of a thin wine—who knew?). Although the quantities used weren't going to kill anyone, the "antifreeze scandal" ruined Austria's wine reputation for two decades. No one would touch the stuff.

The Austrian government could have handled the scandal poorly, but it didn't mess around. From 1985 on, the government has cracked down so hard on producers and become such a watchdog over quality that now most of the stuff coming out of the country is great. Getting rid of the bad seeds means that Austria makes a lot less wine; today it's seventeenth in world production. But small yet good production is not a bad thing.

The more challenging issue for Austrian wine is that it can be hard to pin down the character of the wine: The terroir varies so much that you have to try many different wines from different places before you decide what you like and what you don't. Regardless, I find that the wines of Austria have an acidity and a spiciness that will snap you out of any wine rut you're in.

Because these are fairly specific to Austria, I want to go over the main native grapes.

Whites

GRÜNER VELTLINER (GROO-nah FELT-LEAN-ah): Austria's crown jewel and native daughter, Grüner makes up nearly a third of plantings. This is one of the most interesting, versatile whites you'll find. Ranging from light and citruslike to full-bodied with white pepper spice, tropical fruit, and apple flavors similar to an aged Burgundy, this wine has teeth. It can age if made well. As a personal note, I used to hate the arugula

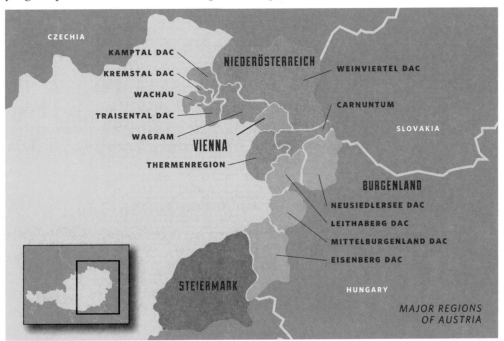

MAJOR REGIONS OF AUSTRIA

bitterness of this wine, but I kept trying and I've acquired a taste for it, so make sure you don't give up. I love it now and recommend it to people looking for interesting whites!

RIESLING: Austrian Rieslings tend to be dry, stony, and full of nectarine and peach flavors. Their acidity is powerful, as with all well-made Riesling, but is offset by a fuller-bodied richness that makes them closer to Alsace Rieslings than German ones in many cases.

Reds

BLAUFRÄNKISCH (BLOW-**FRAHN**-KISH): An acidic red that tastes like black pepper and cinnamon red hots with raspberry fruit, it's refreshing, delicious, and a must-try. The spice will have your mouth singing if you get a good one!

ST-LAURENT (**SAHN** LORE-AHN): A cross of Pinot Noir and an unidentified grape, this wine has berry flavors and is like a rougher, earthier, denser version of Pinot. If you love Pinot's natural, outdoor, gamy flavors, St-Laurent will be a home run for you.

ZWEIGELT (SFY-GELT): In 1922 Dr. Fritz Zweigelt, a professor at one of the wine universities near Vienna, crossed the two other Austrian red grapes—Blaufränkisch and St-Laurent—to get this gem. Today, it's the second most planted grape in Austria (after Grüner Veltliner). It's generally light to medium in weight, with cherry and violet flavors, a hit of peppery spice, and good acid. It's great with food.

The Classification System

Like all EU countries, Austria has a multi-level classification system for wine. It has two main quality levels: the Protected Geographical Indication (PGI), including table wine and country wine, and the Protected Designation of Origin (PDO).

The quality wines—QUALITÄTSWEIN (QUAL-EH-**TATES**-WINE)—are easy to spot. The wine's cap has the red-and-white Austrian flag on top as a guarantee the bottle has been through government chemical and taste testing for typicity (meaning it tastes like what it's supposed to taste like). If it's from a designated region (DAC OR DISTRICTUS AUSTRIAE CONTROLLATUS), specific grapes and style protocols are dictated, similar to the AOP and DOP wines of France and Italy. There are other great regions that are not DACs, and these areas generally have local tasting boards and controls that ensure the wines reflect the style of their winegrowing region.

Austria's *Prädikat* (preed-ee-KAHT) system is nearly identical to Germany's (which I detail in the Germany section, pages 175–87), so you'll see Spätlese, Auslese, Eiswein (ice wine), Beerenauslese, and Trockenbeerenauslese on Austrian bottles, which translate to the levels of ripeness in the grapes. There are some additional designations as well—Ausbruch (owz-BRUCK) is made from botrytized, dried-out grapes, and Strohwein (STROW-wine) is used for sweet wines made from grapes dried on straw mats.

Important Regions of Austria

Austria has great winemaking regions. Vienna is also the only major city in Europe with more than 1,500 acres (607 ha) of vineyards within its limits. Along with Vienna there are three major quality winegrowing areas: Niederösterreich (NEEDA-oh-stir-ike), Burgenland, and Steiermark (STYER-mark). Each area has specified varieties, and to get a DAC status, regions need to show that their wines have terroir-driven characteristics.

Below, I outline the places that produce the highest-quality wine these days, but I encourage you to explore outside these regions.

Niederösterreich (Lower Austria)

The biggest growing area in Austria, Niederösterreich includes a hit parade of winegrowing regions. From the area along the Danube River near Vienna to a warmer part of the Pannonian Plain in the southeast, this huge area makes a variety of wine styles and contains the most famed wine regions of Austria—including Wachau, Kremstal, and Kamptal, detailed below. Other DACs include Wienvertel and Traisental for Grüner Veltliner. Quality areas without DACs are Carnuntum, Wagram, and Thermenregion, and I've had great wines from all these places.

Wachau (vah-HOW)

In Austria's most famed and arguably highest-quality wine region on the Danube River, Grüner Veltliner is the big thing. The best versions have apple and tropical fruit flavors with white pepper spice. Rieslings are full and unctuous. The area's producers are exclusive and have tried to distance themselves from those in the rest of Austria. Wachau doesn't have a DAC of its own but rather a regional honor code and classification system used by some, but not all, producers, with alcohol/ripeness as a guidepost. From lightest to heaviest, the categories are steinfeder (SHTINE-feeder),

federspiel (FEEDER-shpeel), and smaragd (ZMAHR-acht); this last one strangely named after a type of green lizard that hangs around in Wachau.

***

CLOSEST CITIES: *Major wine towns Spitz, Weissenkirchen, Melk, and Dürnstein are 1 to 1.5 hours west/northwest of Vienna by car.*

Kremstal and Kamptal

East of Wachau and also near the Danube River, these adjoining regions have similar styles to Wachau but are much better values. Kremstal is known more for spicy, ripe Grüner and terroir-driven, minerally, lighter Riesling. Kamptal is also known for Grüner and Riesling. Its Grüner is fruity with white pepper notes and high acidity, and the Riesling is fuller in body and fruit flavor. Kamptal is warmer than Kremstal and has a varied climate and terroir. It grows a broader set of grapes—it even grows impressive reds!

***

CLOSEST CITIES: *The Kamptal wine towns of Schönberg, Zöbing, Langenfeld, and Gobelsburg are about 1 hour from Vienna by car. Kremstal's main wine towns of Krustetten, Furth, Gedersdorf, Rohrendorf, Senftenberg, and Stratzing are also about 1 hour from Vienna by car.*

Burgenland

This hot, landlocked region is red wine country: It is the only area in Austria that grows more red grapes than white. With vineyards lying on the shores of Lake Neusiedl (noi-SEE-dle) and on the Pannonian Plain that stretches through eastern Europe, Burgenland has a continental climate. The Blaüfrankisch,

St-Laurent, and Zweigelt tend to be spicy and minerally with great acid and medium tannin. The lake moderates the climate and adds humidity to the air, making botrytis-affected dessert wines (page 57) a big feature of this area (Ausbruch from Rust is famed, as are other sweet wines from here). Taking advantage of lower production costs, new winemakers are setting up in Burgenland, so there's no shortage of high-quality, awesome value wines coming from the region.

Burgenland has four DAC subregions: Mittelburgenland and Eisenberg for Blaufränkisch; Neusiedlersee (NOY-seed-la-see) for Zweigelt; Leithaberg for Blaufränkisch; and whites from Grüner, Pinot Blanc, Chardonnay, and a local variety, Neuberger.

CLOSEST CITIES: *A 1-hour drive south of Vienna will land you in the towns of Rust or Neusiedlersee-Hügelland/Leithaberg.*

Stiermark

Stiermark is the most rustic and remote winegrowing region of Austria, known more for its hot springs and spas than for its wine. This region represents less than 7 percent of vineyard area in Austria, and three quarters of the grapes grown here are white, the lion's share of which are the acidic and sometimes flavorless Welschriesling and Pinot Blanc. The local rosé, Schilcher (SHEIL-shuhr), made from the native Blauer Wildbacher grape, is one to try. This is a more rural, rustic, and less wine-focused area than others, so you won't see a lot of wine from Stiermark outside Austria.

CLOSEST CITIES: *A 2- or 2.5-hour drive south from Vienna will get you to the towns of*

Südoststeiermark *(Fürstenfeld, Bad Radkersburg, and Klöch), the* Südsteiermark *(Leibnitz and the Sausaler Wine Area), and the West-steiermark (Deutschlandsberg, Stainz).*

The Wrap-Up

I've only scratched the surface of the bounty of Austrian wine, which is not short on flavor, variety, or value. The Austrians' dedication to quality is apparent in the glass. These are not blockbuster, full-bodied wines, but don't let their medium texture fool you: The aromas, acidity, and spicy bite in a good glass of Austrian red or white will leave you wanting more. I need to go get a glass right now, just thinking about it!

FRANCE

I feel silly trying to sum up France. It's the motherland of wine. No country has been as influential or essential to wine in the modern era as France. If you read through any of the sections on the major regions that follow this summary, you'll see that each has its own challenges and strengths, but you can't deny that every single one produces famed wines and grapes that have been replanted around the world due to their stellar flavors, textures, and structures. Nearly all the major grapes in the wine world have French names because most are native to France: Cabernet Sauvignon, Sauvignon Blanc, Chardonnay, Merlot, Syrah, Chenin Blanc, and more.

Part of France's success is that it's sort of impossible to get bored with what the country has to offer in wine. It churns out every style possible. And it makes perfect

MAJOR REGIONS
OF FRANCE

NETHERLANDS

UNITED KINGDOM

BELGIUM

GERMANY

LUXEMBOURG

English Channel

CHAMPAGNE

BAS RHIN

PARIS

ALSACE

HAUT RHIN

LOIRE VALLEY

BURGUNDY

JURA

SWITZERLAN

Bay of Biscay

SAVOY

ITAL

BORDEAUX

RHÔNE VALLEY

SOUTH WEST

LANGUEDOC

PROVENCE

LANGUEDOC-
ROUSILLON

ROUSILLON

Mediterranean

SPAIN

sense how and why: With French wine, we're looking at an area that ranges 7.5° in latitude and represents vastly different terroir for grape growing from north to south and east to west. Mountains, oceans, rivers, and the range in climate make France outstandingly varied and, accordingly, the wine styles diverse.

At latitude 42° north in the southern portion of the country, you'll find a Mediterranean-influenced climate where grapes ripen reliably every year, often over a long, lazy growing season. Wines of the southern Rhône, Provence, and Languedoc-Roussillon won't have a shortage of fruit flavor or alcohol—and because of that they are a great jumping off place for lovers of New World wine who are taking France on a first date.

In the western portion of the country, the grapes of Bordeaux and Southwest France at latitude 44° to 45° north range in their ripening patterns depending on vintage. In some years, grape growing is an onerous task, and in others perfect weather makes for beautiful, balanced wines. The Gulf Stream coming off the Atlantic Ocean offsets the coolness that comes with higher latitudes, and complex, distinctive reds, flavorful whites, and sweet wines result.

In the eastern portion of the country and along the north in the Loire Valley region, wine-grape growing gets dicey. At latitudes that reach 49.5° north, almost at the limit where grapes can ripen, miracles of viticulture and winemaking occur. Centuries of learning about the land and winemaking have given vignerons (growers/winemakers) the ability to understand their land so well that even in unlikely areas for grape growing we can enjoy every color and style of wine, all restrained and moderate in body, except for the sweet wines, which are unctuous and irresistible.

Perched on a limestone strip just west of the Saône River is Burgundy, a place with hail, rain, and inconsistent weather that makes viticulture a labor of love. And yet for thousands of years, people living in this eastern central portion of France have understood and obsessed over the idea of terroir—that the grapes and the land have an intimate relationship that are unique to that place.

What would seem like difficult winemaking is not so hard in Alsace on the German border. This stretch of vineyards makes fat, full, rich whites due to abundant sun despite a latitude of 48.5° north.

The Riesling from here was my gateway into wine—something unlike anything I've ever tasted—and it made me want to know everything about fermented grape juice.

And Champagne, well, I don't need to say too much about Champagne. It's in a class by itself, but if not for undulating terrain, unique soil, and a bit of stubbornness by winemakers, there'd be no wine made here—at latitude 49° north, with hail and unpredictable storms, it's a wonder they get grapes to ripen at all.

I could go on and on about what France has to offer in wine, but why do it here when I'm going to do it by specific region! This little gush was just to give you a taste of what you're about to learn. Sorry if I got too excited, but France is fascinating and I want to make sure I convey it to you before you do a deep dive into any of the regions.

A Brief History

I'd be remiss if I didn't give a brief background into how France wound up with the crown for Queen of Wine (hint: it didn't wear a bikini in a pageant). A lot of people were making wine and doing it well before the Gauls (the folks who inhabited France during Roman times) got into the game, but how they rose to the top is the important story.

France entered the wine scene the same way everyone else in western Europe did—globalization! The Greeks brought viticulture here, most likely to the southern port of Marseilles in 600 B.C., and the Romans started plowing their way through in the second century A.D. Each conquering group brought a love of the drink and a know-how of viticulture. The locals made fermented drinks, but they learned new techniques from their conquerors, and it was the ingenuity of the French people (or the prelude to the French people) that took winemaking from a rough-and-tumble operation to an elevated art and science.

After the Romans set up vineyard infrastructure in every nook and cranny of the country, the Christians took over and took things further. Various sects of monks classified vineyards and learned the differences between sites, solidifying the idea of terroir. The Papacy, during its time in Avignon, planted vines at Châteauneuf-du-Pape and made coveted wine for the pontiff. The thirsty British had a taste for Bordeaux, shipping it all over their colonial empire, and helped Champagne get over its embarrassment about bubbles in the wine due to frozen fermentations to make a multi-billion-dollar industry of twice-fermented grape juice. Royalty, dukes, diplomats, and heads of state from far and wide, over the course of history, sought French wines—both for quality and for reputation. Truly, the French elevated wine, making it an integral part of their culture and of their economy.

France Now

I've heard people talk about how France's best wine days are behind it, or say that there are so many options of what to drink that the nation has lost its edge in the wine world. I'd argue that France has been and continues to be at the forefront of innovation—many of the modern technologies you see at New World wineries originated in France. From screw cap closures to the use of concrete eggs for fermentation and aging, to micro-oxygenation that speeds the softening of tannin, and so much more, the French continue to innovate, and their passion and contribution to the world of wine are as strong as ever.

And if you think they've lost relevance, consider this:

- France produces about 4.5 billion liters of wine each year—that's 16 percent of world wine production.
- France has the most valuable wine market in the world, with 29 percent market share, or $9.27 billion (€8,2 billion) of the global profit.
- More than 90,000 wine growers work in France, tending 1.93 million acres (785,000 ha) of vineyard land.

Although it's true that there are now more choices from winemaking nations, from China to Chile, that vast selection means all roads lead more strongly to France. Because after you've dabbled in the New World and enjoyed what it has to offer, you begin to wonder where these grapes came from. If you start to listen, you'll hear the best winemakers in the New World discuss the origins of techniques or grapes in the Old World. Serious wine enthusiasts will always return to learning about France and its contribution to winemaking.

I don't want to gloss over the challenges that France has. In some ways, the AOP classification system (for more on this, see Chapter 4) has failed miserably in its pursuit to keep quality standards high—many producers circumvent the rules or follow them and still produce crap wine. Some producers ride their reputation and don't improve, staying stuck in old ways, which leads to dirty wineries, substandard wines, and damage to the reputation of the industry. Overproduction has formed seas of bad bulk wine that put an economic strain on the country for decades, as subsidies encouraged this practice to continue. Although this is starting to change, France has a declining rate of per person wine consumption, due to an abundance of other beverages flooding the market and cultural shifts in how people take their meals (on the go, rather than sit-down).

Say what you will about France, but you can't deny that the country makes some of the most distinctive wines in the world. People continue to pay top dollar for wines of Bordeaux, Burgundy, Rhône, and Champagne for a reason—try as they may, no one can make French wine except the French. It is the original—the one to which many winemakers around the world aspire, and regardless of trend or fad, wine lovers will never abandon the motherland of wine. It is now, and always will be, relevant to those who love wine—whether they drink French stuff or not.

And now to the regions. Take these as you need them—there's too much to digest to just power through them like a novel. As in all parts of this book, I try to be as honest as possible with you. My goal is to give you a framework or reference point to work with. If I think something is over-rated or bad, I let you know, but I've got to say that nearly every region of France has something to recommend it. Each is distinct from the next and will probably have something you'll fall for. Explore one, understand its importance, its nuance, and move to another.

Alsace

When I first learned of Alsace in the Boston Center for Adult Education wine class that sparked my interest in wine, it was like discovering a secret waterfall in the middle of a forest. Discovering the wine of Alsace was one of the true joys of my life.

Alsace is a fascinating region; take its history: If there was a contest to find a

wine region with the maximum bloodshed and conflict in Europe, this small French area would be a top contender. Germany and France have been fighting over Alsace for centuries. I'd love to tell you that it was because of the vineyards, but it's just old-fashioned imperialism and landgrab.

Why? Location, location, location. Alsace is nestled between the Vosges (Vohz) Mountains on the western French side and the German Rhine River in the east. The land has been part of a ping-pong match between these nations for centuries. Most residents speak three languages—German, French, and their own dialect, Alsacien (which I'm sure was devised to talk about the French and German imperialists without them understanding). That said, Alsace wines show strong French influence through their rich yet delicate style.

There are 2,000 growers in the Alsace, and 90 percent of the wine is white. The Vosges block the rain and storms from continental France, so Alsace has a long, dry, sun-laden growing season. The vineyards are high on hills, and the whites grown here have time to ripen slowly. The result is a style that's often aromatic and, with some varieties, fat and oily in texture. This vinous utopia produces wines with juicy flavor but still a great dose of minerality with a mouthwatering texture.

Part of the reason I love French wine is because most is blended. That means you get the best of all worlds because the flavor of each grape complements the others. Every rule, however, has an exception, and Alsace is it for me. Nearly all wines are 100 percent of the grape variety and they're remarkable in their pure flavors. Most are labeled with the grape name, making it easy for you if you're just getting into wines named by region.

A bunch of different grapes are grown in Alsace, but only four are considered high class or "noble": Riesling (the most widely planted), Gewurztraminer, Pinot Gris, and Muscat. Others include Pinot Blanc, Sylvaner, Chasselas (SHAS-la), Auxerrois (Ox-air-WAH), and Pinot Noir. Pinot Blanc is often bottled alone, but I find it lackluster except when made into Crémant d'Alsace (CRAY-mahn dal-SAHZE), which represents nearly a quarter of production here and is a tasty alternative to Champagne for a much more attractive price.

One last tip on finding these wines before we get to the details. A lot of wine stores lump Alsace wines with German wines for no other reason than shelf configuration: Tall bottles of the store unite! Keep your eyes peeled for these gorgeous whites. They are great values for what you get (they start at around $18 and great ones are only around $30), and most are to drink now, not to age, so they're a hedonistic pleasure. If you're at a loss for an occasion to buy them, know that these whites pair with all sorts of food, especially Indian or spicy Southeast Asian cuisine.

The Wines

Many of Alsace's whites have a spicy bite. Although some are off dry or sweet, most of the top producers make their wines completely dry. That's considered the "classic" style, but make sure you read up or ask the shop what you're getting, as there's a (disturbing) trend to sweeten these wines to increase their fruitiness and fullness, which is counter to tradition and muddies the waters when trying to shop for this delicious delight.

As I mentioned, the wines are 100 percent of the grape listed, except if the bottle is a proprietary blend or says "Gentil" (JHAHN-tee) or "Edelzwicker" (Ay-dells-VICAR), which is a blend of any of the grapes from the region. The four "noble varieties" have distinctive flavors.

RIESLING: If you haven't had a Riesling from Alsace but have had one from somewhere else, you're going to have to try to clear your memory of that experience. This is Riesling like you've never experienced it before. Similar to others, it's aromatic—with lemon cream, pear, peach, white flowers (jasmine always comes to mind), and a slight spicy bite like anise or crushed poppy seeds—but the texture is something totally different from what you may think of when you think of Riesling. It's fresh and acidic but also fat and broad when it hits your tongue. The Alsace version coats your mouth and feels like liquid velvet. Yet it's dry. It's kind of a barn burner for me because it does what a sweet wine would do but finishes dry. As it ages (and better quality ones can age decades because of the acid), you'll find more mineral and petrol (gasoline) flavors.

GEWURZTRAMINER: The French version is written without the umlaut (ü), and much like Riesling, it redefines Gewurztraminer. This wine is often dark yellow because the grapes have richly pigmented skins, and it smells like a bowl of ripe peaches in a bath of spicy orange tea. It's most unique characteristic is its lychee scent (get some lychees at your grocery if you can and you'll see this is spot-on) with pineapple and fresh-cut roses. This wine has lower acid and higher alcohol than the others in Alsace so its texture is purely fat and oily without much brightness to counter it. Silky, aromatic, and just decadent, this isn't for you if you don't like aromatic wines, but if that's your bag, run out and get an Alsace Gewurztraminer, now! And grab some Indian food while you're out, since it's a great match for the wine.

PINOT GRIS: If there was ever an argument for the effect of terroir on a grape, here it is. This is the same grape as Pinot Grigio, and in many cases the same clone, but it tastes nothing like the Italian version. Dark and brassy in color (it can even have a pink tinge since some bunches are pink or purple) and not so aromatic, the wine saves its impact for the flavor. Flavors range but can include honey, honeysuckle, petrol, tangerine, minerals, and white flowers. Alsace Pinot Gris is often smoky, herbal, and nutty. The texture is always full-bodied but with enough mouth-cleansing acid to keep it fresh. This is a white wine that can be swapped in for a red—it's got the "meat" to hold up to dishes that usually pair with red wines.

MUSCAT: Unlike virtually every other region in the world, Alsace makes dry, rather than sweet, Muscat. For me, these wines are much simpler than the Riesling, Gewurztraminer, and Pinot Gris. Muscat tends to be the grape that tastes the most "grapey." So the wine tastes like eating a grape but with honeysuckle and orange notes. Usually a lighter style, this is a good sipper and a nice way to taste the grape from which all others most likely derived.

Special Wines of the Region

Beyond the basic varietal bottlings, there are several special wines from Alsace to know about, including two sweet wines.

ALSACE GRAND CRU AOP: At 4 percent of production, these wines are from individual vineyards deemed distinctive. There are 51 different grand cru AOPs that feature the name of the vineyard—*lieu dit* (LEE-ew dee)—on the bottle. The lieu dit generally has higher standards for winegrowing—lower yields, varietals planted, grape maturity requirements, and more. With only one or two special exceptions, only the four noble grapes of Alsace are permitted in a grand cru. Although some of these grands crus are legit, it's widely agreed that many have no distinguishing characteristics. Don't throw your money away unless you're sure you're getting something distinctive from a better great producer like Trimbach, Zind-Humbrecht, Domaine Weinbach, Domaine Josmeyer, or Hugel et Fils.

CRÉMANT D'ALSACE AOP: Want a cheaper alternative to Champagne? Look no further. Alsace has been using the Champagne method to make sparklers for a century. The winemakers do it well, using mostly Pinot Blanc but sometimes Pinot Gris, Riesling, Pinot Noir, and Chardonnay. These will remind you of Champagne except on your receipt—they are a fraction of the price (like $20 vs. $45).

VENDANGES TARDIVE (VAHN-DANZH TAR-DEEV): Made from overripe grapes that are picked after the main harvest, the wine is sweet. In some versions and in some years, the grapes have been affected by botrytis (page 57), so the wine can take on a beeswax quality. Producers only use noble grapes to make these, so the flavors are consistent with the descriptions of those four grapes, only sweetened and with a waxy, honeyed note. Vendanges Tardive have great acid and are fabulous with dessert.

SÉLECTION DE GRAINS NOBLES (SELECT-ZEE-ohn DE GRAHN NOH-ble): This sweet wine is made from individually picked berries. (Vignerons go through the vineyards and pick the ones they think are ready. Then they do it a few more times! Labor-intensive? Yes!) The wine is harder to make, more intense, and rarer than Vendanges Tardive. The criterion: The grapes must have noble rot, or botrytis, so the wine comes out honeyed, rich, and super sweet.

CLOSEST CITIES: *Strasbourg, Mulhouse, and Colmar are the major cities in Alsace. The region is a 4.5-hour drive or a 2.25-hour train ride east of Paris.*

Bordeaux

What can I say about Bordeaux? We don't exactly think of it as *Wine for Normal People* material. It kind of *sounds* expensive. Wine people talk about it all the time and go on and on about vintages and banks (not the kind you store money in, you gotta figure) and châteaux. Makes you want to throw your hands up and walk away.

Don't do it!

There's a lot to know if you want to become an expert, but trust me on this one: Four basic points should make you feel like you've got a handle on Bordeaux. These things will make it manageable enough so you'll want to take a chance on buying a bottle or ten and wind up with something awesome at a great price.

Let's cover these points and then hit the big appellations you need to know to get good stuff. That should be enough to get you started. The big four on Bordeaux: grapes and wine styles; geography; the importance of weather and vintage; and the classification systems.

If you were wondering what the hype is, the following box should give you a good picture. It behooves the Bordelaise to keep quality high. Most of the time they do. Of course, with the amount of wine produced, there is going to be variability, and since more than 50 percent is everyday drinking wine made under either the Bordeaux AOP or Bordeaux Supérieur AOP

WHY IS BORDEAUX SUCH A BIG DEAL? THE NUMBERS.

Maybe this won't further your drinking satisfaction but I think a quick fact-check will help answer this essential question. Check this out:

The area is about 280,217 acres (113,400 ha), far bigger than New York City, for example, which is only about 205,000 acres (82,900 ha).

•

Bordeaux makes 59 million cases of wine per vintage on average. That's about 10 percent of France's output and 25 percent of the country's protected appellation wine (AOC).

•

If it were a country, Bordeaux would rank twelfth in wine production, with nearly double the production of New Zealand or Austria.

•

It produces several billion dollars in revenue annually. Billion. It's big business.

•

There are approximately 6,300 wine-growers in Bordeaux and hundreds of châteaux, or winemaking operations.

(the same geographical areas but *supérieur* has half a percent higher alcohol, so theoretically it's fuller in body), not all of it is good and some is really bad.

1. Grapes and Wine Styles

Grapes

It's not as easy as Burgundy, where there are only three main grapes to know (Pinot Noir, Chardonnay, and Gamay), but Bordeaux deals mainly in nine grapes: three whites and six reds.

Almost all Bordeaux wine is a blend of two or more of the grapes above. Why? First, blends add complexity to the wine and intensify flavor, which is what differentiates these wines. For instance, without the softening touch of Merlot, Cabernet Sauvignon could be too harsh and taste nasty. Cabernet Franc adds a grounding earthiness to bright, fruity Merlot. The blends give the winemakers a palette of flavors with which to craft their masterpieces.

The second reason is far less romantic: It's farming, plain and simple. Each grape ripens at a different time so by blending, winemakers have a hedge: If anything goes wrong with any single variety they can make up for it with others. Smart thinking. Remember that in a place near the Atlantic Ocean and prone to a passing rainstorm, hailstorm, heat wave, or rot-inducing humidity, you've got to do *something* so you don't wind up with *nothing* in the bottle.

Wine Styles

All Bordeaux red is dry and makes up the majority of wine produced in the region. When the wines are Cabernet Sauvignon dominant, they tend to taste like earth, tobacco, black pepper, baking spice, and blackcurrants and other black fruit. If the flavor of blackcurrant is unfamiliar, think of an Asian pear crossed with blackberry (I must explain because if you're in the United States, where blackcurrants have been banned for decades because of an infectious plant disease they carry, you

RED (ABOUT 89% OF ALL GRAPES PLANTED):

Merlot (63%)

•

Cabernet Sauvignon (25%)

•

Cabernet Franc (11%)

•

Malbec, Petit Verdot, and Carmenère (less than 1%)

WHITE (ABOUT 11% OF ALL GRAPES PLANTED):

Sémillon (54%)

•

Sauvignon Blanc (39%)

•

Muscadelle (7%)

Although a small percentage (8 percent) of the wine made in Bordeaux, excellent dry white blends of Sauvignon Blanc, Sémillon, and Muscadelle can be had. They're grassy, herbal, and citrusy with soft acidity and a wax texture (not like eating a candle but more of a smooth, silky feeling). These are reliably good and usually under $20. That is not always the case with red Bordeaux, which is less predictable in terms of quality until you hit the $25-plus range. The region makes rosé and sparkling wine but you won't see much outside France.

Now you'll know that when you see a bottle of Bordeaux, it's a blend of grapes. Knowing is half the battle—you'll feel more confident picking up a bottle, since it's made of grapes that are probably already in your wine-drinking rotation.

probably don't know). The wines generally have mouthwatering acidity and mouth-drying tannin and often need age to mellow out. When these wines are made mostly of Merlot, they're lighter and floral with earthy, black cherry, black raspberry, and spice notes. They generally have lighter tannins and acid and don't age as well as the Cabernet-driven wines. An important distinction: Even the boldest reds aren't like New World Cabernets—they are subtler, emphasizing earth over fruit, with less overt oak influence.

One of the crown jewels of the sweet wine world, Sauternes is made from grapes affected by botrytis (page 57). These wines made from Sauvignon Blanc and Sémillon have outstanding honeyed, citrusy sweet-ness with strong acidity to keep them fresh and elegant.

2. Geography

I'm not going to be too detailed, because there are around sixty appellations, each with its own nuance, but geography is key to getting up to snuff on Bordeaux.

The name Bordeaux originates from the French phrase *au bord de l'eau*, which means "along the water." It's not just a fancy name—the area *does* lie along the banks of three rivers: the Dordogne in the north and the Garonne in the south, both of which flow into the Gironde, which then flows into the Atlantic Ocean.

From a climatic standpoint, the area is ideal for grapes. The warming influence of the rivers, along with a pine forest in the south, helps protect this otherwise exposed area from the nasty Atlantic weather and severe frosts that can come in early spring. The maritime climate is great for grapes that like a warm climate during the day but a cooler one at night.

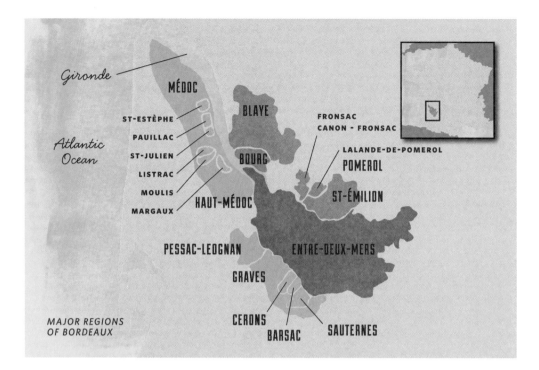

The rivers are a dividing line for the types of grapes that grow best on each side. Here's where "bank" comes into play—banks are sides of the river. On either side the adage is that top châteaux can see the river from their properties. The farther you get from the river, the more variation in the soil and the less consistent the wine.

The three main areas of Bordeaux are named as such because if you were making your way to the Atlantic from an inland destination, you'd find this:

The Left Bank on the Garonne and the Gironde includes the Médoc, where the most famous châteaux are located. It is known for wines made with a significant amount of Cabernet Sauvignon, always blended with a big hit of Merlot and a little bit of the other grapes for tannin, acidity, earthiness, and color. The two major areas of the Left Bank are the Médoc and Graves. The Médoc is closer to the Atlantic, and includes some of the most famous villages and communes (defined winegrowing regions that center around a village) for wine in the world. Because it is a large area, the flavor profiles vary. Graves is a gravel-rich area, whose best wines come from the subregion of Pessac-Leógnan.

The Right Bank is on the Dordogne and the Gironde Rivers (including the famous areas of St-Émilion and Pomerol) and is known for Merlot with Cabernet Franc and Cabernet Sauvignon as supporting players.

Entre-Deux-Mers (translated as "between two seas") is the area in between the two rivers before they converge and is known for affordable and lighter dry white wines. The area makes a ton of cheap red, too, which is almost always lackluster and is labeled just with the Bordeaux appellation.

3. The Importance of Weather and Vintage

I am an animal lover, so I hate to beat a dead horse, but I will say it again: Grape growing is agriculture. Some years Mother

Nature is kind; some years, not so much. In years where it works, prices rise and wine geeks get excited. If you pay attention to weather conditions, then you'll understand vintage—it's very simple, but it's something people love to complicate.

With that horse flogged, a note on aging. Bordeaux are known for their ageability. A good wine from a good year can age for decades because the tannins and acid act as natural preservatives. Over time, the tannins lose a lot of the "fight" in them as they chill out in the semi-anaerobic environment of the closed bottle. As discussed in Chapter 3, older wine tends to be softer and have more complex flavors, because the chemical compounds change over time and combine with other elements in the bottle.

Can all Bordeaux age? No way. Most shouldn't and won't. Drink young white Bordeaux within a few years and less expensive red Bordeaux within five years. Don't hold on to it unless it's high quality, or you'll lose the enjoyment it can offer you now. Not all wine is better with age, and there's certainly no glory in holding something only to open it and be disappointed. That said, for top Bordeaux, fifteen to twenty years is usually not enough time in a cellar!

4. The Classification Systems

OK, the final and most complicated point: Bordeaux is obsessed with classifying its châteaux (wine producers) by perceived quality. There are four main classifications in this large area, and none is without controversy. They are St-Émilion, Graves, Cru Bourgeois, and, most importantly, the 1855 Classification.

THE 1855 CLASSIFICATION originated when Emperor Napoleon III requested a ranking of the best red and sweet wines of Bordeaux for his Exposition Universelle in Paris. The result: The Syndicat of Courtiers, a group of wine merchants and brokers, created a ranking of the châteaux by the price they "fetched." It was a simple demand-driven strategy, and not entirely foolhardy. There were sixty-one red wines classified into five levels or "cru," which means growth. Four châteaux were at the top, and the rest fell in the other four buckets until a price point was reached that they didn't feel was worthy of classifying. Twenty-seven sweet wines were classified from Sauternes and Barsac in three levels: Premier Cru Supérieur (superior first growths, with only one wine, Château d'Yquem), Premier Cru (first growths, eleven), and Deuxièmes Cru (second growths, fifteen).

This seemingly logical method incited much of the resentment and anger that still

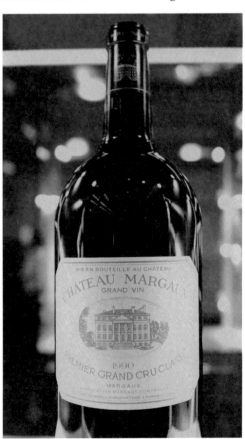

exists today for classified reds in Bordeaux. Why? Bias. All the châteaux included were on the Left Bank, and all but one (Château Haut-Brion in Graves) were in the Médoc area. Organizers shunned the entire Right Bank, as well as other parts of Bordeaux that churn out high-quality wines. To complicate issues further, since 1855, officials have only made two significant changes—Château Cantermerle was added as a fifth growth in 1856 and Château Mouton-Rothschild was elevated from a second to a first growth in 1973 after Baron Phillipe Rothschild petitioned the minister of agriculture, arguing that his wine was valued at a level similar to the first growths. Even though châteaux have changed hands and quality ebbs and flows, no other changes have taken place. And lest you think this is a huge part of Bordeaux production, less than 5 percent comes from these vineyards. There is a sea of other great wine outside this small universe.

Nevertheless, the top five crus (Château Margaux, Château Mouton-Rothschild, Château Lafite-Rothschild, Château Latour, and Château Haut Brion) still garner the highest prices and are considered among the best wines in the world. History reigns supreme here.

ST-ÉMILION is a Merlot-dominated quality area on the Right Bank. It has had a rough go on its classification. First done in 1955, it was meant to be a living classification that changed as wine quality changed, which would be a contrast to the "set-in-stone" nature of the 1855 Classification. This went smoothly for a while, but when an attempt was made in 2006 and then again in 2012 to make changes, châteaux contested their standings, and legal challenges rendered the classification moot. There are three levels of classification: Premier Grand Cru Classé A, Premier Grand Cru Classé B, and Grand Cru Classé. Just in case anyone offers you these wines, know that Premier Grand Cru Classé A, Châteaux Angélus, Ausone, Cheval Blanc, and Pavie are the undisputed top of the heap in St-Émilion.

The GRAVES classification is a little tamer. Officials listed the top sixteen châteaux in 1953 and amended the list in 1959. Look for Cru Classé on the label if you are curious, but know that it is a useless list: It does not provide a ranking of which wines are better than the others, which is important to know if you're trying to compare wines based on some "objective" measure.

The CRU BOURGEOIS is named for the Bourgeois, who lived in Bourg, a Right Bank town of merchants and craftsmen. These folks lived a sweet life with all sorts of perks, including no tax on wine. After the French Revolution (post 1799), they were stripped of much of their privilege, but by that point they'd already acquired a bunch of vineyards all over Bordeaux and that legacy remained. Ironically, today this classification is only for Left Bank red wines of the Médoc.

After many meaningless classifications since first formalized in 1932, in 2003 the French minister of agriculture finally approved the first real classification of the Crus Bourgeois du Médoc, which deemed 247 châteaux worthy of the title out of 490 applicants. That should be the end of the story, but it's not. Given the litigious nature of the châteaux in Bordeaux (all modern organizers of classification systems get sued it seems, which is probably why they fail to hold any weight), the wineries that didn't make the cut sued, and it took until 2009 for Cru Bourgeois to get started again.

Today, members of the Cru Bourgeois must reapply every year for inclusion in the classification. Wines, not châteaux, are

BORDEAUX PRONUNCIATIONS

BLAYE	BLY
BORDEAUX	Boar-DOUGH
BOURG	bou-gkh (my poor translation of the guttural, back-of-the-throat sound!)
CHÂTEAU D'YQUEM	Sha-TOE deek-EM
CRU BOURGEOIS	Crew boojh-WAH
DORDOGNE	Dohr-DOAN-ya
ENTRE-DEUX-MERS	AHN-truh deh MARE
FRONSAC/CANON-FRONSAC	FROHN-sack/canon FROHN-sack
GARONNE	gahr-OHN
GIRONDE	zhir-OHNDE
GRAVES	GRAHV
HAUT-MÉDOC	oh MAY-dok
LAFITE-ROTHSCHILD	La-FEAT rauth-SHIELD
LÉOVILLE-BARTON	layo-VILLE bar-TAWN
LÉOVILLE-LAS CASES	layo-VILLE lass CAZ
LÉOVILLE-POYFERRÉ	layo-VILLE pwah-fehr-RAY
MARGAUX	mar-GO
MÉDOC	MAY-dok
MOUTON-ROTHSCHILD	Moo-TAWN
PAUILLAC	POI-yak
PESSAC-LEÓGNAN	Pay-SAHK lay-yon-NAHN
POMEROL	PALM-er-AHL
ST-ÉMILION	Sahnt A-meal-EYOHN
ST-ESTÈPHE	Sahnt es-TEFF
ST-JULIEN	Sahnt ZHUL-ee-ahn
SAUTERNES	Saw-TAIRN

included in the ranking, so producers must choose their best wares to be judged. An independent tasting board tries the wines for quality. If the wine passes muster, the bottle receives a sticker with a QR code and a Cru Bourgeois logo, which is easily recognizable and something you should look for because these 250 or so wines are usually high quality.

OK, now let's detail the top areas, so you know what to look for when you shop for this stuff!

Left Bank Wines: Cabernet Sauvignon–based Reds, Dry Whites, and Sweet Wines

MÉDOC: As mentioned above, Médoc includes the entire Left Bank that is not Graves. That means it stretches from near the Atlantic Coast inland to the start of the Gironde River. As is always the case, the larger the appellation, the more variable the quality. Wines from Médoc will often have a high proportion of Merlot and sometimes resemble wines from the Right Bank with an earthy, red fruit quality and a soft texture. Since the sourcing area is large, it's sometimes hard to know what you'll get. Some of these are fruit bombs that are reminiscent of New World wines, so if you like a sense of place in your wine, caveat emptor!

HAUT-MÉDOC: This large appellation varies in quality but is a better "catchall" than Médoc because it's more defined, including just fifteen areas, some of which make the best wines on the Left Bank (and are mentioned in the following sections). Like Médoc, the area is big so it's hard to pinpoint a single style. You can be assured of the earthy essence in the wine, but whether it's red fruit from Merlot or black fruit from Cabernet depends on

the château. Some are in the 1855 Classification, some are Cru Bourgeois, and others are just ordinary red wine. Most have earthy, blackcurrant, herbal, and spice notes with softer tannin and acid, but more serious ones can be complex and age-worthy.

ST-ESTÈPHE: Travel to the northernmost tip of the Left Bank and you'll find St-Estèphe. It's an area with heavy soils, and in the past these wines were strictly for aging because they were so intense, earthy, and tannic that it took forever for them to gel. Lately there's been a move away from dense, heavy Cabernet to a larger percentage of Merlot in the wine, making it drinkable earlier. St-Estèphe wines can be like earth, floral, blackcurrant, mushroom, spice, and licorice. Wines here are medium weight but mouth filling. One of the best wines I've ever had is from here—Cos d'Estournel (about $200 but so worth it). Cos and Château Montrose are both "Super Seconds," a group of wines ranked lower in the 1855 Classification with quality on par with that of the first growths. Look for Cru Bourgeois (page 112) from here—they're great values and are usually tasty wines.

PAUILLAC: At the highest elevation of the Left Bank communes, Pauillac is the home of three top crus from the 1855 Classification—Latour, Lafite-Rothschild, and Mouton-Rothschild. It's unique in the world of the Left Bank because it is the only commune in which châteaux own lots of contiguous land. In most of the other places, châteaux own a plot here and there, because they acquired different vineyards over the years to increase production or allow them to grow their own grapes rather than buying from local growers. Cabernet Sauvignon is the star in Pauillac—when it's

grown here and aged, it is powerful, flavorful, and bold. Merlot, Petit Verdot, and Malbec are also used. For Cabernet lovers, look to Paulliac for your fix. The wine can smell and taste like earth, incense, pencils, cedar, blackcurrant, and black fruit with smoke, cedar, and loads of stuff like sandalwood, tamarind, and cumin. These ageable, tannic wines make no apologies for their boldness!

ST-JULIEN: The smallest of the four major regions in the Haut-Médoc produces wines that are mainly Cabernet Sauvignon with Merlot and Cabernet Franc. They are known for their floral, spicy, blueberry, blackcurrant, licorice, baking spice, and tobacco aromas, and bold acidity and softer tannins. Although the region is located right next to Margaux (see right), the wines are nothing alike in style. The most famous châteaux here are Léoville-Las Cases, Léoville-Poyferré, and Léoville-Barton, considered "Super Seconds" by many. Las Cases is the best of the bunch.

MARGAUX: This southernmost appellation of the Haut-Médoc is one of the most famous communes in Bordeaux—mostly because Château Margaux, a first growth in the 1855 Classification, has created a positive halo around the area. The wines of Margaux are known for subtle, floral notes and red fruit flavors, instead of being super powerful, rich, and full of dark fruit. They tend to have a mineral, spice, and sometimes pencil lead and "exotic" notes like myrrh and other incense used in dark medieval churches. One of my all-time favorite châteaux is here—Château Palmer, a third growth that has a lot of Merlot in it, giving it softer tannins than others from Margaux. Palmer is a "Super Second."

GRAVES: Named for its gravelly terrain, Graves is known for wines that fittingly have an earthy, gravelly quality. The appellation is usually Merlot—rather than Cabernet Sauvignon—dominant. Apart from crushed rocks, the red wines taste like black fruit, earth, and black pepper, and are better with age. Dry whites are also a specialty of the region. These Sémillon, Sauvignon Blanc, and Muscadelle blends tend to be grassy and herbal from the Sauvignon Blanc, yet apple-y and floral and heavier with a waxy, full, creamy but crisp texture from the Sémillon.

PESSAC-LÉOGNAN: Feeling that the best châteaux were in a separate cluster of Graves that used a higher proportion of Cabernet Sauvignon than Merlot, producers carved out this appellation in 1987 for reds and dry whites. They often have mineral, gravel, nut, and smoke notes with violet, red berry, earth, and spice, too. The whites are dry, full, and viscous and are often aged in oak barrels. They've got staying power: The best can age for ten or more years. The most famous château here is Château Haut-Brion, a first growth in the 1855 Classification and the only one from Graves/Pessac-Léognan. Wines from this subregion make up most of the wines in the Graves classification, so if you want high quality, look for Pessac-Léognan on the label.

SAUTERNES: Also located within Graves is this sweet wine–exclusive area. Sémillon and Sauvignon Blanc are the primary grapes. To produce the wine, the grapes have to be affected by botrytis (page 57), to make the honeyed, sweet, viscous yet acidic wine that is Sauternes. The vignerons go through the vineyard time and again to pick only the grapes that have been affected by rot, leaving the ones that are old and raisined.

As you can imagine, desiccated fruit that's perfectly affected by a specific rot is not high yielding, so making Sauternes is labor-intensive, and sometimes has little or no payoff. In years where the botrytis

Q+A

Why do you need rotted grapes to make Sauternes?

Even though it's gross to think about using rotted fruit for wine, here it pays off! Botrytis not only thins out the skins of grapes, causing water to evaporate and concentrating flavors; it also changes those aromas and flavors. For example, in Sémillon it creates dried apricot, honeycomb, baked apple, nut, and white flower aromas and flavors. Rot-affected Sauvignon Blanc is used in Sauternes for aromatics and high acidity, and to balance the richness of Sémillon.

levels are inconsistent, the best châteaux don't even make Sauternes. It's a tough business. But when it's good, it's great: Sauternes and its neighbor Barsac create sweet wines that are balanced by bright, mouth-cleansing acidity. The best of these wines can age for fifty-plus years and are a treat to drink alone or with cheese or custard-based desserts.

Right Bank Wines: Mainly Merlot-based Reds

POMEROL: These powerful wines pack a punch of tannin and have tons of fruit flavor. Pomerol has the clay and gravel soils that Merlot loves, so these wines are usually 70 to 80 percent Merlot with some Cabernet Franc. They can be harsh without time to age, but with age Pomerols are soft, fruit filled, and elegant. The most famous wine from here is Pétrus. Typically, the wine is like dark violets with strong savory herb, dark fruit, mushroom, chocolate, spice, and tobacco flavors. It usually has medium mouth-drying tannins, is luscious and full, and can be excellent after five to eight years of age, a lot sooner than its siblings on the Left Bank! Watch out: This area shouldn't be confused with LALANDE-DE POMEROL, which is a lower-quality appellation whose best wines come from producers who also make great Pomerol or St-Émilion.

ST-ÉMILION: In this UNESCO heritage town, known for its ancient buildings, diversity reigns. Given the varied soils and land, it's hard to give you a single description of the wines. Flavor can depend on the soil and the slope of the vineyard. Closer to Pomerol in the west, the wines are spicier, darker, and earthier. In the east, they are more floral, like red fruit with soft tannin. Ultimately, the producer has a lot of say in the style, too: Some producers make something closer to a soft, fruity California Merlot in style, and some focus on earthy, tannic flavors, which is more classic. The wines are mainly Merlot with some Cabernet Franc and Cabernet Sauvignon. Good wine from St-Émilion is medium weight and leaves a soft, cheek-coating quality—for me, the sign of a great Merlot.

St-Émilion has a few "satellite" appellations—similar, close-by areas that make good to great wine. They are Lussac-Saint-Émilion, Montagne Saint-Émilion, Puisseguin Saint-Émilion, and Saint-Georges Saint-Émilion. Montagne and Saint-Georges are the best of the group.

FRONSAC/CANON-FRONSAC: Lying north-west of Pomerol and St-Émilion, Fronsac is a high-potential area that has seen recent investment from other Right Bank producers in particular. Made mainly of Merlot with some Cabernet Franc and Cabernet Sauvignon, the wines are like red berry, red currant, black pepper, and spice. Although both are full-bodied and tannic, Fronsac tends to be more rustic, and Canon-Fronsac is lighter bodied but more complex.

Other Stuff You'll See on Bordeaux Labels

BORDEAUX/BORDEAUX SUPÉRIEUR: Made from anywhere in Bordeaux, but mainly from Entre-Deux-Mers (page 110). These Merlot-dominant wines have a range of flavor and can be floral, like black fruit, like red fruit, like earth, like cedar, or just like a really boring, standard red wine. The grape-growing area is so large that I can't begin to tell you what you may find in the bottle. Are there great producers? Sure, but you've got to hunt for them.

CÔTES DE BORDEAUX: This family of five regions, which make up 10 percent of Bordeaux's production, makes wines of quality between basic Bordeaux and fine-classified wines, which means they can be excellent value for the money. The Côtes have much in common: They are each along the Right Bank in hilly, historical winemaking areas that have close proximity to the rivers (Gironde, Garonne, or Dordogne); have similar well-draining soils of gravel, clay, and limestone; have similar moderate climates; and predominantly use Merlot to make their reds (97 percent of production).

In 2007, the appellation began to unite the disparate regions that were struggling to market their wines solo. Together, they have managed to raise the quality level and attract new talent, which means producers are making wines that have a more modern (fruity, less earthy) style. Here are the five to seek out and the differences between them:

- Blaye Côtes de Bordeaux: The largest Côte; this area makes fruity reds and soft whites of mostly Sauvignon Blanc. They're variable in quality, but some can be serious Merlots and others tasty sippers that are great with food.
- Castillon Côtes de Bordeaux: Château owners from Saint-Émilion are buying up parcels in neighboring Castillon while the getting's still good. Some of these wines are strikingly similar to Saint-Émilion but a lot less money, and hence are considered the top of the heap of the Côtes de Bordeaux.
- Francs Côtes de Bordeaux: The smallest region; Francs makes excellent whites and reds that can age, and have great depth and body.
- Cadillac Côtes de Bordeaux: Possibly the most classic of the Côtes; the reds are richer and bolder than the others, making them age-worthy.
- Sainte-Foy Côtes de Bordeaux: A newer area; the wines are still establishing their identity.

BOURG: Right near Blaye is the slightly better Bourg, home of the former Bourgeois. This area should be part of the Côtes but for unknown reasons didn't join. It produces earthy, red-fruited, Merlot-dominant wines.

ENTRE-DEUX-MERS: Between the Garonne and the Dordogne, this land "between two seas" appellation is only for dry white wines, mostly Sauvignon Blanc with some Sémillon. They can be great summer sippers and are also fabulous intros to Sauvignon Blanc for people who can't handle the high acid of the grape when it grows in Sancerre (Loire Valley) or New Zealand. The Sémillon softens the wine and makes it rounder and plusher in your mouth, but the wine maintains the aromatics and flavors of Sauvignon Blanc. Delicious, especially with seafood!

That's Bordeaux in a nutshell: rivers, banks, châteaux, blends. The châteaux are top dog. The best happen to be on the best land, can see the river, and therefore produce the best wines. Ultimately Bordeaux is a caste system, not a meritocracy, because of the classification systems. That said, there is a spectrum of great affordable wines. The region pumps out 900 million bottles a year, and most of it can give normal people a glimpse of what it must be like to have the $700/bottle stuff that those who live high on the hog enjoy nightly.

CLOSEST CITIES: *The city of Bordeaux is the hub of the region and is on the Left Bank. St-Estèphe, the commune farthest downriver, is 1.25 hours by car. Most of the other communes are about an hour away, with the exception of Graves, which is only about 15 minutes from the city of Bordeaux. St-Émilion and Pomerol are about a 45-minute drive from Bordeaux.*

Burgundy

Bougogne (Boor-GON-Yuh) is a hard topic. As with Bordeaux, there have been tomes, articles, blogs, and probably even sonnets written on this small region. But unlike Bordeaux, which has an abundance of vineyards, big production, and strong marketing, Burgundy is about farmers,

Q+A

Schneider! Why are we even talking about this? I can look on a map!

Because if you want to know how to get good Burgundy and appreciate it, you've got to know that geography and geology are king, queen, emperor, and every other kind of royalty here. With no understanding of those things, you'll be completely lost when it gets more complicated.

tiny plots of land, and little differences in the wines based on nuances of that land, a.k.a. terroir.

Wine nerds say that the final destination in learning about wine is Burgundy because you can never know everything there is to know about this place. I agree.

Thankfully, we're not trying to know it all. For our purposes we'll talk about the keys to understanding Burgundy so it's easier to try and buy. Once you figure out the basics, I wager you'll want to explore this confounding French world further. Even if not, it's still worth knowing about. I'm not saying you have to become a Burgundy scholar, but in your exploration of the wine world, this region of France is a mandatory stop.

I'll break down Burgundy in as normal a way as possible, but it's no easy task. To start, there are six things you need to know about Burgundy to get your bearings.

1. Where Is Burgundy? Geography and a Word on Climate . . .

Burgundy is in central eastern France. It's a disjointed, narrow strip of land stretching from 115 miles (186 km) southeast of Paris, down 178 miles (288 km) to the city of Lyon. It's inland, and like all continental locations, it has extreme weather. Winter is cold, summer is short and warm, spring and fall can be frosty, and crazy rain and hailstorms can pop up at any time of the year, diluting grape flavor and destroying crops. The vines can get a great balance of sugar and acid when things go well, but it's a nail-biter every year to see what Mother Nature is going to dole out; vintage is huge in determining quality.

Burgundy has five distinct subregions, each with its own character. I list them here from north to south.

- **Chablis** (Sha-BLEE), and no, it's not a jug wine, but a historic fine wine region

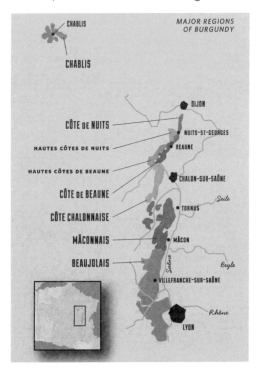

- **The Côte D'Or** (Coat Door), made up of the Côte de Nuits (Coat-deh-Nwee) and the Côte de Beaune (Coat-deh-Bone)
- **The Côte Chalonnaise** (Coat Shallow-NAZE)
- **The Mâconnais** (Mah-coh-NAY)
- **Beaujolais** (boh-zhoh-LAY), only administratively part of the region (think *Sesame Street* "one of these things is not like the other")

Of these areas, the most complex part of Burgundy, and what most people get geeked up on, is the Côte d'Or, "golden slope," which is named for the color of the leaves in the fall but should bring to mind the serious coin producers make by churning out some the most expensive wines in the world (Domaine Romanée-Conti's Romanée-Conti, a Pinot Noir, routinely goes for more than $10,000 a bottle).

2. Grape Types and Wine Styles

The grapes of Burgundy are where it gets simple and also where it gets hard. Unlike Bordeaux, with nine grapes to keep track of in an endless permutation of blends, there are only two main grapes in Burgundy, and a third if you count Beaujolais.

If you're drinking Burgundy, you're drinking Chardonnay if it's white Burgundy, Pinot Noir if it's red Burgundy, and Gamay if it's Beaujolais. Done. (Aligoté, Melon, Pinot Blanc, and Pinot Gris—all whites—can be found but are minor players.)

The hard part is that there is a huge variation in style based on where in Burgundy the grapes grow. Terroir changes everything. But we'll save that for point 3 and in the detail on the communes and towns. For now, here are Burgundy's five

regions again, this time with what kind of wines they make.

CHABLIS:
Steely Chardonnay

CÔTE D'OR:
Côte de Nuits: The most famous Pinot Noir in the world

Côte de Beaune: The most famous Chardonnay in the world

THE CÔTE CHALONNAISE:
The most underrated Pinot and Chardonnay in Burgundy

THE MÂCONNAIS:
Affordable, tasty Chardonnay

BEAUJOLAIS:
Great wines from the floral, acidic Gamay grape

3. Terroir, the Special Sauce of Burgundy

The idea that a specific place—an area as small as a row of vines, for instance—has a distinct character was born in Burgundy.

Burgundy has varied terrain, sun exposures, altitudes, and microclimates, but the thing that distinguishes it is the variability in the soil from which the vines derive nutrients and flavor. The geology of the region over the last 200 million years has created such diversity in dirt that in an area as small as a plot in a vineyard, the soil can change dramatically and substantially alter the flavor and character of the grapes. Chablis in the north has chalky soil, the Côte d'Or is a limestone escarpment that has amazing drainage and marine sediment, the Côte Chalonnaise and Mâcon are a mix, and Beaujolais has a lot of granite. I once read something that described Burgundy as "a mosaic made up of thousands of plots of land." It's a perfect description.

Given this, it should be no surprise that the most coveted and expensive wines of Burgundy come from the best plots with the best combination of sun, slope, climate, soil, etc. Generally those top sites are on the middle of the slopes, with better-drained soils, and great sun exposure.

To harken back to points 1 and 2—you've got to know your stuff when it comes to geography in Burgundy and the style of wine you like, because unlike anywhere else in the world, a matter of a few meters can alter the character of a wine (and sometimes the price!) so much that you won't believe it's made from the same grape. To get started buying and trying Burgundy's wines you don't need to know the differences in vineyards and terroir, but you do need to know that variability exists.

Bottom Line: Because of this nuance in Burgundy, within the world of nonsparkling Pinot Noir and Chardonnay, the region has nearly limitless possibilities in wine style, so don't write anything off immediately. Keep on trying!

4. Burgundian History: Catholic Guilt and a Short Warmonger

Wine has been made in Burgundy for millennia, but the earliest archaeological records we have are from the second century A.D., when the Romans controlled the area. Things ticked along and various regimes rose and fell, yadda yadda, and then a big change took place that set up Burgundy to become what it is today.

In the 900s, the middle of the Middle Ages, Burgundy found religion. The Roman era gave way to the Catholicism of the dark ages. The religious zeal was in full throttle here, and the guilt of the church loomed large. What a boon for wine! Landowners bequeathed Burgundian monasteries their holdings in the form of tithes and indulgences in an attempt to make it to the pearly gates. And with that land, the Benedictines (known for their love of luxury, BTW) created a form of heaven on earth with wine at their monastery at Cluny.

Blessed with nothing but time on their hands and the ability to read and write, this ostentatious, wine-loving sect set about cultivating grapes as more of a science project than a means of creating sacramental beverages. They kept meticulous records of every vine, vineyard, and area they planted. About two hundred years after the

Q+A

C'mon Schneider! First geography and now history? Why do I need to know the history of this region to appreciate the wine? I don't need to know the history of Monte Carlo to go lose my shirt at the gambling tables. Can't I just drink the stuff?

Sorry. You gotta know about this. I don't know if history matters to the modern-day structure of any wine region more than it matters to Burgundy. I'll try to be quick on the facts, but if you hate history, this still may be too much for you. C'est la vie.

Benedictines had a monopoly on Burgundian wine, the Cistercians got in on the act, and these two sects created the foundation for modern-day Burgundy.

Men of the cloth from both sects began recording some very cool, weird stuff about the vineyards: namely that each small *climat* (KLEE-mah), or vineyard, produced totally different wines even if planted with the same grapes. These dudes were the first to recognize and describe terroir, and to delineate vineyard areas and separate the best from the second best. That classification still exists in Burgundy (told you it was relevant!).

Burgundy's fame spread all around Europe. Then, in the fourteenth century, the noble Dukes of Bourgogne, who owned the majority of vineyard land, went on a marketing binge for the wines. They elevated the status and sales of the Pinot Noir, in particular, by pouring it at every major diplomatic fête they could muscle in on. The wines gained status among the European aristocracy, cementing Burgundy's position as one of France's most expensive and coveted wine regions.

There is just one more wrinkle before we leave the history of the place. And this is where Burgundy gets complicated to the point of craziness. The small vineyard plots certainly would be confusing enough since, as you'll see in the classification section, there are a ton of them, but if each were owned by a single person or group, it would be easier to understand. Alas, that short, warmongering guy couldn't leave well enough alone: In his antimonarchy opus, the Napoleonic Code, Bonaparte convoluted Burgundy beyond belief.

Issued in 1804 as a bird flip to centuries of aristocratic rule, which had helped spread the reputation of Burgundy, the code stated that any property left behind by parents at their death had to be distributed equally among the kids (of any gender). That legacy lives on today, with some growers owning a few rows of vines, and with the most famous vineyard sites having dozens and dozens of owners.

5. Producer Matters

The Napoleonic Code standards led to the rise of the négociant (neh-go-SYAN) (page 59) because there often weren't enough vines owned by individual owners to make wine.

How does this matter? Well, even if you know that a specific vineyard is amazing, if the right négociant doesn't buy the right mix of grapes from the right part of the plot that combine harmoniously, the wine may not be worth the money. Some of these négociants only source grapes from the best growers; others take whatever they can and mix it all up. If you own the best rows or sections of the best vineyards, and you don't mess up in the cellar, you're going to outshine producers that own portions of the vineyard that grow less tasty grapes. In Burgundy you've got to keep your eye on the region, the vineyard, and the producer/négociant to make sure the wine is decent.

The best tip I've ever received about shopping for Burgundy was from my friend Ryan Mullins, a smart, passionate wine pro who works for Winebow in Atlanta, loves Burgundy, and has tasted his share of "unicorns" (a term for those astronomically priced Burgundies that you'll rarely, if ever, see open on a table for you to taste): The best way to initially explore Burgundy is by getting the best basic wines you can afford from the best producers. If you get the basics in a great year, it could be far better than a premier cru from a mediocre producer. This will show you what the region has to offer.

Grand Cru

So what should you look for? The top Burgundies have supple, soft, balanced fruit with spice or earth or another complementing element (leather, gaminess) that makes you want to sip them forever.

A flip through Tom Stevenson's *Sotheby's Wine Encyclopedia*, which has recommended producers with pictures of the labels, may help you get the best sense of the great producers of each town or vineyard you're considering trying.

6. The Classification System

Burgundy's classification is all about land—and given what we've just gone over, this focus should make sense. The labels of Burgundy subjugate brand to land—you'll see the name of a village or town before you see who made it, another clue as to what matters here. The vineyards are classified in four main quality levels. There's an inverse relationship, like everything in the world: As quality goes up, quantity goes down.

The bad news: I find there's not much "value" here. The chasm between great Burgundy and not-great Burgundy may be bigger than in any other region. With high-end buyers prebuying the wines, and producers being so small, most great Burgundy is out of reach in price. This makes me wish I'd been a wine lover in the 1980s

and 1990s when many wines like this were a stretch, but not a-few-months'-rent stretch, as they are today!

Now to the classification levels so you can go out and test these assertions for yourself.

GRAND CRU (GRAHN CREW): The best of the best. There are thirty-three vineyards that are classified grand cru (great growth). This level represents only 1.5 percent of the wine made in Burgundy. Of the thirty-three grands crus, thirty-two are in the Côte d'Or; the other is in Chablis. The other regions of Burgundy got snubbed and fall to the lower end of the quality pyramid.

How do you know if something's a grand cru? The label is required to say "grand cru" and include the vineyard name. How else do you know? It's ridiculously expensive! With these wines, each layer of flavor is transparent—you feel like you're looking through sheer, layered fabric as you notice new, tasty flavors and how they blend together.

PREMIER CRU (PREM-EE-AAY CREW): There are about 645 of these, and they vary in quality. Many are amazing, and some are as good or better than the grands crus. These wines are grown in smaller, superior vineyards, called *climats*, and have more distinctive character than village wines, the next level down. They make up about 10 percent of all Burgundy wine, and you can always tell a premier cru because the label states the village name, says "1er Cru," and has the vineyard name (like "Pommard-Rugiens" or "Vosne-Romanée—Les Suchots," where Pommard and Vosne-Romanée are villages and Rugiens and Les Suchots are climats/vineyards).

If you see the commune name and "premier cru" on the label, instead of a specific climat, the wine is a blend of grapes from various premier cru vineyards.

In general, premiers crus can be expensive, but you can find some in the $30 to $50 range. In my opinion, this is the best bang for your buck but, as noted above, you have to study the geography/wine style of the region before you buy to make sure you'll like the style of the one you choose.

VILLAGE (VILL-AHHZHE) OR COMMUNE LEVEL WINE: OK, here's where things can get even more confusing. Like the premier cru

wines, these labels have the name of the commune listed on them. Often the label looks exactly like that of a premier cru, so you really have to know what to look for to see the difference. You can usually tell it's a village wine because of the price (lower than a premier cru) and the absence of the "1er Cru" notation. This level represents about 38 percent of wine in Burgundy.

These wines give you a taste of Burgundy without a huge bite out of your wallet. The Chardonnay is crisp, minerally, and sometimes fruity. They have a little less going on than in a premier or grand cru wine but more than most other Chardonnays for the price. The Pinot is more touch and go for me—sometimes it's thin and acidic; sometimes it has great earth and red fruit flavor. I can't say it enough: Vintage, village, and producer each contribute to what you get in a bottle.

REGIONAL WINES: This is the most general Burgundy classification. The grapes can come from all over Burgundy, and that

| Premier Cru | Village | Regional |

BURGUNDY CLASSIFICATION AND CAR MODELS

As I was trying to explain this very difficult classification system to my dad, my first-pass editor on the book, he raised the point that cars are nearly the same as the communes and vineyards of Burgundy.

He's right! Car shopping is maddening. There are endless permutations and ways to get what you want. Burgundy is similar. Here's an imperfect but quick way to look at Burgundy through the lens of cars, which I think is easier to understand than wine.

BRAND BURGUNDY	V.	BRAND TOYOTA
REGIONAL APPELLATIONS		**CAR TYPES**
Chablis	⟷	Cars and minivans
Côte de Nuits	⟷	Trucks
Côte de Beaune	⟷	SUVs
Chalonnaise, Mâconnais	⟷	Hybrids
COMMUNAL/VILLAGE WINE		**CAR BRAND**
e.g., Puligny-Montrachet	⟷	e.g., Camry
PREMIER CRU		**MODEL OF CAMRY**
e.g., Puligny-Montrachet "Le Cailleret"	⟷	e.g., Camry LE
GRAND CRU		**TOP-OF-THE-LINE CAMRY**
Le Montrachet	⟷	Fully loaded Camry Hybrid XLE

In car shopping, the only way to decide what you want is to rely on research, the salesperson, and friends to help you decide, and to take a test drive. Bringing it back to Burgundy, if you can try a wine by the glass at a restaurant, go for it!

usually means middling quality areas. You'll often see AOC Bourgogne Rouge (red) or AOC Bourgogne Blanc (white) on the label, although there are twenty-three regions allowed (51 percent of wine produced).

These wines are affordable and some are good, but I think the négociants lose a lot of the Burgundy magic in the lower tier. They can taste generic—like "just red wine" or "just white wine." Again, producer and vintage make the world of difference here, so find the best producer making AOC Bourgogne in a great year and you'll get a delicious bottle.

The Devil in the Details: The Communes of Burgundy

No dorky wine book would be complete without an overview of some of the top areas of Burgundy. Before we launch into this, please know that this section isn't for you to memorize or read all the way through. It's for you to use when you need it. When you're thinking about shopping for Burgundy, this summary and commune list should help you figure out what to look for. The descriptions are general and plots, producers, and vintage will all have an effect on flavor.

Chablis

Small and detached from the main drag of Burgundy (i.e., the Côte d'Or and down to Beaujolais), which is 85 miles (137 km) to the south, Chablis's remote location doesn't stop it from rocking the world of Chardonnay. This far north, the weather is chilly and grapes don't always hit peak ripeness so acidity is high in these wines. The Serein (seh-RAHN) River flows in and around the area, having a warming effect but not enough to take out the acid bite from the grapes.

The best soil in Chablis is chalky limestone (Kimmeridgean, if you want to get technical), and you can usually taste that in the wine (no joke—think of beating chalk erasers together). A small sea once covered the vineyards here, and you can still find fossilized marine animals in the dirt.

Although unpopular for many years due to the (ab)use of its name for nondescript, sweetened white jug wine by a major winery in the United States, Chablis has since recovered its reputation. You can't keep a region down that has continued farming for thousands of years despite the fact that they have to put little burning smudge pots in the vineyards or sprinkle the budding vines with warm water to keep them alive during spring cold snaps. *That's* an elevated form of dedication.

As far as fruit flavor—a little lemon, lime, and green apple fruit flavor is the most you're gonna get. Chablis is less about fruit and more about other notes—minerals, waterfalls, even leaves in the fall or a briny sensation. It's bone-dry and rich, but mouthwatering with a tartness that you won't notice when you have it with food. Producers inhibit malolactic fermentation (page 27), and these wines are rarely aged in new oak, if at all, which allows you to see what the Chardonnay grape tastes like in its pure form with no window dressing (hint: nothing like New World oaky, buttery Chardonnay). A few producers favor fermenting in old oak or doing light oak aging in newer barrels to add complexity and a softer texture to this tooth-enamel-stripping wine, but it's not as common as stainless-steel aging.

Personally, I'm not a fan of the oaked versions because I feel they ruin the subtlety of Chablis, but you'll have to try both styles to see what works for you.

Chablis is classified differently from the wines of the Côte d'Or.

- **Petit Chablis** is at the low end and from sites that were part of an expansion of the appellation decades ago that's still controversial today. The soils are different from the rest of the area, which makes for less delicate wines that can sometimes be harsh and tart.
- **Chablis** can range from amazing to lackluster depending on producer. This area has also expanded outside traditional borders, so although it's better than Petit Chablis, you still need to watch who's making the wine to ensure quality.
- **Premiers Crus** are aplenty—there are nearly ninety—but many aren't all they're cracked up to be. Good ones will have floral, mineral, citrus notes with underbrush and chalky notes with age. These vary in quality; research before buying.
- **Grand Cru** is odd. Even though Chablis is considered one grand cru, there are seven vineyards that make up the grand cru. They are always listed on the label unless the wine is made from a combination of these vineyards, in which case it will just say "Chablis Grand Cru." Each is slightly different, but on balance these are mouth filling, with more dried fruit, honey, almond, and mushroom flavors and an awesome balance of refreshing acid and bolder fruit. They can age for decades and still be delicious. (See page 336 for a list of Grands Crus.)

My take on the levels of Chablis: I never buy Petit Chablis and I make sure that someone who produces solid higher-end wines is making my regular Chablis. Premier cru and grand cru are usually worth the money.

And about "the money": Higher-tier Chablis is not prohibitively expensive. Is it a splurge? Sure. But most are less than $100. Even though the grand cru wines only represent around 3 percent of production in Chablis, you can actually find them in a good shop, which is more than you can say for high-end Côte d'Or wines.

CLOSEST CITIES: *The city of Chablis is about a 2-hour train or car ride southeast of Paris. Chablis is about 1.75 hours northeast of Sancerre in Loire and 2.25 hours south of Epernay in Champagne by car.*

Côte d'Or

As we dive into the place where the most famous and expensive wine grapes in the world grow, a couple of explanations of common confusing things.

- You'll see the *clos* (KLOW) in vineyard names. The word means "enclosed" and refers to the fact that when monks owned these vineyards they built walls around them to protect them from animals and theft. Today, those walls are often nowhere to be seen, but the names aren't changing anytime soon, so it is what it is.
- You'll also see vineyard names appended to town names. This became very stylish in the late 1800s. To get a marketing bump for their towns, many with grand cru vineyards added their top vineyard name to the existing town name. Now, hyphens are the order of the day in Burgundy. Confusing? Yes. Overdone? Maybe. But at least we usually know what the best vineyards are in each place without doing research, so we've got that going for us.
- There's a quirk in the law about what grapes are allowed in red Burgundy. Even though nearly every red wine is 100 percent Pinot Noir, vignerons can technically use up to 15 percent Chardonnay, Pinot Blanc, or Pinot Gris in the blends. Why? People used to throw everything from the vineyard in together in "field blends." With time, vines got isolated, but Pinot Noir still can mutate into Pinot Blanc or Pinot Gris in the vineyard. The rule is a CYA (cover your a**), so if there happens to be random white grapes in the Pinot or Chardonnay, no one gets in trouble under French law.

Côte de Nuits

Now to the land of the most famous Pinot Noir on earth and a mneumonic device to use when shopping (see Tip).

Growers put the best Pinot on the middle of steeper hillsides, where the sun hits the vines perfectly to allow for ripening. What's amazing about this area is that the style can vary so much from one adjacent patch

tip

Remember that *nuit* means night; night is dark, so red reigns in this skinny 15-mile (24-km) strip of land. Of the wine produced, 80 percent is Pinot Noir, and 20 percent is Chardonnay or rosé.

of land to another. In some areas, the Pinot is dark colored, full of dark cherry, black plum, and blackberry fruit. In others it's more like raspberry, cherry, and strawberry fruit. Much of the better Pinot has spicy (like cinnamon and licorice), earthy, and even meaty notes. Because of the terroir differences, some wine is much lighter and more like a violet floral perfume or incense, with Indian/East Asian spices.

There are so many communes in this Pinot Noir heaven, and much to explore. To get you started, I'll classify the communes in broad strokes of how the wines generally taste.

Communes with Bolder Styles:

GEVREY-CHAMBERTIN (JEH-**VRAY** SHON-BEAR-**TAHN**): Minerally Pinots with dark fruit, earth, and strong tannins.

Gevrey-Chambertin was the first to hyphenate its town (Gevrey) with the name of its most famous vineyard (Le Chambertin). Might this practice also lead us into thinking we're getting a great deal on a famed Chambertin when we buy the village level wine? Sure. Do the producers care? No! They sell more wine, don't they? Keep it on the list though; there is a lot of good, affordable Gevrey-Chambertin village wine to be found!

MOREY-SAINT-DENIS (MORE-AY SAN-DENNY): Powerful wines with subtle incense, woodsy notes. This is one of the smallest and most underappreciated villages. Seek it out!

VOUGEOT (VOO-ZHO): The wines grown in this larger area of Côte de Nuits have dark flower, nut, herb, spice, and earth aromas and flavors. They are lush with moderate acid and tannin but quality varies.

Communes with Medium to Light Styles:

VOSNE-ROMANÉE (VHONE RHO-MAH-NEE): These famed wines are earthy, minerally, and smoky, with red fruit notes or, in denser wines, dark fruit with spice.

Vosne-Romanée is the land of the wine unicorns! The most sought-after Pinot Noirs in the world are made in Vosne-Romanée, and it's as it should be; the place has almost universally great growing conditions. The rarity and high prices make it nearly impossible to buy wines from the six grands crus, but if you are connected or have $2K to $20K to spend on a bottle, one could be yours! Burgundy groupies agree this is the place for the best Pinot Noir, hence the price tags.

The good news: The Vosne-Romanée village-level wines, which include wines from the great area of ÉCHEZEAUX, too, can be great and have a decent price (starting at around $40), so we can catch a glimpse of the untouchable for a small splurge.

CHAMBOLLE-MUSIGNY (SHAM-BOWL MUSEN-EE): The lightest and most elegant Pinot Noir of the Côte de Nuits, these are like red fruit, spice, earth, and flowers. Pinot obsessives believe the vineyards here, with the top vineyards of Vosne-Romanée and Gevrey-Chambertin, produce the best Pinot in the world.

The Côte de Nuits ends at its namesake village, Nuits Saint-Georges, where many négociants blend their AOC Bourgogne or village-level wines. Almost right where Nuits Saint-George ends, the Côte de Beaune begins. Whereas the Côtes de Nuits is mainly Pinot Noir and contains a scant nine winemaking communes but twenty-four of the thirty-three grand cru vineyards (all listed on page 336), Beaune has eighteen communes and makes both Pinot Noir and Chardonnay with only eight grand cru vineyards. Which do you think is more prestigious?

CLOSEST CITIES: *Dijon marks the northernmost point of the Côte de Nuits. It's a 1.5-hour train ride southeast of Paris or a 3.25-hour drive by car. This area is so small that if you take the slow route near the vineyards it still only takes 40 minutes to drive from Dijon down to Corgoloin, the southern point of Côte de Nuits.*

Côte de Beaune

You want to taste a Chardonnay like you've never imagined? Look no further. With more gentle rolling hills, it's slightly warmer and wetter here than farther north, and for that reason Chardonnay loves the Côte de Beaune. In an area less than 3 miles (5 km) wide and 16 miles

tip

When I think of Beaune, I also use a mnemonic device—bones are white, so Beaune is most famous for white wine.

(26 km) long, the region is a continuation of the Côte de Nuits limestone escarpment, which protects the vineyards from wind and has an abundance of warmer south-facing slopes that allow grapes to ripen fully.

The Côte de Beaune can be divided into the northern area and southern area, with the northern area containing some famous Pinot Noir and the southern area boasting the most famous Chardonnay in the world (see page 336 for a list of the Grands Crus of Côte de Beaune). Below we'll hit on the wines from the communes most widely available in stores.

Bold Reds of the Communes Surrounding the Grand Cru Corton

In the northern part of the Côte de Beaune are villages around the hill of the Corton vineyard, the only grand cru appellation for Pinot Noir in the Côte de Beaune. It's the largest grand cru in all of Burgundy, so the wine is variable in aromas and flavors. Although expensive and hard to get from the top producers, these grand cru wines are much more affordable than the Pinot of the Côte de Nuits, so keep an eye out for them. The village wine can be excellent. Look for these three:

PERNAND-VERGELESSES (PEAR-NAH VEHRGE-A-LESS): Variable but sometimes outstanding floral, earthy Pinot Noir and acidic, minerally, herbal, floral Chardonnay that ages well.

ALOXE-CORTON (AHL-OS COHR-TAHN): Juicy, fruity Pinots with serious earth and refreshing acid. Red berry and black fruit, leather, and earth flavors. The Pinot acquires floral, spice, and nut flavors with age.

LADOIX (LA-DWAH), an adjacent area, is mainly sold as Aloxe-Corton or as Côte de Beaune Villages.

Mainly Red Wines Made Around Beaune

The wine capital of Burgundy is Beaune. This is where most of the large négociants are located. Beaune may be most famous for its charity wine auction called the Hospices de Beaune, which takes place at the fifteenth-century hospice, the Hôtel-Dieu, an elaborate, memorable building (it's got a geometric, kind of psychedelic roof). The importance of the auction can't be overestimated: The prices people pay at the auction, held the third Sunday of November, set the prices for each vintage in Burgundy. The communes to look out for here are:

BEAUNE (BONE): The third-biggest appellation in the Côte d'Or (after Gevrey-Chambertin and Meursault), this area has hit-or-miss quality. More red (80 percent of production) than white is made. There are more than forty premier cru sites, and many are fabulous. Keep the subregions on your radar for tasty, affordable reds and whites:

- CÔTE DE BEAUNE: A bunch of areas around Beaune that make reds and whites.
- CÔTE DE BEAUNE-VILLAGES: Fifteen quality areas producing Pinot Noir only.
- HAUTES CÔTES DE BEAUNE: A few valleys west of town that make fresh whites and reds that age well.

Beaune has two nearby (*les* meaning "near") areas with similar wines.

SAVIGNY-LÈS-BEAUNE (SAA-VAH-NEE LAY BONE) and CHOREY-LÈS-BEAUNE (SHORE-AY LAY BONE): Both make mainly Pinot Noir that's often not as good as its neighbors, for about the same price. Although in Chorey, especially, the Chardonnay shows promise.

Prestigious Reds from a Valley South of Beaune

It's puzzling why there are no grand cru vineyards for Pinot Noir in this warmer valley nestled in the Côte de Beaune, since the wines are lauded and quite popular. But this is an advantage for us—although they can be pricey, these wines are more available and usually worth the money you pay. They rock.

POMMARD (POE-MAHR): Bold but nuanced Pinot Noir with spice, dark fruit, and tannin. Look for Rugiens and Epenots, two premier cru vineyards, for the best wines.

VOLNAY (VOLE-NAY): Some describe this wine as wispy, delicate, or elegant, although I've only ever found it to be too light to really enjoy. If you like very light wines with just an impression of flavor, this is for you.

MONTHÉLIE (MAWN-TELL-ee): A bolder, stronger, cheaper version of Volnay. Good Chardonnay, too. These are great values to seek out.

The Powerhouse White Wine Villages of Beaune

We've arrived, finally. Just a tad south of Volnay and Monthélie is Chardonnay country, but this isn't your grandma's Chardonnay (my grandma's Chardonnay was Kahlua, so maybe that's not the best example, but you get the point).

If you've eschewed Chardonnay for its heavy, oaky, cloying nature, it's time to take another look. Even the heaviest wines in this area aren't anything like the fruit-and-oak bombs you may be thinking of. This wine deserves your attention.

In each of these communes, the whites have just enough oak to add complexity and to balance the stony, tart flavors intrinsic in these wines. Oak is never the star player here; Burgundy rarely uses oak as a flavoring component, but rather as a vehicle to add texture to the wine. Producers usually limit new oak to 35 percent for village and premier cru wines and to 50 percent for grands crus, which have more fruit so they can better handle oak without losing their identity. Limestone is dominant in the soil, ideal for minerally, acidic Chardonnay with some citrus and apple fruit.

Bold Styles

MEURSAULT (MARE-SO): An oaky, fruity, yet balanced Chardonnay style. These wines always have a line of mineral flavor running through them. New World producers aim to emulate Meursault, an impossible feat since the terroir is so distinct.

AUXEY-DURESSES (OH-SEE DEHR-ESS): A great value that tastes like Meursault but costs less; look for this wine!

Medium Styles

CHASSAGNE-MONTRACHET (SHA-SAHNH-YAH MAHN-RAH-SHAY): Honeysuckle, lemon, hazelnut, fresh butter, flinty, with a mellow, full body. Also full reds with noticeable tannin.

PULIGNY-MONTRACHET (POOL-EE-NEE-MAHN-RAH-SHAY): Lighter style than Chassagne, with hazelnut, lemon, almond milk, flint, and honey notes. Puligny improves with age.

These southern Burgundian villages make some of the most famed Chardonnay on earth from their Grand Cru vineyards (page 336). Since those cause sharp wallet pains, I go for the village-level wines.

Although they seem similar because each added the name of their famous vineyard, Le Montrachet, to the name of their towns, they are different (unlike other areas, both Puligny and Chassagne wanted dibs on the name, taking a devil-may-care attitude on how it confused us wine lovers). Puligny makes almost exclusively Chardonnay on its steep, limestone slopes, which catch coveted morning rays. The terroir around Puligny gives its wines a more mineral, acid-driven quality than those of Chassagne.

Chassagne is larger and more variable than Puligny. Its production is 65 percent Chardonnay and 35 percent earthy, red berry–driven Pinot Noir, which can be a great value. The area has limestone soil on its slopes but also sand and marl, particularly in the less desirable flat areas (something Puligny lacks). Chassagne Chardonnay is softer, fuller, and more floral than Puligny but still quite acidic and minerally. I actually prefer Chassagne, but I am definitely not with the critics!

The Reds and Whites of the Southern, Value-Packed End of the Côte de Beaune

The tail end of the Côte de Beaune contains two areas that make value wines to buy in good vintages.

SAINT-AUBIN (SAHNT AW-BAHN): Floral, flinty, almond-like Chardonnay with sharp acidity that mellows with age.

SANTENAY (SAHNT-IN-NEIGH): Spicy, fruity Pinot Noir. Light Chardonnay that's not as good as that of St. Aubin.

Santenay and its lesser-known, more southern neighbor MARANGES, which specializes in spicy Pinot Noir are the last stops in the Côte d'Or. So that concludes our look at the hard part of Burgundy. Easy, right?

CLOSEST CITIES: *Fittingly, Beaune is the big city in the Côte de Beaune. It's a 35-minute drive from Dijon or a 20-minute train ride. If you get the fast train, it's about a 2-hour trip from Paris or a 3-hour drive southeast. From Beaune to Santenay, it's a 20-minute drive south.*

Farther south in Burgundy are more straightforward areas where you can get great value, which is a relief after the confusing intricacies of terroir in the Côte d'Or. Let's go to the Côte Chalonnaise and the Mâconnais now.

Côte Chalonnaise (Coat shall-oh-NAZE-ah)

Just south of the Côte de Beaune, west of the Saône River, and near the town of Chalon-sur-Saône (shal-OWN seahr SOON) from which it gets its name is the Côte Chalonnaise.

You have to know about this place. Why? Because it is just south of some of the best Pinot and Chardonnay areas in the world, and the terroir in some parts of Chalonnaise isn't that much different. The climate is only slightly different—it's less sheltered from wind so the grapes need more sun to ripen—and although the Côte d'Or has the benefit of being a contiguous limestone slope with awesome soil all along its route, Chalonnaise has the same stuff, just in a different, less elegant form: It's clumped on a few limestone mounds.

Côte Chalonnaise's rolling hills and valleys create microclimates. Lots of terrain variation means quality varies, too, but this area has a distinct purpose for normal wine drinkers. These are mostly early-drinking, affordable, less complex bottles that are fruity in their youth and become toasty and smoky with a little time (less than five years). Chalonnaise will give you a sense of what that other stuff from the Côte d'Or tastes like, but at a less offensive price.

There is a general Côte Chalonnaise appellation, but because it's less well known than the Bourgogne AOP, most of the wines use that larger designation. However, five village appellations are clearly labeled and make distinct, sometimes great wine. I list them here.

The Predominantly White Wine Villages of Côte Chalonnaise

BOUZERON (BOO-za-ROH): The only approved village appellation for Aligoté (al-ah-goat-TAY), a native white grape that always loses to Chardonnay for the best vineyard sites. Aligoté is acidic, herbal, and sometimes like white pepper. Although it's grown all over Burgundy and sold as Bourgogne Aligoté, Bouzeron makes the best examples.

RULLY (ROUL-LEE): Full-flavored Chardonnay, smooth Pinot, and excellent sparkling.

MONTAGNY (MAHN-TAH-NEE): Chardonnay styles range from lean to heavy, so read up before buying! The mantra holds: Producer, land, and vintage matter.

The Primarily Red Villages

GIVRY (JIV-REE): Value Pinot Noir region for floral, red-fruited, spicy Pinot with

tip

Côte Chalonnaise is where we go when we don't want to shell out for Côte d'Or wines.

medium tannin and acidity. Also try wines from the neighboring COUCHOIS (KOOSH-WAH), where the Pinot is less refined, but also cheaper.

MERCUREY (MARE-CURE-AY): Full-bodied, fruity Pinots that can rival top Côte de Beaune Pinots. The best are earthy and minerally with bolder tannins.

If you want to explore Burgundy before dropping a ton of money on the wines of the Côte d'Or, Chalonnaise is your stepping-stone. Much of the flavor, none of the price.

CLOSEST CITIES: *The heart of Chalonnaise is the town of Chalon-sur-Saône, a 20-minute drive south of Beaune or a 40-minute drive or train ride south of Dijon. Paris is about 3.5 hours northwest by car or train.*

The Mâconnais (mah-cone-NAY)

With 80 percent of plantings going to Chardonnay, we can comfortably say that this is white wine country. And it should be: The town of Chardonnay is located in the Mâcon!

Mâcon has 17,000 acres (6,880 ha) of rolling slopes. The more southerly location means fruit gets riper than it does farther north. If the producers can restrain themselves, they make rich, full, fruity Chardonnay with a nice dose of acidity for balance. The problem is that too many let the grapes hang too long on the vine and then go nuts with the oak, killing any shot at terroir expression in the wine.

The general appellation of Mâcon covers basic, light Chardonnay, Pinot Noir, Gamay, and rosé of Pinot Noir. Mâcon-Villages is for Chardonnay only, unless it specifies the name of a village and then it can be used for red and rosé. Mâcon's wine is a bit lackluster in my experience unless you get it from a specific quality area (*a lieu dit*). Look for these top areas to get great Chardonnay:

- **Pouilly-Fuisse (Poo-EE Fwee-SAY)**
- **Pouilly-Loche (poo-EE lo-SHAY)**
- **Pouilly-Vinzelles (poo-EE ven-ZEL)**
- **Saint-Veran (sahnt vahr-AHN):** (all of the flavor for less money)
- **Viré-Clessé's (vear-EE cleh-SAY):** similar to St. Veran

Mâcon is worth exploring for value, but I add a bigger caveat emptor for these wines than for anywhere else in Burgundy. It's easy to go amiss in this region since there are large négociants who sacrifice quality for value. Do research and you can get good stuff.

CLOSEST CITIES: *The city of Mâcon is the center of the Mâconnais and is* *equidistant from Chalon-sur-Saône and the gastronomic paradise of Lyon in the south. Both are about 40 minutes by car and a little less by train.*

Beaujolais (bo-zho-LAY)

Baaaa! Ah, the black sheep of Burgundy. It's not really part of Burgundy, but its administrative seat is here, so we'll include it. The main grape of Beaujolais is Gamay, which hasn't had an easy run of it—it's always being compared to its complex, famous sister, Pinot Noir. It couldn't get more humiliating for this poor grape—it's the only one I know of that has been publicly slandered. It was banned from Burgundy, said to be bad for human health, and pulled up en masse in 1395 by one of the Burgundy dukes, Phillip the Bold, even though it's capable of making delicious wines.

Beaujolais is just north of the gastronomic heart of France, the city of Lyon. It's 34 miles (55 km) long and about 8 miles (13 km) wide and has the distinction of being the well-kept secret of wine dorks

the world 'round. We love it because if you know how to shop for it, Beaujolais can blow your mind—and it's seriously undervalued.

What will you find here? Wines that are light- to medium-bodied with great acid, and strong cherry and beautiful violet notes. The wines usually have warm spice flavors and clean, bright textures. Many of the Beaujolais-Villages wines, especially, are summer reds—great after some time in the fridge. These wines will either say Beaujolais-Villages on the label or call out one of the thirty-eight villages permitted to use the appellation. Any are better than the basic Beaujolais AOP, which can have nondescript banana or floral notes. And although it's tempting to buy Beaujolais Nouveau, that bubble gum–tasting wine released the third Thursday in November (regardless of when harvest happened) is usually more like a wine cooler than a wine.

If you want in on the dork's secret: The best Gamay from Beaujolais comes from the ten cru villages, each with its own terroir. Below I group them by weight and how long they can age before they're at their prime. All have beautiful mouth-watering acidity and are aromatic. These wines will change your perception of Beaujolais forever.

BEST ENJOYED YOUNG (two to five years after harvest/vintage date on the bottle)

- **Brouilly** (brew-YEE): Red berry and dark fruit notes.
- **Régnié** (WREN-EE): Fresh and aromatic with red berry, mineral, and pepper notes.
- **Saint-Amour** (Sahnt a-MORE): Either like Brouilly (see above) or spicy and herbal, with red fruit, floral, and pepper notes.

BEST ENJOYED AFTER SOME AGE (four to ten years after harvest/vintage date on the bottle)

- **Chiroubles** (SHEER-ohblah): Grapey, floral, and light with red cherry and dark flower notes.
- **Côte de Brouilly** (coat duh brew-YEE): Slightly higher quality than Brouilly. Grapey, floral, peppery.
- **Fleurie** (flahr-EE): Sounds flowery, right? They named it well! Light but complex with violets and mineral.
- **Chénas** (SHAY-na): Floral, spicy, woodsy flavors, and a silky, complex finish.
- **Juliénas** (zhul-EE-ennah): Earthy with berry, floral, and baking spice notes.

BEST ENJOYED WITH LOTS OF AGE (ten-plus years—yes, some Beaujolais can age like that!)

- **Morgon** (more-GOH): Rich with red and dark fruit and a peach note.
- **Moulin-à-Vent** (moo-LAHN AW vah): "King of the Crus," the wines are floral, fruity, and spicy in youth but they can pick up truffle, earth, and decayed leaf notes with age.

CLOSEST CITIES: *The main quality wine areas of Beaujolais are about 1 hour north of the city of Lyon by car and 20 to 40 minutes south/southwest of Mâcon by car.*

Champagne

Take the fast train 75 minutes (about 88 miles/143 km) northeast of Paris and you'll wind up in Épernay, the heart of the beautiful, wine-obsessed Champagne region. Nearly every nook and cranny of suitable land here is planted. No joke: Here you'll find 84,000 acres (34,000 ha) planted with the three grapes that go into this often blended, always bubbly wine—Pinot Noir, Pinot Meunier, and Chardonnay.

No other wine in the world tastes exactly like Champagne. A combo of the distinctive terroir and the northern location, plus centuries of winemaking experience, gives Champagne a flavor that you can only get there. (Plus, as I've mentioned before, it's weird to call something by a place name if it's not from that place.)

Think all bubbly is created equal? It's not. Taste Champagne side by side with sparkling wine from another region. You may not like it as much, you may like it more, but you'll concede that Champagne is not the same as other sparkling wines.

What's the secret sauce? Three main ingredients: the land, the winemaking, and the history of the people who farm and make wine here.

The Land

The 19,000 grape growers of Champagne live on the edge. This region is at one of the highest latitudes in the world for grape growing (latitude 49.31° north) with one of the lowest average temperatures (50°F/10°C). It's crazy that grapes can ripen enough to make wine here. But similar to other northerly vineyard locations, Mother Nature provides some help.

First, breezes from the English Channel and the forests surrounding Champagne moderate the climate, warming overall temperatures. Second, the sloping vineyards, graded from 12 to 59 percent, create areas with stellar access to sunlight. Growers maximize light and heat by planting vineyards on south- and east-facing slopes, so grapes can ripen enough to make a decent base wine for sparkling. Champagne doesn't require the level of ripeness or fruitiness that a still wine needs—moderate sugar and high acid do the trick—so the climate is perfect for sparkling grapes. Although the threat of spring frosts and hailstorms is still strong, climate change has helped increase the overall ripeness levels of grapes, so Champagne has become fuller-bodied over the last several decades.

The final advantage for grape growing in Champagne is its white chalky soil. Chalk retains moisture, so during the summer when there is little rain, the vines have a water reserve to slurp up. Because the soil is well drained, grapes get only the amount of water they need to flourish. White chalk also retains heat and radiates it at night to keep grapes warm during chilly evenings. During the day, the soil reflects heat onto the vines, which also helps the wine taste lighter and more nuanced.

Classification and Subregions

The slopes, the climate, and the soil vary slightly from place to place, so the area from which the grapes hail is important to the final flavor of a Champagne. This won't be on the bottle, but in case anyone mentions it in a tasting or on a visit to France, there are five main areas, each with its own character.

MONTAGNE DE REIMS (MOHN-TAN-YA DEH HREHMZ): Reims is where the kings of France used to be crowned, and this area mainly grows the royal Pinot Noir (38 percent). The grapes are used for acid

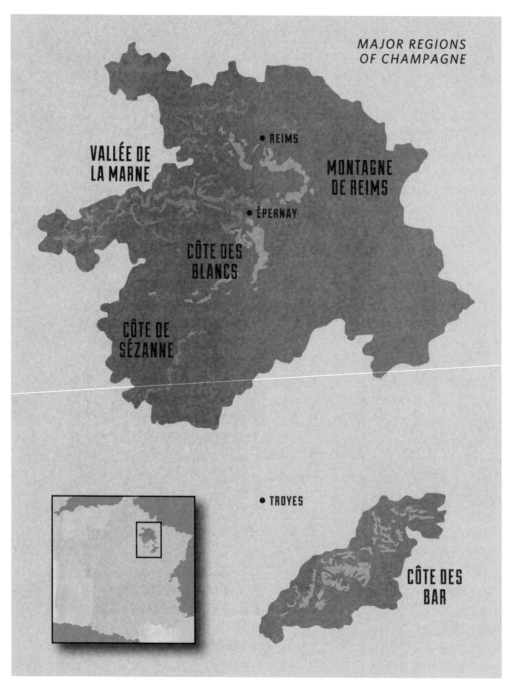

MAJOR REGIONS
OF CHAMPAGNE

VALLÉE DE
LA MARNE

REIMS

MONTAGNE
DE REIMS

ÉPERNAY

CÔTE DES
BLANCS

CÔTE DE
SÉZANNE

TROYES

CÔTE DES
BAR

and aroma, and most big Champagne houses source fruit for their top wines from here. Fruity wines with powerful acidity define Montagne de Reims grapes.

VALLÉE DE LA MARNE (VAHL-AH DEH LA MAHRN): Sixty-one percent of plantings in Vallée de la Marne are the red grape Pinot Meunier, which is hardier than Pinot Noir and Chardonnay and can survive the all-too-common frosts in this valley. If grapes hail from warm, south-facing slopes, this area creates the ripest, most aromatic wine in Champagne. If not, the wines are subtler and less flavorful. You'll find both. This is a big source of grapes for nonvintage

Champagne, which needs the kick of bold fruit and fullness for earlier drinking.

CÔTE DE BLANCS (COAT DEH BLAHNK): Aptly named because this is where Chardonnay (the white or blanc grape) does best—96 percent of Côte de Blancs is planted with this grape. The Chardonnay grapes from here are light and nuanced yet flavorful.

CÔTE DE SÉZANNE (COAT DEH SAY-zhanne): Planted with 64 percent Chardonnay, with about equal parts Pinot Noir and Meunier in the remainder, this area is similar to the Côte de Blancs, but the flavors are not quite as distinct, acidic, or refined.

CÔTE DES BARS/AUBE (COAT DEH BAHR/ OHB): Formerly a second-class citizen of Champagne mostly because it has some clay in the soil (the nerve!), the Aube has been abused, and attempts have been made to banish it from the Champagne region (see History, page 143). This area is now home to an increasing number of grower-producers. It's where terroir-oriented winemakers are growing their reputations, as many of their brands, which taste more of the limestone-based land and less of the winemaker's hand, capture the attention of people looking for something more than just an expensive celebration wine. Eighty-five percent of the grapes are Pinot Noir. Similar to Meunier in Vallée de la Marne, large producers use Aube Pinot Noir for full fruit flavors that make their nonvintage wines yummier in their youth. This area also has two still wine appellations: Coteaux Champenois and the rosé appellation, Rosé des Riceys.

Q+A

I'm looking for high-rent Champagne, how do I know what to get?

Here are the top Grand Crus villages.
- In the Montagne de Reims: Mailly, Verzenay, Verzy, Ambonnay, and Bouzy
- In Vallée de la Marne: Aÿ and Tours-sur-Marne
- In the Côte de Blancs: Le Mesnil-sur-Oger, Oger, Cramant, Avize

A Note on Grand and Premier Cru

Within these five areas are seventeen grand cru villages, considered the best sites, and forty-five premier cru villages that also are worthy of separating from the pack for their quality. I'd love to tell you this was devised in some romantic way, where the grapes were so good they made people weep with joy, but wine is a business: The classification of these vineyards started as a way to set prices for grapes.

Producers and growers developed a ranking system (*Échelle des Crus*—ladder of growths) that sets the value of the grapes based on the historic quality of fruit from these villages. There is discussion around changing the system to center on vineyards rather than villages, to model the Burgundy or Alsace system, but as of now it is what it is.

Champagne Winemaking

I may be thick, but I never even thought about how Champagne was made before I became a wine nerd. I just knew it went down way too easy and was fun to drink on special occasions. It wasn't until I started on the path to wine dorkery that I realized three things.

#1: Champagne is a blended wine, usually with no vintage on the label (I never noticed before I took my wine class in Boston!).

#2: It's really hard to make.

#3: Not all Champagne is the same.

I don't want to bore you with too much detail, so I'm going to hit the highlights: how Champagne is made, the different kinds of Champagne, and why some types cost more.

THE BLEND: As a repeat, the three main grapes used in Champagne are Chardonnay, Pinot Noir, and Pinot Meunier. Chardonnay is used for elegance, acidity, and ageability. The longest-lived wines in Champagne usually have a high percentage of Chardonnay. Pinot Noir gives the wine berry flavors, body, and fullness. Pinot Meunier, or "miller's Pinot" (because it looks like the leaves have white flour all over them), is used for abundant floral and fruit aroma that the other grapes can lack.

Champagne is made like every other fine wine, except that after you make the regular wine, some other stuff happens that is not at all like other wine. In late September or early October, growers harvest the grapes and bring them into their wineries to press them. (There's a very gentle first press that goes into the best wines. There is a slightly more vigorous but still gentle second press that goes into the regular Champagne that most of us slug.) Since the grapes usually aren't very ripe, the yeast eat all the sugar, and instead of making a delicious wine that we want to sip immediately, the result is a dry, low-alcohol, acidic wine that's not so tasty.

Then things go off the rails in Champagne. The *chef de cave*, or Champagne winemaker, blends together a bunch of "base" wines (the blending is called *assemblage*, easy to remember because it's effectively an assembly) from different vineyards and vintages to achieve a consistent wine style. The winemaker can use up to two hundred or more lots to make it happen. Each vineyard produces wines of its own character—some have great mineral flavors and some have more fruit, for instance. Older wines give richer flavors to the blend. It's an incredibly difficult, intricate process to blend, and you need skill and foresight to do it.

FERMENT IT AGAIN, SAM: After that's done, individual bottles (the very same ones we drink from) are filled with the blended wine and a little something called *liqueur d'tirage*. This is a mix of wine, yeast, and sugar that will cause a second fermentation in the bottle.

Sealed with a beer bottle cap, the wine is shut off from air. It hangs out with the yeast for a minimum of fifteen months but can sit for ten years or more.

In that time, two things happen. Yeast munch on the sugar, making alcohol and killing themselves in the bottle. They also produce carbon dioxide. The CO_2 has nowhere to go so it becomes one with the wine—here's your sparkle. This is very different from carbonation, where you inject bubbles that dissipate quickly. These bubbles are more integrated and fizz continuously for a long time after you crack open the bottle.

To get the bready, nutty, rich flavors that are characteristic of Champagne, those dead yeast cells have to break up and their flavors need to permeate the wine in the

CHAMPAGNE SUGAR LEVELS

The levels are listed here from low to high.

- **Brut nature or brut zero:** No sugar, just base wine. The grapes have to be harvested later, when they are riper and have more fruit flavor, a big risk with the frost threat beginning in the early fall.
- **Extra brut:** Pretty dry and austere, with little sugar to balance acidity, similar to brut nature.
- **Brut:** Acidic, but smoother because there is enough sugar to offset the acidity without the wine seeming sweet. Most Champagne is brut.
- **Extra sec/extra dry:** Medium dry, with noticeable sugar. Good to drink alone as an aperitif or after dinner as dessert.
- **Sec/dry:** Strange that a wine called "dry" is actually semi-sweet, but it is. You will taste the sugar, but good ones have powerful acidity to balance it.
- **Demi-sec:** Sweet, but not quite a dessert wine, so it is a good pairing with fresh fruit or fruity desserts.
- **Doux:** A sweet, nectarlike dessert wine, but given the trend away from sweet wine, not really produced anymore, sadly.

bottle, a process called AUTOLYSIS. The longer the time sitting with the yeast (sur lie aging, page 20), the richer and more interesting the flavors are in that wine. Regular, standard nonvintage Champagne spends at least fifteen months on the lies, the French name for dead yeast. Vintage Champagnes age for five to six years. *Tête de cuvées* (page 143) spend seven or more years on the lies.

GETTING RID OF THE BODIES: Now you have great flavors and bubble. Who could ask for more? But there's a problem. Not all the yeast breaks down and integrates into the wine. That means yeast remnants are hanging around in the bottle. It's not going to kill anyone but it's gross. You've got two ways to prep for clean up.

The harder, more traditional way is with *remuage*, or riddling. Here, you take big sandwich board things with sixty slanted holes called riddling racks, or *pupitres*, and insert the bottles neck-first. You hire a bunch of people (*remeurs*) to hang around in 50°F (10°C) cellars all day. You have them first lightly shake the bottles to get the yeast off the sides and then have them turn the bottles ever so slightly. Over the course of two months, the bottles have been turned over completely. At this point, all the yeast remnants accumulate in the neck of the bottle, which is where they need to be if they are going to exit! You move to the cleanup step.

Then there's the easy way. You stick five hundred bottles in a big machine called a gyropallate that slowly turns the bottles, automating the process of remuage so it takes eight days.

Most chefs de cave I've spoken to say there's no difference between the two methods, yet they still use remuage for their top wines, so it doesn't add up. There must be a difference in how gentle the remeurs are with the wine for the finest bottles or they wouldn't do it. But that's just my speculation. I have yet to get a good answer, but I'll let you know when I do!

CLEAN IT UP: After riddling, you're ready to de-gunk the wine! Once you get all the dead yeast into the neck of the bottle, you've got to get it out, refill the missing wine, and stop the bottle back up so it you can sell it. The Champenois have it figured out—they freeze the yeast and the wine in the neck of the bottle while it's upside down. When they pop off the beer bottle cap, the pressure inside the bottle shoots out the frozen dead yeast slushie. The cellar master replaces the missing wine using the same base wine blend in the original wine and usually a little bit of sugar, called *dosage*. This final step determines the wine's sweetness (see Champagne Sugar Levels, page 141), which is often determined by how acidic the base wine is. For example, if it's searingly acidic, you may need more sugar as a counterbalance.

After that, you're done! The wine then goes back to the cellar to relax and bond with its newly added wine for several months or more, then it takes a trip to the store shelf.

Champagne Types

Styles vary by house, but as a general guide these are the types.

- *Nonvintage/multivintage (NV/MV):* A blend of wines from several different vintages, vineyards, and grapes, this is the most common wine type in Champagne and is the flagship of the region. It shouldn't be stored—pop and pour this wine!

- **Vintage:** You'll see a year on the bottle, which will cost nearly double what the nonvintage costs. Given what I've said about Champagne's climate, you've got to know that it's not always a great year in Champagne. But a few times a decade, magic happens in the vineyard. When it does, the houses make a wine from grapes of that year in addition to their NV/MV. Given how special and rare this is, the wines are expensive. Because of this, sometimes vintages are declared when they shouldn't be. Watch the reports before you buy. If people are mad at other houses in Champagne for declaring, it's probably not a great year. Vintage Champagne should have a distinctive character and an ability to age for a decade.
- **Blanc de Blancs:** The "white of whites," these are 100 percent Chardonnay and are the most ageable of all the Champagnes when from the top villages of the Côte des Blancs. They will usually be lighter but more complex than the Blanc de Noirs.
- **Blanc de Noirs:** The "white of blacks," these are made of Pinot Noir or Pinot Meunier or a combo of both. They can be rich and fruity when made well.
- **Rosé:** Either made like regular rosé, with a light press of dark-skinned grapes (Pinot Noir or Pinot Meunier) to get a bit of color out of the grapes, or in a way that you're not allowed to make rosé anywhere else in France: by chucking a little red wine into the white until you get the color and flavor you want. These wines can be tasty, but because they're popular, they're also more expensive than nonvintage Champagne.
- **Tête de cuvée/prestige cuvée:** This super deluxe Champagne started with Cristal from Roederer, which was made only for czars and then trickled down to the rest of us lowlifes by the mid-1900s. Tête de cuvées can be vintage or nonvintage, but all are meticulously crafted from vineyard to cellar. That justifies (sort of) the 500 percent price increase over regular nonvintage Champagne! Krug Grand Cuvée, Dom Pérignon, Pol Roger's Cuvée Sir Winston Churchill, Belle Époque from Perrier-Jouët, and Grande Dame from Veuve Clicquot are examples.
- **Grower Champagne (Recoltant Manipulant):** Some of the 19,000 growers actually make their own Champagne. Usually earthier and less polished, these wines are a great way to taste the land of Champagne—for good and sometimes for bad. Some producers export unique, tasty products, so it's worth seeking these out because they're becoming easier to find. They are usually priced in the $40 to $60 range.

History

Although I haven't gone into extensive detail on the history of many other regions, I think it makes sense to wrap up Champagne and all of its quirks by taking a look at how this unusual wine came to be. The discoveries that led to the wine we drink today were not as straightforward as you'd think. It's certainly worth a minute to explore how things like white wine made from red wine, bubbles in wine, sweetness levels, and the evolution of the Champagne trade popped up.

As in most regions in France, around the fifth century A.D. Romans made their way to Champagne and got busy planting vineyards. Despite the enormous disparity in temperature from Rome, they saw similarities, so they named this place after their own hilly, beautiful land, Campania, south of Rome near Naples. The region got a big bump in status when, in 987, Hugh

Capet was crowned king of France and kicked off an eight hundred-year tradition of monarchs being crowned in the cathedral at Reims. The boon for wine: Glasses of the local, light pink Pinot Noir always accompanied that ceremony. So regardless of the wine's (dubious) quality, the association with the monarchy gave early status to Champagne's wine.

But quality was, indeed, an issue. The Champenois made wimpy, acidic wines. And they had a complex about it. They were seriously jealous of their rivals to the south, Burgundy, who had more heat and sun and could make awesome wines of every color.

Champagne didn't have the climate to ripen grapes that would yield rich, flavorful red or decent white wine. Producers struggled to sell their wines to big wine markets in Holland and Great Britain, which happily shelled out for Burgundy and Bordeaux.

But beyond this problem of thin reds and whites, the Champenois were guarding a dirty little secret. Often during the cool falls and cold winters, fermentation stopped in the cellar. Yeast was still hanging around in the bottles only to come alive again in the warmer spring temperatures. This meant another fermentation would take place, creating a buildup of carbon dioxide that would result in an effervescent wine that sometimes exploded the cheap bottles in which the wine was placed postharvest.

The Champenois tried to hide what they perceived as a massive fault and looked for other ways to make wine that could compete on the world market. In a smart move, they decided white was the way to go. In the sixteenth and seventeenth centuries, their pursuit of market differentiation led to a new method: making white wines from red grapes. Although better than the reds, these wines were more gray or pink—none too appetizing when you're marketing a "white" wine.

By 1662 the British, who rather liked the bubbles in Champagne, figured out how to motivate the secondary fermentation and get fizz in the wine more reliably and with more force. Five years later, a Benedictine monk named Dom Pérignon became the Hautvillers Abbey cellar master. He

perfected the technique of making white wine from red Pinot Noir grapes. His motivation: He thought red grapes were less likely than whites to create unwanted bubbles, something he spent his entire career trying to combat. His techniques of gentle grape handling, softer pressing, and better vineyard management improved wine quality dramatically. Still, Dom Pérignon was never fully able to eradicate the "scourge" of a second fermentation and the bubbles that resulted from it. (As an aside, if the guy came back today and saw that his name adorns one of the most expensive and coveted sparkling brands and that it uses Chardonnay in addition to black grapes, he'd need to have a fabulous sense of irony!)

English merchants captured the interest of wine drinkers in London and grew demand for Champagne through the late 1600s. The taste for bubbly spread to the French courts, and the English worked to figure out how to construct bottles thick enough to withstand the enormous pressure that would result from secondary fermentation elevating carbon dioxide in a bottle.

The Champagne trade grew in the 1700s. Private merchants bought grapes from growers and began to make, bottle, and sell Champagne to Europe's elite. Technology improved: The widow (Veuve) Clicquot and her cellar master devised the process of riddling in the nineteenth century and the ingenious idea of tailoring the sweetness level to customers' preferences by changing the sugar in the dosage. Perrier-Jouët introduced the brut style, with very little sugar (which many termed "brute" and said was too harsh), and different styles evolved.

Then, as in all of Europe, the evil wine vine killer phylloxera (page 45) attacked Champagne. The growers of the Aube subregion were hit particularly hard, with many growers destitute. Needless to say, they were ready to get back into the swing of things and start earning a living again once they grafted their vines onto resistant American rootstocks. But the big Champagne houses of the Marne district, especially, had another idea. They didn't want to pay a premium for the ripe grapes of their own region to bolster their often thin, acidic wines. Instead they wanted to use the new railroad system to import cheap, fruity grapes from the western Loire, the Languedoc, and other parts in the south.

With no appellation system in 1910, the big Champagne houses could legally bring in grapes from Timbuktu if they wanted. Understanding they had a fomenting rebellion on their hands, the French government tried to appease the impoverished, screwed-over growers of Aube by making a federal law that required a minimum of 51 percent of grapes be from Champagne. But the law wasn't enforced and the status quo remained in place. Growers from Aube rebelled, destroying warehouses, chucking wine barrels into the river, setting buildings on fire, and creating enough mayhem to require the French government to send in 40,000 troops to quell the riots.

Then the French government took a misguided step by creating new borders for the Champagne region that completely excluded Aube. It doesn't take a rocket scientist to predict what happened next: Aube producers rioted again.

In all its wisdom, the government redrew the lines yet again to include Aube. The producers of the Marne rioted because they didn't want Aube included. We can't say many positive things about a world war, but in this case the "Champagne Riots" were all but forgotten when France entered World War I. When the appellation system was put into place following the war, producers of the Marne, Montagne de Reims, Côte de Sézanne, Côtes des Blancs, and the Aube were all included.

Today, Champagne is highly regulated. The appellation laws set strict standards for yields, harvest dates, and winemaking. Although much of the twentieth century was difficult for the region and for Europe in general, Champagne thrived. Today, the biggest challenge for Champagne is protecting its brand and satiating worldwide demand. The Comité Interprofessionnel du Vin de Champagne (CIVC) protects the Champagne "brand" around the world by promoting the home of bubbly, litigating against any use of the name on bottles or products not from Champagne, and dealing with issues that arise around the Champagne trade.

A Word on Style

Before we finish with Champagne, I want to say something about the specific styles of each Champagne house because it's important to recognize that each has its own flair. Some are fuller and fruitier; some more mineral driven and austere. Still others (the very expensive Krug comes to mind) are full and rich from barrel fermentation. If you were like me and never thought about anything beyond the brand "Champagne," and thought all the base brands were the same, you should try around. These wines are like any other—there is great variation in style based on place, blend, and winemaker influence. If you venture away from your standby, you may just find a style that you prefer. Take a chance and try something new!

CLOSEST CITIES: *The heart of Champagne is Reims, a 50-minute train ride or*

1.5-hour drive east of Paris. Épernay, the other major center of Champagne, is a 1.5-hour drive or train ride east of Paris.

Languedoc-Roussillon

When I first started working at the big hulking winery, I got put on their latest shiny toy: a gimmicky wine sourced from the Languedoc-Roussillon (Laung-DAWK ROO-see-ohn) region of France. It sold a lot of cases (about 300,000) in the first vintage, and as we began to bottle the second one, the brand was on a rocket ship ride and seemed unstoppable.

In the mid-2000s, wines of the Languedoc-Roussillon were like the second coming. Everyone launched a brand sporting some cute label with a bistro, a bicycle, a beret, lavender, whatever. It was the French version of Aussie "critter wine." And like Australia's first vintages of Yellow Tail, much of the wine was good. I know ours was.

At the time, I learned the basics of the Languedoc-Roussillon region—that it was in the south of France around the Gulf of Lyon, that it was warm and beautiful, and that it was an ancient, historic winegrowing area. I bought the story that the wines were all high quality, excellent value, and the little secret of the wine world. But I always scratched my head at why the region received so little ink in the wine books I respected.

Then I figured it out. While the story is a lovely one for wineries to tell, it's not exactly the truth. It turns out that this "little undiscovered gem" makes about a third of France's wine and therefore is the biggest wine-producing region in the world. Yes, it stretches across ancient, beautiful villages from the Mediterranean coast near Spain to Provence in the east, but there are

700,000 acres (283,280 ha) planted; this is the home of mass-produced wine in France.

It wasn't always like this for the Languedoc or Roussillon, which should be treated separately. We know that vineyards were here in 125 B.C., making this winemaking region the oldest in France and one with a stellar wine reputation. For most of history, the area was separate from France. Languedoc became part of France in the thirteenth century, and France acquired Roussillon from Spain in the mid-seventeenth century.

During the Industrial Revolution, demand for wine by factory workers all over France was at an all-time high, and someone needed to supply it. With a sun-drenched climate, Languedoc and Roussillon seemed obvious candidates to produce bulk wine. And once phylloxera killed many of the older, tastier vines of the region, growers chose the money play—they left behind the high-quality, expensive grapes and went for the high-yielding, lower-quality stuff, namely Spain's Cariñena grape, called Carignan here. It paid off—the World War II wine rations (yes, the French had wine rations in every war they ever fought) came from the Languedoc-Roussillon.

But after decades of industrial wine production, demand started to wane. Soldiers went home to their respective countries and, as they had before the war and the Industrial Revolution, the French enjoyed their locally made wines. Languedoc-Roussillon was stuck with a crapload of vineyards and a crapload of lower-quality vines with insufficient buyers. Over the last decades of the twentieth century, Languedoc was almost solely responsible for France's "wine lake," the oversupply of wine that's distilled into industrial alcohol because there's no other use for it.

Q+A

Is there any stuff out of the Languedoc that is better than the basic stuff?

Several additional subappellations of eastern Languedoc produce wines of slightly higher quality. Here's a list for reference: Sommières, Grés de Montpellier, Saint-Drézéry, Saint-Christol, La Méjanelle, Saint-Gorges-d'Orques, Montpeyroux, Saint-Saturnin, Terrasses du Larzac, Pézenas, and Carbrières.

The saving grace for the Languedoc-Roussillon was its classification as a Vin de Pays (VAHN deu PAAY-ee), now IGP or Indication Géographique Protégée (ahn-DEE-cah-SEE-yohn zhe-oo-gra-FEEK pro-toe-ZHAY), in 1979 (page 92). This raised the quality of the wine by restricting yields and allowed producers greater freedom to experiment with growing different grapes. Maybe most significantly, the category offered flexibility to market wines named by grape instead of by place, thereby giving the wine mass appeal in New World markets.

Although I hear the repeated cries that the Languedoc-Roussillon is full of gems and is a goldmine of delicious wine, I haven't seen much evidence of that. With few exceptions, most of the still, nondessert red wines I've had from Languedoc-Roussillon have been either nondescript or overly fruity and hot from the alcohol. I have yet to find one that I feel could stand up to most wines of Rhône or

Bordeaux, for example. I'm sure they exist, but I want to add this caveat because, after polling more than a few others in the industry, I'm not the only one who acknowledges that if there's potential, none of us has seen it on shelves stateside. (I'm told the selection is better in the UK, but I have a feeling not by much.)

The Appellations

The Languedoc is mostly Mediterranean in climate, except in the far west where it's more Atlantic influenced. There's huge variation in terrain and altitude and, most importantly to us, in style. Wines range from Bordeaux-like in structure (moderate, tannic, layered) to bold and rich like the southern Rhône. Here are a few subareas that may be of interest.

Languedoc

This gigantor appellation covers white, red, and rosé wines from one-fourth of the vines in France (wine lake, anyone?). Seventy-five percent is red from Grenache, Syrah, Mourvèdre, Carignan, and Cinsault, but these last two can never make up more than 40 percent of a blend because the appellation is trying to improve quality by limiting what's considered to be "lesser" grapes. If you get a wine that has "Languedoc" as the appellation, just be aware that the variability in terroir and quality of vineyards, and the fact that the appellation covers both east and west Languedoc make it useless in giving you information about what to expect of the wine.

The action in the Languedoc is in the subappellations. The below are in the eastern Languedoc. Occasionally you'll find the wonderful underbrush scent (think of the smell underneath shrubs)—an herbal, earthy note native to this part of the world and referred to by the French as *garrigue* (gahr-EE-guh), but that is only in the top wines.

PIC SAINT-LOUP (**PEEK** SAHN-**LOU**): These are reds from Syrah, Grenache, and Mourvèdre with red fruit flavor, herbal notes, and good acidity, which is often in short supply in Languedoc.

PICPOUL DE PINET (**PEEK**-POUL DEH PEEN-**ET**): Whites from the Picpoul Blanc grape range from lemony, herbal, and full if picked at the right time to thin and sharp if picked too early. A nice weekday white— I'm a big fan.

FAUGÈRES (FO-**ZHERE**): These red wines are similar to Rhône wines, and dry rosés are mainly of Cinsault, but the best are zesty and refreshing whites of Grenache Blanc, Marsanne, and Vermentino.

Stretching from the town of Béziers down the southern Mediterranean Coast and covering dry, mountainous, and hot coastal land, the wines of western Languedoc can be good quality.

SAINT-CHINIAN (**SAHN**-SHIN-**YOHN**): White, dry rosé, and red are all made here. The whites are full fruited but snappy and are made of Grenache Blanc, Marsanne, and Roussanne. The dry rosé and red are from Syrah, Grenache, Mourvèdre, Cinsault, Carignan, and Lladoner Pelut (furry Grenache). The better wines are from the northern mountains, which yield highly acidic and earthy wines, but not all producers will specify where the wine is from, so be careful when buying these.

MINERVOIS (**MEAN**-EH-VWAH): Reds (85 percent of production) and rosés (12 percent) are made from the standard Grenache, Syrah, and Mourvèdre with a shrinking amount of Carignan and Cinsault. The reds are generally moderate in body and alcohol, rather than bold and rustic as they can be in other nearby appellations. Sweet wines from the whites are tasty, including a botrytis-affected wine (page 57) called Minervois Noble and the Vin Doux Naturel Muscat de St-Jean-de-Minervois, made from the Muscat grape.

CORBIÈRES (CORE-BE-AIR): Reds of Grenache, Syrah, Mourvèdre, and Carignan are similar to Minervois but less refined, and with more obvious fruit and alcohol.

FITOU (FEET-TOO): On the border with the Roussillon, the reds are similar to the rustic Corbières, and the region grows Grenache Gris, Grenache Blanc, and Muscat to make Rivesaltes and Muscat de Rivesaltes, white, honeyed Vin Doux Naturels of Roussillon.

LIMOUX (LEE-MOO): Near the Pyrenees Mountains, Limoux is an anomaly—it's cool enough to produce high-acid grapes for bubbly. BLANQUETTE DE LIMOUX (BLAHN-KET DE LEE-MOO), made from the Mauzac grape with Chenin Blanc and Chardonnay, is like an apple peel, pears, and grass. CRÉMANT DE LIMOUX from Chardonnay, Chenin Blanc, Mauzac, and Pinot Noir is made in the traditional method like Champagne and is citrusy, floral, and biscuitlike. The slightly sweet, old-school Blanquette de Limoux *method ancestrale* is like a cloudy sparkling apple cider but grapey.

For still wines made under the Limoux AOP, you'll likely find oaky Chardonnays with good acidity and mild, boring reds of mainly Merlot with Bordeaux or Rhône grapes blended in. Very meh.

CLOSEST CITIES: *The eastern Languedoc appellations are a 1-hour drive from the city of Montpellier. The western Languedoc appellations are all within a 1-hour drive of Carcassonne.*

Roussillon

Once officially part of Catalonia in Spain, the Roussillon region has only been part of France since 1659, and despite the passage of time, the people still consider themselves Catalan. The region is grouped with its eastern neighbor, Languedoc, but apart from geographical proximity, it's quite different in the wine world.

For starters, Roussillon is effectively in the Pyrenees—the steep mountains that divide France from Spain. Second, with the exception of a few producers,

WHAT ARE VINS DOUX NATURELS?

VDNs are just like Port, only with less alcohol added. Fermentation is halted when the winemaker adds neutral-tasting brandy to stop the yeast from converting all the sugar into alcohol. That means the wines keep some of their sweetness and are a little higher in alcohol (around 15 to 18 percent alcohol by volume). They usually aren't aged for as long or in as many complex ways as Port, but the two wines are both fortified and are quite similar. This wine is historic—Arnau de Vilanova from the University of Montpellier discovered this process in 1285.

Roussillon is not known for dry whites or reds. You'll usually find these wines under the catchall Côtes du Roussillon appellation. The real stars of Roussillon are the Vins Doux Naturels (Vahn dew natur-EL), or VDN, or the sweet wines (see page 149). The Roussillon is where more than 80 percent of France's VDNs are made. Areas like BANYULS (BAHN-YULES) and MAURY (MORE-EE) harvest old Grenache Noir to yield raisined, sweet, and chocolaty wines. Banyuls is like Port and comes in similar styles, including *rimages*, which is similar to vintage Port. It's the best pairing with chocolate (milk or dark, really) you'll find. Rivesaltes makes lovely honeyed VDNs that are awesome with custard desserts, too!

CLOSEST CITIES: *Most areas are a 30-minute to 1-hour drive from the town of Perpignan.*

The Wrap-Up

There is good stuff to be had in the Languedoc and Roussillon regions, but for me it's like a needle in a haystack. I want to like these wines, but clearly I've had a hard time. Sometimes they have nice fruit flavor, occasionally spice, and rarely earth, but they almost always lack structure. They are often hot from the high alcohol and flabby from low acid and tannin content. With fuller body and interesting flavors and textures, the whites show more promise than the reds, although they're harder to find. Frankly, with so much great wine available from so many places around the world, it's hard to make a case for these wines. That said, I'm including them because they are on shelves everywhere and you should know what you're getting before you put down your hard-earned cash.

Loire

Of the major regions of France, for me, Loire (LWAH) is the least accessible. I mean that on a number of levels. First and most practically, it's hard to find the stuff. Although it's become trendier as the "low alcohol" crowd has been clamoring for wines like those from Loire that fall into the range of 11 to 13 percent alcohol by volume, these people are still a minority, so shops and websites don't tend to have big sections of Loire wine. When you do come across bottles, there are often gems, but since almost all of it is labeled by place name, you have to know what you're looking for to shop. To draw an analogy, I think of Loire like Sonoma County in Northern California: great area, but so vast with so much variation that it's hard to know the various subregions intimately.

People have been making wine in this 620-mile (997-km) strip along the Loire River and its tributaries since at least the first century A.D. The Dutch, wanting the winemaking prowess they couldn't have (too cold in the Netherlands), invested in this nearby region, as did the British. Winemaking thrived. But as Bordeaux grabbed the wine world's attention around the 1150s and other growing regions around Europe started winning popularity contests, the Loire turned inward and mainly produced for the locals. We live in a world of marketing excess so if you don't toot your own horn, and no one is tooting it for you, you'll never get the credit you deserve. Loire's modesty meant that in modern times, the region never had the name recognition that Burgundy, Bordeaux, or Rhône experienced.

And then there's the other problem: There's no Loire sound bite. Trust me, I've tried. Despite my attempts to package Loire in a pithy "five things you need to know" list, I can't do it. It's not like Loire

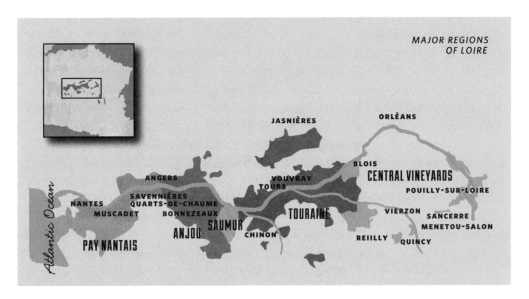

has a "thing." Champagne's got sparkling. Burgundy has terroir. Bordeaux has its blends and its châteaux. Rhône has accessible flavors and easy-to-pronounce names. Then you get to Loire. It has three distinctive white grapes that are sometimes treated well but are often abused (Melon de Bourgogne, Chenin Blanc, Sauvignon Blanc). One big red that gets little credit, except as a blender (Cabernet Franc). Good sparkling. Awesome sweet wines that no one knows about. And rosé that's ubiquitous but often not representative of the quality the region can produce. A motley crew, to say the least.

Geography

To understand the flavors of Loire, you need to know about the land.

Over this large region, the climate of the Loire ranges from continental to Atlantic as you travel the river from the center of France to the Atlantic coastal vineyards. The soil and terrain is vast and disparate. The region is at the northern limit of where grapes can grow (latitude 47° north), and that spells big problems for growers who face crop-devastating frost in spring and fall and potential precipitation throughout the growing season. It can be cool and cloudy; some years the grapes get ripe, some years they don't. This is especially critical as Loire winemakers have put themselves at the forefront of the noninterventionist wine movement, where they try to let natural forces make the wine (ambient yeast for fermentation, natural bacteria for malolactic fermentation, no filtration); the vineyard is "speaking" through the bottle every year whether it has nice things to say or not!

With that said, in a larger context it seems like the subsections of this region are less cohesive than other regions of France. To understand Loire, it's better to put out of your mind that it's one region. In this case Loire is more easily digested as a quartet of places, with only a river to connect them. Following, I give the lowdown on this orchestra of four.

1. Pays Nantais (PAY Nan-TAY)

Also called Muscadet (moose-cah-DAY) and known for high-acid, light wine that's a dream pairing with seafood.

We'll start at the mouth of the Atlantic and at an area that's devoted to one grape only—Melon de Bourgogne (may-LON deh boo-GOHN-ya), also known as Gamay Blanc. You're on the right track if you guessed this interloper came from Burgundy, but it wasn't to produce glorious white wine! It came from necessity when a deep frost in 1709 killed most of the red wine grapes growing in the Pays Nantais. Dutch traders who controlled the area needed a source of cheap, flavorless, frost-resistant white for brandy making. They found the unremarkable yet hardy Melon growing in Burgundy and brought it closer to home.

Muscadet has some quirky things about it. First and foremost, Muscadet is not a grape (that's Melon de Bourgogne) and it's not named for a place. Muscadet is actually a description of the wine—"musky tasting." I could accept this, but the wine is *not* musky tasting. At its base, it's just lemony, salty, and acidic. Weird name.

Second, it's the only wine in France that the government restricts to a maximum alcohol content (12 percent). This ensures it's always a light-bodied wine, regardless of how great the weather was that year and how ripe the grapes got—not a lot of creative license on style for producers!

Third, Muscadet is one of the only wines where the winemaking process sur lie (page 20) can be part of the name of the wine. For producers to put "sur lie" on a bottle of Muscadet, the juice has to sit on dead yeast until at least the March following the harvest. The wines can't be filtered. Odd that you'd call out how a wine is made right on the label (I wish it was more common, actually), but that's Muscadet.

Today, Muscadet is the most produced wine of the Loire, and until recently it's been pretty nasty. Producers made terrible bulk wine and the reputation of the area suffered as a result. It's a real shame, given that this region has a moderate maritime climate, varied terrain, and diverse soils— all great components for successful grape growing.

But there is great hope for Muscadet. A few years ago I tasted the wines of Jo Landron of Domaine de la Louvetrie, a passionate Frenchman with a handlebar mustache (not meant to be ironic, as far as I could tell). He proved to me that if grown in the right area of the Pays Nantais and cared for properly, these wines have a fruity, floral, honeyed flavor behind their strong minerality that makes them far richer and better than the swill producers have traditionally pumped out. In the past five years, I've seen more producers jump on Landron's bandwagon. As techniques evolve, we can look forward to wines from other dedicated producers who will make the Melon grape shine.

Subregions of Muscadet

There are four different regions of Muscadet, but only one of high quality and it produces nearly 85 percent of the wine:

MUSCADET SÈVRE-ET-MAINE (sev-RAY MEN), named after two tributaries to the Loire (Sèvre and Maine). About half of the wines from this area are aged sur lie. The wine tastes like brine or seawater (not fishy, but like being at the beach), fresh green herbs, apple, bread, and mineral. Some versions are floral and fresh, like laundry hanging out to dry. The best are acidic yet creamy and nutty. With its high acidity, Muscadet is a food wine, so attempts to sip it alone may yield "sucking on a lemon" faces.

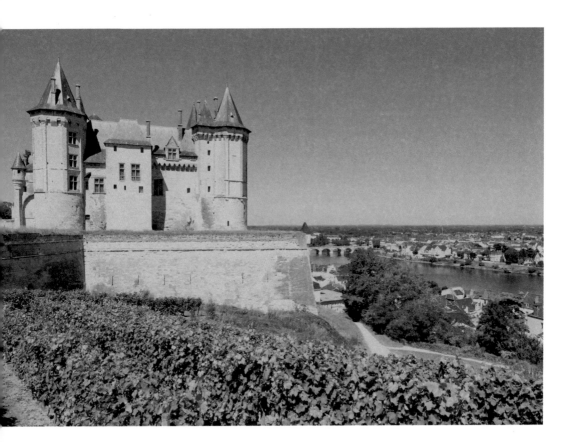

Although you'll rarely see them, here are the other regions of the Pays Nantais:

- *Muscadet Coteaux de la Loire* (apple-like, richer)
- *Muscadet-Côtes de Grandlieu* (lighter, minerally)
- *Muscadet* (lower-quality wines)

CLOSEST CITIES: *The city of Nantes, a 2.25-hour train ride or 4-hour drive slightly southwest of Paris, is the heart of the Muscadet region.*

2. Anjou-Saumur (Ahn-ZHOU Sahm-MYOOR)

The subregion that produces a little bit of every type of wine the Loire makes, but does dry and sweet Chenin Blanc best.

Double name, double (or triple?) identity. From a winemaking perspective, Anjou-Saumur is a hodgepodge. This western-central region of Loire makes every kind of wine—you can find sweet, off dry, dry, white, red, sparkling, and rosé here. Is it all great? No. But you can get good stuff in each category and, personally, I find that impressive.

Chenin Blanc and Cabernet Franc are the pillars of the region. In some years these grapes make awesome wines. Remember that with the Loire being so far north, weather has a heavy hand in what goes on— it's the ultimate decider on wine quality in a given year. If you start getting into these delicious wines, you're in for a ride. No two years are the same and no two wines are the same, even if they're from the same producer. If you're a gambler, this area is for you. Following are the notable wines.

Anjou: Land of Excellent Chenin Blanc

Anjou is full of rivers that reflect light onto the gentle slopes of vineyards, helping to ripen grapes. This is Chenin Blanc (or Pineau de la Loire as it's called here) territory. Although Anjou is very far north, the heat and light during the growing season allow grapes to ripen and lovely dry wines to result. In some areas the terrain has pockets that capture the mists rising off the rivers. That humidity produces botrytis, or noble rot (page 57), which changes the flavors of Chenin Blanc into honeyed, apricot-like, sweet deliciousness. Some red is made here as well, and lackluster rosé often from the bitter Grolleau (ghro-LO) grape. Look for pinks from Cabernet Franc or Cabernet Sauvignon, if you want something tastier. The Anjou hit list is in the subregions.

SAVENNIÈRES (SAH-VEN-YAIR): This tiny region has about forty growers who exclusively produce whites of Chenin Blanc. Save the rare exception, this area makes dry Chenin with high acid and tons of flavor. Expect apple, honeycomb, vanilla, and mineral notes in a full-bodied yet searingly acidic wine. Savennières has another cool feature: Producers often purposefully include grapes affected by botrytis. Many add these to tame the bitter, tart acid that comes from marginally ripe Chenin. Although it can be pricey, Savennières is a must-try—one of the most interesting whites around.

COTEAUX DU LAYON (COAT-TOE DEU LAY-OHN) AND ITS SUBREGIONS CHAUME (SHUM), QUARTS DE CHAUME (KAH DEH SHUM), AND BONNEZEAUX (BON-ZO): The premium sweet wine appellations of Anjou are in areas where the grapes are routinely affected by botrytis or where the dry conditions allow for late harvesting without the threat of mildew. The sweetness varies from simple semisweet wines, found mainly in the larger COTEAUX DU LAYON, to intense, botrytis-affected, sweet, oily wines with good acid from the subregions of CHAUME, QUARTS DU CHAUME (considered the best), and BONNEZEAUX. Expect flavors of honeycomb, peach, baked apple, orange, and lychee. Most of the wines will have minerality and bright acidity that keeps them from being cloying. For a similar sweet wine at a lower price, look for wines from the emerging neighbor, COTEAUX DU AUBANCE (coat-TOE deu oh-BANCE).

CLOSEST CITIES: *The city of Angers, a 3-hour drive slightly southwest of Paris, is the heart of Anjou, and it's about 25 minutes by car to the surrounding wine regions.*

Saumur: Good Sparkling Wines and Cabernet Franc–Based Dry Reds

Sandy *tuffeau* (soft yellow rock) soil in Saumur made it easy for Romans and everyone after them to create underground cellars for wine storage. It was nice to have them, but since the soils of Saumur produce wines of a lighter character, the caves aren't really needed for extended aging. Saumur's strength is early-drinking sippers that go well with food.

Basic SAUMUR BLANCS of Chenin Blanc with Chardonnay can be fruity with high acid or bitter and sharp, depending on the vintage and producer. I usually find it's the latter and steer clear. The basic SAUMUR ROUGE is dry and light-bodied, and can be tannic with green pepper and earth notes in cool years and floral, fruity, peppery, and like pencil lead in warmer years. These wines consist of Cabernet Franc with up to 30 percent Cabernet Sauvignon or the bitter, less good Pineau d'Aunis (PEE-no doo-NIECE). Quality varies, but from a good producer, this wine can be refreshing, tasty, and a great value.

CRÉMANT DE LOIRE (CRAY-MAHN DAY LWAH): Sparkling produced in the Champagne method, Loire's Crémant can be made anywhere in Anjou, Saumur, or Touraine (see following section) from a variety of grapes, but it's usually Chenin Blanc and Cabernet Franc, and it's usually made in Saumur. Grapes are hand harvested, the yields are restricted, and the wine must be aged longer than other sparkling wines in the region, making this the top dog of sparkling in the Loire at a surprisingly low price. This wine is always in the rotation at my house.

SAUMUR-CHAMPIGNY (SAHM-MYOOR SHAM-PIYN-EE): This wine, 90 percent Cabernet Franc with 10 percent Cabernet Sauvignon or Pineau d'Aunis (most producers don't use the latter), is sometimes overpriced and overoaked, but good versions are medium-bodied and taste like violets, dark fruit, earth, herbs, and black pepper. Watch for a good producer and you'll be happy with the flavorful, medium-bodied style of this wine.

CLOSEST CITIES: *Saumur is the heart of this region and is a 30-minute train ride or 45-minute drive southeast of Angers. Saumur is 3 hours by train and 3.25 hours by car slightly southwest of Paris.*

3. Touraine
Loire's best Cabernet Franc–based reds and often the best Chenin Blanc–based whites.

Touraine is a tourist mecca, the land of beautiful châteaux built during the prerevolution era (French Revolution, that is), when the rich reigned supreme. But Touraine wine isn't just lipstick on a pig. There's bacon here: The area has beauty and the best red wines of the Loire. Depending on vintage, it even has some of the best whites. The main reds are Cabernet Franc (called Breton locally); Cabernet Sauvignon; Côt (COAT), which is Malbec; Pinot Noir; and Gamay. The main whites are Chenin Blanc and Sauvignon Blanc.

The red grape areas have two soil types. For the lighter wines, gravelly, alluvial soils produce fresh wines that taste like berries, herbs, and licorice. Those growing on a local, porous, well-draining soil (*tuffeau jaune*) create richer, spicy wines with earthy flavors and dense fruit. Chinon (SHEE-noh) and Bourgueil (boar-GHEYL) have both soil types, and regulations require both to be a minimum of 90 percent Cabernet Franc with up to 10 percent Cabernet Sauvignon permitted, but not always used.

In a world where heavy, ageable reds are praised, this cool region that produces medium-bodied, complex reds can be overlooked: Don't make that mistake! Here's what you can expect from each subregion.

CHINON: Two styles of Chinon are made—one is lighter and full of juicy fruit flavor. It's usually aged in stainless steel to maintain fruit and can be served lightly chilled. These wines taste like red cherry, berry, fresh cut herbs, and violets with moderate tannin and bright acidity. Occasionally you'll taste a touch of green pepper, especially in cool years. The other style is made from grapes grown on tuffeau in warmer areas. They're fuller and more ageable, with earthy, mineral notes, dense black fruit, sweet oak, and occasionally spice and smoke. These wines can have strong tannins, so make sure you have protein-rich food handy before you crack them open.

BOURGUEIL: Similar to the denser style of Chinon, Bourgueil is a medium-bodied yet tannic Cabernet Franc–based wine. These wines are earthy, spicy, herbal, and smoky with red fruit. Bourgueil reminds me of a cru Beaujolais (page 135).

Neighbor ST-NICHOLAS DE BOURGUEIL is similar in flavor to Bourgueil but with sandier soil, so it produces lighter, aromatic wines.

VOUVRAY: CHENIN BLANC HUB: Terroir and weather play a huge part in what you'll get from a bottle of Vouvray, Touraine's Chenin Blanc powerhouse. This area is replete with chalky, soft, porous limestone tuffeau, which helps retain water during drought but drains well enough to prevent vines from drowning. South-facing slopes provide good sun exposure to ripen the grapes in tough years. But inconsistency can arise because there is climate variation—the area is somewhat maritime and somewhat continental. The Chenin Blanc can come from a large area surrounding the town of Vouvray, so big it leads to great variability.

Vouvray's main challenge is that it relies nearly exclusively on the fruit for its flavor and texture—there's no malolactic fermentation and no oak aging apart from the rare producer. It's naked. So when the weather doesn't cooperate and grapes don't ripen,

you'll get lots of dry and sparkling Vouvray. In hotter years the wine will be off dry, sweet, and even botrytis affected.

In theory, this is fine—to have a wine region that makes sweet, dry, still, or sparkling wine based on nature—except that much of the time the producers don't care to tell you how sweet the wine is, so you never know what you're going to get. You need to steer clear of bad producers, who will sweeten a wine to hide the searing acid. These bad versions sometimes have a yucky wool or wet hay character and green stem flavors in poor years. Look for producers who spend the time to label the wines with sweetness levels ranging from *sec* (dry) to *demi-sec* (off dry) to *moelleux* (meaning "mellow," but is sweet) to *doux* (sweet). Domaine Hüet, Domaine Pichot, and Domaine Vincent Carême are top names.

In good years, Vouvray is worth the trouble. When the wine is good, it's aromatic, with apple, pear, chamomile, and floral notes. As Chenin ages, which it does well since its high acid preserves it, those flavors mellow into honey, honeysuckle, and baked apple with a waxy, soft texture. Vouvray from a good producer in a good year is awesome, but you have to have the discipline to follow vintages and the patience to wait around for a good one!

CLOSEST CITIES: *Tours is the center of this region and is just an hour on the fast train southwest of Paris or a 2.5-hour drive. Chinon and Bourgueil are about 45 minutes west of Tours by car. Vourvray is a 15-minute drive east of Tours.*

SOILS

In this farthest eastern part of the Loire and in the Center of France (hence the name, Central Vineyards), soils range and dictate styles.

- **On clay-flint,** the wines have a gunflint (just-fired gun) note to them.
- **On white limestone with clay,** the wines are more robust and fuller-bodied.
- **Limestone** with more pebbles produces fruity yet acidic wines.

4. Central Vineyards
The Sauvignon Blanc Capital of Europe.

About two hours south of Paris are two little areas that are most people's first introduction to the Loire, whether they know it or not: wines of 100 percent Sauvignon Blanc from SANCERRE (SAHN-SAIR) and POUILLY-FUMÉ (POO-EE FU-MAY). Although there are other vineyards in this area, these two are at the epicenter of quality.

When you think of these regions, think pure citrus fruit flavor, herbs, minerality, and strong acid. Being right across the river from each other, these regions are similar but different. In Sancerre, you'll get a more austere Sauvignon Blanc with biting acid and fuller citrus and mineral flavors. In Pouilly-Fumé, you'll find wines with more fragrance, smoke, and floral notes. If you want to understand the nuance of Sauvignon Blanc, you've got to have wine from both areas.

POUILLY-FUMÉ VS. POUILLY-FUISSÉ

The world "Pouilly" comes from the name of the former Gallo-Roman estate Pauliacum Super Fluvium Ligerim from the fifth century A.D., but we all knew that. The name was co-opted by the Benedictine monks and brought south to create Pouilly-Fuissé, a move made only to confuse us all.

I've always used a ridiculous way to remember that Pouilly-Fumé is different from the Chardonnay-based Burgundy wine Pouilly-Fuissé: Fumé is like fumes. Fumes are smoky, which is also an aroma found in Pouilly-Fumé because of that gunflint quality. (In truth, Sauvignon Blanc takes on a gray hue at harvest, which looks like smoke, and which is why producers refer to it as "fumé.")

If you don't like that, remember that Burgundians are a little *fussier* about their Fuissé wines, and that should help you remember the difference.

If you're looking for the highest-quality Sancerre, look for the top villages of Chavignol (SHA-vyn-yol) or Bué (BWAY) on the label, which produce fruity, minerally, steely wines.

A small amount of good rosé from Pinot Noir and still red Pinot are made here as well. They're light and berry flavored. You can also find lesser quality but less expensive Sauvignon Blanc from Quincy, Reuilly, and Menetou-Salon, with the last sometimes rivaling or exceeding Sancerre or Pouilly-Fumé.

CLOSEST CITIES: *Sancerre (and the winemaking areas of Quincy, Reuilly, and Menetou-Salon) is about a 2-hour drive east of Tours, a 1.5-hour drive south of Joan of Arc's former haunt Orléans, and a 2-hour drive or train ride south of Paris. Sancerre and Poully-sur-Loire are about 20 minutes by car from each other.*

Provence

Beautiful, breathtaking, pleasant Provence has a lot going for it and always has. It's sunny in both climate and personality. It is close to Italy, and people have made wine in this lavender- and sunflower-dotted paradise since Roman times but, sadly, it's never been taken very seriously. That seems to be changing: Lately Provence has stepped it up and the wine keeps getting better.

Provence spans 150 miles (241 km), stretching from the Rhône in the west to the Côte d'Azur near the posh country of Monaco in the east. Although we think of Provence as Nice, Cannes, and St-Tropez—tanned bodies on beaches, celebrities on yachts, and beautiful, colorful towns—in the wine world it's far more than that, encompassing some cool areas like Coteaux Varois where producers are growing cool-climate Pinot Noir and Syrah, and warm areas like Bandol where sun-loving Mourvèdre thrives. Needless to say, styles vary.

Provence is known for its ubiquitous rosé, which is delicious when made well—fresh, herbal, acidic, and great as a sipper or with food. Commonly produced from a blend of Grenache Noir, Cinsault, Syrah,

Mourvèdre, and Carignan, Provence rosé is the world's gold standard of pink wine. The best wines reflect the terroir in the area, and always seem to have that thyme, lavender, shrub, and herb character, known locally as garrigue.

To get the best out of Provence, it helps to dig into the labels. Most people shop rosé by color, but that's not always the best indicator of what you're going to get in the bottle. All that tells you is about the grape variety used and how long the juice sat with the grape skins! Through excessive sampling (I'm a rosé monster in the summer), I can attest that the best Provence rosé comes from great producers who often put a subappellation on their wines. The more specific the terroir, the more character you often get.

Main Appellations

You'll see three main appellations on your Provence rosé: the large, very general CÔTES DE PROVENCE (Coat de Pro-VAHNCE), COTEAUX D'AIX-EN-PROVENCE (Coat-OH DEX-en-Pro-VAHNCE), and COTEAUX VAROIS EN PROVENCE (Coat-OH vah-WAH en Pro-VAHNCE).

As can be expected of an area encompassing nearly 50,000 acres (19,600 ha), Côtes de Provence has the best and worst wines in the area. Pay attention to producer and you'll get something herbal, fruity, and acidic. Even better, find a wine from one of the subappellations of Côtes de Provence: look for SAINTE VICTOIRE, FRÉJUS, or LA LONDE for wines with more of a stamp of terroir and layered flavors, for (oddly) around the same price.

Coteaux d'Aix-en-Provence makes mainly floral and berry-flavored rosé, which can be excellent because of the ripeness of the grapes, but many I've had have been boring, lacking fruit and acidity. Coteaux Varois is a cooler area, and the rosés have excellent acidity and more layers of flavor due to a long growing season.

A small appellation that makes whites of Clairette, Marsanne, Ugni Blanc, and Sauvignon Blanc called CASSIS is growing in popularity. It's an herbal, full, delicious wine of great value but is hard to get due to limited vineyard land. Grab some immediately if you see it. It's tasty and rare!

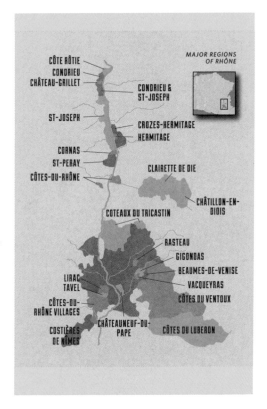

CLOSEST CITIES: *Aix-en-Provence is only about a 30-minute drive north of Marseilles. Brignoles in the Coteaux Varois is about 1 hour from Marseilles and 1.5 hours from Nice by car.*

Bandol: The Red Revelation of Provence

Most wine in Provence (more than 85 percent) is rosé, but there is one gem from here in the world of reds: BANDOL (BAHN-DOLE). This area's reds and rosés are made mainly (at least 50 percent) from Mourvèdre with some Grenache and Cinsault. The opposite of the light rosé of the region, this is a fireplace wine—brooding, full, chewy, and in need of decanting before you drink it.

Some Bandol is rustic, some fruity, but most is tannic with soil, herbs, and ripe black fruit notes. These wines often smell like smoked meat and taste like licorice and spice. Track some down and store it to let the tannins settle down—it will be better after relaxing in a cool, dark place for a year or two.

Bandol rosés are also made from Mourvèdre and, thanks to the strong character of the grape, can age for a few years before losing their zip. Because of

this quality, Provençal winemakers are looking to the success of Bandol's ageable rosés and the price premium they command to make their own more age-worthy Mourvèdre-based rosés.

CLOSEST CITIES: *Bandol is a 45-minute drive east of the port city of Marseille.*

Rhône

If you're just getting into French wines, Rhône (ROAN) should be your first stop. Why? More than any other, these wines are both easy to like and easy to find. It's simple to grab a decent Côtes du Rhône at your shop and be satisfied with your choice. But like everything else in this book, that's not enough for us! Even if you're new to it, I want you to get more out of this region, so we'll dig into the nuances and quirks to do that.

From a style perspective, the Rhône is a funny place. The area is split into parts that make wines with little in common; the (creatively) named northern Rhône and southern Rhône. The northern Rhône, north of the town of Montélimar, has a continental climate, with hot days and cool nights. Its best vineyards are perched on the Rhône River's steep banks, and the wines they produce are age worthy and layered, and have earth-driven, nonfruit flavors. Often, they're so complex that they have you questioning how the liquid silk in the glass could result from fermented grapes! This contrasts sharply with the hot, dry, Mediterranean climate of the south, which yields juicy, easy-to-drink wines. The best vineyards of the south mainly lie in foothills away from the Rhône River and produce wines from hot weather–loving grapes, notably Grenache Noir and Mourvèdre.

Despite the differences, both areas are simultaneously victim to and beneficiary of the defining characteristic of the Rhône: the strong, cold wind known as the *mistral* that blows intermittently throughout the year. Particularly in winter and spring, this northwesterly current blows hard and fast (it can reach up to 115 miles [185 km] per hour), keeping the vineyards clear of mold, mildew, and pests, preventing winter frosts, and bringing sunny days. Although mainly good, the wind at the wrong time can snap shoots and rip berries off a vine in short order. For good or bad, to make good wine in the Rhône, producers must find a way to work with this key climatic feature.

Rhône History

To understand the Rhône's significance, let's take a dorky historical look at it. We'll start with the most salient point: Smack in the middle of the wine region lies the navigable, prime-for-boat-traffic Rhône River, which meets the sea at the southernmost point of the region. Given this fantastic access, over the millennia the area has seen a lot of foot traffic. During the days of Roman rule, the main period of European viticultural expansion, vineyards popped up in the Rhône so wine could be sent upriver to slake the thirst of Roman soldiers pillaging in lands without a vinous tradition. Centuries later, the region's proximity to Italy made it a thoroughfare for trade and the natural asylum for people, more specifically popes, fleeing the political messiness of Rome yet desirous of the comforts of home (the Babylonian Captivity in 1305–1377 saw seven French popes rule from the southern Rhône city of Avignon).

As you can guess, those popes had some influence on taste-making in Europe, and their love of Rhône wines raised the status of and demand for them. By the 1600s, Côtes du Rhône was such a coveted wine that, to prevent wine fraud, barrels were stamped with C.D.R. to prove they were legit. The Rhône cemented its place as a wine powerhouse centuries ago, and today it is wine royalty. But the region has something really important going for it: It's not overhyped. That means you can get wines from meticulous producers for a fraction of the price you'll pay for coveted wines from other places.

Getting your arms around Rhône will take time and patience—I mean, it is the second-largest appellation in France after Bordeaux, with 173,875 acres (70,365 ha) under vine. And then there's the bigger problem. The strength of the region is its weakness: diversity of grapes, quality, and flavor. You need to know what you like and what to look for to make the Rhône work for you. Totally doable!

Northern Rhône

The northern Rhône has the world's best vineyards for Syrah. From the northern city of Vienne south to Valence, the small area (about 5 percent of the Rhône's output) is constrained in growth because top vineyard land on the steep slopes flanking the river is at max capacity. This is good for us as wine lovers because the limited space and hard work to farm mean that there isn't much crap wine—most of it is decent at worst. But the size also means bottles are in shorter supply and therefore usually expensive.

The grapes of the northern Rhône are easy to remember because there are few—the only red is Syrah; the whites are Viognier, Marsanne, and Roussanne. Red wine producers use Syrah on its own, but in many appellations, they blend in white grapes and sometimes the result is magic (see Côte Rôtie, following). Like all whites of the Rhône, northern Rhône's versions are underrated and worth tracking down. If you think white wines are either acidic and thin, or oaky and buttery, these beauties will dispel that thought instantly. Rhône whites are substantial with fat texture, flavor, and lower acid and are mind-blowing.

Famed Red Appellations

CÔTE RÔTIE (COAT ROW-TEE): Producing red wines with black fruit and floral flavors or black pepper, dried herb, olive, and bacon notes, Côte Rôtie is one of the most famed wines of the northern Rhône. Located on baked-in-the-sun "roasted slopes" on the right bank of the Rhône, these terraced vineyards are worked by only about a hundred vignerons (winemaker/growers) in sixty vineyards. This is the only area in the northern Rhône where Syrah grows alongside Viognier in the vineyard. Up to 20 percent of the white grape is permitted in the blend. It stabilizes Syrah and gives it more longevity, and when vinified together the combination is a knockout. When the wines are Syrah alone, they're still stunners—like olives, bacon, black pepper, and leather—but I'm a sucker for the Viognier addition.

HERMITAGE (ERM-EE-TAJH): On the left bank of the Rhône, in a warm, high area with a Mediterranean influence, lies what may be the best climate and terroir for Syrah in the world. Named for a soldier who sought solitude following a gruesome experience in a Crusade of 1224, this legendary slab of granite atop a hill had vineyards long before the warrior-turned-hermit Gaspard de Stérimberg took up residence and planted his vines there. Today, the wines must be at least 85 percent Syrah, but producers often blend in up to 15 percent white Roussanne and Marsanne. These wines are among the best reds in the world and prime for aging since their flavor transforms drastically over time, changing from tannic and full of black fruit to bold but softer with bacon, black pepper, olive, lavender, and leather flavors.

The whites aren't shabby either. About 25 percent of Hermitage wines are age-worthy Marsanne and Roussanne combos that taste like peaches, nuts, and vanilla. A sweet, traditional wine made from raisined Marsanne is a local specialty that has been around since Roman times.

White Appellations

CONDRIEU (CON-DRAY-OOO): On the right bank of the river, Viognier shows its stuff with full-flavored, dry white wines with peachy, floral, and citrus notes. Condrieu's steep vineyards are a labor of love to farm. And it's a good thing locals love Viognier—

if not for a few passionate producers in the 1950s, the grape wouldn't exist here. Viognier almost went the way of the dinosaur after several world wars and vine disease outbreaks. Thankfully, due to a few keeping it going, we can enjoy its beauty, even if it is a little expensive (more than $40).

CHÂTEAU GRILLET (SHA-**TOE** GREE-**AY**): The smallest appellation in the Rhône (only about 8.5 acres [3.4 ha], this Viognier-only vineyard is owned by one producer (a.k.a. a *monopole*).

For centuries, this small area on the right bank of the Rhône produced wines similar to Condrieu, but with more mineral notes and a great ability to age. Sadly, after the brand rode its reputation for years, the quality fell. Although improving under new ownership, Condrieu is still a safer Viognier for less money.

ST-PERAY (SAHN PEAR-**AY**): This white-wine-only area grows Marsanne and Roussanne, and one-third of the wine is sparkling and made like Champagne. In my experience, the wines are pretty meh, so I skip them when I see them on the shelf.

Wines Not Completely Out of the Budget

ST-JOSEPH (SAN JHZO-**SEF**): In this decent value area, you'll mainly find Syrah-based wines that taste like bacon, black pepper, lavender, shrubby underbrush (garrigue), and black fruit. They have complexity but restraint and are decadent when well made. Ten percent of the wines are whites of Roussanne and Marsanne, with the former favored for its richer tropical fruit and honeysuckle flavors and waxy texture. Because it's larger and more wine is produced, this is one of the more affordable appellations of the northern Rhône.

CROZES-HERMITAGE (**CROWZ ERM**-ee-**TAJH**): This is the largest area in the northern Rhône (50 percent of production!). The wines are the most affordable and most variable in quality. Although the area uses the same grapes and has about the same red-white breakdown as St-Joseph, the flatter vineyards in Crozes-Hermitage aren't as consistently good so quality is more variable. From a great producer, you get phenomenal wines that taste just like what I described for St-Joseph. From a mediocre one, these are nothing special. Read up before you buy—I've had some of both.

CORNAS (KORN-**AHS**): Nestled in a steep, natural amphitheater that maintains heat and protects vineyards from the mistral, Cornas only makes rich reds from Syrah. The wines have black fruit notes with licorice, earth, and herb flavors, and are known to be great agers given their consistent flavor and quality. You'll pay a higher price for Cornas ($40 plus) than for St-Joseph or Crozes-Hermitage, but they're underrated so the quality for the price is outstanding.

CLOSEST CITIES: *The small city of Vienne is the most northern part of the northern Rhône. It's 20 minutes from Ampuis, near Côte Rotie and Condrieu. The towns of Cornas, Tain l'Hermitage (near Hermitage), Crozes-Hermitage, and Mauves (St-Joseph) are 15 to 30 minutes from Valence, which is 1 hour south of Lyon.*

Southern Rhône

Whew! After the complexity of the northern Rhône, it feels good to move on to the south. Côtes du Rhône? We've got that one down! And even if you're not a Beastie Boys fan (totally inexplicable if not) and haven't heard "Body Movin'," you may have heard of Châteauneuf-du-Pape, the most famous wine of the southern Rhône. Easy stuff! I can say we've officially entered the Rhône comfort zone.

Or have we?

Argh! No! The wine of the southern Rhône is much more of a gamble than that of the northern Rhône. If we start with the most accessible thing (mostly) from the south—Côtes du Rhône—and look at the production zone, we see that grapes can come from 79, 138 acres (32,036 ha) across the whole Rhône. That's a whole lotta land, and not all of it grows delicious grapes. And though there is a consistent Mediterranean-influenced climate in most parts, there's a huge range in terroir. You've got to watch the vintage, producer, and blend (if you can track it down online

or on the label). Even then you may not know what you're in for.

If we move to the grape arena, it gets even crazier. Côtes du Rhône allows use of twenty-seven different grapes—fifteen reds and twelve whites. Although the majority of red blends have to be Grenache, Syrah, and Mourvèdre (often called GSM, the base of wines in every region detailed here), the other twenty-four make a difference. For example, low-quality Carignan can hijack a blend and make it taste like eating prunes on a bed of dried hay.

When it's good, the GSM blend works because each player contributes unique flavors. Grenache is the star player, producing high-alcohol, berry-flavored, acidic wines. Syrah tempers the exuberant Grenache, adding color, spice, acid, and tannin. Mourvèdre, grown on the hottest sites, adds wild berry, earthy, and meaty-flavored notes and tannin to the blend. The other grapes provide nuance or support for whatever the big three don't deliver.

Given those wild cards, I approach the southern Rhône with skepticism: From experience I know that I could luck out and get something amazing or I could be out cash for something I pour down the sink.

So I have work-arounds. I look for Côtes du Rhône Villages or a wine from one of the nine crus, both of which I'll detail here. These areas have stricter requirements for farming and production than general Côtes du Rhône wine. If those aren't options, I hunt down blends with more Syrah than Grenache; Syrah is hard to grow in the southern Rhône (it likes cooler sites and much of the south can be too hot), and the producers who use it as a majority of the blend often get delicious results. Even with those heuristics, Côtes du Rhône is unpredictable.

But let me stop the negativity parade and say that when you get a great wine from the southern Rhône, it's decadent, fruity, full, and earthy. When done right, these are some of the most delicious everyday French reds. The whites and rosés are food friendly and unique in their texture and flavor profiles.

Frankly, once you know what to look for, Rhône has the best quality for the price in France. With that, let's get to the nitty-gritty so you can drink better Rhône wine.

The Nine Crus of the Southern Rhône**

CHÂTEAUNEUF-DU-PAPE (SHA-TOE-NEWF DU PAHP): The hot, dry, former home of seven popes is the place where winemakers create France's boldest wine.

The vineyards of Châteauneuf-du-Pape take up about 7,740 acres (3,133 ha) between the towns of Orange in the north and Sorgues in the south. Although there's variability in flavors, the warm temperatures,

high quality of the soil (much of which contains large, light-reflecting rocks to speed ripening, see photo), and strict regulations keep producers in line and yield grapes that are nearly uniform in their potential to make fabulous juice. The thing that most Châteauneuf-du-Pape wine has in common: The terroir is palpable in the wine. And for the guarantee of quality and the sense of place, you'll pay the price—the best start at $50 a bottle and just keep going up.

I'll point out that I said consistent *quality*, so you can rest easy that from a winemaking perspective the wine will be good. But what distinguishes one wine from another is the *flavor*, and that's a different story. Up to thirteen grapes are allowed in the Châteauneuf-du-Pape blend (but different colors of the same grapes are counted as single ones). For reds, Grenache (Noir) dominates, with Mourvèdre and Syrah as runners-up. Also allowed are Cinsault, Vaccarèse, Counoise, Muscardin, and Terret Noir. White and pink grapes are Clairette (Blanc and Rosé), Grenache again (Blanc and Gris), Picpoul (Blanc and Gris), Bourboulenc, Roussanne, and Picardin. With the exception of a couple of châteaux, no one uses all thirteen, but as with all southern Rhône wines, proportions and blends affect flavor.

More than 90 percent of Châteauneuf-du-Pape is red. Some versions are full, high in alcohol, tannic, and full of black fruit, baking spice, pepper, and leather notes. Others are lighter and fruitier, and aren't meant for long aging. Regardless, you should watch alcohol on these wines: Heat-loving Grenache can rack up the sugar on the vine and the wines can hit more than 16 percent alcohol in warmer years, making the wines feel hot in your

**Unless otherwise specified, the main grapes are Grenache, Syrah, and Mourvèdre.

mouth. That's rare, though; on balance, these wines are spectacular.

Red gets all the status, but Châteauneuf-du-Pape blanc is one of my all-time favorite whites. It's responsible for one of the best pairings I've ever had—with halibut in an herbed butter sauce at a (now-closed) restaurant in San Francisco. It was heavenly! Made mainly of Roussanne or Grenache Blanc with Picardin, Clairette, and Bourboulenc, the wine is full, fragrant, herbal, honeyed, and spicy. Although it's harder to find, it's worth the hunt!

Similar to Châteauneuf-du-Pape for Far Less Money

GIGONDAS (ZHEE-GONE-DAHS): This hot, sunny region is at the base of the Dentelles de Montmirail (don-TELL day muen-me-RAYH)—limestone rock pyramids that shelter this region from storms and allow ample sunshine to lengthen the growing season to create fully ripe grapes. Gigondas are full-bodied reds that taste like dried and black fruit, licorice, earth, herbs, and spice. The wines are tannic and can age, but many are great for immediate gratification, too. The best part: Good ones start at $25 and rarely exceed $50. Watch the vintage on these wines. Gigondas can be subject to harsh weather, making them thinner and less impressive in some years.

VACQUERAS (VACK-ERR-AHZ): Like Gigondas, only lighter, fresher, and a little more variable in quality, this area is also in the foothills of the Dentelles de Montmirail. At its best, it's full of dark flowers, earth, licorice, spice, black pepper, and dark fruit, with fresh acidity. I find Vacqueras can be great or can be sharp and rustic, but it's also less expensive than the more reliable Gigondas. Sometimes you get what you pay for!

The Other Outstanding Crus

CAIRANNE: The villages of the Côtes du Rhône truly are the training ground for future crus, as Cairanne's 2016 promotion from "Cotes du Rhône Villages—Cairanne" to "Cairanne" proved. Although it seems minor, the move validates that the AOP is distinctive and on par with other high-quality areas. I think it's true! Cairanne is a few kilometers west of Gigondas and Vacqueras, so the mainly GSM reds are known for their ripe fruit, herb, black pepper, and baking spice notes in the vein of these esteemed places. Five percent is white from standard Rhône whites. These wines are delicious and a great value!

VINSOBRES (VAHN-SOBE): "Wine sober, or sober wine, drink it soberly" was the motto of Vinsobres for centuries. In good vintages, these crowd-pleasing wines are juicy, jammy reds with black fruit and herbal notes. In less good ones, they are pretty boring. But, in exciting news: Vinsobres is undergoing a bit of a rebirth, as young winemakers are experimenting with a higher proportion of heat-loving Mourvèdre, realizing that it may play a better supporting role to the star of the wine, Grenache, than the old wingman, Syrah. Watch this space!

RASTEAU (RAS-TOE): Rasteau makes strong, spicy, earthy, ripe red wines and has since at least 30 B.C. These tasty reds are spectacular values. In warmer areas with south-facing slopes, raisined grapes of fifty-plus-year-old Grenache Noir vines produce Rasteau's Vin Doux Naturel (Vahn DOO nah-too-RELL; page 149), which comes in two styles: sweet, light-colored, honeyed, and nutty or sweet, bold, and jammy and like baked pie. Both make stunning dessert wine.

BEAUMES DE VENISE (BOAM DE VEN-EAZE): In the Dentelles de Montmirail, this area makes blends of mainly Grenache and Syrah. Watch the alcohol, since I've found these wines feel hot in some vintages. They normally have red and black fruit, earth, and baking spice flavors and aromas and can have up to 10 percent white grapes blended in to make them brighter and zestier. Similar to Rasteau, this area makes a Vin Doux Naturel: Muscat de Beaumes de Venise (MOO-skaht de BOAM de Ven-EAZE) is a sweet yet acidic wine that smells like white flowers and tastes like grapes, apricot, orange, and ginger. The Muscat-based wine is not meant to age. It's best when it's young, fresh, and cold.

LIRAC (LEE-RAHK): The lovely, sunny, Mediterranean vineyards of Lirac date back more than 2,000 years. Most of the wine is red with black fruit, spice, and earth flavors. Nine percent is white with citrus, tropical fruit, and herbal notes. Sound good? I'll level with you: I've had a few Lirac in my time and find reds and whites are usually not worth the more than $20 you'll pay for them. The exception is the rosé, which is similar to Tavel, though not as ageable, and is one to seek out.

TAVEL (TAH-VELL): Rosé, baby. That's all Tavel does, and it does it well! Using mostly Grenache Noir and Cinsault, these wines are mouthwatering yet full in texture with berry, citrus, herbal, and pepper notes. The big kicker: You can age Tavel for a few years and it will become more complex, rather than flat and gross like most rosés after more than a few months in the bottle.

CLOSEST CITIES: *From the beautiful walled city of Avignon, Châteauneuf-du-Pape, Lirac, and Tavel are within a 25-minute drive. Avignon is a 3-hour ride south on the fast train from Paris. About 13 miles (21 km) north of Avignon is the ancient town of Orange, from which Gigondas, Vacqueryas, Cairanne, Beaumes de Venise, and Rasteau are 15 to 20 minutes east.*

Big Regional Rhône Appellations

CÔTES DU RHÔNE: Welcome to wine flavor and quality roulette! The Côtes du Rhone regional appellation includes nearly the entire Rhône—north and south from Vienne to Avignon—although most of the vineyards are in the Mediterranean-influenced south that's mainly hot, dry, and sunny.

Given that twenty-one grape varieties are authorized for use, producer is the most important factor in selecting a Côtes du Rhône—the grapes and the winemaker's skill in blending them determine the quality of the wine. Nearly 90 percent of Côtes du Rhône is red with Grenache Noir, Syrah, and Mourvèdre as the leads. Those grapes plus Cinsault make up most of the rosés of the region. The whites—mostly made of Grenache Blanc, Clairette, Marsanne, Roussanne, Bourboulenc, and Viognier—are often unpredictable; unless the wine is from an exceptional producer, I usually skip it and buy something from one of the crus.

A Few Subareas You May See on the Shelf

CÔTES DU RHÔNE VILLAGES: Seventeen villages within the Côtes du Rhône area have been called out for being better than the basic CdR. Even though they use the same grapes as basic Côtes du Rhône, each has distinctive features that make the

HOW OLD IS WINEMAKING IN FRANCE?

Look at the famed vineyards of Muscat de Beaumes de Venise to see. Artifacts show that Greeks settled here long before the Romans arrived and that they brought viticulture with them. The latter brought their own innovations: The grapes still thrive on narrow *restanques* or terraces, originally set up by the Romans.

wine better than average. These wines can have more spiciness, herbal character, or earthiness. If you're curious, look for these village names appended to Côtes du Rhone on the label and give them a try.

- *In the mountains and foothills in the east:* Rochegude, Rousset les Vignes, Saint Maurice, Saint Pantaléon les Vignes, Gadagne, Massif d'Uchaux, Plan de Dieu, Puyméras, Roaix, Sablet, Séguret, Valréas, and Visan.
- *On the Right Bank of the Rhône:* Chusclan, Laudun, and Saint Gervais, and Signargues.

COSTIÈRES DE NÎMES (COAS-TEE-AIR DEH NEEM): In the land where van Gogh painted some of his most famous works (between Nîmes and Arles) lies an area with potential to become the next great Rhône region. Why? The terroir—with flat areas, large stones, and well-draining soils—is reminiscent of Châteauneuf-du-Pape. With these features and the quality I've had lately, I think we'll be hearing about the rise of this region in short order. More than 50 percent of the wine is red, currently featuring the rustic Carignan or Cinsault, but producers are shifting to the GSM blend and yielding wines that taste like black fruit, lavender, and black pepper. Sippable rosé (35 percent of production) is dry, fruity, and herbal, and I adore the white made from the standard Rhône grapes; it's full, stunning, and a killer value!

The More Variable Regions

VENTOUX (VAHN-TWO): In and around the steep Mount Ventoux, the Tour de France cyclist killer, is a huge higher-altitude, cooler southeastern appellation that makes lighter, fruitier wines of the standard southern Rhône grapes. The area spans fifty-one communes and more than 30 miles (48 km). Ventoux churns out mainly reds with some refreshing whites and rosés. I'm sure you know what I'm going to say: Quality is variable so seek out wines from small, local producers rather than co-ops if you can find them; otherwise pass on these.

LUBERON (LOO-BEAR-OHN): Lying on the Provence/Rhône line, with cool nights to keep acidity bright, Luberon makes simple red wines and whites worth looking into. If you want a better-than-usual red, get one with a bigger proportion of Syrah, which thrives in the cooler areas. The citrusy, herbal, full whites of Grenache Blanc, Clairette, Vermentino, and others are delicious. Rosé ranges in flavor depending on the producer and the proportion of each grape type used, so proceed with caution.

CLOSEST CITIES: *To the southwest of Avignon, Costières de Nîmes is about 45 minutes by car. Farther-flung regions of*

Ventoux and Luberon are about 1 hour east of Avignon, with Ventoux in the northeast and Luberon in the southeast.

The Wrap-Up

Is your head spinning yet? It's a lot of information and a lot of places to know. Just remember that the northern Rhône churns out complex Syrahs that taste like bacon and olives, and whites that are rich, floral, and fruity. The south, with its hot, dry Mediterranean weather, makes juicy, fruity, higher-alcohol reds and whites that run the gamut in flavor due to loose blending rules. Some experiments in the southern Rhône result in beautiful wines, others not so much! It's a big area with lots of hills, mountains, rivers, slopes, and climate variation. We won't love every wine from here, but the good news is that there's plenty to choose from, with good value for the quality, and there's no reason to stop trying!

EVERYWHERE ELSE IN FRANCE

There are lots of other regions in France and some of them make great wine that you may even see occasionally in a store or at a restaurant. But what's obscure wine BS and what's actually something you may run across and want to try? Even as I'm writing this, I'm fighting with myself about Gaillac vs. Jurançon vs. Irouléguy (which didn't make the cut).

So where I've come down is here: I think that in the next few years, the following regions may become more available. Right now, they may seem oddball, but with increasing interest in off-the-beaten-path varieties, I can tell you that in better wine shops I have found many of the regions listed here. The more obscure ones can be found online fairly easily. Someone is exporting the stuff out of France, and since it tastes good, I think we stand a chance of seeing more in the next few years. The regions included here are not going to light the world on fire, but if you travel to these areas or are interested in seeking out rare gems, this section is for you!

Southwest France

Up the rivers from Bordeaux lies a bunch of winemaking regions that have enormous potential. Collectively, in the wine world, these are lumped into the unglamorously named "Southwest France" area. This region is dotted with a few cool appellations that make great wine, often from native grapes with unique flavor profiles.

Southwest France has two main kinds of winemaking regions: those that are close to and similar to Bordeaux and those that are closer to the Pyrenees mountains, which use mainly native grapes to create different and sometimes outstanding wines. Below are some of the best appellations to seek out.

Places Near Bordeaux

Throughout history, Bordeaux has had a lot of assets: three rivers to moderate warm summer temperatures, forests for weather protection from erratic storms, and, most importantly, a spot right on the Atlantic Ocean from which traders could launch ships full of wine and get them straight up to the UK and out to anyone else in the world who wanted to imbibe.

For its more-than-2,000-year history, this situation gave Bordeaux a natural leg up on competitors in the wine trade, and that, coupled with great-tasting juice, helped the region become the powerhouse it is today.

There's that. Oh, and then there's the fact that the merchants screwed everyone upriver on the Gironde, who had delicious and sometimes better wine, out of the opportunity to sell their wares to the thirsty English and Dutch by slapping on a tariff so high that it made little sense for these upriver producers to even try exporting.

That was the sad state of the Haut Pays (O PAAY), the name in the Middle Ages for the older winemaking regions of southwest France with warmer climates. The area made stronger, often better wines than Bordeaux in those days and was shut off from export until the Bordelaise had sold their entire vintage of often thinner, less tasty wine. Although they had varied terroir, rivers for transporting their barrels, and more predictable weather—warm, with Mediterranean, Atlantic, and continental influence—Bergerac, Gaillac, and Cahors became walled off and their wines denied access to the world market.

I know this is nerdy history, but as with many things in wine, the effects of something that happened in the Middle Ages live on. You know Bordeaux, but what do you know about Bergerac? My guess is not a lot. Once Bordeaux rose to prominence and aligned with the English, who wanted wine from these other areas besides locals? No one. Who cares if they tasted better? They weren't "Brand Bordeaux." And with time, and lack of investment, eventually these wines began tasting less good. Such is the case today.

Although there are decent wines from the regions below, many—with the exception of Cahors, which caught a lucky break by being a Malbec-centric appellation at a time when Malbec is the popular kid—are similar to Bordeaux. While the wines are better than a lot of basic Bordeaux for around the same price, these regions will probably never recover from the Bordeaux whipping of the Middle Ages.

BERGERAC (BEAR-ZHURE-AHK): Located on the Dordogne River, not too far from the Right Bank and Entre-Deux-Mers, is the prolific and best known of the Bordeaux-like wines of Southwest France, Bergerac. The area makes red, dry white, and sweet white wines. The climate is warmer than that of Bordeaux so the reds are mostly heat-loving Cabernet Sauvignon blended with Merlot. The white grapes are Sémillon and Sauvignon Blanc. You'll find that these wines are labeled Bergerac or CÔTES DE BERGERAC, an appellation that makes more complex wine from slightly better terroir.

Within Bergerac is the red wine appellation of PÉCHARMANT (PAY-SHAR-MAHN), which I find makes ordinary red that has less character and balance than Bordeaux Supérieur AOP for the same price. The sweet botrytized (page 57) whites of Sémillon, Sauvignon Blanc, and Muscadelle from MONBAZILLAC, modeled in the image of Sauternes, are quite good and are a fraction of the price. Dry whites are similar to good-quality Bordeaux Blanc.

CLOSEST CITIES: *Bergerac is a 1.5-hour drive east of Bordeaux.*

GAILLAC (GUY-AHK): Gaillac may have been one of the first winemaking centers of Gaul back in the first century A.D. It likely predated the Romans, and producers shipped wine down the River Tarn and out of the Bordeaux estuary for centuries before Bordeaux started winemaking. It's a shame that the Bordelaise made it impossible for Gaillac to get its wines out to the world, since the region has gems that should have been widely available and that we should all be drinking.

Red is the star of this area. The local Duras (DHURE-aas) grape with black pepper, licorice, and dark fruit notes and a full body tastes unlike anything else you'll find. Also fabulous is Fer (FAIR), another local grape that's like red plums, strawberry, and black pepper when good (or rustic, if not allowed to fully ripen, with harsh tannin and piercing acid). These two grapes must make up at least 40 percent of Gaillac Rouge, with supporting players Syrah, Gamay, Merlot, Cabernet Franc, and Cabernet Sauvignon used in lesser proportions. Prunelard is another native that creates dark-fruited, black pepper, and cinnamon-tasting wines with firm tannin and high acid. Although good with food, many of the reds of Gaillac are sharp with acidity and can lack fruit flavor, so I wouldn't try to sip them solo unless you are someone who licks lemons for fun (no judgment—just informing others who don't do that).

The whites of Gaillac are full bodied and flavor packed. The dry whites are generally blends of the floral, citrusy, acidic Len de L'El with the pearlike, softer Mauzac (mo-ZACK; also in Blanquette de Limoux, mentioned in the Languedoc section, page 149), floral Muscadelle, and Sauvignon Blanc, which tends to be herbal in this part of the world. A third of white wine production is slightly sparkling GAILLAC PERLÉ (guy-AHK pear-LAY) made of Mauzac. Sweet, mainly late harvest wines are another feature of the area, with Len de L'El, Mauzac, Muscadelle, and the local

Ondenc grape matured in oak and turned into balanced GAILLAC DOUX.

CLOSEST CITIES: *Gaillac is a 2.5-hour drive southeast of Bordeaux and 45 minutes northeast of Toulouse by car.*

CAHORS (KAH-OR): Cahors is one of my favorite reborn appellations. Riding on the back of its signature grape, Malbec—Auxerrois (ow-say-WAH) or Cot (COAT) as it's known here—Cahors is the clear star of Southwest France, the breakout hopeful that many of us may have actually heard of. This warm area makes concentrated and bold wine. In fact, Malbec from Cahors is so dark in color that it used to be called the "black wine of Cahors." In poor vintages of the nineteenth century, Cahors sold its wines to Bordeaux to beef up the chateaux's anemic blends.

Cahors makes reds of Malbec blended with Merlot and Tannat, although 100 percent varietal wines are growing more common as Malbec has become a grape of choice for many in the US and UK. The clone here is different from Argentina's Malbec. Rather than juicy, plummy fruit, Cahors is rich, earthy, herbal, and minerally with black cherry, coffee, and leather notes. The wines can be tight, tannic, and acidic, especially when from the Causses, the high, dry plateau here. They are fruitier and softer when from the Coteaux, an area with gravel and sand near the river. If you haven't had a brooding, black wine from Cahors, crack one open on a cold winter night with hearty food and enjoy it in all its earthy, tannic goodness. It's a favorite winter wine of mine.

CLOSEST CITIES: *Cahors is a 2- to 3-hour drive southeast of Bordeaux and 1.5 hours north of Toulouse by car.*

Parts Farther South

If Gaillac was piquing your interest for its different-ness, you're going to love reading about these next few places, which have

grapes you'll rarely find elsewhere. I'm not saying these are for everyday drinking, but if you get a wild hair and you want to try something out of the ordinary, these will fit the bill!

FRONTON (FROHN-TAWN): Fronton is mainly a red wine appellation distinguished by use of the Négrette (NEIGH-gret) grape. The wine tastes like black and red berries, pepper, violets, and licorice, and can be rustic or even steaky in flavor, but can also be fruity and light depending on the terroir and the blend. Négrette must be 50 to 70 percent of the reds and rosés, with Syrah, Cabernet Sauvignon, Cabernet Franc, and the peppery Fer making up the rest of the blend. Flavors vary based on the proportion of each grape used, but I find these wines don't disappoint.

CLOSEST CITIES: *Fronton is a 40-minute drive north of Toulouse.*

MADIRAN (MAH-DEER-OHN): In the far southwest corner of France at the foothills of the Pyrenees Mountains that separate France from Spain lies Madiran, an area known for its strongly flavored food and strong wines to match. Nothing fits better than the highly tannic, acidic, full-flavored Tannat grape (also currently making a splash in Uruguay, page 257). Madiran wines are 60 to 80 percent Tannat, with Cabernet Sauvignon, Cabernet Franc, and the local Fer each playing a part to temper this tannic beast. That's saying a lot: Cabernet Sauvignon is extremely tannic, yet it's used to calm the astringency of Tannat.

Special care is taken in Madiran to coax a drinkable wine from Tannat—not an easy feat. Producers use the full arsenal: picking later to ensure ripeness, destemming, handling grapes gently to prevent the skins from giving off too much tannin, barrel aging, and micro-oxygenation, a practice that began here (see sidebar for more detail).

CLOSEST CITIES: *Madiran is about 2 hours south of Bordeaux and 2 hours west of Toulouse by car.*

JURANÇON (ZHUR-OHN-SOHN): In the foothills of the Pyrenees, the Jurançon wine region is historic: From the fourteenth to nineteenth centuries, demand soared for the sweet wines of the area and producers shipped it all over Europe and the United States. The wine hit its peak in the mid-1500s when priests rubbed the future French King Henri IV's lips with it during his baptism. Can't ask for better PR than that!

Sadly, from these great heights, Jurançon fell in reputation. Phylloxera (page 45) destroyed the vineyards in the mid- to late 1800s, and the area still hasn't fully recovered from that misstep, but producers are trying.

White grapes dominate in this high-altitude, cool region, and Jurançon comes in a few styles. Jurançon (sec) uses mainly the Gros Manseng grape. The wine is acidic, complex, and dry with green apple, honey, herb, and crushed rock notes. The most famous wine is the sweet stuff (Jurançon doux) made mainly of the soft, floral Petit Manseng, which is picked when the grapes have raisined on the vine.

CLOSEST CITIES: *Pau, the main city, is a 2-hour drive south of Bordeaux and 2 hours west of Toulouse.*

SOFTENING WITH OXYGEN

Micro-oxygenation is when the winemaker allows oxygen to permeate a wine during fermentation to build a healthy yeast population and after fermentation to stabilize the wine. Winemakers use a small wine oxygen pump to regulate the amount they let in. Micro-oxygenation is also used during aging to mimic barrel maturation, which makes the wines drinkable earlier and saves producers money by decreasing the time wine spends in barrels. This technique was devised in 1991 by Madiran producer Patrick Ducournau to tame Tannat but is now used around the world by producers looking to control and speed the aging process so they can get softer, drinkable wines to market quickly.

Corsica, The (Italian) French Island

Napoleon Bonaparte's mountainous Mediterranean homeland isn't just a beautiful rock, although 50 percent of the wine is labeled Ile de Beauté IGP—the Island of Beauty; it's making some increasingly good wine from its varied climates and soils. The Italian influence here is striking. One-third of the grapes are Nielluccio (neal-LOOCH-o), a.k.a. Sangiovese. It shows the earthy, floral, herbal side of the grape but is unmistakably Sangiovese. Fifteen percent of grapes are Sciaccarello

(see-ahc-ah-RELL-o), also known as the mainly Tuscan grape Mammolo, which adds spice and violet notes to Sangiovese. Cannanou or Grenache is often earthy and simple, and the white grape Rolle, or Vermentino, is a stony, smoky, citrusy wine. In addition to these Italian and French grapes, the island boasts a bunch of native grapes, but none of the wines made from them is exported. Look for VIN DE CORSE AOP wines if you want slightly better quality than Ile de Beauté IGP.

CLOSEST CITIES: *There's a 4-hour fast ferry from Nice to Calvi, or flights from regional carriers out of London, Paris, and other major European cities.*

Alpine Wines

The Alps aren't just for skiing. They're also for fabulous wines. Recently I've found them readily available in the United States, and that's a great thing. They're tasty for a nice weeknight wine. Nothing heavy, nice flavors, and great with light to medium food. There are two main winemaking areas in the French Alps, both small and good.

JURA (ZHURE-AA): Situated between Switzerland and Burgundy in the mountains of eastern France, Jura is isolated and small. Producers march to the beat of their own drums when it comes to wine. The common thread: The wines are lovely and light.

A quarter of the wine is Crémant de Jura made from Chardonnay and Pinot Noir—light, crisp, apple-y, and less bready than Champagne due to a shorter time aging on the lies (page 142). In addition to Chardonnay, Jura producers also use

Savagnin (SAV-ahn-yan), a floral, aromatic, textured grape to make a dry white that is like a lighter-style white Burgundy. Reds of the peppery, floral, red fruit–flavored Trousseau (true-SO) grape or the rustic, barnyard-like Poulsard (phoul-SAHR), or a blend of both, are tasty. I love the spice, tannin, and tangy acid on red wines from ARBOIS, the main appellation of Jura. It's a little pricey (more than $25) but good for a splurge every now and again.

Worth mentioning are the rare specialties of the region. VIN JAUNE, or "yellow wine," is made sort of like Sherry from Spain—with a veil of yeast covering the wine and lots of oxygen getting into the barrel for exactly six years and three months. It tastes nutty, spicy, smoky, and mushroomlike. Another local treat is Vin de Paille, a sweet wine made from grapes that are dried on straw mats to concentrate the sugars of the Savagnin grape.

CLOSEST CITIES: *The town of Arbois is 1 hour southeast of Beaune in Burgundy or 2 hours from the city of Lyon by car.*

SAVOIE (SAV-**WAH**): The vineyards of Savoie are just south of Lake Geneva on the Swiss border. The small growers of this region make wines with lots of character and, of late, have been pushing them for export. The whites dominate, with the most interesting being Roussette de Savoie made from the Altesse grape. It's floral, acidic, and citrusy but has a counterbalance of creaminess. Roussanne of Rhône fame is also grown here, but masquerades under the name Chignin-Bergeron (sheen-YAH bear-ZHER-ohn). The grapes don't get quite as ripe as in Rhône, so aromatics are more floral and peachy than honeyed.

The wine has higher acid and lighter body than Rhône wines, but you still get the cheek-coating texture that goes well with lighter food in cream sauces and cheese fondue, which is ubiquitous in this Swiss-influenced area. Jacquère (ZHAK-ere) is a widely planted white that makes light dry wines (the most meh wine for me). One of my favorite off-the-grid reds is Mondeuse Noir (mahn-DOOSE nwah), one of the most overtly peppery, spicy wines I've ever had. Fresh acidity and spice dance on your tongue! It's fantastic!

CLOSEST CITIES: *Chambéry is a 1.5-hour drive southwest from Lyon and a 1-hour drive north of Grenoble.*

The Wrap-Up

There are so many pockets of interesting, local wines everywhere in France. It can be overwhelming . . . or it can be exciting! To appreciate France, you have to make the choice to be thrilled by all you don't know and have yet to discover. New producers, new grapes, new wines—when it comes to France, you can keep trying and learning. As long as you have an open mind, you'll discover a universe of wine that can never be fully comprehended or mastered, which makes it all the more fascinating. There's a certain magic in the wines of the vinous motherland, and your exploration could take you down figurative and literal roads you never imagined.

GERMANY

In my youth, I traveled a bit through Germany. I drank not a drop of wine. Instead I consumed mass quantities of beer in enormous steins. Oktoberfest tents in Munich presented a bevy of beverage choices—lagers, ales, stouts—and a dramatic scene of debauchery (my butt has never been grabbed so often in so short a time). A visit to Nuremberg included a flaming drink called a B-52 and more beer. No vinous delights.

It was probably for the best. If I'd had one glass of Riesling, I probably would have dismissed it as inferior to all the Italian wine I was drinking while living in Florence. It could have closed the book on my fascination with German wine.

My how things have changed! I'm a huge fan of Riesling. But I am fully aware that Riesling has a lot to overcome because for decades all that was available was sweet, cheap wines that were imported en masse and had nothing to recommend them.

In this section, I've got a big job: to debunk your ideas about Germany as a producer of nasty Riesling. I'm hell-bent on success because if you can get behind Riesling and specifically German Riesling—which has 50 percent of the world's plantings of it—then you'll unlock one of the most magical grapes of the wine world. I'm not going Pollyanna on you; I'm being honest. Riesling is the most versatile white grape and most of the stuff exported at the $15-plus level is going to be consistently great, which is more than you can say for Chardonnay or Pinot Grigio. If after you read this I fail to convince you and you don't drink German wine regularly and never will, I'll settle for convincing you that

it's important to know about this historic, quality winemaking nation. Do we have a deal? OK.

A Word on German History

As in every other winemaking country north of Italy, the Romans pillaged Germany, tasted native grapes, and made wine from them. Those grapes are ancestors of what we drink today. By the eighth century, monks were classifying the best vineyards in Germany (this wasn't just a Burgundian practice). Up until about A.D. 1500, there were vines in every corner of Germany. That's when the weather got a little cooler, beer became a little easier to make, and France and Italy marketed their rich red wines to Germans, who welcomed them with open arms.

Things clicked along, with Riesling beginning her reign as the benevolent queen in 1435 and "field blends"—different grapevines growing next to each other, then being harvested and fermented together—dominating winegrowing. Then in the late 1800s, phylloxera (page 45) decimated the vineyards, killing many of those native grapes (this is a good thing in that some sucked, but a bad thing in that we'll never know what good ones were lost).

Hot on the heels of phylloxera were world wars and ongoing political turmoil. Germany has had major winemaking setbacks for decades, but today the German wine industry is thriving. That's saying something since it's hard to grow grapes here.

Germany Today

You've got to respect German winegrowers. They have challenges others don't have.

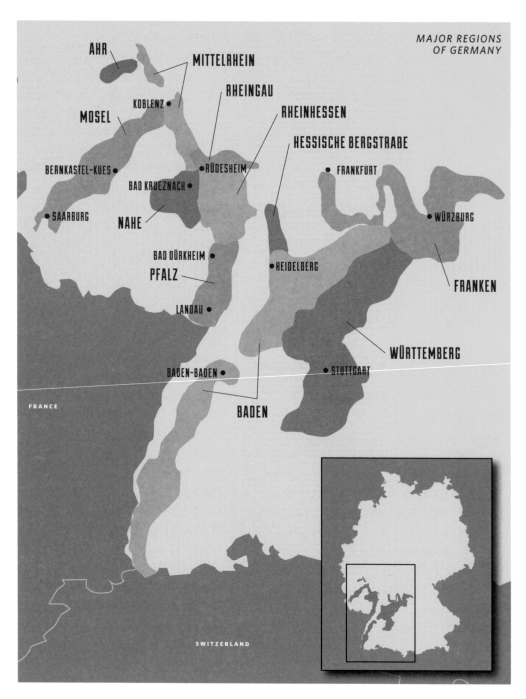

AHR

MITTELRHEIN

RHEINGAU

RHEINHESSEN

KOBLENZ •

HESSISCHE BERGSTRAßE

MOSEL

• FRANKFURT

BERNKASTEL-KUES •

•RÜDESHEIM

BAD KRUEZNACH •

• WÜRZBURG

• SAARBURG

NAHE

BAD DÜRKHEIM •

• HEIDELBERG

FRANKEN

PFALZ

LANDAU •

WÜRTTEMBERG

BADEN-BADEN •

• STUTTGART

FRANCE

BADEN

SWITZERLAND

Growing grapes just below the fiftieth parallel, growers need to think about things like: Will my grapes ripen? Will everything freeze before I have a chance to harvest or at the right time so I can make Eiswein? How many workers will get injured or die hand harvesting grapes on the 70 percent graded vineyard sites along the Mosel River? (I'm not kidding—it happens.) These are not concerns for those in Bordeaux or Chianti.

Winter can be bitterly cold, and summer only brings moderate warmth. Consider this: The most southerly vineyards of Germany are at the same latitude as France's most northerly ones (Baden, the farthest south, is similar to Champagne and Loire). If not for the warm Gulf Stream, steep slopes with good sun exposure, and close proximity to rivers that reflect light for additional ripeness, German viticulture wouldn't exist.

Now back to Riesling. It's no surprise that red wines are needier than whites. They require more sustained heat and sunlight to develop the pigment and flavor that make the grapes ripe. So that means white wines are Germany's gig. Riesling is 22 percent of all plantings, and whites like Müller-Thurgau (mehler TUR-gaw) and Silvaner (zil-VAHN-er) are popular, too. In more southern areas with warmer pockets, producers make acidic reds like Pinot Noir, called Spätburgunder (SHPATE-boor-gun-dah), and lighter-style reds like Dornfelder and Lemberger (a.k.a. Austria's Blaufränkisch). With climate change, these wines are getting better,

but don't expect them to rival Austrian or French versions of the same grapes—they are lighter versions. You may see German sparkling wine, called Sekt, too. It's not made in the Champagne method, but is tank fermented like Prosecco (page 54), to maintain the grapes' fresh flavor. It can be a nice sipper, especially when made from Riesling.

The Top Wine Regions of Germany

There are thirteen quality wine regions in Germany, and I could go into detail on a lot of them, but two are the rulers of the German quality wine world: Mosel and Rheingau. I also feel the need to mention the up-and-comer, Pfalz. Here's what you need to know about these wines. I'll get into a little more detail later on the other areas.

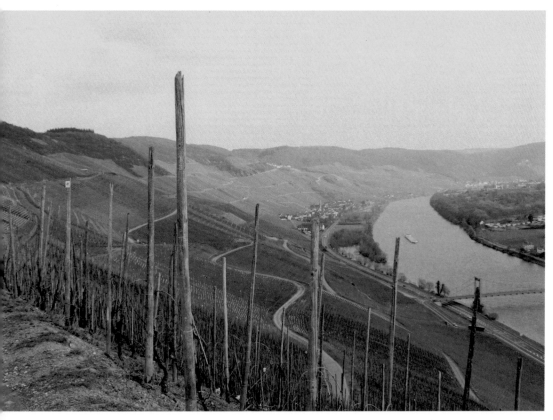

Mosel

If you know any area in Germany for wine, you probably know Mosel (MO-zle). Critics widely agree that the wines of the region, with their high acid and distinctive flavor, are the top of the Riesling heap. Could it be that there's credence to the alleged healing powers attributed to the wine in the thirteenth century, giving one of its famous vineyards its name (Bern-kasteler Doctor)? Or is it just that this crazy place makes stellar wine? I'm going with the latter.

To set the stage for Mosel, I'll say that even if you have just a passing interest in wine, this is one of the most amazing places you could visit. It's a feat of mankind and of nature—a true viticultural miracle that you can't comprehend until you see it yourself.

Why? The main part of the Mosel is practically a vertical ledge of vines that seems an impossibility to farm, until you see the backbreaking manual labor taking place. It's also picturesque—full of slate-covered slopes that run to grades of up to 70 percent and tower over the Mosel River. These blue slate soils atop limestone impart flavor and aroma in the wine and give them a distinct bite with a mineral/spicy/mountain stream note that can't be attained anywhere else in the world.

What I've described is just one part of the Mosel. The region is actually a combination of three distinct areas: Middle Mosel, which I've described above, Saar (ZAR), and Ruwer. For its beauty and awesome wines, the Middle Mosel is best known. Middle Mosel has excellent terroir in parts away from the river as well: The best vineyards have south-facing slopes to capture the sunlight that is so precious at latitude 50° north.

Saar is as well esteemed as Middle Mosel. Sitting on the Mosel River tributary, the Saar River, the area is also full

of steep hills that allow the sun to hit the vines directly, helping ripen the grapes. The conditions are similar to those in Middle Mosel, but the wines tend to be more elegant and lighter.

Ruwer is also located on its namesake tributary of the Mosel. The area has flatter land and less slate in the soil, and these wines have a slightly different, frankly less distinctive character than those from Middle Mosel and Saar.

The rivers in all areas play a big part in the wine of the region. In combination with the jet stream, they circulate fresh air through the vineyards with their continuous

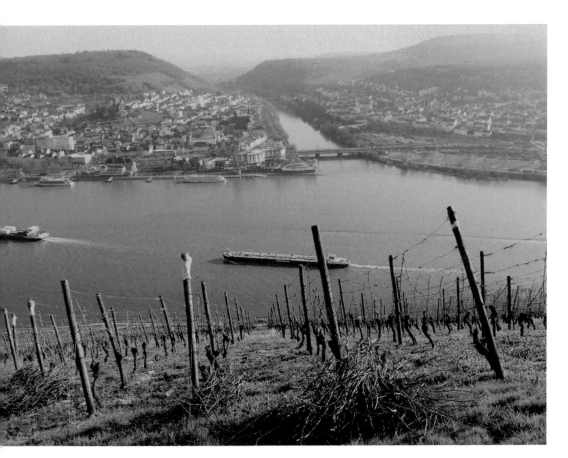

movement. The sun reflects off the water, giving the vineyards additional light to assist with photosynthesis.

I know I'm dorking out on the terroir stuff but, to give you a sense of how important it is, the vineyards are celebrities in Mosel. There are "Hollywood" signs with the vineyard names all over Mosel; a reminder that terroir is the star and, as in Hollywood, the producer's job is to make it shine. The great thing is that the producers are largely successful, although not without lots of work. The terraced vineyards high atop mountains where vines are individually staked to the ground so they don't blow, float, or get carried away are dangerous to harvest. Maintenance of these vineyards is constant—for efficiency, spraying of pesticides is done by helicopter, and after the rainy season workers collect the slate topsoil that has been washed to the

bottom of the hill to put it right back where it came from. And there's that pesky issue of latitude—even though the overall climate has warmed and ripening in many parts of Mosel is more of a sure thing, the weather can be erratic and some years are certainly better than others (vintage matters!).

But it's all worth it. The flavors of a classic Mosel Riesling range from light and limey to herbal and minerally to tropical, nutty, and like petrol (a characteristic that's in the grape and increases with age). The acidity in a Mosel Riesling against the fruit and minerality makes this wine complex and layered. Mosel Rieslings have the clearest, cleanest flavors imaginable: e.g., they're purely apricot or purely lemon and their notes are easy to call out. In a world where vocabulary and flavor confounds many people, the clarity of Mosel Riesling makes this wine a great one for understanding how flavor expresses itself in a wine, especially if you're just getting started!

CLOSEST CITIES: *The Mosel wine town of Koblenz is about 1.5 hours northwest of Frankfurt by car. The famed town of Bernkastel-Kues is about 1 hour east of Luxembourg City in Luxembourg and 2 hours west of Frankfurt.*

Rheingau

Rheingau (RINE-gau), or "Rhine district," represents only 3 percent of vineyard area but packs a punch in reputation.

You may have no idea what Rheingau is or why it's important, but I bet if you've glanced at the Riesling section you noticed that some wines say "Johannisberg Riesling." That's because in a little enclave in the Rheingau there's a 1,200-year-old estate called Schloss Johannisberg that makes some of the most fabulous Riesling in the world—so good that other people are using its name and town as an indicator that it's the "true" Riesling, as opposed to the many clones or crossings that use Riesling in the name but aren't the real stuff.

The former Benedictine cloister in Johannisberg is so legendary that it is its own geographical designation and nothing else is required on the bottle besides the name Schloss Johannisberg. Spätlese (shpate-LAY-za), or late harvest Riesling, was invented here in the 1700s (by mistake—they waited too long to harvest the grapes because of a late messenger, a story for another time). For centuries this wine was available only to royalty. Today, one-tenth of the harvest still goes directly to the Hapsburgs in Austria. When you drink this wine, you drink a piece of wine history.

If that's not enough reason to know about Rheingau, know that Cistercian monks hopped over from Burgundy in about the 1100s to continue their work on terroir and vineyard classification. The monks likely brought Pinot Noir from Burgundy, which makes a totally different wine (lighter, less complex, less good in my opinion) but is still a force in Rheingau, especially in the town of Assmannshausen (the immature side of me just loves this name, for obvious reasons). With all the positive attributes of Burgundy, Rheingau likewise joined in the difficulties of its French counterpart—Napoleonic land ownership laws applied here. That means when large landowners died they were legally bound to break up their properties equally among their children, and they to their children, and so on for generations. The result is exactly as it was in Burgundy: wine producers can own half of a hectare here and another in a separate village, and there isn't any consolidation. This proves to be a huge obstacle for producers thinking about expenses in managing a harvest (you have to drive all over the damn valley to get to your sites!), and it's nearly impossible for people looking to do organic (when your neighbors spray and you all own tiny parcels, it's inconceivable the spray won't get on your grapes).

With nearly 80 percent of the vineyards planted to Riesling, this small region is single-minded. It's a miracle grapes even grow at around latitude 50° north. It wouldn't be possible but for a little quirk in the flow of the Rhine River. Inexplicably, it takes a jog from its northerly path for 19 miles (30 km) and flows west, forming southern-facing slopes that gather sunlight and heat.

Insulating the grapes even more are the Taunus Mountains to the north, which deflect nasty polar winds, keeping in heat and providing much-needed humidity when it's dry in the summer.

Another helper for viticulture: In parts of this region, the land rises from the river to nearly 1,000 feet (305 m) on sharp slopes with 20 to 70 percent grade. Most of the vineyards are located either in the high slopes or on the slightly flatter (but not flat) land lower down. The vineyards aren't next to the Rhine, but begin above the towns and continue high up the slope until they reach the Taunus forest.

Rheingau wines, when made well, are elegant and, in their youth, shy, to put it mildly. Frankly, some of these wines taste like nothing when you put them in your mouth—except maybe tart with a rocky note and, in the sweet wines, a little peachy. Rheingau is not a wine for today; it's a wine for tomorrow. The fruit, the minerality, the character—all come out after six or more years. Here, you have to gain an ability to discern what components will mature into something outstanding. They need time to come out of their shells.

As a closing big reveal, the most shocking factor in Rheingau winemaking is that even though the wines absorb no flavor from it, the top producers age or ferment their best Riesling in . . . wait for it . . . oak. These are not small barrels nor do they have the same purpose as what we think of when we think of oak. They hold anywhere from 500 to 2,400 liters (132 to 634 gallons) or more. The most common size in Rheingau is the 1,200-liter (317-gallon) size, called the *Stükfass*. The barrels are not toasted; they're steamed, and many are treated with water and other neutralizers for a year or more to remove any chance of oak flavor seeping into the wine. Why use oak? The barrels allow natural micro-oxygenation (page 173) and a slight tannin transfer to provide these highly acidic wines with more body and

fullness. The wines are nearly all aged sur lie (on the dead yeast cells) as well, some even for years, to add more body (winemakers do this in Mosel too, with smaller barrels!).

CLOSEST CITIES: *Rheingau is really close to Frankfurt. You can get to Rüdesheim or Weisbaden in the Rheingau in 30 minutes by car.*

Q+A

What's the answer to "how do I get into German wine if I hate sweet stuff?"

Pfalz, a predominantly dry wine region on the rise.

Pfalz

Pfalz (FAAL-tz) Riesling was served at the opening of the Suez Canal in 1869, but the wine fell notches in reputation over the next hundred or so years, as it became known as a region producing lots of bulk, blah wine. Today, this warm, arid area is experiencing a renaissance. In the last decade, it has attracted some of Germany's best young talent, and these people are determined to make Pfalz known for the best dry-style Riesling in the country. All indications are they are on their way.

They're certainly playing in the right playground: Pfalz lies between the Rhine River and the Haardt Mountains, which are a southern continuation of Alsace, France's Vosges range. It's a sizable region divided into two parts. The northern Mittelhardt makes Riesling similar to that of Alsace, France. The southern regions specialize in red wines, like Pinot Noir (sometimes called Spätburgunder here) and Dornfelder, both of which are often fruity, earthy, light summer sippers.

Of the two areas, Mittelhardt has raised the reputation of this winemaking region, which has made wine for at least 2,000 years. In this northern section, conditions mimic Alsace: This is one of the sunniest, driest winegrowing regions in Germany. Pfalz experiences a similar rain shadow from the Haardt Mountains as Alsace does from the Vosges. These conditions allow Riesling to ripen fully, so producers can ferment the wine dry to alcohol levels of 12 percent or more, achieving fuller-bodied, concentrated, fruity styles.

One-fourth of all wine produced here is Riesling, and most of it is dry, with flavors and aromas of white flowers and citrus. But be aware Pfalz is also the most planted area for Riesling in Germany, and some of the vineyards aren't in great spots. There's lots of crap wine alongside the good stuff. In short: Producer matters! That said, because land is plentiful and less expensive, you can get excellent wines at a great price from Pfalz. Seek out young, emerging producers and you won't be sorry with the Riesling or the reds from this up-and-coming region.

CLOSEST CITIES: *The town of Bad Dürkheim is a 20-minute drive west from Mannheim.*

❶ Grape	❹ Dryness Level
❷ Vintage	❺ Alcohol Content
❸ Region Name	

❶ Town and Vineyard	❸ Grape	❺ Old Vines
❷ Vintage	❹ VDP = Special Association	

Skip Here!

If you're done with Germany and know enough, skip right to the next section! If you want to know more, keep reading, but it's going to get weedy!

Complicated German Label Jargon

For those of you who are huge dorks or have lots of curiosity about all things wine, here's some bad news. You may need a guide when you first shop for German wine. German wine labels offer TMI (too much information). They look like a German novel, and for most normal people, this is off-putting. If you think Californian or Australian wines lack information (I do) or that French script is intimidating (but it does look pretty, doesn't it?), Germany's labels will make you sick.

Truth be told, it's not *that* bad once you know what to look for. Let's filter through so you can buy a bottle and feel good about what you're getting. To start, I'll break down the stuff you'll see on the label. Then I'll get into detail about what, exactly, it means.

Let's start with the obvious items on the label and then get into more German-specific stuff.

- **The grape:** Even if nothing else looks familiar, this will be. Riesling is Riesling!

- **The vintage:** Just a year—easy to spot! Given the erratic weather of the regions, this is important.
- **The region name:** The regions are called Anbaugebiete (AHN-bowg-ah-beet-ah). There are thirteen. I've talked about three and I list the rest in the following pages. These are akin to regions like Loire, Bordeaux, Burgundy, etc. Once you recognize them, they'll be easy to spot on the label.
- **Dryness level:** If you're looking for a dry wine, keep your eyes peeled for *trocken* (TRAHK-en) or "dry" on the label. *Halbtrocken* or *feinherb* usually mean off dry.
- **Alcohol content:** This is huge. Generally wines that are sweet have lower alcohol levels because the wine wasn't fermented all the way. If you see levels below 11 percent and the label doesn't specify dry, expect sweetness. Wines that are more than 13 percent will almost always be dry. It's a great way to guide your purchases when the bottle doesn't tell you jack.

Now the more German-specific stuff.

- **The village and/or vineyard name:** This info on a bottle isn't specific to Germany, but the way it's displayed is. If the wine is a better one, you may see a village on the bottle. It could say Johannisberg or Erbach, for example. If there's a vineyard associated with the village, the label will

usually give the village and the vineyard. The village will have an "er" attached to it, which indicates something is a resident of the place. For example, it may say Wehlener Sonnenuhr, which means the town of Wehlen's Sonnenuhr vineyard.

- **Ripeness level:** If the wine is a premium wine or a Prädikat (Preed-ee-KAHT, kind of like "fraidy cat"), it will be classified with a ripeness level, which I'll detail in a second. A basic wine will say QbA, which is not from specific sites or estates and is like a regional wine—think Napa Valley in California or Hunter Valley in Australia.
- **Special associations/logos that indicate quality:** If it's a high-quality wine, you may see a black eagle and the initials VDP, to indicate the winery is a member of the Association of German Prädikat Wine, two hundred or so of the top producers, according to themselves, BTW. It's a voluntary organization and fairly elite. These producers have their own classification that's similar to Burgundy's classification.
- **Regional wine** is called Gutswein (GOOTS-wine).
- **Wine produced in a specific village** is Ortswein.
- **Premier cru** wines on some of the top sites are Erste Lage (Ehr-STE LA-gah) or Erste Gewächs (Ehr-STE ghey-VEX) if from Rheingau only.
- **Grand cru vineyards** (the top of the heap) are Gross Lage (gross LA-gah) or Grosses Gewächs (Grosses ghey-VEX) for dry wine from grand cru vineyards. They can be red or white wines, but yield is dictated by the rules. Producers refer to Grosses Gewächs as GG, so it's OK just to call it that and spare yourself the pronunciation headache!

If the wine is estate bottled, you may see the confusing words Erzeugerabfüllung (aht-SOW-gehr-ahb-FA-lung) or Gutsabfüllung (GOOTS-ahb-fa-lung). These mean the wine was grown on a premium, specific site, and it's usually good.

The Other German Regions

Now, let's take a quick tour of those ten remaining regions (Anbaugebiete). Of the ten, Nahe, Baden, and Rheinhessen deserve a bit more explanation. The rest I'll bullet point with the noteworthy grapes and areas, in case you want to explore them further.

Nahe

The rural area Nahe (NAH-ha) makes high-class Riesling, Müller-Thurgau, and Silvaner with fresh, bright acidity. Reds Spätburgunder and Dornfelder are rising in popularity but are a small part of the pie. Nahe's size limits production and raises the price, but it's one to seek out since the region can create layered, delicious wine similar to Rheingau with more body.

CLOSEST CITIES: *The wine town of Bad Kreuznach is 1 hour southwest of Frankfurt by car.*

Baden

The region Baden (BAA-den) is right across the mountains from Alsace, so the wines should be similar, but those I've tried aren't close. Pinot Gris (Grauburgunder) and Pinot Noir (Spätburgunder) are the main grapes. In my opinion, they need a little more flavor and balance to compete on the world market. That said, *they are trying*, so *I'll keep trying their wines periodically to see if there is any improvement!*

CLOSEST CITIES: *Baden-Baden is the start of the picturesque and tourist-friendly Baden Wine Road that stretches for 124 miles (220 km) through parts of the Black Forest and ancient towns. The spa town is a 50-minute drive south of Heidelberg and a 1-hour drive west of Stuttgart.*

Rheinhessen

Down the hill and across the river from Rheingau is a vast flat area that's Germany's biggest wine region in terms of vineyard area: Rheinhessen (rine-HESS-ehn). Because it churns out copious amounts of wine, it's a gamble in terms of quality. Excellent (and very blah) Riesling, Müller-Thurgau, and Silvaner are made, along with occasionally good Pinot Noir, Portugieser, and Dornfelder for reds. Good producers make delicious stuff, so read up before buying and you could be up for a great wine experience.

CLOSEST CITIES: *Mainz is a 40-minute drive southwest of Frankfurt or a 50-minute drive north of Mannheim.*

AHR (AR): Ahr makes Riesling with reds Portugieser and excellent Pinot Noir, called Spätburgunder.

FRANKEN: Bottled in funny, flasklike bottles called *Bocksbeutel* (BOX-boy-tel), the specialties are whites Müller-Thurgau and Silvaner.

HESSISCHE-BERGSTRASSE (HESS-EH-SHEH BERG-STRAH-SSAH): Fruity dry or off-dry Riesling, Müller-Thurgau, Grauburgunder, and red Spätburgunder come from this tiny region.

MITTELRHEIN (MITTEL-RINE): Riesling, with the floral white Kerner and Müller-Thurgau.

WÜRTTEMBERG (VERT-EM-BAHG): East of Baden is this mainly red wine area with light, acidic red Trollinger, Pinot Meunier (from Champagne fame), and Lemberger as the stars. Schillerwein (SHILL-er-wine), a local rosé, is popular. Riesling is the main white.

In the former East Germany, these areas focus less on fine wine and more on slaking local thirst.

SAALE UNSTRUT (ZAA-LAY UHN-STRUT): The most northerly wine region of Germany. Silvaner, Weissburgunder, and Müller-Thurgau are most common in Saale Unstrut.

SACHSEN (ZACHS-EN): In this, the smallest German wine region, Müller-Thurgau, Riesling, and Weissburgunder are most popular. A local specialty is a Riesling-Muscat crossing, called Goldriesling.

To recap the classification section (page 89), like every place in the European Union, Germany has two main wine quality levels. The first is Protected Geographical Indication (PGI), a simple category that includes table wine (Deutscher Tafelwein) and the slightly more restricted country wine (Deutscher Landwein). The next level is Protected Designation of Origin (PDO), which includes the two categories you'll commonly see. QbA, or QUALITÄTSWEIN BESTIMMTER ANBAUGEBIETE (qual-eh-TATES-wine besh-TIMM-teh AHN-bowg-ah-beet-ah), is for basic good wines from the main regions. QmP, or QUALITÄTSWEIN MIT PRÄDIKAT (qual-eh-TATES-wine mit preed-ee-KAHT), is for good wines with Prädikat or special attributes, meaning they come from riper, fruitier grapes and can often be sweet.

The Prädikat

If you're willing to venture into German wines, you need to know the Prädikatsweine. Because of the cooler temps in Germany, it should come as no surprise that top German wine is ranked by how ripe the grapes were when they were picked. Before I tell you what these levels of ripeness are, you should know that at the first two levels of this ranking what you get in terms of sweetness or dryness is roulette unless it's specified. Remember this tip: Check alcohol levels—higher alcohol wines will most likely be dry (more than 11.5 percent); lower alcohol ones (11 percent or less) will probably be sweet.

On the plus side, most of these wines are going to have powerful acid, and they'll be great with food. The following terms are on the label.

KABINETT (CAH-BEEN-ETT): These wines are made from ripe grapes, but you have no idea if they'll be sweet or dry unless it specifies trocken, or dry. Usually light in body. Check the alcohol by volume (ABV) on the bottle.

SPÄTLESE (SHPATE-LAY-ZA): These "late harvest" wines are usually fruity and can be dry. If the label doesn't say trocken, or dry, the wine will have a touch of sweetness with a counterbalance of acidity.

AUSLESE (OWZ-LAY-SA): These "selected harvest" wines use even riper grapes than Spätlese and often have intense fruit flavor and sweetness. Auslese need some age to taste great (at least 3 to 5 years).

BEERENAUSLESE/BA (BEER-EN-OWZ-LAY-SA): You won't see BA wines on most store shelves or in everyday restaurants. They are sold in small dessert wine bottles and are made from grapes that have a honeyed aroma from botrytis (page 57). This wine ain't cheap—the fruit is all hand selected, berry by berry. Lots of manual labor = a high price.

EISWEIN: Said like "ice wine," this is another one you'll see in a skinny dessert wine bottle. The producers use overripe grapes that freeze on the vine. Winemakers press out the frozen part of the juice (ice/water), leaving sugary, acidic goodness. These wines can age for decades but are produced in tiny quantities—most grapes are about 85 percent water so if you squeeze that out you don't have a whole lot left to work with. Again, lots of labor translates to a high price for ice wine (see page 260).

TROCKENBEERENAUSLESE/TBA (TRAHK-EN-BEER-EN-OWZ-LAY-SA): If you break down the name, it means dried (trocken) selected harvest berries (beeren = berries, auslese = selected harvest). If you look at the price, you may pass out. This ultrasweet wine is made from almost-raisined, botrytized fruit that's dried on the vine. It can take a day to pick berries for one bottle of this richly fruity wine. It's got great acid so it's still fresh despite the sugar. It's rare and delicious.

The Wrap-Up

I hope I've convinced you to give German wine a try. The history, the complexity of the flavors, and the ability to taste the land so clearly through the glass make Germany an ideal one for armchair travel. Crack open a bottle, close your eyes, take a sip, and envision yourself on a steep vineyard in the Mosel. For $20, you'll be transported!

GREECE

I'm a wine nerd so I love the details of wine—the history and the culture surrounding winemaking and consumption are fascinating. Because of that, it may be surprising that Greek wine, with its 4,000-year legacy, is a conundrum for me. I'll take it a step further to say that given the wine history of this country and its influence on Italian winemaking, particularly, I find the modern story of wine here disappointing and in dire need of a reboot.

For around 3,000 years, Greek winos were going strong. In ancient times, household wine production was huge. People worshipped Dionysus and had cults, festivals, and artwork dedicated to the god of the vine. Hippocrates praised the medicinal effects of the fermented drink and freely prescribed a glass for a wide range of maladies. (Why are we just rediscovering this now?)

Wine was also big business for the Greeks. They figured out how to ship wine in amphorae, which preserved it and allowed producers to make big bucks by selling the good stuff all around Europe—from Switzerland to Spain, from southern France to Sicily. Native Greek grapes spread around the Adriatic, and Croatia, Macedonia, and Italy still make wines from grapes of Greek origin. For example, the grapes of Southern Italy, Greco di Tufo, Malvasia, and Moscato, were likely brought to Italy by the Greeks. Up until the mid-1200s, at the end of Byzantine rule, Greece was a wine powerhouse. But when the country lost momentum, its wine fell off the map and hasn't regained ground since.

Although Crete, Cyprus, and the Peloponnese continued making wine, in most of Greece, wine tradition faltered with new regimes (especially with the teetotaling Ottomans). Wars and economic turmoil didn't help. Cooperatives ruled the wine trade after World War II, and these wine factories made seas of undistinguished plonk that no one outside Greece wanted to drink. It wasn't until the 1980s that the efforts of a few quality-minded producers landed wine back on the agenda, and not until the 2000s that quality wine was available for export.

That 800-year gap in wine culture for Greece is problematic. Because even though it's technically an Old World country, most of the action in Old World winemaking took place in those eight centuries when Greece *wasn't* a player.

I can't deny that Greek grapes have a long legacy, but the winemaking and the flavors of the wine are, for me, more New World than Old World. So in my mind, it's easier to think of Greece as a New World winemaking country that happens to have had a history of winemaking long ago and far away. This lets me judge the wines as new, fresh products and takes away any lurking expectation that the winemakers should follow a style or tradition as I expect from Old World producers in France, Spain, Italy, Germany, and

Portugal, for example. I say this to set your expectations as you get into Greek wine and maybe to lower the bar for them.

But enough Greek critique. With European Union support, the Greek wine industry has awoken. Although it hasn't yet achieved mass popularity abroad, I think most people are aware that Greece makes wine, and some even think that it can be good. That's a solid foundation, and for the wine adventurer, that knowledge is enough to allow us to take a chance on grapes we may have a hard time pronouncing.

Because Greek wine is labeled by grape, it may be more helpful to understand the grapes than the place. I detail them here and mention now that there are three big quality areas to watch in Greece: Santorini, Neméa in the Peloponnese, and Náoussa in Macedonia. These places have high-quality standards and special terroir, so if you need to pick a wine by place and see one of these three, go for it!

Here's a list of the top white and red grapes.

White Grapes

ASSYRTIKO (A-SEER-tee-ko): A dry, acidic white with a range of flavors from lemon-lime to peach and apricot with a mineral note. I've found this wine ranges from delicious and interesting to overly acidic and thin. It's originally from Santorini, where it's more tart, but is also grown in Thessaly, Macedonia, and Attica, where it's softer and fruitier.

ATHIRI (AH-THEE-ree): An ancient grape from the island of Santorini, it can be peachy but it's often blah in flavor—sort of like Italian Pinot Grigio. I'm not a fan.

MALAGOUSIA (MAH-LAH-GOU-ZYA): A versatile white grown mainly in Macedonia that can make wines with fresh mint, jasmine flower, and citrus flavors or ones that are tropical with oak notes from barrel fermentation.

MOSCHOFILERO (MOS-KO-FEEL-EROH): The best and most consistent white of Greece, it's floral and spicy, with orange flavors and great acid. Moschofilero is from the Peloponnesian Isles.

ROBOLA (RO-BO-LA): Made mainly on the island of Cephalonia, Robola has lemon and peach flavors with stony and smoky notes. You'll see it on Greek restaurant wine lists. It's great with spanakopita.

RODITIS (RO-DEE-TEES): Similar in taste to Athiri, Roditis doesn't have much flavor going on, but it can be a great summer sipper if it's chilled.

SAVATIANO (SA-VA-TYA-NO): I only mention the "Saturday wine," as it's translated, because it's the basis for Retsina, the wine aged in pine resin to give it a "distinctive" flavor (for me, it's a yuck). If you go to Greece, you'll see this everywhere. I had it once when I was there, and that was enough for me. Forever.

Red Grapes

AGIORGHITIKO (AH-YOR-YEE-TI-KO): Translated as "St. George's Grape," this grape is similar to Beaujolais's Gamay, with black cherry and violet flower notes, low tannin, and a punch of acid.

XINOMAVRO (KSEE-NO-MA-VRO): The "acid black" red of Macedonia, the wine can be floral with olive and spice notes and high tannin. Some people compare it to Nebbiolo of the Piedmont in Italy but I think it lacks the earthiness that makes Nebbiolo so special.

OTHERS: You may also see Mavrodaphne (Mav-ro-THAF-nee), which is the base of a sweet fortified wine, or Mandeleria (Mahn-dee-lar-EYA), which is a tannic, harsh grape alone and does better when blended with other, softer grapes.

The Wrap-Up

Until the Greek wine industry makes further inroads in exports, that's the story. Slow and steady wins the race, and if the producers can keep quality high and compete on their individuality rather than churning out yet another Chardonnay or Cabernet, they'll gain more traction with those of us looking for cool things to try.

ITALY

Something is amiss if you don't love Italy in some respect. Am I judgmental in thinking that? Hell yes, but given the beauty in countryside, in language, in food, in art, in attitude, and especially in wine, it's hard to understand someone who doesn't love the place.

I spent a semester of my junior year of college in Florence, and to this day I remember the important lessons I learned. Stuff like lines at the post office in Italy are what we called mobs in the United States. That "one-way" is an optional street sign. That football (soccer) games result in brawls. And that wine is a part of everyday life.

While there, I drank it every night with my host family and with every dinner I had with friends. It was food—like olive oil, bread, and pasta—so it was at the dinner tables in Florence that I learned to truly enjoy wine.

I wish I'd known or cared more about wine then because I could have explored the bounty of wine regions that were a train ride away. I was a normal student (albeit dorky since I used to roam the streets of Florence after class looking at Renaissance art and architecture): I just wanted to have fun and learn a few things about the world. Wine wasn't more than another interesting, delicious part of Italian life for my twenty-year-old self. But it permeated me somehow. A few years later, I was inspired to attend a spectacular Italian wine tasting with my alumni club that gave me another push on the wine path. So please keep in mind that despite all the smack I'm about to talk about Italy, it holds a special place in my heart.

Four paragraphs of glowing endorsement and now I have to level with you. Despite my homage to Italy, the country is one of the most messed-up places for wine in the world. Case in point: I know of no other wine nation where they can't seem to decide whether they want to name the wines by grape (Pinot Grigio), by place (Chianti), or by both (Brunello di Montalcino). You may find France confusing, but at least they've got a method to the madness—most quality areas, with the exception of Alsace, name their stuff by where it's from. Italy has nothing standardized in terms of naming or anything else in the wine world, really.

Still, history is on Italy's side. The Romans were responsible for all the current Old World winemaking regions we know and love. They mastered the art of winemaking and then spread it all over their empire. The Romans did more to further winemaking in the world than anyone before or since, and the Romans were effectively Italian. Given that, I find it sad that the abundance of wine has meant that many people take it for granted. Even historically amazing wine regions have been defiled by opportunistic producers and unethical exporters. And if you've been to Italy, you may have realized that the Italians aren't afraid to thwart the law, so it's not as if the government regulations deter the degradation of great areas. In the 1960s through the 1990s, mass-producers fought to have the boundaries of classic, premium areas expanded so they could cash in on the names of prestigious regions. As you read through the regions, you'll see me refer to the distinctions between the Classico areas and the general ones. In almost all cases, the historical, Classico

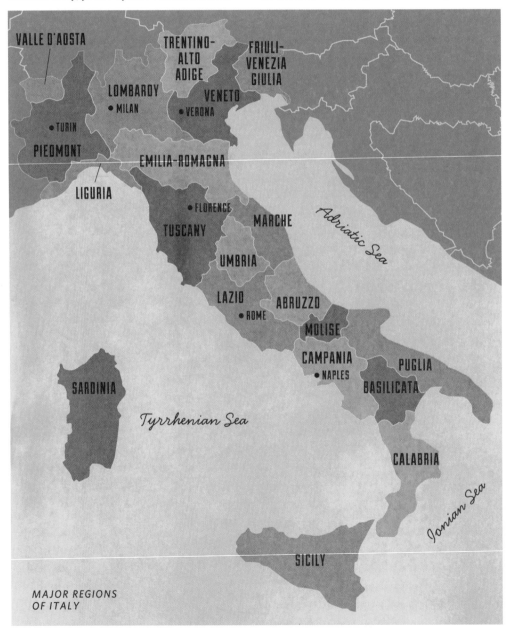

MAJOR REGIONS
OF ITALY

regions are the better choice and are worth the extra money. The rest is often not worth it.

Although you have to be cautious when shopping for Italian wine, I do feel that the Italians are getting wise to the fact that some of us have lost faith. In the past few years it seems like Italian producers are starting to improve the quality of wine. There is a more consistent quality level out of nearly every region. With that, cost has risen (France may still be a better value, to be honest), but at least now you'll get what you pay for.

With that point-counterpoint on Italian wine, following is a summary of what I think are the most important regions of Italy. Is it exhaustive? By no means. But it should give you enough info to explore the best areas of Italy and keep you busy for a few months or even years.

And as a note, I mention the classifications DOCG, DOC, and IGT in the following sections. For more information on these, please look at the introduction to Old World wines (page 89), which details the classification systems of each country and discusses the differences between them.

Northern Italian Regions

Piedmont

At the foot of the Alps, in rolling, hilly vineyards, is the home of some of the world's best reds and most interesting whites.

In this land of white truffles and Nutella (chocolate and hazelnuts contribute greatly to the economy here—sign me up!), the undulating terrain, hot summers, and haunting, thick, daily fog make the wines of the Piedmont unlike any others. Most wine is high quality, and the grapes here are real homebodies; try as they might, no other region can come close to emulating the reds and whites here. And it's not for lack of trying!

There are a few must-know wines from the Piedmont that are also must-know wines of Italy, since they're coveted the world around for their savory, layered, food-friendly qualities. Piedmont has no shortage of grapes or wines—whites, reds, sparkling, dessert—so the best I can give you is an overview. The variety means there is a little something for everyone, but I like to think of Piedmont wines in two categories: Thinking Wines with complexity and gravitas and Drinking Wines for everyday imbibing.

Thinking Wines: The Complex Red Wines of Piedmont

BAROLO (BAH-ROH-lo): This "king of wines and wine of kings" is made from the Nebbiolo grape, which is hard to grow, tannic, acidic, and in need of age to be drinkable. Barolo is one of Italy's greatest wines. Just southwest of the town of Alba, the best Barolo vineyards are nestled in the Apennine Mountains (Apennine means "foot of the mountain" in Italian), in hilly, southern-facing sites to catch maximum sun for ripening.

Although Nebbiolo itself tends to have rose, herbal, and tarlike smells and flavors (another "sounds weird, tastes great" thing), not all Barolo is created equal. A few basics can help to explain this great wine.

1. *There are different styles of Barolo, depending on terroir.* Barolo is spread over eleven communes but five are tops. In Serralunga d'Alba, Monteforte d'Alba, and Castiglione Falleto, you'll find brawny, bold, harsh wines. Most can't be consumed until they've had time to chill

out in the bottle for ten or more years. From the larger areas of La Morra and Barolo, you'll find softer, more perfumed, and less tannic wines that need more like six to eight years of aging to pair with your mushroom risotto. These regions are often stated on the bottle so look for them.

2. *Barolo has an informal vineyard classification similar to Burgundy, but it isn't official.* Building on the terroir thing, the crus of Barolo are well established, but Italians eschew bureaucracy so you won't find an official classification anywhere. That said, certain sites produce better wines than others, and you should know they exist, even if you don't know them all or want to spend the wad of cash required to get them.

3. *There are "Barolo Wars" between traditional and modern producers.* Dry Barolo has only been around since the mid-nineteenth century. It used to be sweet, because it was harvested late and as the cellar started to get cold in October and fermentations froze up, sugar remained in the wine. As technology improved, the wine was made as it is now—dry, big in flavor, and in need of aging.

Today, the traditional producers of the dry stuff are of the school that tannic, earthy wines with little fruit that need at least ten years of age are the only way to go. They have disdain for the modern producers who use technology (see Softening with Oxygen, page 173) to make fruity, oaky Barolo. Each has benefits and drawbacks. Traditional producers' wines are layered, feature flavors of the grape and land over the oak, and need time to age and major decanting once open. Modernists sometimes get softer tannins, vanilla

MAJOR REGIONS OF PIEDMONT

CAREMA
GATTINARA
GHEMME
ERBALUCE DI CALUSO
BARBERA DEL MONFERRATO
TURIN
BARBERA D'ASTI
ASTI/MOSCATO D'ASTI
ROERO
ASTI
LANGHE
ALBA
NIZZA
BARBERA D'ALBA
GAVI
BAROLO
BARBARESCO
BRACHETTO D'ACQUI
BARBERA D'ASTI

and tobacco flavors, and earlier drinking at the cost of the earthy Nebbiolo flavors. You need to decide what you like and go for producers who make it.

4. *Barolo is ageable, but expect it to turn orangish or rust colored with time.* Nebbiolo doesn't hold pigment but don't let it fool you. Color is no indication of what you're about to taste when you have an aged Barolo—power, texture, and flavor will all be there.

BARBARESCO (BAR-BAH-RAY-SKO): Just 10 miles (16 km) northeast of Barolo and east of Alba, Barbaresco includes the communes of Barbaresco, Treiso, and Neive. Although made from Nebbiolo and similar to Barolo in production methods, Barbaresco has different terroir, and that makes a huge difference. The humidifying influence of the River Tanaro and the lighter soils in the region mean Nebbiolo ripens earlier and has lighter, smoother tannin than Barolo. The floral and tar flavors exist as they do in the big guy, but these wines are generally softer and don't require as much aging. Barbaresco is known for rich, spicy, tobacco, dark fruit, and floral aromas and flavors with a mouth-drying texture and mouthwatering acid to give the wines a fresh quality.

From Barbaresco, I think you get more consistent wines than from Barolo. Barbaresco is one-third the size of Barolo, so it's rarer, but it's usually cheaper and fabulous. Although I'm not talking producers in this book (because it's frustrating for you to see these names and never find them in the store), I will mention the Produttori del Barbaresco, a co-op of sixty grape growers who own some of the best sites and pool their grapes to make outstanding wines. Each year they make a basic Barbaresco, but in better years they make up to ten wines, the basic wine and then one for each of the nine crus or better vineyard sites of the area. Look out for them because when you buy from the Produttori, you're assured great stuff.

Drinking Wines: The Everyday Red Wines of Piedmont

BARBERA (BAR-BAYH-RAH): The most widely planted grape of the Piedmont, Barbera used to get the shaft from producers, as they made little effort to make anything more than basic table wine. Although it still plays a secondary role to Nebbiolo, today producers are planting the grape on better sites. That's allowed this high-acid, darkly colored, cherry, herbal, licorice, and sometimes menthol-flavored wine to shine. It can be a little pricey for an everyday wine ($20 plus) but it's often worth it. Look for ones from Alba or Asti; otherwise you're gambling on quality. And try it with pizza; you won't be disappointed.

DOLCETTO (DULL-CHET-OH): I mentioned in the intro to this section that one of my first wine classes was on Italian wine. I remember tasting Dolcetto, with its contrast of sweet fruit, earth, characteristic bitterness, and smooth acid. It got me hooked on red wine. Dolcetto (translated to "little sweet one" but it's not sweet) is underrated. When it's grown in Alba, Dogliani, or sometimes Langhe, you'll find a consistent combination of black fruit, earth, and bitter chocolate notes. Although it's fallen out of favor with the rise of Barbera, the wine is food friendly and just plain great. Seek it out!

Drinking Wines: The Everyday White Wines of Piedmont

ARNEIS (ARE-NACE): Like many great wines of the world, Arneis is a beautiful, delicious grape that's a huge pain in the ass to grow. Arneis translates to "little rascal" because growers have such a hard time with it. Even when it's grown in Roero, where it's at its best, it can have low acid and acquire off flavors (oxidize) quickly. But as wine lovers have discovered, this aromatic wine can taste like peaches, pears, almonds, and flowers. Because of increased demand, growers have more incentive to do something good with this grape. They've discovered that on certain sites they can get more acidity and citrus flavors from the grape and in others more of those peachy, floral aromatics. Some producers put the wine in oak barrels, but the best ones showcase the grape in all its fruity, floral, nutty beauty without wood.

GAVI (GAH-VI): Made from the Cortese grape, this is the most famous dry white of the Piedmont. I find it ranges in flavor. Some versions (the cheaper ones) can be tart without much character, but the better versions have peachy, lemon aromas and flavors, and strong acidity, with a fullness that makes them awesome on their own or with lighter food.

One confusing thing about Gavi: Some versions just say Gavi on the label and others say Gavi di Gavi. There is a slight difference—Gavi is the DOCG but it's also a confined area within the province where grapes grow. The grapes cultivated within tighter boundaries of the town of Gavi are labeled Gavi di Gavi. As for all Italian wines (and French wines for that matter), along with the origin you have to pay attention to who made the wine; there will be awesome producers in the broader area and crappy ones in the smaller area.

MOSCATO D'ASTI: Before you start your eye roll and think to yourself, "That cheap garbage? I'm not going to drink sweet Moscato!" please read on. There's a big difference between wines made in other places from this ancient grape and the slightly sweet, fizzy, high-acid wines of Asti.

Moscato has serious credibility. It's also known as Muscat Blanc à Petits Grains, the base grape for some of the great sweet whites of southern France. When grown in Asti, it's a high-quality grape with honey, apple, and pear flavors and a mouthwatering tartness. It does particularly well when made as a sweet wine because it can maintain acidity, the key to preventing it from being sticky and heavy. Add a little effervescence to the mix and you have a wow factor, especially when it is paired with fruity desserts. Give it a shot next time you need a dessert wine. You won't regret it.

These regions are the tip of the wine iceberg in the Piedmont. From Ghemme and Gattinara, which are Nebbiolo-dominant wines (sometimes 100 percent, sometimes blended), to the red sparkling Brachetto d'Acqui, to the ancient, reemerging white grape Erbaluce, to the tannic and sometimes off-putting Freisa, you could spend many a night with a glass of Piedmontese wine and be surprised. A perfect region for armchair (or real) travel.

CLOSEST CITIES: *Turin is about 1 hour away by car and about 1.5 hours by train to the larger cities of Asti and Alba, in the heart of wine country.*

Veneto

Veneto is a sea of wine uncertainty. It is, in fact, the largest sea of unpredictability, eclipsing the prolific southern Italian areas of Sicily and Puglia, which previously cornered the market on making oceans of indistinguishable wine in all colors. But with those regions working to reduce vineyard area and focusing on quality, Veneto has the dubious distinction of having picked up the slack.

Part of the issue for Veneto is that it tries to do too much. The area stretches from the Italian Alps in the north to Lake Garda in the west and Venice in the east. The best grapes grow on hillside vineyards, the worst in valley floors that used to grow cereal products before wine grape growing became more lucrative. The good areas are struggling to maintain or regain their reputations. The bad areas are the over-cultivated home of grapes for $7-a-bottle alcoholic lemon water, a.k.a. Pinot Grigio.

There is so much grown in this region and the quality is so bipolar that it's hard to make sense of it. Veneto has areas that make varietal wines (Cabernet Sauvignon, Chardonnay, Pinot Grigio, Cabernet Franc, Pinot Nero, Prosecco, etc.) and then traditional areas that make blends. Since it's easy to figure out varietal wines, I'm only going to address the blends, which

are more difficult to make sense of and, frankly, have better stories to tell.

VALPOLICELLA (VAL-POLE-EE-CHEL-LA): I loved to recommend Valpolicella when I worked in an Italian restaurant in St. John (US Virgin Islands) in the early 2000s. It's a quintessential Italian name and it sounds like it will be delicious. It was my easiest sell—I could usually convince a few poor souls a night to taste it just by putting on my best Italian accent. Sadly, I realized years later that I duped these kind guests, describing the wine as it would be if made by the top producer (our version was not), not how it actually was.

As we'll discuss in Chapter 8 (page 314), remember that you gotta feel out your server before you buy! (I'm sorry if you remember me serving you in St. John and it didn't work out for you. I was learning.)

Do I feel guilty knowing what I know now? Yes. Because in the "Valley of Many Cellars," as Valpolicella translates, the increased demand in the late 1960s for this red created a situation in which producers expanded the growing area to places with no business growing grapes. The wines became boring and generic. The area couldn't recover because prices for grapes were so low that only bulk producers with fertile sites and big crops could make money. Small producers had to abandon the better, harder-to-cultivate hillside areas. It wasn't until Amarone (see following) became a hot commodity in the 1990s that the traditional Classico region in the hills outside Verona bounced back. Today only 40 percent of grapes included in Valpolicella are from these hillsides, so there are a lot of sucky versions out there.

The best grapes for the wine are the sour cherry–flavored, acidic Corvina and the spicy, red fruit–flavored Corvinone. Most producers will also add big proportions of the less flavorful Molinara grape and the bland but high-yielding Rondinella.

There are two main styles of the wine—simple, young versions with sour cherry flavors and high acidity from the valley floor and fuller, dark fruit–flavored, spicy styles from the hillsides. Some of these wines are made with the *ripasso* method, which entails fermenting the wine with skins of higher-quality grapes used in Amarone to theoretically make the wine fuller and richer (I'm not sure I believe that it makes a difference in bulking up the wine but you can judge).

Good Valpolicella exists, but you have to be vigilant about area and producer. If you want to steer clear of the mass-produced, overpriced versions, look for either VALPOLICELLA CLASSICO or VALPAN-TENA, a good pocket for grapes that lies outside the Classico zone.

AMARONE DELLA VALPOLICELLA (AHM-A-RHONE-EH DELLA VAL-POLE-EE-CHEL-LA): This dry, high-alcohol, fruity, expensive red is a real feat of winemaking. It's a ballsy, robust wine that is not for lovers of delicately flavored beverages. To make it, producers pick very ripe Corvina and Corvinone grapes, and then dry them, usually in slatted boxes inside temperature- and humidity-controlled rooms. Doing this intensifies flavors and softens acids and tannins. There's no regulated time for how long producers dry their stuff, yet it determines the wine's fruitiness and weight; if you prefer one producer's style to another, this may be why.

The grapes and growing area are the same for Amarone as they are for Valpolicella, so the importance of site, blend, and producer are the same—the stuff from the Classico region is great, the stuff from the

fertile areas, less so. Producer and vineyard matter.

Because of how it's made, Amarone almost always has a raisin, prune, or dried cherry note and is high in alcohol (14 percent or more because the grapes are dried, losing water, and when they are pressed there is more concentrated sugar, which results in high alcohol). Great ones have herb, tobacco, sweet oak, and spice notes, too. The wines can be tannic and need time to mellow. For me, balance is the key to a good Amarone—tannin, acid, fruit, and alcohol have to be aligned, or the wine can feel hot from the alcohol or taste bitter. That makes sense since Amarone means "great bitter one," although the name was created to distinguish the dry wine from the sweet version of the wine called RECIOTO DELLA VALPOLICELLA, made in the same way but just not fermented dry.

BARDOLINO (BAR-DO-LEE-NO): A simple, light red made from the same grapes as Valpolicella—Corvina, Rondinella, and Molinara—this wine lacks the fullness and acidity of its more famous cousin. The bulk of the region is on a big, flat, fertile plain near Lake Garda, and the terroir is less than stellar for grapes. Even though there is a Classico zone, meant to up the ante in quality, it's far less meaningful here than it is in Soave or Valpolicella. The wine has a higher proportion of Rondinella and Molinara than the high-quality Corvina. Still, it's got a nice, simple sour-cherry flavor and bright, refreshing acidity. It's great when popped in the fridge for a while and served cool on a hot summer day.

PROSECCO (PRO-SAY-KO): The sparkler of Veneto, this simple white wine is made from a grape that used to be called

Prosecco . . . until the wine got popular enough so that New World producers started making it and putting "Prosecco" on their labels. As any good marketers would, the producers in Veneto scrambled to change the name of the grape to Glera, an old synonym, so they could claim Prosecco as a historical, regional name for the wine. It worked, so we'll give these folks credit!

Although they can now guarantee the wine comes from Veneto, they can't guarantee it's good. Most Prosecco is a slightly sweet, nondescript, fizzy wine. The best is from the subareas of VALDO-BIADDENE (VAHL-DOH-BEE-AH-DAY-NAY) and CONEGLIANO (KOH-NEH-L'YEE-AH-NOH) or from the coveted CARTIZZE vineyard. Those designations usually mean that apple, peach, and honeysuckle flavors and bright acidity will be more prominent.

Regardless of quality level, it's useful to know that, even though it's bubbly, Prosecco is not made like Champagne. Its second fermentation takes place in a big vat rather than in a single bottle (the Charmat method). This saves the producers money and preserves the fruitiness of the grape. It's great for a sipper, but less so for food and wine pairing, and not one for aging!

SOAVE (SWAH-VEH): Soave is like the boyfriend or girlfriend you can't quit—when it's good, it's so good, but when it's bad, you wonder why you even gave it a chance in the first place. It's a dry white that's a victim of overexpansion into crap areas, similar to Chianti and Valpolicella but somewhat worse off. Starting in 1968, when Soave became a worldwide wine superstar, until the early 2000s, the wine was not on anyone's wine radar. Why? Because the producers of this once fine white wine churned out so much characterless plonk that Soave soon became the joke of the wine world and no self-respecting wine lover would drink it.

Fortunately for us, in the late 1990s phoenixes rose from the flames of wine conflagration and a few careful producers demanded a reset. These producers worked with the Consorzio Soave to study the terroir of the area and identify the best sites in the hilly Classico portion of the region that traditionally made wines from the native white grape Garganega (gahr-GAHN-eh-ga). In these confined areas, the full body and lemon, spice, mineral, and almond notes of Garganega shine. Augmented by Verdicchio (called Trebbiano di Soave here), Chardonnay, or Pinot Bianco (Pinot Blanc), today's better versions of Soave are full and refreshing with a great range in flavor.

With the pain of the past still hanging around, Soave producers today have a hard time convincing people their wines don't suck. If you buy carefully, they won't. Wine from the Classico zone tends to be mouthwatering, citrusy, and crisp. Fruitier, richer, floral versions come from the west side of the zone. Either way, keep in mind that vineyard and producer will matter more than whether or not the wine is a DOCG, DOC, IGT, or Table Wine, so ask your wine shop person or check descriptions on the web so you know what you're getting.

CLOSEST CITIES: *Most regions are about a 30-minute drive in various directions from the beautiful city of Verona, which is 1 hour west of Venice.*

Now let's turn to Veneto's two smaller neighbors—Alto Adige and Friuli-Venezia Giulia. Together these three areas are sometimes called the Tre Venezie.

Alto Adige

A small, beautiful, German-speaking northeastern province bordering Austria, Alto Adige (ALTO AH-dee-jay) is named for the Adige River that runs through it. The summers are warm, the winegrowing regions are best when high in the foothills of the dramatic Dolomite Mountains, and most of the wine is high quality. The cooler weather makes this white and light red wine territory.

The main grapes are Pinot Grigio, Chardonnay, and the native Schiava (skee-AHH-vah), which makes light red wines. The reds Lagrien (LAHG-ree-en), unique to this region and producing earthy, tannic wines, and Pinot Nero (Pinot Noir, which is unimpressive) are also produced here. You'll most commonly see Pinot Grigio and Pinot Nero out of Alto Adige. If you have to make the choice between a wine from Alto Adige and one from Veneto, choose Alto Adige. You'll get fuller, richer, more interesting wines most of the time. Also explore sparkling from here; there is a thriving bubbly scene, led by Ferrari, the first winery to introduce Chardonnay to Italy. Its traditional method sparkling is excellent, often rivaling Champagne in complexity, but at a much better value.

CLOSEST CITIES: *The main cities of Bolzano and Trento are home to hundreds of wineries and vineyards, big (Cavit, the enormous Pinot Grigio producer is here) and small. The main airport is in Bolzano,* *which is a 40-minute drive north from the charming town of Trento.*

Friuli-Venezia Giulia

This single region, with its mouthful of names, is also in the far northeast of Italy and borders Austria and Slovenia. It has Italian, German, and Slavic cultural, linguistic, and winemaking influences. Accordingly, people from all over planted their native grapes here—Romans, Venetians, Hapsburgs. Like Alto Adige, this cool-climate area is white wine country, and the region makes mostly varietally labeled wines (in the German tradition). This is another high-quality area with a lot of grapes you won't often see on shelves, but you should try them if you go there—especially high-acid reds like Refosco and Schioppettino (ski-YO-pee-TEEN-oh), and delicate, lively whites like Ribolla, Friuliano (free-oo-LAH-no), and Verduzzo (vare-DUTZ-oh), to name a few. Although some Pinot Grigio, Pinot Bianco, and Pinot Nero come from Friuli-Venezia Giulia (free-OO-lee ven-ETZ-ah JEWEL-eya), the more interesting wines are from grapes you don't commonly see outside Friuli.

CLOSEST CITIES: *The coastal city of Trieste is about a 1-hour drive northwest from the main wine areas, Gorizia and Udine.*

Central Italian Regions

Tuscany

In my wine-drinking life, I've visited Tuscany again and again on both personal and wine industry trips. When I'm visiting, the wine is good and sometimes great.

Rarely is it as good at home. I know I'm not alone: I hear this from people again and again. Is it that you're on vacation and everything is better? Maybe. Is it that wine doesn't travel well and tastes different after it's been moved around? Sure. But I think the problem with Tuscan wine—Chianti, Brunello di Montalcino, Vino Nobile di Montepulciano, Maremma, Vernaccia, and even Super Tuscans—is that some of the best bottles from smaller producers rarely reach us (I say this from a US perspective but I think this holds for other markets, too).

One of my saddest realizations while touring Tuscany on a wine trip was that often producers alter the blends to cater to the American market. They're fruitier, less earthy, and less reflective of terroir. Producers ditch sense of place to increase sales. I can't say this is the case for all brands that hit our shores, but it's a depressing trend. At least it explains why the wine tastes different.

Another issue for us in the world of Tuscan wines is consistency. Tuscan producers can be lawless and unpredictable. Blends aren't always up to regulation. What is "typical" of a town or area varies wildly, as does quality. Producer reputation is important, and yet it seems we may not be able to trust that either, since there have been scandals involving prestigious producers who bend the rules to make the wine more marketable abroad.

CHIANTI (KYAHN-TEE): It's probably the most recognizable wine of Italy, but these days you never know what you're going to get in a bottle of standard Chianti. Producers abutting the traditional quality area, established in 1716, have pushed to have their regions included in Chianti. As a result, there are many subpar vineyards making subpar wines with Chianti on the label. You have to research to find a good bottle of Chianti.

If you don't have the patience for Chianti wine roulette, my recommendation is to seek wines from the Chianti Classico designation. This is where Chianti has been produced for centuries and encompasses the best vineyards from Florence to Siena. Look for a black rooster or *gallo nero* on the label to make sure the winery is a member of the Chianti Classico Consortium, the association of local producers.

Classico is required to be 75 to 100 percent Sangiovese, the high-acid, cherry, and sometimes orange peel–flavored grape. The remaining grapes are commonly the native Canaiolo and Colorino, sometimes with grapes like Cabernet Sauvignon and Merlot added in. The blend is a factor in the flavor of the wine so you'll have to try different producers' versions to discover what you like best. Also, research or ask your wine shop person for bottles that come directly from estates rather than from négociants (page 59)—that way the producer has had control over where and how the grapes were grown, which is usually the difference between good and bad Chianti.

How do you determine what makes a good Chianti? Aromas and flavors of red, black, and sour cherry and floral and cinnamon notes are typical. Sangiovese always seems to have an orange-peel flavor, earthiness, acidity, and mouth-puckering tannin. All that makes this wine the ideal pairing with Italian food. A good Chianti can age for decades and develop dark leather and spice aromas with time. A regular one will kick butt with most Italian food and enhance your meal!

CLOSEST CITIES: *Radda, Gaiole in Chianti, Greve, and Castellina are the main towns in Chianti Classico and are about 1-hour drive southeast of Florence.*

BRUNELLO AND ROSSO DI MONTALCINO (BROO-**NAY**-LO; RO-**SO** DEE MON-TALL-**CHEE**-NO): Drive an hour and a half to two hours south from the Chianti region and *bam*! You hit another of the greatest wine towns in Italy: Montalcino. Brunello, meaning "little brown one" for its skin color, is a clone of Sangiovese, and although it's a close relative, the difference is striking. In a warm, dry climate, on slopes surrounding the medieval, walled city of Montalcino (where you can find me during my retirement, with any luck), the vineyards produce different wines depending on the terrain, soil, and slope. Brunello tends to share standard Sangiovese's black and red cherry flavors, but with fruitier, more layered flavors like black licorice, earth, tobacco, leather, and forest flavors from longer oak aging. It's tannic and acidic, but with ten years of age, the wine gets richer in flavor and smoother in texture.

The best producers have vineyards at altitude on cooler north-facing slopes and on warmer south-facing slopes. They seek areas with different soil types. Blends of grapes from different areas create wines with a balance between acid, tannin, fruit, and earthy aromas and flavors. Like Barolo and Barbaresco, the vineyards are not officially classified by the government, but there are subzones in the region that make distinctive styles of Brunello (see sidebar). Although you shouldn't count out those that don't do this, a producer who puts a subzone on the bottle or on the back label is telling you they understand that not all Brunello is created equal—a great sign.

ROSSO DI MONTALCINO: This wine is how the Brunello producers bankroll Brunello. Since good Brunello must age in oak for three or more years, and because it's only made from the best grapes in Montalcino, there's a two-fold problem. First—financing inventory-holding costs. It's expensive to sit on reserves of wine year after year. Second—what do you do with grapes that don't make the cut for Brunello?

The solution for both? Sell a fresh, fruity wine that requires less aging, of course! Charge $20 or $25 vs. $50 or more for Brunello. And now you have Rosso di Montalcino, a younger wine with ripe cherry flavors that's a simpler version of Brunello.

CLOSEST CITIES: *Montalcino is about 50 minutes southeast of Siena by car and 1.75 hours southeast of Florence.*

tip

For its consistency and price, I usually grab a Rosso di Montalcino rather than a Chianti when shopping for Tuscan wine. It's usually a way more reliable sipper for the money.

PROPOSED BRUNELLO DI MOTALCINO SUBREGIONS

Although this move is not yet formalized, a group of producers in Montalcino argue that the prestigious region requires subzones so enthusiasts can discern the subtle, terroir-based differences between the wines. Wines growing at altitude, they reason, are far more aromatic and soft than those growing on the valley floor. Further, *vigna*, or single-vineyard wines, are labeled, so the extra information on the label about zone shouldn't be an issue. Others argue that it will devalue excellent wines made from a blend of grapes from various subzones. To date, nothing has come of this movement, but it's something to watch since it seems that it is destined to happen. These are the proposed subzones.

Montalcino North
•
Montalcino South
•
Castelnuovo dell'Abate
•
Camigliano
•
Tavernelle
•
Bosco
•
Torrenieri
•
Sant'Angelo

VINO NOBILE DI MONTEPULCIANO (VEE-noh NOH-bee-lay dee MON-ta-pool-CHEE-AH-no): I know it seems like I'm saying every wine in Tuscany is famous, but that's because it's kind of true! From the town of Montepulciano (not to be confused with the plummy, full wine from the Montepulciano grape of Southern Italy), this wine has to be at least 70 percent Sangiovese but is generally more like 100 percent.

Instead of the bright cherry flavors you find in Chianti, Vino Nobile has more dried fruit flavor with an earthy, forest, mineral, decayed leaf note. It has mellower tannins and milder acidity. You can taste the darker, heavier soils of this growing area vs. the bright fruit and high acidity in Chianti. The bonus of Vino Nobile: Because it's lesser known than Brunello or Chianti, quality for the price is awesome.

CLOSEST CITIES: *Montepulciano is about 1 hour southeast of Siena by car and a 1.5-hour drive southeast of Florence.*

SUPER TUSCAN: Made from French grapes—Cabernet Sauvignon, Merlot, and Syrah, with some native Sangiovese—Super Tuscan blends vary in style and flavor. The top producers are located in coastal Tuscany, in and around the town of Bolgheri. The style is generally modern—rich and bold, with full black fruit like blackberry, black plums, and black currant, and a good hit of oaky vanilla flavor.

Top producers started making these wines in the 1970s to experiment with different regions and grapes outside those permitted by rigid Italian wine laws. At first, these famed wines—Sassicaia, Ornellaia, and Tiganello, to name a few—were classified as table wines because they didn't fit in the Italian classification system. The

Q+A

So what's the lesson on Tuscany? Is it good or bad?

When the wines are great, they're outstanding. When they aren't, they are a fiasco (literally—that cheesy straw bottle holder of cheap Chianti is called a fiasco!). I find myself proceeding with caution when buying Tuscan, but there is lots of quality to be had. I've tried to provide structure to this erratic wine region in this guide to the major areas and what, in my experience, these famed red wines should taste like.

Super Tuscans were routinely more than $300 per bottle and met peerless critical praise, yet were classified alongside nondescript everyday wines. Partially out of embarrassment for this discrepancy and partially out of a need for flexibility, the IGT (Indicazione Geografica Tipica) category was created to allow producers to "color outside the lines," using different grapes and winemaking techniques and still boast high-quality wine. The Super Tuscan phenomenon proves that Italians are nothing if not adaptable, especially when it comes to wine law!

CLOSEST CITIES: *Bolgheri is a 1-hour drive south of Pisa and a 1.75-hour drive southeast of Florence.*

Like Piedmont, many great wines come out of Tuscany. The historic CARMIGNANO, which has rustic wines of Sangiovese with Cabernet Sauvignon and Cabernet Franc; MORELLINO DI SCANSANO, a fruitier Sangiovese-based wine from the southern coastal hills; VERNACCIA DI SAN GIMIGNANO, a dry, citrusy, refreshing white wine; and VIN SANTO, the wine made from dried Malvasia and Trebbiano grapes that ranges in style from dry to sweet are blockbuster wines, too. There are countless others I can't cover here, but when you're in Tuscany, don't be surprised if you find that every town has a quality wine to offer. Try them all.

Umbria

It's hard to believe that a historic wine country like Italy has any big, bold wines that aren't known around the world. But every region has different strengths, and Umbria (UUM-bree-ah), the verdant, landlocked province, has more fame in its saints (St. Francis of Assisi, St. Clare) and artists (Perugino, Raphael's master) than in wine.

Even though much of the wine made is from Tuscan superstar Sangiovese, Umbria has an arrow in its quiver that no other region has: Sagrantino. And although there are few producers who make wine from this black grape, the ones that do make magic. Umbria can be a mixed bag but stick with the reds, especially the four below, and you'll be pleased.

MONTEFALCO SAGRANTINO (MON-TEE-FAHL-KO SAH-GRAHN-TEE-NO); SAGRANTINO DI MONTEFALCO (SAH-GRAHN-TEE-NO DEE MON-TEE-FAHL-KO): There are only about eighty producers of this red wine and they only farm about 250 acres (101 ha) of

Sagrantino around the hills of Montefalco; production is limited and wines can be pricey (more than $30) but are generally worth it. Sagrantino, native to Umbria, packs an aromatic punch of red cherry, black cherry, and oranges. The wine smells like a forest and can taste spicy, with black pepper and tobacco flavors. Sagrantino is tannic and acidic, so it's great with food but watch the alcohol levels—they can creep up without your tasting them because the wines are so well balanced. That one element could crush a subtler dish if you're having the wine with food.

ROSSO DI MONTEFALCO (ROE-SO DEE MON-TEE-FAHL-KO): This is where things get confusing. The di Montefalco means "from Montefalco." So this wine translates to the red (rosso) of Montefalco. It's different from Sagrantino because it's just 10 to 15 percent Sagrantino with between 60 and 70 percent Sangiovese and the rest of the blend from a long list of approved grapes. Despite a similar name, this wine is more like a richer version of Chianti than like Montefalco Sagrantino. It's got red cherry, sour cherry, and orange peel aromas and flavors with refreshing acid but with rich, earthy overtones and a mouth-drying tannic bite from the Sagrantino. This wine is more reasonably priced than Montefalco Sagrantino, but it's also more hit or miss, since the vineyards are more uneven in quality.

TORGIANO ROSSO RISERVA (TOUR-JEE-AHN-NO ROE-SO REE-ZERV-AH): Made mainly of Sangiovese with some Canaiolo, this red can have up to 10 percent of the white grape (!) Trebbiano and the reds Ciliegiolo and Montepulciano. It sounds like a cheap Chianti blend, but growing farther inland on different soils, the grapes for this wine become more flavorful than generic Chianti—like blackberry jam, black cherries, and black raspberries. The wine can have pepper or vanilla notes from oak aging, with mouth-drying tannins and refreshing acid typical of Sangiovese. If Chianti is too earthy for you but you like the fundamentals of the wine, Torgiano Rosso Riserva is your wine.

ORVIETO (OR-VEE-YETO): Hailing from the beautiful hilltop town of Orvieto in the southern area of Umbria is this white that is mostly made from the bland Trebbiano Toscano grape with the fuller Grechetto and other local whites thrown in to make it palatable. I know that producers are trying to improve the quality of this wine, which I think is one step up from acidic water, but unless you notice the producer is using more of the flavorful Grechetto grape, with its acidic backbone and lovely citrus aromas, I would steer clear of the whites of Orvieto. I still haven't met one I'm excited about.

CLOSEST CITIES: *Montefalco is a 1-hour drive south of Perugia, and Torgiano is about 20 minutes south. Orvieto is 1-hour southwest of Perugia by car.*

Southern Italian Regions

Campania

Campania (cahmp-AH-nyah) is my favorite Italian region no one has heard of, especially for whites. If you think white wine tastes like butter and vanilla, cat pee, or just a step above grain alcohol, I suggest you pick up something from this region. Campania's whites (along with those of the Rhône and Alsace, France) will give you a new appreciation for white wines you never dreamed possible. And the stunning reds in this southwestern Italian region will surprise you with their blend of New World fruitiness and Old World depth, earthiness, and texture.

Close to the famed Mount Vesuvius, this area's vineyards are still covered in ash from the volatile volcano. Vineyards are mainly around the volcano and in Avellino, a remote location in the Irpinian Hills, east of Naples. In this warm region, the grapes develop plenty of plump fruit flavor and round, cheek-coating body, but also an ashy, mineral quality that can only be ascribed to a certain something in the soil.

The crazy thing about this area is that all these grapes, many of which are ancient in origin, were almost extinct a few decades ago. In the mid-twentieth century, people abandoned the rural, financially depressed, inland areas like Avellino as they searched for jobs in the cities. The vineyards went feral, turning from neatly pruned rows into overgrown bushes, with traditional grapes growing on hillsides roamed by wolves and goats. The Falanghina, Greco, Aglianico, and Fiano grapes modestly grew, and producers made small quantities for local consumption. Then a big earthquake in the 1980s wound up reviving the area.

EU government money for the rebuilding effort plus the efforts of one family, the Mastroberardinos, who worked tirelessly to keep these ancient grapes alive and to popularize them, transformed the region, and now we can find the wines I'm about to describe. Beyond the tourist destinations of Napoli, the Amalfi Coast, and Capri, this area is a lesser-known wine mecca for you!

Many of the wines are labeled by grape name and are some of my favorites.

Reds

AGLIANICO (AHL-LYAHN-EEK-O): The wines made from Aglianico, the most widely grown red grape in Campania, are awesome and underappreciated. They can be more medium bodied—with strawberry, cherry, and herb notes and light acid and tannin—or they can be huge yet balanced with tons of tannin, acid, and black fruit, licorice, spice, and smoke notes. These are serious wines and they can age well, too. If you buy one, wait until it's at least a few years old to drink it—the payoff is a balanced, complex wine that changes with every sip. You can find basic Aglianico under the AGLIANICO DEL TABURNO and IRPINIA appellations or from TAURASI, the big daddy of Aglianico.

PIEDIROSSO (PEE-DEE-RO-SO): An up-and-coming grape, Piedirosso is fresh and aromatic, with red fruit, earth, and herbal notes. When it's good, it's like a Gamay from Beaujolais, France. It's mainly a blending grape, but quality is improving and now you can find great stand-alone versions. The two big areas for this grape are CAMPI FLEGREI and LACRYMA CHRISTI DEL VESUVIO ROSSO. Both are mainly Piedirosso with another local grape, Sciascinoso, and Aglianico. Both wines have smoky, cherry, and mineral flavors, but Campi Flegrei is softer and fuller.

Red Region

TAURASI (TAOW-RAH-ZEE): In and around the small town of Taurasi are vineyards sitting atop steep mountains on volcanic soils. Mostly made of Aglianico, which thrives in this soil, Taurasi is dark colored, with earthy, tobacco, licorice, and dark cherry and black raspberry flavors. With time it can acquire chocolate and coffee notes, too. It's got huge tannin and acidity, and could use time decanting before you drink it. Full-bodied, ageable, and flavorful, Taurasi is for you if you like big wines. They're not cheap, but they're a steal compared to other wines with similar heft (expect to pay around $40 for a good one).

Although I'm not going to detail the BASILICATA province near Campania, another very similar wine grown just 40 miles (64 km) away, AGLIANICO DEL VULTURE, is produced there, and it's as good as Taurasi and about the same price.

Whites

FALANGHINA (FAH-LAWN-GHEE-NAH): A history dork-out for you: This grape was most likely the basis for the white version of the first cult wine, the Roman Falernian, which was as rare as it was expensive back in the Forum. Growing north of Naples, Falanghina is lighter than the other whites of Campania and has citrus (specifically orange), floral, and pear aromas and often a strong mineral note. One word of warning: I find Falanghina to be less consistent than the other whites of the region, so if you taste one and it's thin and watery, try another producer or move on to one of the other whites!

CODA DI VOLPE BIANCA (KO-DA DEE VOLE-PAY BEE-AN-KA): Coda di Volpe translates to "fox tail" because the shape of the bunches just looks like one! This white, which usually has lots of mineral, peach, pear, and light Indian spice notes, is used mainly in blends, but I have tried a few awesome stand-alone versions, too. This ancient grape is an "old is new again" project of producers, especially in VESUVIO and LACRYMA CHRISTI (DEL VESUVIO) DOCs. The latter translates to "the tears of Christ on Vesuvius," named so because people believe that as Jesus ascended to heaven he looked at the Bay of Naples and wept tears of joy for its beauty, which fell upon Mount Vesuvius and show through in the wine (*I don't get much salinity from it, but you can judge!*). You'll see this grape in blends all over Campania, so keep an eye out.

White Regions

FIANO DI AVELLINO (FEE-AH-NO DEE AH-VAY-LEE-NO): Fiano is an ancient grape variety that was probably the basis for another famed Roman wine, Apianum. Why do we think that? Because apianum refers to the Latin for "bees," and bees love the sweet smell of Fiano—the vines in Avellino literally buzz during flowering. Sadly, the grape is a pain to grow—low yields, disease prone, etc.—but continuing with the bee motif, when it makes good wine it tastes like honey and nuts with floral notes. My favorite versions have a spicy, fresh, herbal bite that's mitigated by the waxy texture. Like all the whites of this area, Fiano is a bold, mouthwatering white. This is my favorite wine of Campania.

GRECO DI TUFO (GRAY-KO DEE TOO-FO): Growing around the town of Tufo, Greco, presumably of Greek origin, is dark yellow and full-bodied. The wine has a strong herbal note, but sometimes tastes like peaches and white flowers. I find it always has a chalky, ashy note, probably from the volcanic soils on which it grows. That ashy, herbal, citrus flavor and mouth-filling texture make this unlike any other white I know, in a good way.

CLOSEST CITIES: *Avellino is about a 45-minute drive east of Naples, and Taurasi is about 1 hour west.*

Sicily

Sicily is Italy's third-largest wine-producing region. This hot Mediterranean island makes more white than red, which is totally counterintuitive when you consider that most other hot places specialize in red grapes.

Although they've been making wine in Sicily since around 1500 B.C. and making serious stuff since the Greeks landed in the eighth century A.D., in modern times Sicily has made seas of crap wine. Why? Easy money. The fertile, volcanic soil is great for growing lots of fruity yet flabby bulk wine sold in mainland Italy to beef up wimpier wines from cooler, northern places.

Despite recent history, we can't write off Sicily as a winemaking force: In the last decade or two, enormous efforts have been made to improve winegrowing and winemaking, and it's paying off. In the 1990s, local talent broke free from the co-op structure that dominated, and started leveraging the native grapes—the reds Nero d'Avola, Frappato, and Calabrese and the whites Cataratto, Grillo, Inzolia, Zibibbo (Muscat of Alexandria), and Moscato Bianco—and adding French favorites like Syrah, Merlot, and Chardonnay. The result is impressive!

Even better, some of the wine coming out of Sicily from smaller producers is more than a delicious victory for us—it's a political one, too. Many of these people have waged a quiet war against the Cosa Nostra (mafia) and the "tariffs" they impose to do business there. Some have risked life and limb to do so, and finally we get to see what independent winemakers can do when they are free to create wines they want.

Because it differs from most of Italy and is almost a winemaking country of its own, and because much of the wine is labeled by grape variety, below I address the major grapes you'll encounter when venturing into Sicilian wines and what they'll probably taste like.

Reds

NERO D'AVOLA (NEH-ROH DAV-OH-LA): The "black of Avola" is a wonderful native grape of Sicily, with red fruit flavor, but it can lack acid and be overly alcoholic in the wrong hands. It may be the most underrated red on the market these days, and you can get it for a song (around $18 for a decent one), which makes it a fabulous weeknight wine, especially with southern Italian food like pizza or pasta in tomato sauces. It usually tastes like black cherry, raspberry, and fresh flowers with chocolate and spice. Nero often has strong mouth-drying tannin and enough acid to make it ideal with food.

Look for Nero on its own or in CERA-SUOLO DI VITTORIA (CHERA-SWO-LO), a Sicilian wine required to be a maximum of 60 percent Nero d'Avola and 40 percent or more of the fruity red Frappato. Cerasuolo, whose name derives from *cerasa*, or "cherry," in a local dialect, is appropriately named since the wine tastes like cherry, strawberry, and cranberry.

NERELLO MASCALESE (NEH-RELL-OH MAH-SKA-LEH-ZEH): Found mainly on the slopes of Mount Etna, Nerello is dark skinned with red, black, and sour cherry notes, herbal flavors, and a distinct earthy quality that roots it in the land. When at its best in Etna, it's planted at high elevations of up to 3,280 feet (1,000 m). The vines benefit from cool nights, giving them a lighter, more refined aroma than stuff grown in the hot valleys of Sicily. Nerello Mascalese makes up the majority of the blend in the ETNA ROSSO DOC (from the side of the volcano) and the FARO DOC (in the hills above the city of Messina). Both appellations produce some of my favorite Italian reds these days.

Whites

The following Sicilian *whites* are made as stand-alone wines or are blended into Marsala:

CARRICANTE (KAHR-E-KAHN-TEH): This ancient grape has likely been growing on the high altitude, volcanic slopes of Mount Etna for a thousand years or more. The grape shines in its native environs, producing wines that are rich in mineral, green herb, salt, and citrus flavors. With excellent acidity to preserve it, Carricante can age well, taking on complex Riesling-like kerosene notes, with savory herbs and a persistent saline quality. The wines are sometimes aged sur lie to counteract their acidity. ETNA BIANCO DOC contains a minimum of 60% Carricante. Etna Bianco Superiore has 80% of the grape.

CATARRATTO (KAH-TAH-RAHT-TO): Giving you a sense of how much wine comes out of Sicily, Catarratto is the second most widely planted grape in Italy even though it's almost exclusively grown in Sicily. Growers generally overcrop it, so it has a neutral taste, but when it's made well, this grape can be medium- to full-bodied with rich lemon notes. This is the stuff that cheap Marsala is made from, so it's not high on my list of Sicily's finest.

GRILLO (GREE-LOW): Grillo can have lemon-lime flavors and a rich, full body, but it's not aromatic or distinctive. I've been unimpressed by all the versions I've tried. To me, it's Sicily's answer to the low-quality Pinot Grigio from Veneto, and that's nothing to brag about.

INZOLIA (EEN-TSOH-LEA): Nutty, with pear, apple, and melon notes, Inzolia can be a nice wine if the heat of the Sicilian sun doesn't bake out the grape's acid. Inzolia is often fresh and complex, but to get a good one you have to watch the producer and you may have to shell out more than $25.

MARSALA (FORTIFIED): An Englishman, John Woodhouse, created this wine in the late 1700s and named it after a town in Sicily. It uses some combination of Catarratto, Inzolia, and Grillo, with the best versions using only the last two. Much like Madeira, Sherry, or Port, winemakers add brandy to halt the wine's fermentation and bring the alcohol to 15 to 20 percent. There are a bunch of different styles classified by color, sweetness, and time aged. The best tend to be aged longer (e.g., VERGINE and VERGINE STRAVECCHIO are both aged like Sherry) and make good aperitifs or cheese pairings.

The issue for Marsala is that no one really wants it these days. As demand has declined, so have the number of quality producers. Most people associate it with cooking wine used to sauté onions or shallots, or make chicken Marsala or sweet desserts like zabaglione. I hope it will eventually see a renaissance before all the great producers are gone, but it doesn't look good.

CLOSEST CITIES: *From the main city of Palermo, the wine regions are as close as 1.5 hours (Marsala) by car or as far as 3.5 hours (Mount Etna, Noto).*

Abruzzo

Abruzzo (ah-BRUTZ-oh), on the east side of Italy's boot, boasts plenty of Adriatic coastline and substantial mountains. Its gem is the Montepulciano grape, and the area has great potential to make lovely sippers with it. The problem: Abruzzo is economically poor, and out of necessity, producers focus more on quantity than quality so they can eke out a living. Most of the wine is made by large, often careless cooperatives. The wines suffer as a result. Montepulciano d'Abruzzo can be a serious, flavorful treat if the winemaker cares to take the time, which sadly few do. When treated well, it can be light, plummy, and rustic, or more layered with leather, black pepper, and blackberry flavors with good tannin. There are a few boutique producers (Valentini is the most famed), who make expensive and, by all accounts, excellent wines of Montepulciano, Trebbiano (white), and Bombino Nero, but they're a rarity.

As a reminder, the Montepulciano grape has nothing to do with the Tuscan town that churns out awesome Sangiovese-based blends (Vino Nobile). Confusing enough? I don't make the names—I just tell you about them.

CLOSEST CITIES: *The wine regions are around the towns of Pescara, Chieti, and l'Aquila. Pescara and Chieti are about a 20-minute drive apart; l'Aquila is a 1-hour drive west from both places.*

Puglia

Puglia (POOL-ya) occupies the high heel of the Italian boot. It's a historic, beautiful region in the southeast coast of the Adriatic. The region has endless coastline but most of the wine grapes grow in the hot interior. The center of the province grows the native Uva di Troia and Primitivo (Zinfandel), and the heel specializes in the native Negroamaro (NEH-gra-MAHR-oh). Primativo is grapier and earthier, although often less nuanced, than many California versions. I find Negroamaro, meaning "bitter black one" to be the best thing out of Puglia. SALICE SALENTINO (SAH-lee-CHEY SAHL-EN-TI-NOH), a red wine made of Negroamaro, is probably the most commonly exported wine from this area. Good ones taste like ripe cherries, berry, and bitter dark chocolate, with healthy doses of alcohol, medium tannin, and acidity.

In the last decade, investment from international Italian market makers like Antinori (who make Tormaresca) and Zonin (the Masseria Altemura brand) have brought more Puglian wines to market, but that hasn't changed the fact that, like Abruzzo, this is an indigent area and most of the wine trade is run by co-ops with an eye toward volume, not quality. Although there is a growing group of independent producers, the lesson (again) is read up on producers before you start buying wines from Puglia or you may wind up with crap bulk wine that has little to recommend it.

CLOSEST CITIES: *Wineries are scattered all up and down the back of the boot through the heel, but Bari and Brindisi are about a 1.5-hour drive from each other, and a strategic drive will allow you to see many of the wineries.*

The Wrap-Up

Italian wine is endless in its breadth and scope. Hopefully this primer will help you get your feet wet beyond Chianti and Pinot Grigio if you haven't ventured past the basics. There is far more to learn and explore, but for now, the preceding section should be enough to keep you busy, and get you excited to drink better and more interesting Italian wines.

PORTUGAL

What does the world's biggest supplier of cork and maker of arguably the best fortified wine in the world (Port) have to offer the wine world besides those two contributions? A lot, but the country has yet to strike it big in the global wine market, and we have to see if it will.

Although it's in a rebuilding phase now, Portugal had a wine heyday. From discovering much of the New World then exporting wine to colonies, to becoming a huge supplier to the wine-loving Brits, the place was at the top of its wine game at one point. But its relative isolation on the western front of the Iberian Peninsula and its (pretty awesome) resistance to using nonindigenous grapes for blends has shoehorned Portugal into a tough place in the global wine market. It seems that if it isn't Port, Vinho Verde, or Madeira, we don't know it, don't understand it, and only want it if it's cheap. And, given that Portugal's stars are specialty wine types and don't exactly fit in with everyday consumption, that leaves the country in a tough spot in terms of getting people interested in trying its dry wines.

This stinks because with hundreds of native grapes and big variations in terrain and soils, Portugal is a treasure trove of great wine. And it's a place on the rise: Since it joined the EU in 1986 and got an infusion of money, Portugal has slowly modernized its facilities and vineyards, setting up the country to make a go of it in the wine world.

But the way I see it, Portugal faces a sticky business issue that "emerging" wine regions face: Even if you wanted to shop your way around Portugal and try wines from Bairrada or Dão (more to come—don't worry if you have no idea where those are), it's not easy to find this stuff. Portugal is part of a chicken and egg problem: The wines aren't widely available so we don't shop for them. No one selling wine is going to waste money on carrying something that won't sell, so wine shops don't carry the wine from every region. Hence, shoppers get limited access to great bottles, unless the wine shop is willing to take on these wines as pet projects. Market dynamics are tough.

That said, with more interest in blends these days, Portugal is slowly becoming the place for people looking for new wines to enjoy. Trends show encouraging pickup in Portuguese wines from a number of regions—all good news.

To learn about Portugal, you need to know that the country is essentially split in half in terms of wine style. The north produces wines that are easier to find, buy, and try. The south, which arguably is more important for its massive cork production, is making fruitier wines and working on raising quality levels.

There are hundreds of native grapes and dozens of Denominações de Origem Controlada (DOCs)—small, more restricted wine-producing regions. With time, we'll see more of these regions on the shelf as younger, dynamic producers and outside investment in Portugal improve the wine. For now, there are five main regions you should know.

Vinho Verde

"Green wine," as Vinho Verde (veeng-YO vehrd) translates to, refers not to the color of this fun, young wine, but to its age. These wines (most commonly white, with reds and rosés mostly for domestic consumption) are young when released in their acidic, often fizzy state to us. Reds are fruity and use the Vinhão grape. Whites have a low-alcohol level, normally below 12 percent, and use lighter-style grapes like floral Loureiro, acidic Trajadura, creamy Avesso, and minerally Arinto. Higher-class versions often use 100 percent of the Alvarinho grape, better known as Albariño in Spain. Vinho Verde, frequently made spritzy with a shot of carbon dioxide before bottling, tastes like limes and nectarines and is perfection in the summertime when chilled and served with light cheeses, shellfish, or pesto. Although not much is exported yet, the small subregions of Monção and Melgaco on the Spanish border are the areas to seek out for exceptional Vinho Verde.

CLOSEST CITIES: *Driving distance from Oporto, the southernmost part of the region, will depend on the city you decide to explore. Guimarães, Vieira do Minho, and Viana do Castelo in the heart of the Vinho Verde and are about 1 hour north of Oporto.*

The Douro

The hot, arid Douro (DOOR-oh) basin, which grows the grapes for Port production, is arguably Portugal's most important wine region. Top sites are on steep hills surrounding the river Douro (Duero in Spain, both meaning "river of gold"), and have to be farmed manually, making this a costly, difficult place to grow grapes.

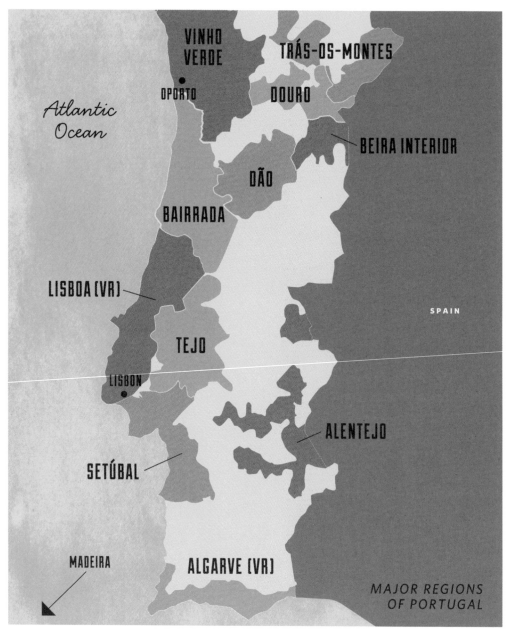

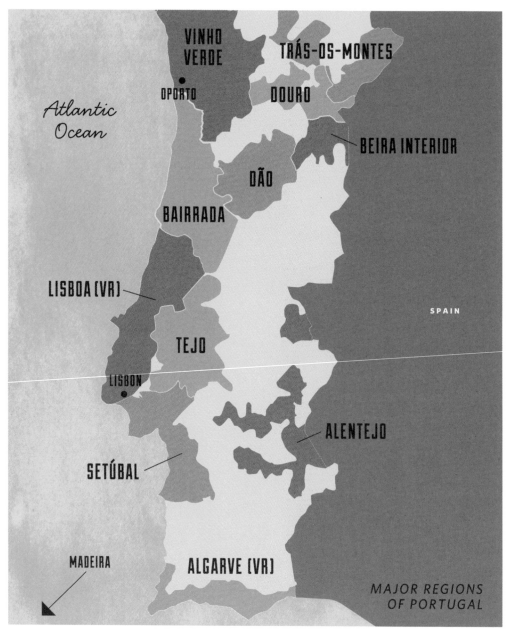

VINHO VERDE

TRÁS-OS-MONTES

OPORTO

Atlantic Ocean

DOURO

BEIRA INTERIOR

DÃO

BAIRRADA

LISBOA (VR)

SPAIN

TEJO

LISBON

ALENTEJO

SETÚBAL

MADEIRA

ALGARVE (VR)

MAJOR REGIONS OF PORTUGAL

The Douro is also big, and alongside the ideal places on slopes are less than perfect sites for growing multiple varieties of lower quality levels. Given this difference in terrain and microclimates, there's actually a system that ranks the vineyards by quality and determines the price farmers will receive for their fruit (similar to Champagne, [page 139] actually). This is why you see some Port that costs hundreds of dollars and some that costs $15!

It's widely agreed that five main grapes are Douro's best:

- Touriga Nacional (tour-EEG-ah NAH-see-oh-NAL)
- Tinta Cão (CHIN-ta COWM)
- Tinta Roriz (CHIN-ta hoar-EEZ), a.k.a. Tempranillo
- Touriga Franca (tour-EEG-ah FRANC-ah)
- Tinta Barroca (CHIN-ta ba-HOAK-ah).

Not by chance, it's these grapes that go into the top Port wine blends.

The DO authorizes eighty grapes for Port, although only the big five mentioned are best for reds. Each of the red grapes that go into Port has a different character—some are floral, some spicy, some earthy. The combination, along with the winemaking, which we'll cover in a second, gives Port its flavor.

Port can also be white, using the grapes Gouveio, Malvasia Fina, and Viosinho, but most white Port is for everyday, domestic consumption so don't expect it on store shelves unless you're in Portugal.

Once grapes are harvested in September, the fruit is crushed (occasionally by foot, commonly by gentle press) and fermented until half the sugar turns to alcohol. Then the grape soup gets drunk on brandy! The winemakers pour in a clear, potent, young brandy to stop fermentation. It mingles with the crushed grapes until spring, when the wine moves down the Douro River to be aged, blended, bottled, and sold (see Port Production in Oporto).

Although fortified wine is the cash cow of the Douro and the most important product, this area didn't start out growing grapes for Port. Until the late 1600s when Port became a preferred drink of the English and an industry was established to buy grapes from this area, producers made dry wine. They never stopped, and today quality is rising, as the best labels are using more than just the leftovers from Port production to create memorable dry reds—especially of Touriga Nacional and Tinta Roriz. Douro reds have intense fruit aromas and flavors and tend to be higher in alcohol with firm tannin and acid. If you love a full Tempranillo from Spain or a hearty Cabernet from Napa, this may be your next favorite region.

CLOSEST CITIES: *The Douro is northeast of Lisbon. It's 3.5 hours by car, 5 hours by train with connections in Oporto.*

Port Production in Oporto

Situated on the coast, this city is weird because no grapes grow here, yet it's a wine hub. After growing grapes, crushing them, and fortifying them in the Douro Valley, producers (or shippers, as they're known) ship or truck the fortified, unfinished wine west to age in LODGES (wineries) in a suburb of Oporto called Vila Nova de Gaia (VEE-lah NOH-va deh GUY-uh).

The largest shippers are mostly of English descent—Cockburn, Sandeman, Taylor Fladgate, and Symingtons—since the English were the first to exploit Portugal's fortified winemaking prowess, creating a giant export market for the stuff back home.

You should know the styles of Port so you can shop for it. The world of Port is divided into how it's aged once it reaches

Oporto and Vila Nova de Gaia: It is either mostly in an oak cask or mostly in a bottle. Oak-aged Ports are ready to drink on release, but those matured in bottle are the responsibility of the buyer—it can take two or three decades before they're ready to go, so you have to store them and have patience not to drink them. If you're shopping and don't have this book with you, price will be a tip-off here—bottle-aged Ports will drain your wallet. Oak-aged, not so much.

Port changes with age, and how it's aged changes the flavor of the wine. With time, harsh tannins and overt fruitiness mellow out. Here are the main categories with notes on flavor.

Mostly Oak-Aged Port

RUBY PORT: Simple, cheap, and ruby in color with red berry and dark cherry flavor. Ruby Port is sweet, and good ones have nice balance between fruit and acid. They're great with Cheddar cheese and anything chocolate.

LATE BOTTLED VINTAGE PORT (LBV PORT): From a single year and aged in wood for four to six years, some LBVs are unfiltered and need to be decanted before serving. Some are similar to vintage Port at a lower price. Although these were created by Taylor Fladgate in 1970 as an affordable "drink now" Port that had vintage Port qualities, don't expect too much—these wines generally have less character than the high-end stuff. The style varies by lodge, but expect dark fruit and sometimes earth or licorice notes. They're generally soft and sweet but have enough acidity and tannin to prevent them from being flabby. Try these wines with soft cheese or with chocolate-raspberry desserts.

TAWNY PORT: Many styles fall into the Tawny category, but the original was called tawny because ruby Ports were aged in oak and turned brownish or tawny in color. Over time they gained nutty and less fruity characteristics. These days, greedy producers have cut corners and the wine is

Q+A

How long can Port stay good after being left open?

Although there are variables and you should taste the Port for yourself to make sure you don't throw it out too early, here is a quick guide that may help you figure out how long you have before you need to ditch a half-consumed bottle.

Bottle-aged Ports: These are like red wine. You need to consume them within three to four days, maximum, for them to be good. The older the wine, the quicker you need to drink it, because the deterioration of flavor and structure starts as soon as you pop the cork and progresses quickly.

Basic ruby and tawny: It may be cheap, but this stuff can last a month or so in the fridge, so it's a good investment to make!

Quality tawny: If refrigerated, this can last up to a month after being opened.

Late-bottled vintage: This will last a week or two, if refrigerated.

just like ruby Port—young and not aged for long. It's now tawny because it's made from lighter-skinned grapes grown in cooler vineyards, not because of long aging. Producers still make the original kind but even this is shifty. You'll see an age on the bottle—ten, twenty, thirty, or forty years—but in a real dishonest move, this isn't how long the wine has aged; it's just a "target profile" for how old the producer wants the wine to seem. That said, real tawny Port wines are delicate, great when chilled, and go well with nutty cheeses and fruity custard or honey desserts.

COLHEITA PORT: Tawnies from a single year, bottled with a vintage and aged for more than seven years are colheita. These have to be consumed within a year of bottling to be good. The bottling date is on the label so look for it.

WHITE PORT: White Port is much less popular than red. When aged in casks, these wines are amber, nutty, and dry. But if you happen upon one, be careful because they can be sweet, even if labeled dry. White Port is great with nuts, olives, and a view of the Portuguese coast.

Mostly Bottle-Aged Port

VINTAGE PORT: The most expensive and coveted of all Ports, vintage Port represents only 1 percent of production. This is the stuff that's aged in a bottle for most of its life. In great years in the vineyard, the Port is made, aged for two to three years in an oak cask, and then released for the buyer to sit on for twenty or so years before drinking. Only three vintages in ten are generally "declared" to be worthy (another parallel to Champagne). When you open one of these, expect a giant amount of sediment (it's been twenty

years, so you have to expect that the wine has grown a proverbial long, white beard, no?). You have to decant these thick, fruity, and chocolaty wines that have a good amount of tannin and acid. The classic food for vintage Port is blue cheese, especially Stilton, but if you're like me and can't do blue, sheep's milk cheese or other salty, tangy foods are great stand-ins.

SINGLE QUINTA (SINGLE ESTATE): In years when a vintage isn't declared for vintage Port, estates will make wine that includes only grapes from their property. Generally this single quinta Port is aged by the producer. An increasing number of small producers are making their own versions, which will taste more like the land it grew in than the wine from the large shippers (similar to grower Champagne vs. big-brand Champagne). Depending on age, these can also pair with blue or sheep milk cheeses.

CRUSTED PORT: If you love sediment and are an expert at decanting, crusted Port is for you. These relatively rare wines age for a few years in a large cask and then spend time in a cellar until they're released. They aren't filtered so they "throw" a crust or make a bunch of thick sediment over time. They have the dark, dried fruit and chocolate flavors of a vintage Port but aren't quite as refined. They're also cheaper.

GARRAFEIRA: This strange kind of Port is from a single vintage and is bottle aged, but it has to be aged in a specific type of glass bottle called a demijohn. Garrafeira can be aged for two to four decades and then taste like a soft, tawny Port—spicy and toasty, with dried fruit and tobacco notes, and soft tannin. You can pair a Garrafeira with nuts and baked fruit desserts, similar to a tawny.

CLOSEST CITIES: *A straight shot north up the coast, Oporto is 2.5 hours by train or 3 hours by car from Lisbon.*

Bairrada

Unlike most of the wine regions of Portugal, this Atlantic-influenced, hilly place is the only large region where one grape dominates. That's the Baga grape, which can make nasty stuff—acidic, tannic, bitter, darkly colored, and just harsh—or, in the hands of the right producer, wines that have red and black fruit flavor, earthy nuance, and good balance. To get a good wine from Bairrada (BUY-haad-eh), watch the producer. It's the difference between sludge and excellent reds that can age for decades. Although the region is mostly known for reds, the white grape Bical is making serviceable wines and is a big contributor to the sparkling made here.

CLOSEST CITIES: *It's a 2-hour drive north from Lisbon to the small city of Mealhada, the center of the region.*

Dão

East of Bairrada is Dão (DOW), a landlocked, warm, north-central region that can create mighty blended red wines. After years of a failing co-op system that produced nasty wine, in the 1990s EU money helped the region modernize, and the wines are improving, with smaller quintas making high-quality reds and whites. Only 5 percent of Dão is dedicated to vineyard land but an endless number of grapes grow here, with Touriga Nacional, Tinta Roriz (Tempranillo), and a few other indigenous grapes leading the pack. The region has

been called the Burgundy of Portugal because the wines vary greatly depending on where they are grown. They tend to be subtler—ranging in flavor from light and spicy to fuller and fruity, but always with a lighter touch than wines of the Douro, for example. The Encruzado grape blended with other whites has great potential for almondlike, citrusy, cheek-coating wines, too.

CLOSEST CITIES: *Dão is about a 3-hour drive north from Lisbon.*

Lisboa and Setúbal

You don't have to go too far from Portugal's capital of Lisbon to hit vineyards. This vast area north and west of the city used to be called Estremadura, but the name was changed in 2009 to capitalize off the familiar name of the main city. Lisboa (LEESH-bo-ah) is classified as a Vinho Regional (VR), which is like Italy's IGP or France's Vin de Pays. It has several DOCs within its boundaries, but I've found the VR wines to be tasty and satisfying, which you can't always say about wines from larger appellations.

Lisboa runs alongside the Atlantic, and the best regions are inland from the coast in hills and mountains, which provide protection from fierce ocean winds. The main red grapes are Alicante Bouschet, Aragonez (Tempranillo), and the native Castelão, Tinta Miúda, Touriga Franca, Touriga Nacional, and Trincadeira. In the Vinho Regional of Lisboa, international grapes like Cabernet Sauvignon, Merlot, and Syrah are also permitted and complement the rich, fruity, spicy native grapes well. The whites, especially of native grapes Fernão Pires, Arinto, Malvasia, and

Vital, make spectacular full wines similar in body to those of the Rhône Valley but with a distinct combination of tropical, citrus, nut, and honey notes you'll only find here.

SETÚBAL (SEH-TO-BAHL), across the Tejo estuary from Lisbon, makes reds of Castelão (also known as Periquita) and sweet wines of Muscat, called Moscatel de Setúbal.

CLOSEST CITIES: *Each vineyard area is 35 to 40 minutes by car from Lisbon.*

Madeira

On a little volcanic island off the coast of Portugal is what was once the hub of wine shipments to Colonial America. Since this was the last place to stock up before ships made the voyage across the pond, wine needed to be included. And it wasn't just to make sailors jolly—it also helped fight scurvy! Who could ask for more?

But something else was strange about the wine from this island. Whereas most wines spoiled and tasted horrible after crossing the ocean, the wines from Madeira improved. The heat and the motion of the ship gave this wine a baked quality that suited it. It was a favorite of George Washington and perhaps the greatest American wine aficionado of the time, Thomas Jefferson.

Today, producers make the wine by storing it in hot stoves for a few months and then aging it for years in casks. The effect is the same as the ocean voyage— that baked quality remains the distinguishing feature. So if you hear someone say a wine tastes *maderized*, it means it has a baked-fruit quality.

Although Madeira isn't popular these days, you should be the lone buyer of it in your wine shop because it rocks. It ranges in style from dry to sweet and goes well with everything from nuts to cheese to dessert. It's worth trying a glass if you see it on a menu, or buying a bottle and serving it to friends to surprise them.

Another bonus: Good Madeira keeps getting better in the bottle and can be opened and then consumed over the course of a few months without being worse for wear! Some of the best Madeiras have been aged in a bottle for more than 150 years.

Madeira of any quality is going to be labeled with a year, which is an average of the vintages of the grapes harvested for the wine. You'll commonly see three, five, ten, fifteen, twenty, thirty, or forty-plus years on bottles. You'll see single vintage (FRASQUEIRA), which is wine from one grape, one vintage, and is aged for twenty to one hundred years. Colheita spends five years aging in oak. Top-quality versions come from one of the four grapes named in the sidebar.

CLOSEST CITIES: *The island of Madeira is in the Atlantic, southwest of Lisbon. It's a 2.25-hour flight.*

The Wrap-Up

With all Portugal has going for it—history, native grapes, interesting blends—it's a country on the brink of mass popularity, if it can get the marketing and export ducks in a row. Let's keep our fingers crossed for a Portuguese invasion!

SPAIN

In college (and high school, actually) I traipsed around Spain with my sister. We drank plenty (of wine and other stuff), but there were two problems. First, we weren't sophisticated enough to know what we were drinking. More importantly, we were in Spain at a time when wine, with the exception of Rioja and Sherry, was pretty bad. Second, we were about to kill each other on

LABELED BY GRAPE

The best Madeira is labeled with one of four top-quality grapes.

SERCIAL (SIR-SEE-AHL):
A dry-style wine, similar to a fino Sherry. Good with nuts or cheeses or alone as an aperitif.

•

VERDELHO (VER-HA-DEYL-oh):
Off dry or slightly sweet. You'll taste the smoky, baked, honeyed flavors typical of Madeira in this wine, which is great with hard smoked cheeses, nuts, or alone.

•

BUAL (BOO-AHL):
A sweet wine but lighter in style, smoky, and honeyed with great acidity and a light tanginess. This will be interesting with not-too-sweet cheesecake.

•

MALMSEY (A.K.A. MALVASIA):
Super sweet, brown, rich, honeyed, baked, and tangy, but the best ones have terrific acidity, making them ideal with fruit-based desserts like apple cobbler or cherry pie.

both trips, so that impeded any learning we may have done about the vinous pleasures of the area (a story for another book or for a therapist's office somewhere).

My how things have changed on all fronts (my sister and I are best buds)!

On the wine front, Spain is the opposite of bad. The Spanish are smart. They didn't waste the chance to modernize their wine industry and export market after receiving an infusion of money from the EU to improve viticulture and winemaking in the 1990s and early 2000s.

Like most of the Old World, wine is integral to Spanish culture. The country has been making wine since 4000 B.C., and even Moorish domination with its tee-totaling ways didn't stop winemakers or wine drinkers. Despite a lull in participation in the modern wine world due to some murky political leadership (the Franco dictatorship, lasting from 1939 to 1975, did the industry no favors), it should come as no surprise that Spain is a wine powerhouse and is only improving.

When Spain reentered the wine world in a significant way in the early 2000s, it didn't put on a wussy show. It went for it, guns a-blazin'. Producers entered the commercial export world with unabashed strength and confidence, and we wine lovers drank it up. It didn't matter that a lot of the stuff being sold was made from native grapes, blends, and regions we had never heard of before. The country showed no fear in introducing its authentic wares instead of using French grapes to pander to the "market."

Today, Spain is known for red blends, fresh whites, and fabulous stand-alone grapes. The quality for the value is impressive. The wines are accessible, pronounceable, and, when from warmer places, fruity and reminiscent of wines from the New World. The product and the attitude of the Spanish producers and distributors created an ideal situation for Spain and for those of us willing and wanting to try what the country had to offer. As Spain continues to modernize and improve its vineyard practices and winemaking techniques, the wine goodness gravy train is unending. With hundreds of native varieties, we can continue enjoying the bounty of this Iberian treasure.

There are so many great regions and up-and-comers that it's hard to narrow them down, but I'll split the Spanish wine world by mainly white wine regions and mainly red wine ones and offer advice on what to buy from each.

White Regions

RIAS BAIXAS (REE-as BUY-shush): The "low estuaries," as Rias Baixas translates, are known for beautiful beaches and excellent food. One big, important grape comes from this area: Albariño (Al-bah-REEN-yo). Some people say it's like a combo of Sauvignon Blanc and Riesling, but I think that does a great disservice to this grape. Grown by the sea in small estate vineyards, Albariño has lemon, peach, and sometimes tangerine aromas and flavors that contrast with its salty, stony mineral flavors and high acid to give the wine character. It is an ideal pairing with seafood.

My only caution: Make sure you buy from a good producer. In recent years, to appease American tastes especially, some producers have been leaving in residual sugar, letting the wine become creamy through malolactic fermentation (page 27) and, in some rare cases, using oak to enhance flavor, none of which I find to be good additions to this superstar grape.

CLOSEST CITIES: *The city of Pontevedra is about 9 hours by train or 6 hours by car northwest of Madrid.*

RUEDA (RUE-EH-DAH): Located on a high plain in northwest/central Castilla y León, Rueda has some of the best whites, made mostly of Verdejo, a grape that had dropped off the radar of winemakers until recently. The grape tastes like lime and lemon, and generally has an earthy, underbrush/shrubby smell. It has a slight bitterness and great mouth-cleansing acidity but

it's not sharp. In fact, it's usually silky or creamy in your mouth and makes you want to go in for another sip.

You need to know some background before you buy wine from Rueda. Wines labeled "Rueda" are only required to be 50 percent Verdejo; the rest is Sauvignon Blanc and Viura (called Macabeo in other parts of Spain). Wines labeled "Rueda Verdejo" are required to be 85 percent Verdejo, but many are 100 percent and usually indicate so on the bottle. Rueda Verdejo is what I prefer and what I described above, but you should try both to see what you like.

CLOSEST CITIES: *The train trip from Madrid north to Valladolid, which is close to many wineries, is a quick 1.25-hour ride. Drive time from Madrid is a little over 1 hour.*

CAVA: The sparkling wine of Spain, Cava is made in the Champagne method (page 54). It's a Denominación de Origen (DO) that covers eight areas around northern Spain. The regions go as far west as Rioja and Castilla y León (Ribera del Duero), generally considered red-wine country.

The Spanish have been making sparkling wine in the traditional method since 1872, and they're skilled at it. Although I've found that the quality has declined at the lower end (sad, because it used to be awesome), the stuff at the $20 to $25 level is spectacular and at half the price of most Champagne, well worth a try.

In 2017 the Consejo Regulador of Cava introduced **CAVA DE PARAJE CALIFICADO,** a top vineyard classification to give the best Cava makers a way to distinguish their exceptional terroir and wine. Twelve sites were initially approved—a mix of large wineries and small family-owned ones whose top wines go for more than $100 a bottle. To classify as this category, wines are aged at least three years in bottle, are brut or brut nature (page 141), and are vintage dated.

Cava is mainly white sparkling wine, but there is a rosé version that incorporates Cabernet Sauvignon, Garnacha (Grenache), and/or Monastrell. Some producers use Chardonnay and Pinot Noir, the traditional grapes of Champagne, but for the most part, the native Spanish varieties of Parellada (par-a-YAD-a), Xarel-lo (ha-RELL-o), and Macabeo (mahc-a-BEH-yo) are the standards. It's important to think of Cava as its own wine, not a Champagne substitute, since the grape flavors and earth quality make the wine its own deal.

CLOSEST CITIES: *The heart of Cava country, Sant Sadurni d'Anoia, is a 40-minute drive or 1-hour train ride from Barcelona.*

Red Regions

RIOJA (REE-OH-HA): Rioja is Spain's most revered wine region, and with good reason. This place has been a wine mecca for centuries, and I choose the word "mecca" purposefully: When pilgrims made a yearly trek to the holy site of Santiago de Compostela on the northwest coast of Spain, they stopped in Rioja's major city, Logroño, to rest, relax, and (being good Catholics) drink up! This yearly trek created a big market for the wines of Rioja, and the pilgrims helped spread the reputation of the area as a place with high-class wine. There are four important characteristics that determine Rioja's flavor: place, blend, oak, and length of aging.

The combo of grapes and terroir in this northern central plain makes for superb

---

THE IMPORTANCE OF AGING AND OAK

Riojanos love oak, and the traditional producers, especially, equate time in wood to quality. You'll see the following terms on a bottle when shopping.

SAYS NOTHING OR SAYS COSECHA: Probably not aged at all, these wines are fermented and then bottled. These are light, simple reds.

•

JOVEN: Not aged more than six months in oak, if at all.

•

CRIANZA: Aged for one to one and a half years in oak, with an additional year in bottle before release.

•

RESERVA: Aged in oak for one and a half to two years and then another one to two years in a bottle before release. These wines have more fruit and spice notes and are often layered in flavor. A weekend wine.

•

GRAN RESERVA: Aged in oak for two to three years and then another three years in the bottle. They're only made in great vintages, and this should be an expensive, special occasion wine if made with great grapes and high-quality winemaking (not always the case, which is why you can sometimes find these for $12).

---

results. And don't think Riojanos don't know it! In 1635, the mayor of Logroño prohibited horses and carts in the streets near wine cellars, to prevent vibration from wrecking the wine. Smart move, indeed, and certainly a government that supported its local industry!

The region has hot summers and cold winters, and is protected from the violent northern Atlantic winds by the Cantabrian Mountains. Two rivers, the Ebro and Oja, warm the vineyards of Rioja as well. There are three main production areas: Rioja Alta, Rioja Alavesa, and Rioja Baja. Traditionally, the highest-quality grapes came from the cooler hills and mountains of Alta and Alavesa, which have longer growing seasons. Winemakers used the full, fruity grapes from hotter Baja to goose up the fruitiness, body (alcohol), and color of the blend. But the times are changing and that's not the case anymore—great grapes come from meticulous producers in all three areas these days.

It may surprise you that Rioja, though mostly associated with reds, is a multi-colored affair. It's made in white, which is mostly Viura, with Malvasía blanca and Garnacha blanca as supporting players. You'll also find Rioja as a tasty Rosado (rosé), which is usually a blend of Tempranillo and Garnacha. For the reds, Tempranillo is the lead horse, with Garnacha, Graciano, and Mazuelo (Carignan) used for floral and red fruit aromatics, alcohol, and color.

this remote area, and it laid in relative obscurity until the 1990s, when a few key producers burst onto the scene with fruity yet earthy wines made from grapes grown in the abundant sun on the black slate and quartz soils here.

Along with Rioja, Priorat is one of two highly distinguished areas of quality in Spain (Denominación de Origen Calificada or DOCa). Once you taste a great Priorat, you'll know why it deserves the distinction. Priorat is mouth filling, with chewy tannins, dark raspberry and plum fruit flavors, and a healthy dose of minerality. Some have Cabernet Sauvignon, Syrah, and Merlot to add dimension, which often works well with the densely flavored Garnacha that grows here. Although oak aged, most aren't oaky, and that makes the wines and the terroir stand out even more. There are only about ninety producers in the area, so supply is limited and what's around will cost you at least $25, but it's worth it.

Priorat also makes a small quantity of white wine, mostly of Garnacha Blanca (white Grenache) with Macabeo, Chenin Blanc, and Pedro Ximenez sometimes blended in. The best are rich, full wines— like white Châteauneuf-du-Pape blanc, but for a lot less money. If you like full whites, seek these out. I love them!

CLOSEST CITIES: *Logroño is northeast of Madrid, about 3.5 hours by train or car. It is northwest of Barcelona, 4 hours by train, 5 hours by car. You can also fly there from either city.*

PRIORAT (PREE-AR-OTT): Decadent, delicious reds of mainly Garnacha (a.k.a. Grenache) and Cariñena (Carignan) are the specialty of Priorat in northeastern Spain. Although the region has a long history, phylloxera (page 45) decimated

CLOSEST CITIES: *Gratallops, the major wine hub in Priorat, is a 2-hour drive or 2.5-hour train ride southwest from Barcelona.*

RIBERA DEL DUERO (REE-BEAR-A DELL DWEAR-OH): On a high (3,000 feet/850 m), dry plateau just southwest of Rioja but still in north-central Spain lies Ribera del Duero, another Iberian stronghold of red wine. The region is known for dramatic diurnals (hot days, cold nights that can swing 40°F/21°C in a day), and the wines have a combination of fruit and acidity that's hard to rival anywhere in the world. Vega Sicila, one of the most expensive wines of Spain, hails from Ribera del Duero.

I have had good versions, but in my experience Ribera del Duero is unreliable and hard to get a handle on. In every price point under $30, I've found equal amounts of great and terrible stuff with little rhyme or reason. I find Tempranillo, which makes up the base of the wine (called Tinto Fino or Tinto del País here), is erratic in flavor when grown in Ribera del Duero. The high-end stuff is often but not always alcoholic and tannic, and can be overwhelming. Could be the temperature or the windswept soils in these parts, but unless you're dedicated and willing to try and try again, be prepared for a roller-coaster ride when you try the wines from this region. Wine critics go nuts for Ribera del Duero, but of all Spain's well-known gems, this is, for me, the most unpolished, and with so many other great Tempranillo options, I usually pass it up.

CLOSEST CITIES: *Madrid is 1 to 1.5 hours by car or 30 minutes by train to Segovia and Valladolid (which overlaps with Rueda) and 2.5 hours by car or train directly north to Burgos, where many wineries have tasting rooms.*

WHICH CAMP? CHECK THE LABEL

Two camps exist in Rioja. It can be hard to discern them, but if you use the label as a guide, you'll almost always get it right.

LAS TRADICIONALISTAS The traditional style is driven by what's known as the Centenarian Bodegas, which have been around and owned by the same families for more than a century. These bodegas benefited from a huge migration of French winemakers over the Pyrenees, when that vicious serial vine killer, phylloxera (page 45), hit Bordeaux in the 1860s and put them out of a job. The traditional producers have distinct styles—the wines tend to be lower in alcohol and higher in oak, so spicy and woodsy. The main wineries are CVNE (Companía Vinícola del Norte de España), La Rioja Alta, Muga, López de Heredia, Marqués de Riscal, Marqués de Murrieta, and Bodegas Riojanas. They have traditional-looking labels.

LAS MODERNISTAS A younger generation of winemakers has learned techniques from Australian and American winemakers, and the wines taste more like New World wines. In the past, I've found these to be blah—flavorless and boring. But recently, there's been a shift. Producers are making wines that have less spice and oak, and are instead showcasing the fruit and the land, which makes for distinctive wines. These wines are worth a try if you don't want a dark, brooding, oaky wine, as the traditional producers often make. Modern producers' labels are usually artistic, colorful, and simple—more like California wine labels than old school French or Italian ones—so they are easy to spot.

JUMILLA/YECLA (HU-MEE-ya/YAY-cla):
I mention this area because *I* love it, not because it gets a ton of attention. Here, the Monastrell grape (known as Mourvèdre in France) creates wines that are massively fruity, layered, and high in alcohol, but still have balance and an earthy, farmyard character. These wines are often terrific values (you can get solid ones for $15) and taste like dirt-driven versions of Californian or Australian wines that are three times the price of Jumilla. For someone just starting to explore Old World wines, Jumilla/Yecla is a great jumping-off point. And for the price, if it's an epic fail and you hate it, at least you haven't spent a fortune!

CLOSEST CITIES: *Jumilla is only about a 2-hour drive southwest from the coastal city of Valencia. Madrid is 3.5 hours north and Barcelona a little more than 5 hours northeast of Jumilla.*

Fortified Wine

JEREZ/SHERRY: No, Sherry is not just a cooking wine or a sipper for old British ladies! Real Sherry is from the Jerez (her-ETH) area in southern Spain and it's cool stuff ("Sherry" is the English bastardization of the Spanish Jerez). They've been making wine around Cádiz in southern Spain (called the Sherry Triangle by wine dorks) since about 1100 B.C. But Sherry, a fortified wine made in a mind-bogglingly complex way, is what brought fame to the region.

And thanks to some marketing efforts from producers, wine lovers the world over are rediscovering this hard-to-make, different-tasting wine and finding that from predinner to dessert, Sherry can be mind-blowing. I love Sherry and I hope I

can, at minimum, entice you to seek some out to see if you can become a fan.

First, Sherry Winemaking . . .

VINEYARD AND GRAPE: Like all great wine, terroir is a huge part of making great Sherry. The star grape is Palomino, which grows best on the white, chalky, moisture-retaining Albariza soils of the area. Palomino makes up about 90 percent of all Sherry grapes grown and with good reason—it's a bland grape, which lends itself to total manipulation in the cellar. Moscatel and Pedro Ximénez, the backup singers of the trio, grow on darker and sandier soils and are used to provide the aroma and heft that their leading lady lacks. Since Sherry gets most of its flavor from what the winemaker does, not from the grape, this bland characteristic is essential.

WINEMAKING: What's so complicated? Well, once the grapes get pressed and fermented, the wine can go in different directions. After a "base" wine is made, the winemakers taste the batches and determine the quality to figure out which style of Sherry will work for each barrel. Some will turn into delicate, crisp finos,

some will be more robust olorosos, some will become amontillados—but let's not jump the gun by listing the wine types here before we get into the convoluted way this wine gets made.

After each batch's fate is determined, the winemaker fortifies the wine (adding a mixture of half old Sherry and half brandy) to bring it to more than 15 percent alcohol. Then blending and aging throw things into a tailspin.

AGING: Riojanos aren't the only ones who love to age fermented grapes in oak for long periods of time. The folks from Jerez take it to a new level.

There are two big categories of Sherry that most types fall into, or fall in between. These have to do with what happens to the wine once it's in the tank. Biological aging, as it's called, happens to finos. Oxidative aging happens with olorosos.

So, finos (FEE-nos) are a type of Sherry aged in casks that allow a little air to get in. In the marine, salty air of the towns where aging occurs, a special yeast that looks like a flower (and is called *flor*, "flower" in Spanish) grows on top of the wine, completely changing the flavor and removing the juice's acidic bite (see picture, page 224).

The tougher olorosos (oh-lo-ROE-so) don't get any flowery yeast—these are lesser quality and are fortified to an alcohol level that's too high for pretty yeast flowers to grow on the wine. Instead, winemakers age oloroso in open-air casks so the juice can get more concentrated in flavor and in alcohol, as water evaporates.

THE SOLERA: Each wine then enters its own crazy system of aging. Winemakers organize the barrels by age in the cellar (called a *solera*). Every so often (they figure out when the time is right), they move some younger wine and combine it with the next oldest wine. So they take vintage 2013 and combine it with some of vintage 2012, and move some wine from 2012 into 2011, and on and on until they get to the stuff in the oldest barrels. Because they take a fraction of the wine out and replace it with younger wine, the system is called FRACTIONAL BLENDING; basically wine musical chairs.

The wine that's ready to be bottled is labeled with the average age of the combined wines. You may see VOS (very old Sherry, at least twenty years old) or VORS (very old rare Sherry, at least thirty years old) on the bottle to signal that the wine has been hanging around the cellar for longer than the run-of-the-mill stuff.

By doing this fractional blending, the producer maintains its style from year to year. As young wine mingles with old wine, Sherry gains a consistency in flavor and lots of complexity.

Styles

Because the winemaker has so much control over decisions with Sherry, there are seemingly an endless number of styles.

FINO: Fino is dry, pale, straw colored, and strong in alcohol, and has a twangy bite that's hard to describe. It needs to be served cold to be good.

MANZANILLA (MAHN-ZAH-NEE-YA): Manzanilla is fino made in a place called Sanlúcar de Barrameda, which is right on the ocean. Producers believe the salty air gives the wine a saline character. I find manzanilla more interesting than the usual finos.

AMONTILLADO (AH-MOHN-TEE-YAHD-OH):
An aged fino that lost its delicacy in the aging when its flowery yeast stopped working, this wine is nutty and minerally in flavor. Amontillado is my favorite Sherry style. If it develops full, heavy aromas but maintains its lightness, the rare PALO CORTADO style is made.

OLOROSO: Dry, but full, with nutty, dried-fruit aromas, oloroso is amber or nearly brown in color. This style is a full-bodied, higher-alcohol sipper that is the best intro to Sherry for regular wine drinkers because it is most like a combo of wine and hard liquor.

There are also sweet Sherries, which are sweetened olorosos for the most part. Here are a few you may see:

MEDIUM SHERRY AND PALE CREAM SHERRY:
Slightly sweetened. Medium Sherry is a blend of amontillado and oloroso; pale cream is a combination of fino and amontillado.

CREAM SHERRIES: Despite the name, these "cream" wines don't contain dairy. They're just sweet olorosos.

BROWN SHERRY AND EAST INDIA SHERRY:
Low-quality wines, these types are made from cheap oloroso that's heavily sweetened and colored using Moscatel grape extract.

PEDRO XIMÉNEZ (PX) AND MOSCATEL: Made from the backup singers of Sherry, PX and moscatel show their real talent in the form of sweet, brown dessert Sherries that are otherworldly when poured on top of ice cream or enjoyed with a creamy dessert.

CLOSEST CITIES: *Because the region is located in far southern Spain, you will need to fly or take a long train ride from the major northern cities to get here and commit to spending a few nights before returning. The area is only about 1 hour south from the beautiful city of Sevilla by train or car and about 2 hours southwest by train and 2.5 hours by car from Córdoba, if you happen to be exploring parts south.*

The Wrap-Up

There are other great-quality areas in Spain—Toro for rich Tempranillo, Bierzo for spicy, medium-bodied Mencía, and Calatayud and Navarra for Garnacha. Basque country sports Txakolina (chock-o-LEEN-ah), one of my favorite rocky, minerally whites. Málaga and Montilla-Moriles also make Sherry-style wines. And new regions with high-quality wines are cropping up all the time. Your mission: Explore and report back. Spain is full of value and of excellent wines that you'll quickly find are the gift that keeps on giving.

UNITED KINGDOM

Without climate change, this chilly island nation at latitude 51° north (out of the grape-growing band of latitude 30° to 50° north) could never entertain the idea of winemaking, but Mother Nature has obliged and now England has a growing niche market.

People have tried since Roman times to make viticulture work here, but it wasn't until the 1970s that it started to go. The chalk escarpment that runs through Champagne continues west and runs through southern England, and that means the soil types are prime for making crisp, acidic, and minerally whites. Taking advantage of south-facing slopes, and long days of sun during the summer, the grapes can ripen in most years. Although the wines made in these difficult conditions are improving, we do need to keep perspective—only a few years in a decade are solid, and some years are total busts!

More than 80 percent of UK wine is white, and most of the remaining balance is mainly acidic, light, aromatic, and floral rosé. Still wine can be made from a variety of grapes but Chardonnay and Pinot Noir are 40 percent of plantings. Sparkling wine is produced mainly from Chardonnay, Pinot Noir, and Pinot Meunier, the traditional grapes of Champagne.

The UK wine industry is relatively small and largely reliant on tourism to stay afloat, but it is now a serious force and demand for the wines is consistent. From Kent to East and West Sussex to Surrey and into Wales, the wines can and do compete on the world stage and hold their own.

Right now the UK wine industry has 135 wineries that make about 4.5 million bottles. But if it can scale production and if the climate change stays as it is, the UK will surely be an upcoming source of cool-climate whites and sparklers. One to watch, for sure.

CLOSEST CITIES: *Kent is 1 hour southeast of London by car or train. West Sussex is 1.5 hours south by car and train, and Surrey is a 40-minute train ride or 50-minute drive southwest of London.*

Central and Eastern Europe
CROATIA

Here's an up-and-comer with a big history behind it: Winemaking began on the Dalmatian Coast of Croatia in about 2200 B.C., expanded further under the Greeks in A.D. 390, and then again under the Romans. That makes Croatia a country with a far older winemaking tradition than most of western Europe.

This area on the western edge of the Balkan Peninsula has had its share of hardships, so it's been difficult for Croatians to build a strong export market for a sustained period of time. Between Ottoman rule (teetotalers), phylloxera, and world and civil wars, they've had a tough go. But as things have settled down for Croatia politically, tourism on its breathtaking coastline has expanded, and winemaking is growing at a rapid clip.

So what should you seek out? With 130 indigenous grapes, there's no shortage of interesting wine in Croatia. Sixty percent of the wine is white and most of that is made from Malvasia and Graševina (GRAH-shay-veenah), also known as Welschriesling. In the cool continental area, which stretches across the plains to the Danube River in the northeast, you'll find crisp, mineral-driven whites made mainly of Graševina. It's lean, bright, light, and citrusy. Traminac (Traminer), Riesling, and Pinot Bijeli (Pinot Blanc) and medium-bodied reds from Frankovka (Blaufränkisch), Cabernet Franc, Cabernet Sauvignon, Merlot, Pinot Crni (Pinot Noir), and Zweigelt can be had, too.

The higher-quality wine areas are on the coast of Croatia. In Istria, Malvasia Istriana, the local clone of the floral, fruity

Malvasia white grape, is the popular wine. White Žlahtina (zzh-LACHK-teen-ah), grown only on the island of Krk (KIRK), with citrus and pear notes, soft round textures, and low acidity, and the red Teran, full of juicy black fruit flavors and medium tannins, are famed. Istria, which used to be part of the Venetian Empire, has a strong Italian influence, which you may be able to taste in the acidic, herbal nature of the whites.

The Dalmatian area, with its warm, sunny climate, produces a variety of fruity wines from native grapes—look for whites Debit, Pošip (POH-ship), and Maraština (mu-RUSH-teen-ah). Good Debit is like a minerally Sauvignon Blanc but with more lime than grapefruit flavor. With oak age, this wine can be like a medium-bodied Chardonnay. Pošip can be full-bodied with an oily, heavy texture and pear, apple, fig, and peach notes with honey and herbal flavors. Maraština is dry and full-bodied, with peach, nut, and floral aromas and a full, viscous texture. The red Plavac Mali (Plah-VAAHTS MA-lee), the offspring of Zinfandel, is dense, high in alcohol and tannin, peppery, smoky, and spicy.

CLOSEST CITIES: *Venice, Italy, is a 2.5-hour drive to the wine towns of Istria. From the coastal city of Dubrovnik, the Pelješac Peninsula and neighboring wine areas are 1 hour north. Regions farther north are a 2- to 3-hour drive from Dubrovnik. Towns of Slavonia, the most esteemed area, are 1.5 to 2 hours east of Zagreb by car.*

THE REPUBLIC OF GEORGIA

Georgia is a small country at the intersection where eastern Europe meets Asia. It's a fascinating place that's just getting back to wine after years of bad bulk winemaking under Soviet rule, but I include it because the primary wine region of Kakheti in the Caucasus Mountains is considered to be the birthplace of wine, and that's nothing to sneeze at!

Nearly all parts of Georgia produce wine because it has such a wide-ranging climate. It makes lots of different styles but the country is currently trendy because of its tradition of creating ORANGE WINES, which are whites whose grapes are left in contact with their skins for days to months, giving the finished wines a dark color and a tannic bite, similar to a light red. Georgian orange wines have been made for centuries, using *qveri* (KWHERE-vree), 1,000-liter (264-gallon) beeswax-coated terra-cotta jars. These are filled with wine and then buried in the ground, which keeps the wine at the right temperature during fermentation and puts the white wine juice in contact with the skins and seeds, leading to orange wine.

Five hundred or more indigenous grapes grow in Georgia, but primary grapes for wine are the red Saperavi, which makes rustic, rough, dark yet aromatic wines with high acid and alcohol levels, and the white Rkatsiteli (rh-kat-see-TELLY), which is acidic with pear and mineral notes.

CLOSEST CITIES: *Kakheti is a 1.5-hour drive west of Tblisi.*

HUNGARY

Of the eastern European countries trying to become players in the big markets of the west—Croatia, Bulgaria, Romania, and Hungary—Hungary is the one with the highest potential. Hungary, like these other countries, became a satellite nation of the former USSR, but unlike those nations, many of the vineyards remained in the hands of small producers during the country's time behind the Iron Curtain. That meant that although producers needed capital to improve, there wasn't a huge gap in production when Hungary democratized. Although Hungarian wine hasn't hit the export market en masse, today the country makes more wine than Austria. Currently only 20 percent is exported; that could change overnight if the country ramps up its marketing.

Wine has been made here since the Romans set up shop, but the area stumbled in production a few times, specifically during the 150 years of Muslim rule in 1500s to the late 1600s and then when producers lacked capital to modernize during the nearly fifty years under the Communist regime. But there was always a shining light for Hungary: Tokaji.

In the 1700s, this sweet wine from a small plateau near the Carpathian Mountains captured the attention of celebs from Voltaire to Beethoven and of monarchs from Sweden to France. Regardless of Hungary's political challenges, there's been a market for this wine for centuries. The country makes a variety of other wine, but ultimately Tokaji, with its perfectly balanced, honeyed sweetness and acid, is what has kept Hungary on the wine map and relevant to the west when the country could have faded into obscurity.

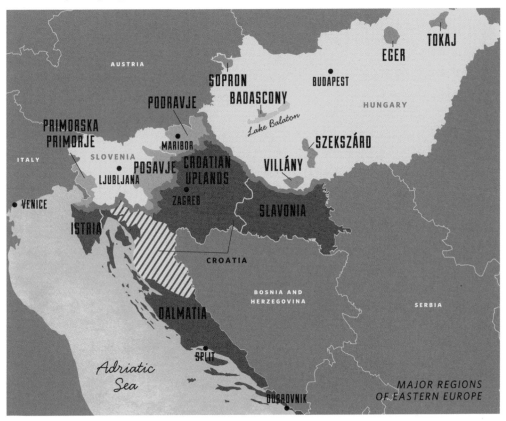

MAJOR REGIONS OF EASTERN EUROPE

with strong acidity that balances the wines and makes them ideal with (or as) dessert.

The rest of the wines made in the Tokaji region are dry or slightly sweet and mainly white. You'll see them named by grape variety: Tokaji Furmint and Tokaji Hárslevelü are most common. Expect the Furmint to be like honey and Golden Delicious apples and Hárslevelü to have a full body and honeyed flavor.

CLOSEST CITIES: *The town of Tokaj is a 2.5-hour drive northeast of Budapest.*

EGER: You may have seen Bull's Blood of Eger or Egri Bikavér on a shelf somewhere. It's normally a cheap red, and its fun name means lots of shops carry it. Based on Kékfrankos (Blaufränkisch in Austria), Bull's Blood can be good, but most of the wine exported is cheap, mass-produced swill, so beware. The producers of Eger are trying to shake the low-rent image but aren't

Although some of the best wines in Hungary are native gems that we won't see without going there, the value and quality of exports are rising so don't be surprised if these wines wind up on your shopping list in the next few years.

Of the twenty-two wine regions in Hungary, two are easy to find on shelves.

TOKAJI: Although it represents less than 1 percent of Hungary's output, Tokaji is responsible for the country's wine reputation on a global scale. Tokaji aszú, known as Tokay in English-speaking regions, is an amber-colored dessert wine made from botrytis-affected (page 57), dried grapes (*aszú* means "dry"). The aszú vary in sweetness (measured in *puttonyos* from three to six, if you see that on the bottle), with *aszú-eszencia* at the pinnacle of off-the-chart sweet wines. The long growing season of the area allows the Furmint grape (the main ingredient in Tokaji) and its floral, spicy partner Hárslevelü to develop botrytis and concentrate sugars. The flavors are nutty, honeyed, and sweet,

HUNGARIAN WINE PRONUNCIATIONS

Hungarian isn't the most intuitive language, so here's an assist.

WINE TYPES:
Tokaji: TOKE–ay–ee
Aszú: ah-SUE
Puttonyos: POOT-on-yos
Aszú-eszencia: ah-SUE es-EN-zia

GRAPES:
Furmint: FOOR-mint
Hárslevelü: HARSH-levelu
Kékfrankos: CAKE-frank-os
Egri Bikavér: EGG-ree beek-a-VER

there yet. Good versions of Kékfrankos are similar to Austrian Blaufränkisch—dark red in color, with black pepper and plum aromas and flavors and soft tannins with good acidity to keep it bright. Eger is also making citrusy, acidic Chardonnay, so don't be afraid to pick some up if you see it.

CLOSEST CITIES: *Eger is about a 1.5-hour drive northeast of Budapest.*

SLOVENIA

Slovenia may have been behind the Iron Curtain, but it never lost its winemaking moxie. The country is on the border of the Friuli region of Italy (page 198), and Slovenian whites were shipped and consumed in Western Europe despite the restrictions under the Communist regime. Stretching from the Italian border down the Adriatic Sea to Croatia, and east nearly to Austria and Hungary, this small country is full of rolling hills that make for ideal winegrowing conditions. Slovenia makes wines of every type—red, white, sparkling, sweet—and much of it is high quality. Despite the potential, Slovenians have issues on the business side—theirs is a fragmented industry and, as a result, Slovenia hasn't been a player in the world wine market.

Slovenia is known for its whites, the best of which can be found from vineyards on the Adriatic Coast near Italy. You'll find Ribolla Gialla, Fruiliano, and Pinot Grigio, which range from light, minerally, and citruslike in the case of the first two, to full and robust in the case of the Pinot Grigio. Styles vary, but winemakers often use malolactic fermentation (page 27) and

have a proclivity for oak, so expect a full, rich style. Orange wine (page 228) is popular here as well.

CLOSEST CITIES: *The main wine regions around Goriška are about a 1-hour drive north from Trieste in Italy. Inland areas are a 1.5-hour drive from the city of Maribor.*

The Wrap-Up

Getting stuck behind the Iron Curtain for decades when the rest of the world moved at a fast clip didn't do central and eastern Europe any favors with regard to many things, including wine. But with these countries working to catch up, they're prime for investment leading to a wine renaissance. I wouldn't be surprised if we saw one or two of them (my money's on Hungary and Croatia) become trendy wine regions in the next decade.

Middle East
LEBANON

The "Wines of Lebanon" website states that there is evidence that winemaking was established in this area in 7000 B.C. That contradicts other info available, but it is clear that the Phoenicians brought wine and winemaking ideas from Lebanon to Greece, Rome, and southern Spain, and from there things took off. Lebanon has had a tumultuous recent history, but the country has a role to play in today's wine world.

Although much of the country is mercilessly hot and dry, the high plateau of the BEKAA VALLEY, at 3,300 feet (1,000 m) elevation, moderates temperatures, yielding quality red grapes. Fruity, rich Cabernet

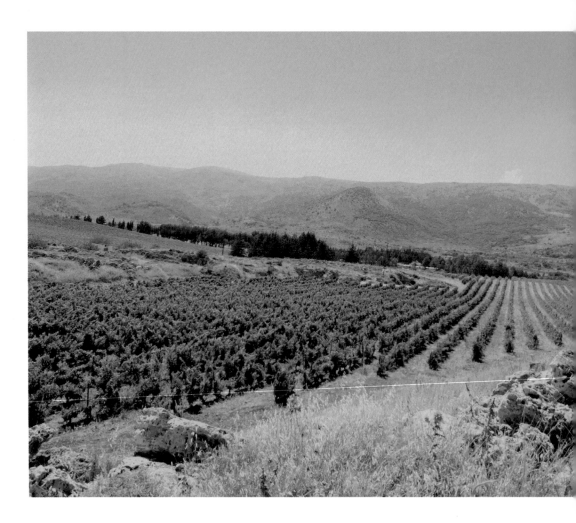

Sauvignon blends are available, but Rhône varieties—especially heat-tolerant Grenache, Carignan, Mourvèdre, and Cinsault—may present the best future for Lebanon. Native grapes exist (the whites Obaideh and Merwah, related to Chardonnay and Semillon, respectively), but these are minor players in production.

Château Musar, established in 1930 and recognized by leading British journalists at the 1967 Bristol Wine Fair, is the most popular winery whose wines are available outside Lebanon, but a handful of other wineries are building the reputation of the region, too.

ISRAEL

With double the plantings and much more export muscle than Lebanon, Israel is also a player in the wine export scene. Various hillside and mountain sites mitigate the hot temperatures, and Golan Heights, Mount Meron near Lebanon, and Galilee have pockets at altitude to help grapes maintain acidity. Quality wineries are producing reds from Cabernet Sauvignon, Merlot, Shiraz, and old vine Carignan that are highly rated and rich, albeit still hard to get your hands on.

tip

Watch out: **Although most wines exported from Israel are kosher, some are not. If you need a kosher wine, do not assume that if it's from Israel it's kosher. Better to google kosher wine and find one that fits the criteria than make this assumption.**

The Wrap-Up

I struggled to decide what should be included in this "other" section of winemaking regions. Should I include China? What about Turkey? Are the Czech Republic and Romania about to light the wine world on fire? What about India? Ultimately, I based my decision on the regions that I feel are up and coming now. Does that mean that in the future Turkish wine or Japanese wine won't be the next big thing? No. All it says is that in my gut and my conversations with trusted people in the industry, these are the regions I think you should know about. There are more—there's always more—but this is a fair representation of places that are showing major promise.

6 | NEW WORLD
REGI

W
RLD
ONS

f the Old World is the "old soul" of wine, the New World is the risk-taking, rambunctious soul. There are fewer rules and experimentation is the order of the day in most New World regions.

Despite differences, the tie between the "worlds" is strong. The influence of the Old World permeates the New World. We see hints of tradition and a harkening back to the past often. For example, the German immigrants who came to Australia planted Riesling in the Eden Valley of South Australia—something that may never be considered today. French varietals are big in Chile because the Chilean elite took a shine to Bordeaux and sought to recreate those wines outside of Santiago, the capital city.

In most parts of the New World, weather is warmer and more predictable, and vineyard sites have traditionally been chosen based on climate, although now more care is paid to soil and drainage, sun exposure, elevation, etc. In general, Mother Nature takes a gentler hand in the New World, so weather (therefore vintage variation) is often less of a roller coaster ride. The careful attention you pay to vintage in Bordeaux or Burgundy, France may not be as crucial to the wine's character in Napa, California in the United States or in Central Otago, New Zealand.

Given how big and diverse New World winegrowing regions are, we can't completely generalize on flavor or style. What we can say is that where Old World wines can throw some funky, unexpected flavors in the mix, New World wines are often more fruit driven and winemaker influenced because of the New World focus on technology. These wines are sippable and easier to understand.

It's for that reason that I always tell new wine drinkers to start out in the New World. You can taste the sun from most New World regions. And the varietal labelling makes it easy to figure out what you're drinking, which can give you confidence when you're starting to learn more about wine.

Similar to the Old World section of the book, this chapter provides country overviews. After the overviews, you'll find larger areas listed first, followed by descriptions of the important subregions. I note this for clarification in reading but also because if you read the Old World section first, you need to know the New World is a different animal. In Europe, the appellation system is driven by laws about yield, winemaking techniques, grapes, blending, etc. There is less guesswork about what's in the bottle. In the New World, we have to be a bit more cautious—there is no DOC versus DOCG or AOC versus Vin de Pays. When you are shopping for New World wines, you need to take note of the region and specifically the size of the region. If the label calls out the larger region, the wine can have some of the characteristics of the smaller ones that lay within, but they are often generic, "meh" bottles. As a rule of thumb, the smaller the region, the better or more typical the wine, which is why you'll want to read about them and seek them out!

The Southern Hemisphere
ARGENTINA

When I was five or six, my sister and I were obsessed with *Evita*, the musical about the rise of the beloved (or reviled, depending on whom you ask) Argentinean political figure Eva Perón. We played the tape (yes, we're that old) 5 million times and sang out of the photocopied libretto until we knew every single word. The glitch was that even though I could sing and she really couldn't, my sister made me perform all the parts of the dudes and secondary characters so she could be Evita. The joys of being a younger sister! Putting that bitter memory aside, all this is to say that I've loved Argentina since then, and accordingly I felt a certain level of preliminary comfort with it when Argentina allowed the rest of us access to their vast and delicious wine treasury.

When these wines hit the market, wine lovers the world 'round were thrilled with the plummy, spicy, smooth, affordable Malbec. The ideal mountain climate of the main growing region of Mendoza, the influence of Italian and French winemakers on Argentina, and the unique clone of a tertiary grape of Bordeaux (Malbec)

Q+A

Allow us access? What does that mean?

Until they were threatened with financial ruin and hyperinflation in the 1990s, Argentines drank almost everything they made. Argentina is the fifth-largest producer of wine in the world, so that's saying something about their love of wine!

gave Argentina serious clout. As a white counterpart to Malbec, Torrontés, a cross of the unimpressive conquistador import, Criolla Chica (called Pais in Chile), and an impressive one, the fragrant, lovely Muscat d'Alexandria, were exported. Argentina led with its strength: unique, likeable grapes.

For clarification, France still grows Malbec. But the type of Malbec in Mendoza has taken a different path from that of Cahors, the French stronghold of the grape. In Argentina, deep, plummy, velvety reds are usually well balanced with soft acid and tannin. The bright sun, cool nights, and abundant snowmelt for irrigation make the wines easy to drink and fruity, unlike their dense, tannic French counterparts.

There's been consistent quality and good news out of Argentina for about a decade now. But like most new regions that get "hot" in the wine business, too many cooks spoil the broth. Sadly, the $10 or $15 Malbec is not even close to the quality of when it launched. As big

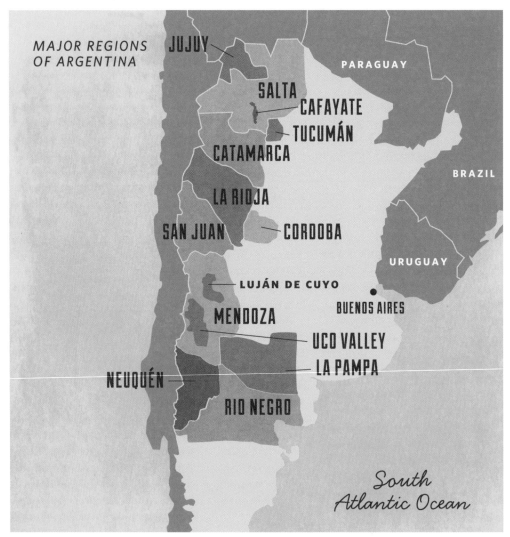

MAJOR REGIONS
OF ARGENTINA

JUJUY

PARAGUAY

SALTA
CAFAYATE
TUCUMÁN

CATAMARCA

BRAZIL

LA RIOJA

SAN JUAN

CORDOBA

URUGUAY

LUJÁN DE CUYO

BUENOS AIRES

MENDOZA

UCO VALLEY

LA PAMPA

NEUQUÉN

RIO NEGRO

South
Atlantic Ocean

companies from the United States, Spain, and France have invested and more people have become Malbec fans, there's a giant volume of wine produced and the quality has suffered. There are still a few winners, but these days I have to spend more than $20 for a good Malbec.

As for other grapes, Argentina has been diversifying its exports but has had a hard time growing the "international" grapes well—I find the Chardonnay to be forgettable and the Cabs to be bitter or simple (there are exceptions at the $25-plus price point, but at that level there are better substitutions around the world for less). So that leaves me with Malbec and kick-ass

Torrontés. I hope Argentina continues to produce outstanding fruity Malbec—it's too great a wine to spoil and only Argentina can do it this well. I believe it will, and with smaller regions like La Rioja and San Juan improving in quality, we may see even more interesting wines to come.

A note as we get to the two most important regions of Argentina: You should know that most of the wine regions are far from large cities. From a travel perspective, this makes it hard to get there, but the distance also avoids the very real issues of pollution or suburban sprawl that can affect grape quality. These remote places create an untouched environment for vines, resulting in wines that have lovely, clean fruit flavors that taste the same in the bottle as off the vine.

Mendoza

Argentina's largest winegrowing region by far, Mendoza is where wine investment, growing, and quality are centered. Grapes thrive at latitude 32° to 33° south because of the altitude—the vineyards are in the foothills of the Andes Mountains. The best areas for Malbec—the Uco Valley and Lujan de Cuyo—are between 2,800 and 5,000 feet (850 and 1,525 m). Uco has seen investment from European winemakers because it's cooler and makes more restrained wines, in line with Old World styles. Lujan de Cuyo has more New World investment for its plumper, richer-tasting grapes. In both areas, higher-altitude vineyards produce higher-acid wines that are less fruity and more complex. Lower down in the valleys, producers make velvety, simple, luscious wines with lower acidity, and often with less distinctive fruit flavors. The moral: Pay attention to what you like and start shopping by subarea, which is nearly always on the label (even if on the back).

Mendoza is a huge region, and although it's known best for Malbec, you can also expect to see other grapes like Bonarda (a light, refreshing red called Charbono in the United States), Cabernet Sauvignon, Syrah, Chardonnay, and Tempranillo on a shelf near you.

CLOSEST CITIES: *Mendoza is a 2-hour flight from Buenos Aires, and the wineries in Lujan de Cuyo are about a 30-minute drive from the Mendoza airport. The picturesque Uco Valley is a 1.5-hour drive from the airport.*

Salta

This is the nosebleed section of winegrowing. The highest vineyards in the world are located in Salta, at around 10,000 feet (3,050 m)! Even the lowest vineyards in Cafayate, the main subregion, are at over 5,000 feet (1,525 m). These vineyards do best growing Torrontés Riojano, the queen clone of Torrontés. When you take a whiff of the wine and get its peachy, honeysuckle, limeade smells, you'll think it's going to be sweet, but the hit of acid, the soft coating of your cheeks, and the long finish will surprise you. It's a great cheese wine and a nice sipper. Growers know that doing this wine right requires hard work in high vineyards and that it pays off in flavor. If you don't believe me, trust the world-famous wine consultants and winemakers who have invested heavily in the area. I'm not crazy about the Malbec vines growing this high up because they lose their ripe fruit character, but Torrontés from Salta is a stunner and a truly Argentinean wine you need to try.

CLOSEST CITIES: *Salta has a small airport and is a 2-hour flight from Buenos Aires. The best wine area of Cafayate is about a 3-hour drive south from Salta.*

The Wrap-Up

Argentina is full of outstanding wine, especially Malbec. The country's launch into the international wine scene has been an uncontestable success. Malbec is here to stay, and Argentina's version is the new benchmark for the grape (sorry France!). Torrontés is a fabulous white counterpart for lovers of dry, aromatic whites. The only gripe I have with Argentina is the inconsistency and price creep as wine production has grown. I hope we can rely on wines above $20 to remain good, but I worry that as demand grows, quality may take another step down. Watch this space.

AUSTRALIA

Where do I begin with Australia? People have made wine in the former penal colony for more than 150 years. There's no doubt that the place has both the land and the skill to make wine the right way. You only have to look at the prices for the country's most famous wine, Penfold's Grange (a Shiraz-based wine from South Australia), to know that this place can make wines that are powerful, complex, and worth a lot to someone.

But Australia is not without problems. I think of the region as a young starlet whose rise to fame was too way fast: It was on a rocket ship ride and then it imploded a bit and became a victim of its own success. In my view, as the country claws its way back, it's currently residing in a no-man's-land for its place in the wine world, its value, and its future. It's a depressing story for right now, but I'm positive that in a few years the narrative will be one of resurrection (we all love that, don't we?). For now, though, I'll give you my take on the story of modern Australia and what that means for how you shop for wine from here.

I still remember, when I was a young-ish tyke, my dad talking about unbeliev-able Australian wine when it burst on the scene in the 1990s with low-priced bottles that were rich in flavor, yet had balanced structure. The reds were decadent and they had acidity and tannin, but were fruitier and softer than the original versions of the grapes: Shiraz (Syrah from the northern Rhône), Cabernet Sauvignon, and Merlot.

The Chardonnay was similar to California Chardonnay but cost less. Semillon, the white of Bordeaux, made some stunning solo appearances in certain areas of Australia, too. The Riesling was outstanding—dry with fruit-first flavors and high acid but easier to understand than German versions. Australia became the prime choice of first-time wine drinkers and for those who needed a break from the more food-oriented wines of Europe.

By the early 2000s, the Australian wine industry was emboldened by the success of an approachable, friendly, yellow-tailed kangaroo. The nation set the audacious goal of becoming the largest producer of wine in the world by 2020 and set about planting grapes to reach that volume. Producers and wine conglomerates planned to ride their ingenious, cutesy marketing plan forever and we, as consumers, seemed on board. They made, and we bought, every wine that had a "critter" on it: a cartoon label with a kangaroo, a boomerang, a koala, a wombat, a dingo, a platypus . . . you get the point.

But, and I don't mean to be bitchy, Australia botched it. Australian wineries thought the critter trend would never end. So they planted, and planted, and planted. In areas where they had no business planting: where grapes wouldn't produce great-tasting wine. Apparently they forgot something: Early critter brands initially succeeded and gained a following because the wine was surprisingly much better than what it cost.

The fact is that Australia's fame and fortune did end. And it left the country with a bigger problem than inclusion in the latter portion of *US Weekly*'s "What's Hot/What's Not" column. A very simple supply and demand problem existed: Wine producers had too much wine that too few people wanted.

Australia exports 60 percent of its wine, so when its largest customers—the UK and US markets—grow uninterested, the wineries have problems. When there's more wine than you can sell, the folks selling it need to get rid of it. They reduce the price. Then we as wine buyers reformulate what we think the wine is worth in our heads and start seeing Australian wine in a bargain-basement way. The wine seems less desirable. With this, you wind up with the situation where Australia produces somewhere between 20 to 40 million more cases than it can sell. Wineries have been forced to "reconcile," as they say in business: shut down wineries and dig up vines to reduce the supply and try to sell as much as they can to thirsty Asian markets while there is demand.

Since the late 2000s, the country has struggled to redefine itself and its strategy. As other value countries, regions, and continents—mostly Spain, South America, and New Zealand—have dominated "new news," Australia is at sea in terms of identity. Are there still people who get excited about the high-end wines? Yes, and they should. Are there still millions of people drinking at the low end? Yes (Yellow Tail still sells around 8 million cases in the United States alone!). But for those of us shopping in the middle, between $15 and $30, it's slim pickin's. Few brands have managed to keep that category alive. And there have been few new players as the whole industry struggles to reduce supply and create a demand for their unique wines.

Despite the mistakes Australia has made, the country has the fundamentals of great viticulture and winemaking. Wine

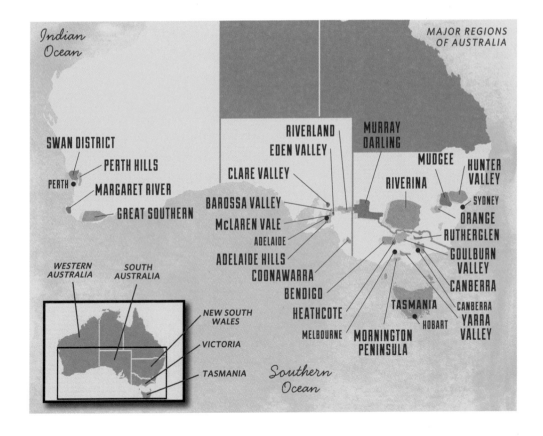

will make it here. Once wineries resolve the supply issue (sadly, some will need to pour the wine down the drain), watch for the individual regions of Australia to feature more prominently on labels and for the push for organic and biodynamic farming to be a point of differentiation.

It may be a few years before we start getting excited about Australia's rebirth, but it's coming. There are signs of life in the UK market, and the United States can't be too far behind.

Australia is divided into large zones, regions, then subregions. Generally lower-end wines contain the zone name (Southeastern Australia, Victoria, Western Australia, Tasmania, New South Wales) and higher-end wines have regions or subregions, which are what I describe in the following sections.

Southeast Australia

Barossa Valley

When you think Barossa, think Shiraz. This is the mecca of the grape in Australia. One of Australia's oldest growing regions and, for a long time, its most underrated, the region finally got its due when the chocolaty, spicy Shiraz made from old vines came to the attention of wine critics worldwide. Now Barossa is one of Australia's most famous wine regions. It does Shiraz best, but its GSM (Grenache, Shiraz, Mourvèdre, à la southern Rhône) blends are great. Look for outstanding, lime-flavored, high-acid, bone-dry Rieslings, made from the cool, higher-altitude EDEN VALLEY subregion.

CLOSEST CITIES: *Barossa Valley is a 1-hour drive northeast of Adelaide.*

Clare Valley

Riesling is the darling of Clare Valley. It's strange that this picky grape can grow where the days are relatively warm, but the valley's cold nights allow the grape to maintain its characteristic acidity. The resulting wine is fruity with tropical notes and a full texture but still acidic and almost always dry. I love it for its food-friendly, reliably dry style. People grow Cabernet Sauvignon, Shiraz, Chardonnay, Semillon and other grapes here, but Riesling is queen and what you should seek from Clare Valley.

CLOSEST CITIES: *Clare Valley is a 1-hour drive northeast of Adelaide.*

McLaren Vale

More than 50 percent of the grapes harvested in this area are Shiraz, and that's a great thing. With its diverse soil and cooling breezes from the mountains and the ocean, McLaren Vale produces Shiraz that often has an elegance or restraint about it that you rarely find in other Shiraz from Australia. Yes, the wine has fruit, but there's usually spice and sometimes earth behind the fruit, which makes this one of Australia's truly differentiated red wine regions.

CLOSEST CITIES: *McLaren Vale is a 40-minute drive south of Adelaide.*

Coonawarra

The aboriginal word for "honeysuckle," Coonawarra doesn't make wines that taste of that delicate flower—it's another blockbuster region, producing Australia's most famous Cabernet Sauvignon from its red, iron-infused terra rossa soil. With a longer, cooler ripening season than other parts of South Australia, Coonawarra is a small area with a maritime climate that's like Bordeaux. It's no wonder winemakers can make such rich Cabernet that's full of fruit but still has a taste of earth from that red clay soil. Although other stuff is grown here, Cab is the star.

CLOSEST CITIES: *Coonawarra is a 4-hour drive southeast from Adelaide and a 4.5-hour drive northwest from Melbourne.*

Victoria

Yarra Valley

Even hot countries like Australia have cool-climate regions, and Yarra Valley is one of the most famous in Australia. Known for Pinot Noir and Chardonnay, and sparkling wines made from the two grapes, this area produces wines that are leaner, more acidic, and more representative of the grapes (less of the traditional New World style, with less oak and no malolactic fermentation [page 27]) than other cool regions of Australia. Cabernet Sauvignon grows on the warmer sites and can be more restrained than Cabernet Sauvignon from regions of South Australia. The rising star of the region is Shiraz, which can be jammy and robust or restrained and interesting. Producers generally label the latter version "Syrah" to indicate that it's a more medium-bodied, savory wine with olive, herb, and bacon notes similar to Rhône versions. Located a short drive from Melbourne, this is also one of Australia's most popular wine tourism hubs, with more than 2 million tourists a year visiting!

CLOSEST CITIES: *Victoria is a 30-minute drive east of Melbourne.*

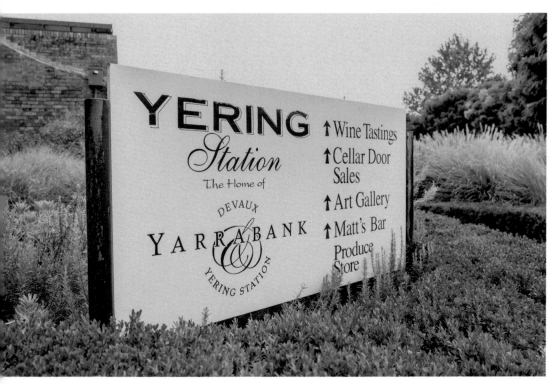

New South Wales

Hunter Valley

For the fact that it's one of the oldest winegrowing regions in Australia, it's close to Sydney, and it churns out amazing Semillon, Hunter Valley is one of Australia's most famous wine regions. Although it makes a ton of Chardonnay, Shiraz, and Cabernet, the hottest property out of Hunter Valley is Semillon, one of the white blending grapes of Bordeaux that does unusual things in this area. The grape is usually low in acid and full tasting with lemon and herb flavors, but in Australia's heat and humidity it somehow creates a higher-acid, honeyed wine that after a decade of aging tastes like a creamy, oaky Chardonnay or even has a cheese rind tang though the wine never sees a barrel or goes through malolactic fermentation. It's a wonder of the wine world, so get some, even if you find (as I do) that most of the Hunter Valley's other widely available wines are meh, at best.

CLOSEST CITIES: *Hunter Valley is a 1.25- to 2-hour drive northeast of Sydney depending on what part of the valley you visit.*

Tasmania

I include Tasmania, the cool island to the south that is whipped with ocean breezes on all sides and sometimes can't even ripen grapes, as a "one to watch." Not much Tasmanian wine is exported, but the sparkling wine and the Riesling, which apparently bears resemblance to some German versions, consistently makes a splash among critics. Acidic yet fruity, Pinot Noir is also turning heads. Although it's not a region that's super popular, it's one I mention because these wines will be food friendly and different from typical Australian wine: less fruity, higher in acid, and earthier.

CLOSEST CITIES: *Wineries in the south are a 20-minute drive from Hobart airport. Launceston and the historic Tamar Valley are a 2.5-hour drive from the Hobart airport.*

Western Australia

Margaret River

On the Indian Ocean in southwest Australia, there is a relatively new (the first wine grapes were planted in the 1960s) but excellent wine area: Margaret River. The region has a Mediterranean climate, and Cabernet, Chardonnay, Sauvignon Blanc, Semillon, Shiraz, and Merlot thrive here. Although it only makes up 3 percent of Australian wine, Margaret River is responsible for 20 percent of the high-end bottles. Winegrowers and winemakers have established high standards and a culture of quality. They let the grape speak for itself rather than covering it up with overzealous winemaking, and what it has to say isn't too shabby. You'll taste full fruit flavors with acidity, mild alcohol, and moderate tannin and get a nice balance of oak and fruit. If you've been off Australian wine for a while and are ready to dip a toe back in, Margaret River is the place to start.

CLOSEST CITIES: *Margaret River is a 3-hour drive southwest of Perth.*

The Wrap-Up

I'm not a gambling person but I'd bet money that there is a great future again for Australian wine. It's a shame that in the United States, at least, the selection has become a polarized hodgepodge of mainly high-tier brands and bottom-of-the barrel, mass-produced bottles. I keep hoping that something will change—a big new brand will emerge in the middle tier that represents Australia's quality, or some effort to bring in smaller producers who make high-quality, balanced wine will enter the scene. As of yet, it's still a hope, but if we follow our friends in the UK, who have taken option two (smaller producers in the middle tier from smaller regions), we'll be in good shape. My fingers are staying crossed!

CHILE

For a long time the story of South American wine *was* Chile. Even though it makes significantly less than its neighbor to the east (Argentina), when Chile went global, it focused on quality and the decision paid off. As the major wineries started exporting, they sent out great stuff for a great price and the world took notice. Chile paved the way for Argentina and for other South American countries that may decide to export on a large scale in the future. But the Chileans also set the bar: We now have high expectations for the quality to price ratio out of this continent.

If you think about it, it should make sense to wine lovers that Chile can produce awesome wine. Fold the world in half at the equator, and its wine regions transpose onto some of the best winemaking areas of California. This skinny, long country runs 3,000 miles (4,828 km) down the west coast of South America, and in about a third of that, you'll find vines.

One of the coolest things about Chile is that its geographic features isolate it and provide protection from all sorts of nasty things that afflict other regions. In the north is the Atacama Desert; in the south, Antarctica; to the west, the Pacific. Then there are the Andes Mountains to the east, which give protection from Atlantic storms and provide ample snowmelt from the mountaintops for irrigation. With all this bounty and the unusual feature of sandy topsoils, Chile has another benefit that few other wine regions in the world can boast: no phylloxera (the vine serial killer bug of the wine world; page 45). Chile's isolation keeps the louse from being transported easily to vineyards through regular commerce with the outside world, and if any critters happen to make it, they can't survive in the sandy soil. It's a perfect storm for Chile.

But there's an irony about phylloxera and Chile. Although it has never been infested, this terrible bug is responsible, in large part, for the success of the country's wine industry.

What? Let me explain.

This story begins in the mid-1800s, when rich Chilean businessmen traveled to Europe and specifically to France to discover more about European culture. They realized that Pais and Moscatel, the grapes that went into most Chilean wines, were pretty bad. These oenophiles wanted wines similar to what they tasted in Bordeaux, and they wanted to make them on their home turf. Being people of action, they took hundreds of the best clippings back home. So Cabernet Sauvignon, Merlot, Cabernet Franc, Carménère, and Sauvignon Blanc, among other vines,

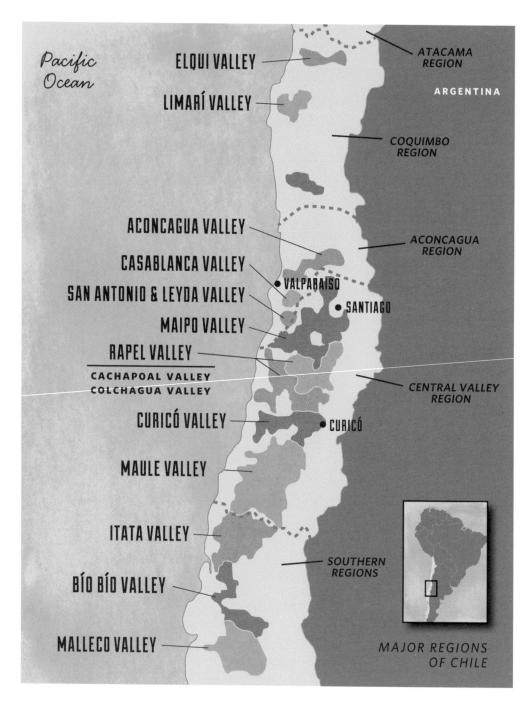

Pacific Ocean

ELQUI VALLEY

LIMARÍ VALLEY

ATACAMA REGION

ARGENTINA

COQUIMBO REGION

ACONCAGUA VALLEY

CASABLANCA VALLEY

SAN ANTONIO & LEYDA VALLEY

MAIPO VALLEY

RAPEL VALLEY

CACHAPOAL VALLEY

COLCHAGUA VALLEY

CURICÓ VALLEY

MAULE VALLEY

ITATA VALLEY

BÍO BÍO VALLEY

MALLECO VALLEY

ACONCAGUA REGION

VALPARAISO

SANTIAGO

CENTRAL VALLEY REGION

CURICÓ

SOUTHERN REGIONS

MAJOR REGIONS OF CHILE

landed in Chile. The grapes thrived in vineyards mostly outside Santiago, the country's capital.

Although it's true you need great grapes to make great wine, you also need some talent to coax tasty stuff from the fruit— sheep need a shepherd. And this is where phylloxera helped Chile big-time.

It just so happened that as guys like Don Maximiano Errázuriz and Don Silvestre Ochagavía Echazarreta (Errázuriz and Ochagavía are still operational today) were importing vines and looking for French talent to help out in Chile, phylloxera and powdery mildew were decimating Bordeaux and leaving talented winemakers out of work.

With few other options at home, French winemakers headed to Chile on sabbatical and created Chile's modern wine industry.

Today, much of the industry is still run by the descendants of those rich guys from the nineteenth century—Concha y Toro, Santa Rita, San Pedro, Errázuriz, and more. Endorsement and investment from the likes of Robert Mondavi from California, Baron Lafite-Rothschild from Bordeaux, and Miguel Torres from Spain only helped to improve quality further.

Chile has come a long way but there's one thing on which they messed up royally: grape identification! In an attempt to figure out why the Sauvignon Blanc and Merlot sucked so much in the '80s, visitors provided some perspective. Chilean viticulturists (vine scientists) had misidentified Sauvignon Blanc as an unrelated, often flavorless grape called Tocai Fruiliano or Sauvignon Vert. The Merlot tasted a lot like green pepper and had none of the silky red fruit you'd expect because it was actually the long-lost Carménère grape, a hard-to-grow Bordeaux variety that was nearly extinct in its homeland but thrived in Chile. *Oops*!

You gotta love the Chileans: They turned liabilities into assets, replanting with good clones of Sauvignon Blanc, which make excellent wines today. They also marketed the hell out of the Carménère to the point that it has become the unique red of Chile.

Today, Chile is a wine-quality center. I find that if you spend $20 on a Chilean wine you'll get something that would be $50 from another region. Cabernet Sauvignon is the king of the reds in Chile, with Carménère as the "signature" red grape. Chardonnay and Sauvignon Blanc are standouts in the world of whites—fresh, light, and herbal. Although you can get some stinkers from the place (I haven't met a great Chilean Merlot yet, for instance), generally great wine abounds.

Before I get into the regions, here's a personal note on Chilean wine style in general. I don't know if it's the clones of the grapes, but I find that many wines from Chile (except at the $20-plus end) have a green pepper note. It's understandable in Cabernet and Sauvignon Blanc, which have methoxypyrazines (the chemical in green pepper that gives it a tangy taste), but I'm not sure why it expresses itself in the other varieties. It may be that yields are too high, resulting in overly green flavors, except from the better producers. Regardless, although it's often there, it doesn't always compete with the lush fruit and great structure of the wine, so it's not a deal killer! I thought you should know in case you taste that too—you're not alone.

The following main, large wine areas are Aconcagua and Valle Central, but I've also detailed subregions and smaller areas because that's where the best wines can be found.

Aconcagua

Casablanca and San Antonio/Leyda

Located in an east-west facing valley that benefits from the cooling air of the strong Pacific Humboldt Current, the coastal subregions of Casablanca and San Antonio are far cooler than their latitude 33° south would suggest. The ocean influence, with its breezes, midday clouds, and marine fog, provides a long growing season that allows these regions to make crisp whites. The areas specialize in oaked but not oaky Chardonnay with tropical, citrus fruit notes and brine and sea salt flavors, and

Sauvignon Blanc with herbal and grapefruit notes and soft textures. A total hit. I always look for these regions when I shop for Chilean white. Pinot Noir and Syrah grow successfully here, too, but I haven't had enough to make a call on whether it's a go.

CLOSEST CITIES: *Casablanca and San Antonio are about a 1-hour drive northwest from Santiago.*

Central Valley (Valle Central)

The Central Valley is huge with major variation in wine quality. My trick for shopping: Look for specific regions, not just "Valle Central." Here are the areas you'll see on a label with a caveat emptor where necessary.

The Maipo Valley

Containing Chile's oldest and most famous wineries, Maipo (MY-po) is the heart of Chilean wine. In this valley that includes part of Chile's capital city of Santiago, more than 50 percent of the vineyards are planted to Cabernet Sauvignon. The area has huge temperature diurnals (difference between day and night temperatures) and low rainfall during the growing season but great access to water from the Andes snowmelt: perfect conditions for red grape growing. The best vineyards in the Alto Maipo subregion are in the Andean foothills at altitude on rocky, well-draining soils that seem to impart earthy, minerally notes. These vineyards produce Cabernet with juicy, dark fruit, floral and earth notes, and a medium body. The once dense, rich, high-alcohol styles that were being made to satisfy certain critics' preferences are on their way out, so look for balanced, lower-alcohol versions from top producers, who are moving up to higher-elevation vineyards in the Andes to revive the old, restrained style of Chilean Cabernet, which resembled French versions.

There are two other subregions: Maipo Medio and Maipo Costa. Maipo Medio is hot and dry, producing smooth, fruity reds. The coastal mountain area, Maipo Costa, is great for fresher, lighter styles of Cabernet and high-acid Chardonnay and Sauvignon Blanc, which are like fuller versions of those from the Casablanca.

CLOSEST CITIES: *The Maipo Valley is a 1-hour drive southwest of Santiago, but if you don't have a car you can take the metro from Santiago right to the wineries!*

Rapel Valley

Just south of Maipo is the large Rapel (rah-PELL) Valley, which has two subregions—Cachapoal in the north and Colchagua in the south. This valley produces the best, and maybe the only distinctive Carménère in Chile. When Carménère is grown on poor sites, and the winemakers aren't careful, I think it tastes like mothballs and rubber tires, sometimes with a hit of sulfur on the side (*yum!*). It reminds me of the Pinotage of South Africa, only fuller. In Rapel, you can get spicy, rich, fruity wines with strong tannins and good acid.

Rapel is excellent for reds. Winemakers are doing well with Cabernet Sauvignon and Syrah in addition to Carménère. Expect full fruit yet spicy, earthy, and medium-bodied wines.

THE CACHAPOAL VALLEY (CA-CHA-POE-AHL)
With a Mediterranean climate and a long, dry growing season, the area has two rivers that provide ample water for irrigation, which is essential in a place with almost no rainfall. The valley has two parts, each suited to its own grape. For Cabernet Sauvignon, the best vineyards and wineries are in the east, in the foothills of the Andes, where temperatures are cooler than on the valley floor. This area also has gravel soils, which Cab loves, so Cachapoal Cabernet Sauvignon is full, rich, and tannic but restrained. Carménère, grown mainly near the coast on more fertile soils, is red fruited and spicy, and actually doesn't taste like tires most of the time.

CLOSEST CITY: *The town of Requinoa, the start of a small wine route, is a 1.5-hour drive south from Santiago.*

THE COLCHAGUA (COAL-CHA-GWA) VALLEY,
in the southwest of Rapel, is much more famous than Cachapoal (probably due to more marketing savvy—it's known as the Napa Valley of Chile). The area also specializes in Cabernet Sauvignon and Carménère with a little Syrah. It's warm here since the valley is at latitude 34° south, but ocean breezes cool things down and rivers give growers ample access to water for irrigation. The slopes of the Andes Mountains in the east provide sharp temperature diurnals (day to night temperature swings) and intense sunlight during the day: They are prime for vineyards so this is where the best, most balanced Cabernet, Carménère, and Merlot grow. Chardonnay and Sauvignon Blanc show promise in the cooler western part of the valley.

CLOSEST CITY: *The wine touristy city of Santa Cruz is a 2.5- to 3-hour drive south from Santiago.*

Maule

A southern, cooler area, Maule (MAOW-lay) is huge and is a hotbed of investment these days. But for a long time, Maule was full of crap wine made from the Pais grape, which was brought by the conquistadors to Central and South America. Investment and interest in the better pockets of this big valley mean that now it's possible to get great reds from here, but there are still seas of cheap, nasty, flavorless wines that have little identity besides being just red wine. Maule's most interesting wine is old vine Carignan, which is soft but earthy and full. The area has potential but it's not there yet so proceed with caution.

CLOSEST CITY: *Maule is a 2.5-hour drive southwest from Santiago.*

Chilean Regions to Watch

With global climate change and increasing investment, some small regions may prove to be some of Chile's best if they can produce enough wine to meet global demand.

North of Santiago

You may see high-acid Sauvignon Blanc and interesting herbal, spicy Syrah coming from the LIMARÍ and ELQUI VALLEYS in the Coquimbo region. Good stuff, but these regions are small and in marginal growing areas because the valleys are so far north. (We're in the Southern Hemisphere so even if they are in cool pockets, in the north the valleys bump up against hot areas, which can bake out the acid in grapes.)

CLOSEST CITY: *The Limarí and Elqui Valleys are a 5-hour drive north from Santiago.*

South of Santiago

Cool-weather grapes like Chardonnay, Pinot Noir, Sauvignon Blanc, and possibly Riesling have promise in the cold southern regions in the south—BÍO BÍO (BEE-YO BEE-YO) and MALLECO (MAH-YAY-co). The short growing season and cold weather will make it a place for tenacious winemakers. If they can figure it out, this may be the next trendy region for high-acid, aromatic whites and balanced, nuanced Pinot Noir. What I've had to date has wowed me.

CLOSEST CITY: *Bío Bío and Malleco are a 3- to 4-hour drive southwest from Santiago.*

The Wrap-Up

Of all the places that have been trendy in the New World, Chile is one of the only nations where quality seems to consistently rise every vintage. Chileans overdeliver on whites and reds, especially in the $15-plus range, and the kind of wine that you get for $50 blows away most wines of a comparable price from other wine nations. Chile has to work on taming yields and perfecting vineyard practices, but producers are on the right track, and for that reason these wines are always on my shopping list!

NEW ZEALAND

Do you know why New Zealand wine is of such high quality? Because it's harvested by Hobbits. Totally kidding. But this is the land where the Lord of the Rings movies were filmed, and it's a vast, varied, and beautiful place. Although it's only

1,000 miles (1,600 km) long, New Zealand is a major force in the wine world for its distinctive bottles.

This small, dual-island wine megastar is divided into north and south islands, with cool weather and a definitive ocean influence everywhere. No vineyard is more than 80 miles (129 km) from the ocean! Relatively speaking, the nation doesn't make much wine. As of 2018, it's the fifteenth-largest wine-producing nation.

It's what they *do* produce that makes them notable—Sauvignon Blanc unlike any other and Pinot Noir that has some of the best traits of Burgundy and California combined. In nearly all the wines there's a pure fruit flavor—a stunning clarity that lets you recognize and taste each flavor with nothing obscuring it. When I taste a New Zealand Sauvignon Blanc, I have no problem telling you exactly what I taste—grapefruit, grass, often jalapeño, and a note that people either call gooseberry (that's the nice way to say it) or cat pee (somehow in the wine it's not bad). There's an unmatched beauty in that intensity.

The thing I love most about New Zealand? It is so damn consistent. There is a character to the wine that you can find nearly each time you drink a bottle. And although the purity and intensity vary based on vineyard and brand, the fundamentals of the wine—the taste of the place—are similar. I can't think of many other regions about which I can say that.

I do have a caveat: As demand has increased, growers in the region have sought out less desirable areas. Although up to this point New Zealand has always wowed me, I've noticed that there is more of a difference between the moderately priced and lower-priced offerings of Sauvignon Blanc and Pinot Noir. New Zealand's beauty is that every wine shows its origin

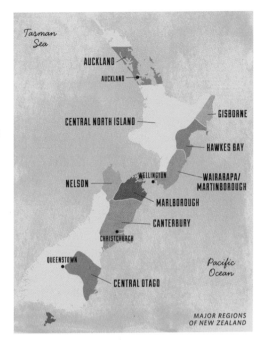

MAJOR REGIONS
OF NEW ZEALAND

in the flavor—the purity is the strength. When that purity is murky or adulterated with sugar to hide tartness, however, you see that too and it isn't pretty. So the lesson: If you get one you don't like for a lower price, move up a tier or two and you'll find there's a world of difference.

But to continue the love fest, I'll give it to the Kiwis. New Zealand isn't a one-hit wonder. It makes fabulous wines apart from Sauvignon Blanc. Pinot Noir, which is great from the big region of Marlborough, is stunning from the most southerly vineyards in the world on the South Island in Central Otago (latitude 47° south). Farther north, even in areas at latitude 35° south, near Auckland on the North Island, the cold ocean influence allows Cabernet Sauvignon and Merlot to take their time to ripen and attain a fruit flavor with an earthy, salty quality that you don't get anywhere else in the wine world.

New Zealand has even more up its sleeve. Next up? I think cool-climate, dry Rieslings and, in slightly warmer pockets, Rhône-style Syrah will start gathering steam. If these wines are as consistently good and as great a value as the current offerings, we'll be lucky.

NEW ZEALAND VS. AUSTRALIA

If you know nothing about New Zealand, it can be tempting to compare it to its distant neighbor in the north—Australia, which is 1,400 miles (2,253 km) away. But don't do it. The two don't have much in common when it comes to wine. In fact, Australia is New Zealand's biggest export market. If the countries were so similar, there'd be no reason for Australians to import Kiwi wines. In my mind, the two couldn't be more different.

South Island

Marlborough

If you want to know New Zealand, you have to know Marlborough. The place makes nearly 80 percent of the wine in the country. It's important.

Located on the east coast and sheltered by a western mountain range, which protects it from strong ocean breezes, Marlborough is the heart of winegrowing in New Zealand. This is the origin of the signature Sauvignon Blanc for which the country is so famous. Many critics and normal wine people consider Marlborough Sauvignon Blanc to be the best in the world. Its acidic, herbal, grapefruit, and jalapeño bite gives the wine a distinctiveness.

The Wairau (WHY-raow) Valley is the main quality growing region. Sunshine is abundant here, but the region is relatively cool, and at night the temperature drops, which is what allows the grapes to build their characteristic acidity. The Awatere (awa-TIER-ee) Valley is cooler and adds acidity and citrus flavors to the wine in years when Wairau is hotter and produces lower-acid grapes. Great Pinot Noir is also grown in these valleys. It's generally a value for such a fruity, earthy, acidic, well-balanced wine.

CLOSEST CITIES: *The Wairau and Awatere Valleys of Marlborough are a 1.25-hour flight from Auckland and a 25-minute flight from Wellington, then a short drive from Woodbourne Airport in Blenheim to the wineries.*

Central Otago

At around latitude 47° south, Central Otago has the most southerly wine regions in the world (meaning, it's cool). Nestled high in the mountains and surrounded by picturesque lakes and ski resorts, this gorgeous area has more of a continental climate (hot summers, freezing winters) than any other winegrowing region in the country. Here, Pinot Noir reigns. The area has big diurnals (difference between day and night temperatures) so complex flavors and great acidity can build as the grapes cool at night. Central Otago's Pinot has been compared favorably to the wines of Burgundy. But with clear berry-fruit flavors, earthy flavor, and great acidity, the Pinot is usually a good value compared to Burgundy. As more people discover how great these Pinots are and as winemakers gain more experience here, I expect the prices will inch up, as they probably should, given what a pain Pinot is to grow the right way. Look out for Riesling as well, which is a newcomer in Central Otago but shows great promise.

CLOSEST CITY: *Cromwell and Alexandra are about a 1-hour drive east from Queenstown, which is a nearly 2-hour flight from Auckland and a 1.75-hour flight from Wellington.*

North Island

Hawke's Bay

New Zealand's oldest wine region—which grows more than 80 percent of the country's Merlot, Cabernet Sauvignon, and Syrah—produces medium-bodied wines with an abundance of black fruit flavor. Gimblett Gravels, the warmest section of this region, is in an area of an old riverbed. In good years it seems to produce perfumed, fruity, spicy wines (although in cooler ones they're sharp and bitter!). Chardonnay is another star here, but I've found it varies in quality—with many having citrus and floral aromatics that heavy oak and cream flavors sadly crush.

CLOSEST CITY: *Hawke's Bay is a 1-hour flight or a 5.5-hour drive from Auckland or a 3.5-hour drive northeast from Wellington.*

Martinborough

A small town on the southern tip of the North Island, Martinborough has a cool climate and mineral-rich soils that create acclaimed fruity, earthy, acidic, and lightly tannic Pinot Noir. The texture and flavors are outstanding, and the value from Martinborough is much better than a lot of Pinot Noir from other New World regions. Although producers make Sauvignon Blanc too, they usually pale in comparison to what's on the South Island.

CLOSEST CITY: *Martinborough is a 1.5-hour drive east from Wellington.*

The Wrap-Up

New Zealand is small but mighty, and its wines are some of the safest bets around—consistent, pure in flavor, and imminently drinkable. As long as the industry remains focused on quality rather than quantity, we can hope to see a further evolution of Pinot Noir, Sauvignon Blanc, Riesling, Syrah, and more from this country. As winemakers get more of a handle on their stellar land and the kinds of wines it has the power to create, we'll have years of pleasant and tasty surprises from more and more regions of this beautiful place.

SOUTH AFRICA

In a time long ago and far away, I had an awesome South African best friend. As part of his awesomeness, he invited me to come to South Africa and get a look at his country. So I did. (The story ends sadly—M.C. Ice and I were deemed bad influences by his wife so I'm not allowed to see him anymore. Maybe it was the wine?)

Apart from Johannesberg (where I learned that the food is outstanding), Kruger National Park (where I learned that elephants can charge safari vans and hyenas look drunk at 6 a.m. as they come in from a night of feasting), and the lion park where I pet a lion cub (so wrong, especially for my animal rights–loving self), I got to see Cape Town. And I got to visit some of the Cape Winelands. Although I had little clue about the treasure in front of me, I remember some key things about the visit and the wines.

South African wines are so diverse that it's hard to put your finger on them. The main quality areas—all in a big zone called the Western Cape—are near the point where the Atlantic and the Indian Oceans meet. The ocean breezes can either warm great areas like Walker Bay, Elgin, and Stellenbosch or cause a whipping wind that chaps your face, knots your hair, and, if you're a winegrower, reduces your harvest. Farther inland, on mountain slopes and in river valleys in areas like Paarl and the Franschhoek district, a Mediterranean climate allows the grapes to develop a rich flavor while maintaining acid and tannin

because of big diurnals (day to night temperature swings). Soils vary dramatically and have a strong effect on flavor.

Despite the diversity, the common thread in most South African wines is a balance between Old World minerality/ dirtiness (in a good way) and New World fruitiness. This may be from the terroir or from the fact that European settlers started making wine here in the 1650s, giving the winemaking an Old World bent. And that's why South African wine is a perfect transition wine for someone looking to get into Old World wines from a life of only New World ones. I recommend starting with the Sauvignon Blanc, Chenin Blanc, and Syrah, and the Cabernet Sauvignon blends. The best examples have excellent fruit character, noticeable but not overpowering acidity and tannin, and a serious sense of the ground they grew in. Who wouldn't want that kind of balance? They remind me of another of my favorite and highly

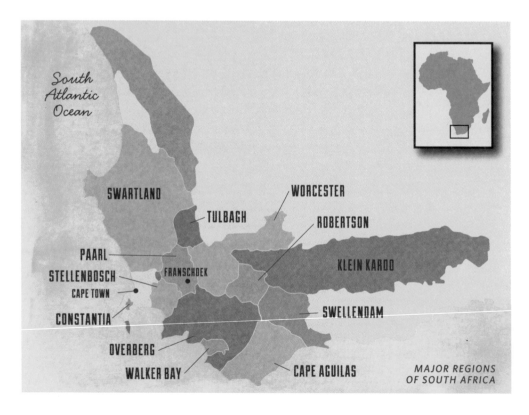

South Atlantic Ocean

SWARTLAND

WORCESTER

TULBAGH

ROBERTSON

PAARL

FRANSCHOEK

KLEIN KAROO

STELLENBOSCH

CAPE TOWN

CONSTANTIA

SWELLENDAM

OVERBERG

WALKER BAY

CAPE AGUILAS

MAJOR REGIONS OF SOUTH AFRICA

overlooked areas—Walla Walla, Washington, which we'll get to later.

What don't I love? The South African grape, Pinotage. In 1924 a viticulturist at the University of Stellenbosch, which has a prestigious winemaking and viticulture program, created this beast by crossing Pinot Noir and the southern French blender, Cinsault. Pinotage often smells like rubber tires and tastes like drying paint, with some raspberry on the side. In what I think is a huge misstep, marketers and wineries have tried to brand this mostly yuck wine (there are a few exceptions of good Pinotage but, in my experience, *very few*) as South Africa's red wine. Why you would do this when you could put a good foot forward with excellent reds that taste different from Australian, American, New Zealand, and South American wines is beyond me, but it's what they did.

South Africa has so much to offer, even if it feels as though most importers have missed the boat on bringing in the best wines. The winemaking areas are divided into regions, districts, and wards. You'll most often see the district on the label, so I've described the best ones here.

Stellenbosch

Atlantic breezes temper this hot, dry area 25 miles (40 km) from Cape Town and keep the heat in check. Stellenbosch is home to top South African Cabernet Sauvignon. Whether alone or blended with Merlot, this is probably South Africa's boldest offering and it's good. Expect the Cab blends to have tobacco, pencil lead, black fruit, and smoke notes with medium tannin. Syrah from Stellenbosch can be peppery and fruity, although not as complex as from Swartland (page 256). Planted closer to the ocean and benefiting from

cool breezes, whites like Chardonnay, Chenin Blanc, and Semillon can be high in acid with tropical and apple/pear notes and all around tasty. Pinotage got its start here at the University of Stellenbosch, but don't hold it against this great region!

CLOSEST CITY: *Stellenbosch is a 35-minute drive slightly southeast from Cape Town.*

Paarl

Northeast of Stellenbosch lies Paarl, meaning "pearl" in English. It was named for how the mountain shines after rain falls. This area is hotter than Stellenbosch with diverse soil types, so the styles are less consistent. Cabernet Sauvignon, Shiraz, Chardonnay, and Chenin Blanc are Paarl's pearls. Full fruited, bold, rich, and often earthy when good, these can also be jammy with little structure when not so good. Since the climate is warm to hot, grapes in the hands of the wrong producer can be flabby. Pay attention to who is making the wine!

CLOSEST CITY: *Paarl is a 40-minute drive east from Cape Town.*

Franschhoek

Named after the French Huguenots who settled here, Franschhoek is one of the oldest and best-quality wine districts in South Africa . . . when it's good. Quality is mixed here but the top wines are fantastic. Surrounded by the Groot Drakenstein, Klein Drakenstein, Franschhoek, and Simonsberg Mountains, this little valley is shielded from wind and, as a result, it's hot. It makes strong reds from Cabernet

Sauvignon and Syrah with juicy dark fruit flavors and spicy, earthy notes, and often has soft tannin and low acidity. Strangely, in spite of the heat, there are cool areas higher in the mountains that produce high-acid grapes for great CAP CLASSIQUE (sparkling wine made like Champagne). The whites, especially the Sauvignon Blanc, tend toward tropical, applelike, and figgy flavors with minerality and high acidity but softer, creamier textures.

CLOSEST CITY: *Franschhoek is a 1-hour drive slightly southeast from Cape Town.*

Swartland

This is the most underrated region in South Africa, for me. It's probably because it grows the world's most underrated grape: Shiraz/Syrah. Swartland means "black land" and is named for the rhinoceros bush that turns black after the rainy season. The area is hot and dry, so the best farmers dry-farm the vines, bush training them instead of hanging them on trellises, and eschew irrigation. This produces fewer berries with intense flavor. Swartland makes some of the best New World Shiraz/Syrah I've ever had. And few know about it. Often these wines have fresh, juicy cherry, and blackcurrant fruit balanced by herbs, lavender, and spice with a medium body. They're complex in flavor and texture and a great bang for your buck! There aren't that many producers, and those wines that are exported are usually outstanding, so get on it.

CLOSEST CITY: *Swartland is a 1-hour drive north of Cape Town.*

Elgin

Located near the South Atlantic Ocean, over the Hottentots-Holland Mountains from Stellenbosch, Elgin has a much cooler climate and longer growing season than its across-the-mountain neighbor. The style and types of wines are similar to those from Walker Bay. Elgin grows high-acid Sauvignon Blanc, Pinot Noir, Chardonnay, and even Riesling and Gewürztraminer.

CLOSEST CITY: *Elgin is about a 50-minute drive southeast from Cape Town.*

Constantia

Constantia (cahn-STAN-sha) is actually a ward (subarea) of Cape Town, but it stands alone because it is one of the oldest and most prestigious wine areas in South Africa. In the 1600s and 1700s, Constantia's sweet wines made from the white Muscat Blanc à Petits Grains grape were shipped to nobility all over western Europe for their unctuous, honeyed deliciousness (Napoleon even ordered some while in exile!). The best dry wines are from Sauvignon Blanc, with tropical fruit (pineapple, guava), melon, citrus, and grass notes, and ample acidity. Cabernet Sauvignon and Chardonnay are solid.

CLOSEST CITY: *Constantia is a 30-minute drive south of Cape Town.*

Walker Bay

Located right on the water on the southern coast, Walker Bay is influenced by cool maritime breezes, which lengthen the growing season and slow the ripening, creating high-acid yet fruity wines. The stars here are the cool-climate grapes Chardonnay, Pinot Noir, and Sauvignon Blanc. The Chardonnay tends to have noticeable oak (vanilla, caramel notes) and a creamy character to offset the acidity. The Pinot Noir often has red fruit, earthy notes, and great acidity. The Sauvignon Blanc is bright, citrusy, tropical, and herbal. Located slightly east, CAPE AGULHAS and OVERBERG are areas with similar climates and wines.

CLOSEST CITY: *Hermanus, the old fishing village near most of the Walker Bay wineries, is a 2.5-hour drive on winding roads southeast from Cape Town.*

The Wrap-Up

South Africa has no problem producing excellent wine. The challenge these producers face is getting more of that high-quality wine exported, more consistently. For a while the big wineries took on South Africa, but they did it in a critter-wine, cheapy way. This got South African wine into the consciousness of wine lovers, but after interest waned there's been little focus on the gems of this land. The wines can be a mixed bag—sometimes they are too alcoholic and fruity with no structure; sometimes they are thin and just bad—but on balance I find there are more moderately priced (under $25), excellent-quality options from South Africa than from, say, Australia these days. You can find some exceptional producers on shelves or online if you seek them out, especially if you're looking for a high-quality sparkler for a good price: For that, Cap Classique has to be on your list.

URUGUAY

Although it's not yet big enough in terms of export or production—producers cultivate just 22,239 acres (9,000 ha)—I want to devote some space to Uruguay because it will, in my opinion, be the next star of the New World. Although at the hot end of the grape-growing belt at latitude 30° to 35° south, Uruguay has a vast Atlantic coastline, and its rolling hills get plenty of cool breezes from the south to offset the intensity of the sun. Most of the quality vineyards are located in the south of the country—notably Canelones, Montevideo, San Jose, and Maldondo are strongly focused on making quality wines rather than pumping out mass quantities at low prices.

It seems like the success stories in South American wine have been about countries adopting their own signature French grape—Chile has Carménère, Argentina has Malbec, and Uruguay has Tannat, originally from Southwest France. Although Tannat probably came from the Basque country between France and Spain in the 1800s, much like Malbec, it has become something far better in the hands of Uruguayan growers. This harsh, tannic grape, when growing in the sunny vineyards of Uruguay, makes fruity, earthy, dense wines but with nice acidity and softer tannins. The best versions I've had are a few years old (five plus), when the tannins have had time to soften. Given the success with Tannat so far, there will surely be more on the market, most likely followed by Uruguayan Malbec and Cabernet Sauvignon.

Look out for Tannat, request it from your favorite store if the shop doesn't carry it, or order it online, and then squirrel it away for a few years so you can enjoy the spoils!

CLOSEST CITY: *Canelones is 1.25 hours by car from Montevideo, the capital, but if you wind up in Montevideo, there are wineries about 15 minutes from the city center. Maldondo is 2 hours east by car and San Jose is 1.75 hours northwest by car.*

The Northern Hemisphere
CANADA

Canada has a two-hundred-year history of winemaking, but for all but the last fifty or so, the country made pretty bad wine from the native species of grapes *Vitis labrusca* and *Vitis riparia*. That means the wines tasted excessively sweet and grapey and nothing like what most of us would want to pour in our glasses. But technology and smarts helped Canadians figure out how to grow *Vitis vinifera*, and once they overcame their political baggage, the industry has been on an upward climb, making some great wines.

After much effort, experimentation, and help from winemakers and growers around the world, Canada now successfully grows *Vitis vinifera* and churns out tasty cooler-climate wine. Although Nova Scotia and Quebec are making gains with their winemaking efforts, the two significant wine regions in Canada are British Columbia, namely the Okanagan Valley, and Ontario, specifically the Niagara Peninsula.

Q+A

Wait a second. Political baggage? Canadians don't have political baggage.

Yeah, they seem to have a lot figured out north of the US border, but Prohibition took hold in the early twentieth century and junked up Canada's wine industry even worse than temperance messed with the US industry. Even though Prohibition ended in 1927, it wasn't until the 1970s that Canada amended its restrictive fifty-year ban on issuing new winery licenses. That ban hamstringed any efforts to build a wine industry until the 1980s. *That's* baggage.

British Columbia— The Okanagan Valley

To give you an idea of how kind the people of Okanagan are, I wrote the wine alliance an email asking where I could buy BC wines in the United States so I could present an accurate picture in the book for you. The organization did one better: They flew me out to British Columbia and let me see the region for myself. I guess when you live in a place that gorgeous it makes you nice! Shout-out to Laura Kittmer of Wines of British Columbia!

So what should you make of British Columbia wine? Well, in the world of emerging wine regions, this is one of the newest. Until the 1990s, only native and French-American grapes grew here. The wine industry was small, local, and pretty bad. But in 1990, a little trade agreement called NAFTA (the North American Free Trade Agreement) opened up Canadian borders to less expensive wines from the United States, and BC wines couldn't compete. To help out, the provincial government offered subsidies to farmers with an ultimatum: rip up the plonk and plant *Vitis vinifera*, or find another crop to grow. Two-thirds of the growers replanted to another crop, leaving just 1,000 acres (405 ha) of vines. Now the BC wine industry is booming, especially in Okanagan, the place with the most potential for premium wine and where 275-plus wineries farm nearly 10,000 acres (4,047 ha) of vineyards planted mainly with Merlot, Pinot Gris, Chardonnay, Gewürztraminer, Riesling, Syrah, Pinot Noir, Cabernet Sauvignon, and Cabernet Franc.

There are a bunch of growing regions within BC, but 84 percent of wine is from Okanagan, the hub of the region. The conditions for vineyards are good—the dry, sandy soils and cool temperatures have prevented major fungus and phylloxera outbreaks, so many vines grow on their ungrafted, original *Vitis vinifera* roots (although I found this made no difference to the flavor of the wine). The area around Lake Okanagan is beautiful, but the wines are just OK. Every wine that captured my attention was from the southern Okanagan Valley.

The unofficial subregion of BLACK SAGE/OSOYOOS and the official SIMILKAMEEN VALLEY region on the US border have warm, long growing seasons and produce balanced, fruity Merlot, Cabernet Franc, and Syrah. The southern area of Oliver contains Vaseaux Lake, which moderates temperature and can yield flavorful Riesling, Chardonnay, Gewürztraminer,

Pinot Noir, and Gamay. In the warmer, southern parts of Oliver, producers churn out excellent Merlot, Cabernet Franc, and Syrah. The best wineries of BC are located in this pocket of Okanagan, and when I visit again, I'll head south: The south of the valley is the future of BC wine.

CLOSEST CITY: *Okanagan is a 4-hour drive east of Vancouver, but Kelowna has an international airport if you want to fly directly to wine country.*

Ontario—Niagra

With 17,000 acres (6,900 ha) under vine, Ontario is a tiny region when you compare it to others around the world. But with 150 wineries and a distinctive flavor profile, the region is going to grow larger.

Although the province makes still, sparkling, and sweet wine, it's best known around the world for ice wine: Ontario has the distinction of being the number one producer of ice wine in the world by volume. Because the temperature is consistently below 17.6°F (-8°C) in winter, which is what's necessary for the production of ice wine, this region is the only one in the world where ice wine can be made every year (see page 260). The top ice wines are made from Riesling, but the more common ones are from the less prestigious but still great French-American hybrid Vidal Blanc. You'll see Cabernet Franc ice wine as well.

Ontario has three Designated Viticultural Areas (DVAs): NIAGARA PENINSULA, PRINCE EDWARD COUNTY, and LAKE ERIE NORTH SHORE. All benefit from the moderating effect of two Great Lakes, Erie and Ontario, but this is squarely a cool-climate wine region. Within the Niagara Peninsula lies the Niagara Escarpment, which has

MAKING ICE WINE

Ice wine is produced from grapes left hanging on the vine long after regular harvest. Whereas still wines are harvested from August through October, ice wine harvest doesn't start until late December or January. When the grapes are picked, they aren't shriveled raisins—they still have water inside them. When the temperature drops below 17.6°F (-8°C), the water in the grape freezes, and producers can easily pop out that ice cube, leaving sweet, fruity, yet still acidic juice to ferment and bottle. As fun trivia fact, it takes 10 shriveled grapes to make 1 milliliter or a fifth of a teaspoon of ice wine and 1.5 regular grapes to make 1 milliliter of still wine. The ice wine biz is labor- and cost-intensive.

some of the best subappellations in Ontario: BEAMSVILLE BENCH and TWENTY MILE BENCH.

Chardonnay, Riesling, Pinot Noir, and Cabernet Franc are the top grapes for still wine. Styles vary, but the region's cooler climate makes the wines lighter in body with high acidity, mineral notes, and lower alcohol levels.

CLOSEST CITY: *The Niagara Escarpment and Niagara-on-the-Lake are each just over 1.5 hours by car from Toronto, and 45 minutes by car from Buffalo, New York.*

The Wrap-Up

Canadian wine is a fast-growing enterprise, with over 800 wineries farming 32,000 acres (12,950 ha) today, but that number stands to grow. If you have the time and budget, visit Canada to see what a new wine nation looks like: 94 percent of the wineries are small enterprises, with hard-working, down-to-earth people in the tasting rooms and making the wine. As it happens in all wine regions that make great wines, the wines of Canada will become more prestigious, the people more experienced and more jaded, and the visiting experience more like established regions of the United States. Visit now, so you can see the evolution from the beginnings and track these regions' potentially great future.

UNITED STATES

Winemaking has been going on in the United States since the 1600s, but if you dust off the brain cobwebs and dig back into American history, you'll recall that public opinion seriously turned against booze in the early twentieth century. Even though California's wine industry was already gathering steam by 1919, the Volstead Act and the Eighteenth Amendment to the US Constitution began Prohibition and killed wine for thirteen years. The effects of that period are still around today.

The problem is that when you prohibit people from doing something they were previously permitted to do, they completely rebel and go to extremes. And that's why you don't hear about people making bathtub wine or getting hammered on wine in speakeasies in the 1920s. It was the hard stuff that people craved when they drank on the sly because it would get them loaded fast and it was the most defiant of Prohibition. Sadly, people became so accustomed to the booze lifestyle that when things got sorted out, the hard stuff was still the drink of choice.

This legacy created a cultural bias in the United States for hard liquor for decades (evidence: The three-martini lunch so popular until the 1980s). Wine couldn't catch up because, for it to get back on the public's radar, the country needed a cultural shift. There was another big problem: Wine is farming. You have to get the land back in order and your grapes producing before you can go out with a product that people want to drink. By the time wineries gained momentum in a meaningful way, it was the 1960s. At that point, beer and hard alcohol had dominant positions and wine was a second-class citizen.

Thankfully, California and some other states had stubborn folks who believed in wine's potential. The real turning point for California and American wine came when Napa Valley wineries Chateau Montelena and Stag's Leap Wine Cellars won a competition in Paris in 1976 that ranked their wines as tastier than leading French wines. Although mostly a show of wine dorkery, the idea that California could beat France's best made the world take notice and started to shift the US consciousness about domestic wine. *Maybe we could make good wine after all!*

About forty years later, the United States now has a culture that's exploring wine and loving it. There's never been a better time for wine in the United States. But tackling American wine is a tough undertaking. The country is huge and great wines come from all over. The leading horses remain the four high-quality regions of California, some amazing areas in Washington State, the wines of Oregon, the wines of New York State, and, in my opinion, the emerging wine areas of Virginia. So with no snub to other areas, here we go.

California

According to the California Wine Institute, California produces nearly 90 percent of wine in the United States. Apart from a few other areas that are making exceptional wines, it's safe to say that California basically *is* wine in the United States.

Spanish missionaries grew grapes in California starting in 1683 (about eighty years after Virginia started work on growing grapes!), and Italian, French, Hungarian, and Swiss immigrants identified the best places for grape growing and imported *Vitis vinifera* vines from Europe

NECESSARY CAVEAT

Since I'm an American, I'm putting a caveat here immediately—inevitably someone will read this section and say, "How could you forget X region or state? That's *my* state! We make the best wine ever! Elizabeth, you're a horrible person." I'll lay it out now. We are going to hit the main regions that produce a significant volume of wine or regions that have great acclaim for being players in the wine world at this time. No offense meant, but I can't do everything here.

I hope no one's feathers get ruffled and we can get onto the fun stuff.

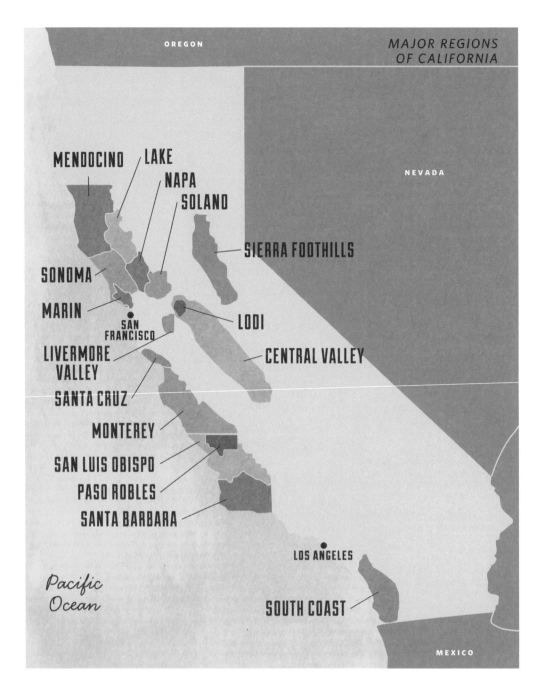

OREGON

NEVADA

MENDOCINO LAKE

NAPA

SOLANO

SIERRA FOOTHILLS

SONOMA

MARIN

SAN FRANCISCO

LODI

LIVERMORE VALLEY

CENTRAL VALLEY

SANTA CRUZ

MONTEREY

SAN LUIS OBISPO

PASO ROBLES

SANTA BARBARA

LOS ANGELES

Pacific Ocean

SOUTH COAST

MEXICO

to California. Blessed with sunshine, varied terrain, and a predictable growing season in most places, California was destined to be the heart of American wine.

Beginning in the 1970s, California became a powerhouse on the world wine scene. Much of that is due to the wineries in the North Coast, a 3-million-acre (1.2-million-ha) mega-AVA (American Viticultural Area) that covers Napa, Sonoma, Mendocino, Lake County, and parts of Marin and Solano Counties. California wine country has expanded greatly since then, including areas east, south, and even north of the traditional areas. Following are details on the big areas, beginning with the three of the North Coast: Napa, Sonoma, and Mendocino.

Napa

There is so much I could write about Napa. My experiences of it have been wonderful and not so wonderful. Folks in neighboring Sonoma will generally tell you that they won't cross the border because of the snootiness, shameless marketing, and emphasis on money and image over wine quality. I can't argue that many wineries are guilty of this, and I'll admit that in recent years the expense and snobbery have stopped me from visiting often, but Napa still makes phenomenal wines.

The main grape of the area is Cabernet Sauvignon, with Merlot, Chardonnay, and Sauvignon Blanc as strong backups. For an area that's about 4 miles (6 km) wide and 30 miles (48 km) long, it has enormous diversity. Napa contains nearly every soil type in the world and has more pockets of cool and hot than you can fathom. Morning fog rolls in from the southern San Pablo Bay and through gaps in the western coastal range to blanket the vineyards and keep the grapes cool in the morning. When the fog burns off in the late morning, abundant sun ripens the grapes. This condition is essential to the high quality of Napa's grapes and wines.

Although the region only makes 4 percent of the wine in California, more than 480 wineries are on that job. *Yikes.* What does that mean for us as buyers of this wine? It can be a crapshoot in terms of flavor and quality: The name "Napa" warrants a higher price tag, so less ethical producers will take full advantage of that, giving you poor quality for way too much money.

The biggest distinctions in Napa are in where the fruit is grown: mountains/foothills vs. valley floor. Wines from fruit grown in the mountains have more concentrated fruit flavors, abundant tannin, and acidity. They're tougher in their youth but more complex with time. The valley floor wines are more for immediate gratification—they're bold, fruity wines with high tannin, low acid, and often high alcohol, making them soft and velvety.

Q+A

What's the deal with bottles that say Napa Valley? I see those a lot—more than any of these areas you just called out.

I mention this in passing on the previous page, but for clarification, the Napa Valley AVA includes *all* the areas mentioned here plus any grape-growing regions outside those appellations. It's an all-encompassing area, and that can mean interesting and great blends can result because winemakers can get a combination of fruit from all over. Usually, however, it's a dumping ground for leftovers—all the wine not fit to go into finer wines. "Napa Valley" on a label allows you to charge a premium, regardless of quality. Once again, producer is the key to figuring out what's good and what's not.

Oh, and while we're on the topic, the same goes for the Sonoma County AVA. (Sonoma Valley is an AVA inside Sonoma County, so it's a different naming convention with the same idea.)

Another major distinction in Napa is between older producers and newer ones. The older ones tend to keep alcohol levels lower (below 14 percent) and try to pick on the earlier side to get more acidity in their wines. The newer ones are generally focused on big and brawny, although they've tempered their approaches as people have demanded more balanced styles.

Even with these cuts to divide the world, given the sunny, beautiful weather in most years in Napa, fruit is always the primary component in a wine. That makes Napa one of the first regions that I recommend for people just getting into wine. The opulent, rich, full flavors are accessible to anyone who has eaten fruit (*'cause the wine tastes a lot like the fruit you know and love*). This quality makes it easier to relate to the wines and the descriptions of them.

Napa has sixteen subareas. Nearly all specialize in juicy, black fruit–flavored, tannic Cabernet with other Bordeaux blending grapes like Merlot, Petit Verdot, and Cabernet Franc mixed in. Chardonnay is the queen of the whites and grown nearly everywhere, which I find odd, since Chardonnay does better in cooler regions, but wineries need to pay the bills and Chardonnay is a big money maker. There is some Sauvignon Blanc (abused and usually an afterthought for these wineries but also a cash cow) and a few others—like Zinfandel, which used to dominate this valley long ago and is generally high quality.

When considering the wines of Napa, there's something counterintuitive to remember regarding the geography: As you go north, it gets hotter and hotter. The southern end of the valley is cool, due to the influence of the San Pablo Bay and the Pacific Ocean breezes and that fog I mentioned earlier. So wines from the south tend to be more moderate in fruit flavor, alcohol, and tannin. Wines from the northern end of Napa are bolder. Also, the mountains are often above the fog line, so they never get that cooling influence and receive strong sun during the day with a reprieve of cool to cold temperatures at night, which can create more layered, intense flavors.

Since I've emphasized growing area, the best way to address appellations is by terrain.

MOUNTAIN AREAS: On the west side of the valley—in the Mayacamas Mountains—Diamond Mountain, Mt. Veeder, and Spring Mountain each specialize in a different style of Cabernet. All have intense fruit flavor and strong tannins.

MT. VEEDER and DIAMOND MOUNTAIN are more tannic with fruit and spice. Veeder tends to be more elegant, Diamond more minerally, although some producers make full, high-alcohol versions on Diamond.

SPRING MOUNTAIN isn't actually a mountain, but a bunch of hills with springs flowing through them. The wines can be luscious and tasty or over the top with too much alcohol and tannin. Because Spring Mountain is spread out with varied terrain, there are pockets where whites grow well—you can find fruity, tasty Viognier, Riesling, and Chardonnay from Spring Mountain producers.

HOWELL MOUNTAIN makes fruity, tannic Cabernet Sauvignon and Zinfandel, but their point of difference is an herbal quality that you can't find from other mountain wines.

CALISTOGA, at the far north end of Napa Valley, is sandwiched between Howell Mountain and Diamond Mountain. It gets hot during the growing season but has cool nights that prevent the grapes from becoming jammy or flabby. Calistoga's diurnals (day to night temperature swings) are the largest in Napa—the temperature can range 50°F (28°C) throughout the day. I put it in this section because these wines are similar to mountain wines: They're plump with ripe fruit and healthy amounts of tannin.

VALLEY FLOOR AND BENCHLAND: The floor of the Napa Valley holds many of the most esteemed appellations in the United States. Here are a few groupings of AVAs that have similar wines.

ST. HELENA, YOUNTVILLE, AND ATLAS PEAK are moderate to full, mainly Cabernet Sauvignon and Cabernet blends that are velvety with restrained fruit, alcohol, and tannin.

RUTHERFORD, OAKVILLE, AND STAGS LEAP DISTRICT are rich, dense, fruit bombs that are tannic, alcoholic, luscious, velvety, and fruit forward, although the better Cabernets, Merlots, and Bordeaux-style blends are more nuanced and have a lighter touch. Napa's reputation for "big" wines was born in these places. Stags Leap is probably the mildest of the crew, Rutherford is known to be earthy but dense, and Oakville is known for its huge (cult) wines that have an herbal or mint quality.

LOS CARNEROS, COOMBSVILLE, OAK KNOLL DISTRICT OF NAPA VALLEY, AND WILD HORSE VALLEY are restrained wines with the only Pinot Noir, acidic Chardonnay, cooler-climate Syrah, and truly restrained Cabernet and Merlot in Napa. These southern areas receive marine influence from the Pacific and San Pablo Bay, making them cooler and the wine lighter than the rest of Napa. Carneros makes sparkling wine as well.

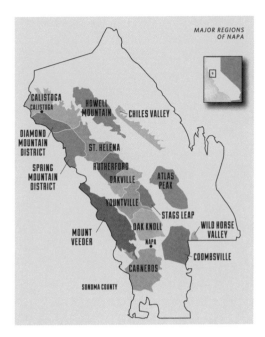

MAJOR REGIONS OF NAPA

CLOSEST CITY: *The Napa wineries are a 1- to 1.5-hour drive northeast from San Francisco, depending on where in the valley you go.*

Sonoma

Sonoma is bigger and harder to get a pulse on than Napa. But I want to be clear: Just because it's big doesn't mean it's bad. Sonoma is different from Napa in climate and terroir, even though they are often (mistakenly) grouped together.

A few defining climate and geographic features make Sonoma unique. The most important one is the role of the Pacific Ocean and the cooling influence it provides to the region. The ocean fog and breezes that sneak in through gaps in the coastal range and from San Pablo Bay in the south keep the grapes on a steady, moderate diurnal swing. Fog comes in and blankets the vineyards, keeping them cool through the night and early morning (and for a longer period than in Napa Valley). The fog burns off, the intense heat gives the grapes needed hours of ripening, and then the cool breezes and fog return. Because of this pattern, much of Sonoma's growing area is characterized by a slow, long growing season.

Sonoma, which has had success but not the kind of commercial acclaim that Napa has garnered, has more farmer-type producers (although of late there has been a buying spree, and both large wineries and folks from Silicon Valley have been snatching up small wineries, making Sonoma a bit more like Napa). You'll get more style variation from Sonoma, and maybe a few more misses than Napa because there's more experimentation and variability in terroir. Also, given how big Sonoma is and how many valleys it contains, there are pockets for every varietal—you'll find Cabernet Sauvignon, Zinfandel, Syrah, Grenache, Malbec, Viognier, Pinot Gris, and Italian varietals growing in Sonoma alongside Chardonnay and Pinot Noir. The variation makes the region hard to pinpoint, but it's worth it to try.

Because the action in Sonoma is in the individual valleys, I'll detail those major areas. This will help you differentiate between styles when you're shopping for these wines.

THE SOUTHERN AREA: SONOMA VALLEY: This is confusing because as I mentioned in the Napa section, the Napa Valley AVA is the kitchen sink blend (sometimes not a bad thing, but grapes come from all over). Sonoma's version is *not* Sonoma Valley; that's Sonoma County. Sonoma Valley is in the southeast corner of Sonoma and it overlaps LOS CARNEROS, the cool southern region of Napa and Sonoma, which I discuss in the Napa section (page 265). In the southern part of the valley, the Petaluma Gap, a small opening in the coastal range near the town

NAPA VS. SONOMA

Let's go back to my original comment about Sonoma folks and their criticism of Napa as being full of snoots who place an emphasis status over wine quality, which I didn't really explain.

Sonoma is full of farmer types. They look at Napa as a place for celebrity winemakers and brand names. It's the Hollywood of wine, and Sonoma is more like the indie film scene. People who criticize Napa say that high-quality grapes are secondary to winemaker tricks (malolactic fermentation, yeast selection, oak and more oak), showy properties, and flashy marketing, and that's not OK. They have a point in some cases. Napa is, after all, home to the cult wine scene—small-production vineyards that make intense wines that score big scores, cost thousands, and are not accessible unless you know someone and can gain access to the mailing list (Screaming Eagle, Scarecrow, Harlan, and Colgin, to name a few). It's also home to huge brands owned by big wine conglomerates like Gallo, Constellation, and large investor groups with big marketing budgets, making Napa wines completely commercial.

There's big variety in Napa, and if you can sort through the BS you'll find wineries with a philosophy you'll hear espoused by many a European winemaker, a good benchmark for land-loving winemakers.

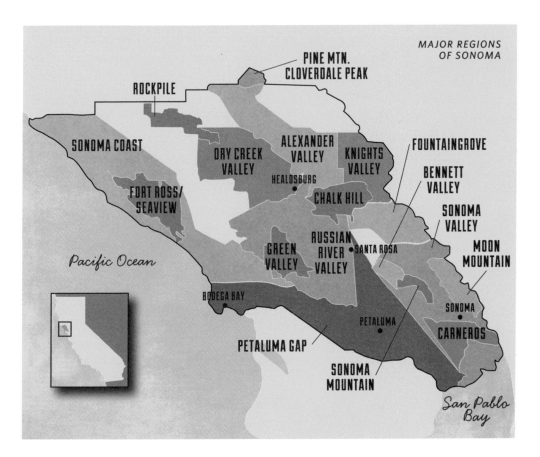

MAJOR REGIONS
OF SONOMA

PINE MTN.
CLOVERDALE PEAK

ROCKPILE

SONOMA COAST

DRY CREEK
VALLEY

ALEXANDER
VALLEY

KNIGHTS
VALLEY

FOUNTAINGROVE

BENNETT
VALLEY

HEALDSBURG

FORT ROSS/
SEAVIEW

CHALK HILL

SONOMA
VALLEY

Pacific Ocean

GREEN
VALLEY

RUSSIAN
RIVER
VALLEY

SANTA ROSA

MOON
MOUNTAIN

BODEGA BAY

PETALUMA

SONOMA

PETALUMA GAP

CARNEROS

SONOMA
MOUNTAIN

San Pablo
Bay

of Petaluma, allows early morning ocean fog to enter the inland winegrowing regions. The fog burns off, the grapes get intense sun to ripen, and then the Pacific breezes lower temperatures in certain parts of the area in the afternoon.

Notice I said "certain parts." This is a problem for Sonoma Valley: It has an enormous range of grapes, temperatures, and terroir, so it's hard for producers to coalesce on a style. Some of the wines are concentrated; some are light. Some are good; some are boring. What you get depends on the part of the valley the producer is in and what that producer decides to do with the grapes in the vineyard and in the cellar. Here are some key areas to look out for.

SONOMA MOUNTAIN is small, tall, and kind of weird. The appellation is defined by elevation—the vineyards are at 400 to 1,200 feet (120 to 365 m). But the mountain

is a two-headed beast! On one side, it's devilishly hot and unaffected by fog. Cabernet Sauvignon is the most successful grape, yielding black-fruited, tannic wines with lower acidity. On the other side of the mountain, which is not technically the Sonoma Mountain AVA, cool Pacific influence comes in and Pinot Noir and Chardonnay, with nice acidity and good fruit flavor, thrive.

BENNETT VALLEY wins my award for up-and-comer in Sonoma. The cooling effect from the Pacific Ocean means grapes have a long growing season in which they can maintain acidity while gathering concentrated fruit flavor. The best wines are Syrah and Rhône-style blends, although Cabernet and Merlot do well here, too. They can be pricey but they are fantastic.

The MOON MOUNTAIN DISTRICT, at elevations up to 2,200 feet (670 m) in the northern hills above the town of Sonoma, is above the fog line, and the grapes bask in sun all day, so it makes powerful, rich Cabernet Sauvignon and Zinfandel with balanced acidity.

CLOSEST CITY: *The Sonoma Valley and Sonoma Mountain areas are a 10- to 30-minute drive from the cities of Sonoma and Santa Rosa and are about a 1.25-hour drive north/northwest from San Francisco.*

THE MIDDLE PORTION OF SONOMA: RUSSIAN RIVER VALLEY: Pinot Noir, Chardonnay, and Zinfandel are the stars of Russian River Valley, which includes the cities of Healdsburg, part of Santa Rosa, and some of Sebastopol in the south. Russian River Valley wines are distinctive—fruity and often with a taste of the marine-influenced soil (almost salty tasting to me). The fog keeps this valley cool, intruding in the late afternoon, so the wines maintain acidity and balance.

Russian River Valley has some phenomenal producers, but it also has more than a few whose Pinot is often more like Cabernet Sauvignon or Syrah. They pick late for maximum fruitiness and supple texture in the wine, and by doing so they lose the subtlety that makes Pinot Noir interesting. Although this has changed in recent years, a lot of Russian River Valley Chardonnays taste manipulated—lots of oak, lots of creamy butter notes from malolactic fermentation (see page 27). I'm in a minority on this one, but if you're with me and don't like huge-alcohol, fruit-forward Pinots and Chardonnays, know that there are producers who lay off that stuff and make a different style wine. You need to do research to find those, however, because they aren't the norm. There are two subregions of the Russian River Valley.

CHALK HILL is a warm, elevated sub-appellation (its highest point is 1,300 feet [400 m] in the eastern Mayacamas Mountains). The best wines are grassy, herbal Sauvignon Blanc and fat, creamy, oaky Chardonnay.

GREEN VALLEY OF RUSSIAN RIVER VALLEY is quite the opposite of Chalk Hill. It's blanketed in pea-soup-thick fog for much of the day, and it barely heats up before the cool breezes and fog roll back in during the late afternoon. Great sparkling and still wine of Pinot Noir and Chardonnay come from Green Valley of Russian River Valley (there's another, hotter Green Valley in California, which is why this place has the long name). Cool-climate Syrah from here is one to watch.

CLOSEST CITY: *Russian River Valley is between the cities of Sebastopol, Santa Rosa, and Healdsburg, which are a 1.25- to 1.5-hour drive from San Francisco and about 20 to 25 minutes from one another.*

THE NORTHERN PORTIONS OF SONOMA: DRY CREEK VALLEY, ROCKPILE, ALEXANDER VALLEY: Small and compact, Dry Creek Valley is fun to explore and has some of the most dynamic producers of Sonoma. Although it gets fog, it's mostly a classic California winegrowing climate, with warm days and cool nights—excellent for Zinfandel, the valley's signature grape. This is an old grape-growing area that has historically been dominated by family-owned wineries, and still is. Expect plummy, spicy but balanced Zinfandel with good acid and moderate tannin. A growing number of small producers make tasty red southern French (Syrah is outstanding) and Italian varietals, so look out for them. Overly fruity, low-acid, high-alcohol Sauvignon

Blanc and Chardonnay are also popular (but I'm hoping the update of this book will say white Rhône varieties like Viognier and Grenache Blanc have taken over, since they'll be more successful!).

ROCKPILE is a Zinfandel paradise in a northwest pocket of land adjacent to Dry Creek Valley. The name of the appellation says it all—soil is rocky and spare, making the grapes dig for nutrients and packing them with flavor. With its own specific clone, Rockpile Zins are usually dripping with juicy plum fruit and a hit of earth, black pepper, and moderate tannin and acid. Most people agree that this is some of the best Zin in the world. Solid, dark-fruited, rustic Petite Sirah comes from here, too.

A huge, warm valley that's more agriculture focused than tourist driven, ALEXANDER VALLEY is known for Cabernet Sauvignon. I would argue that some Alexander Valley Cabs are better than Napa Cabs. Rich, dark fruit flavors and powerful tannins with soft acid make this a classic California Cab appellation. Although many are still more than $75, this is the place for value if you're looking for a Napa style at a non-Napa price. Old vine Zinfandel, Merlot, Chardonnay, and even Sangiovese also grow in pockets. Within Alexander Valley is the sunny, warm PINE MOUNTAIN-CLOVERDALE PEAK appellation, which grows nearly all fruity, tannic Cabernet Sauvignon above the fog line at 1,600 to 3,000 feet (485 to 915 m).

Next to Alexander Valley and Calistoga in northern Napa, KNIGHTS VALLEY produces figgy, melonlike Sauvignon Blanc, and Cabernet Sauvignon with enormous fruit flavor, tobacco, and cedar notes and often little complexity or acidity, given how warm the vineyards are.

CLOSEST CITY: *Dry Creek is a 5-minute drive from downtown Healdsburg, as is Alexander Valley, where there are fewer wineries to visit. Healdsburg is about 1.5 hours from San Francisco, and parts of the valleys above can take more than 2 hours to reach, given the windy, rural roads.*

THE MASSIVE SONOMA COAST What can I say about an AVA that contains more than 500,000 acres (202,343 ha)? Not all are planted, but still it's huge! It follows a coastal range of mountains that spans from the southern tip of Sonoma in the San Pablo Bay to Mendocino County in the north. This area is craving to be carved up into smaller, more meaningful sub-AVAs, given the number of microclimates and temperature variations. As of 2019, two discrete areas have been carved out of the Sonoma Coast AVA. FORT-ROSS SEAVIEW, which is a warmer, sunnier area above the fog line, produces acidic, yet fruity Pinot Noir and Chardonnay. The PETALUMA GAP AVA includes parts of northern Marin County and is a cool, windy, foggy area. These breezy vineyards, which specialize in acidic, earthy, crisp Pinot Noir, Chardonnay, and Syrah, sit in a break in the coastal mountains (wind gap) that allows cool marine air to filter into the rest of Sonoma County. The Petaluma Gap wines are some of California's best cool-climate wines.

CLOSEST CITY: *There aren't many wineries on the Sonoma Coast and it's hard to get to! You'll need to make an appointment with specific wineries rather than just exploring and then allow 2 hours from San Francisco and 1 hour from Santa Rosa.*

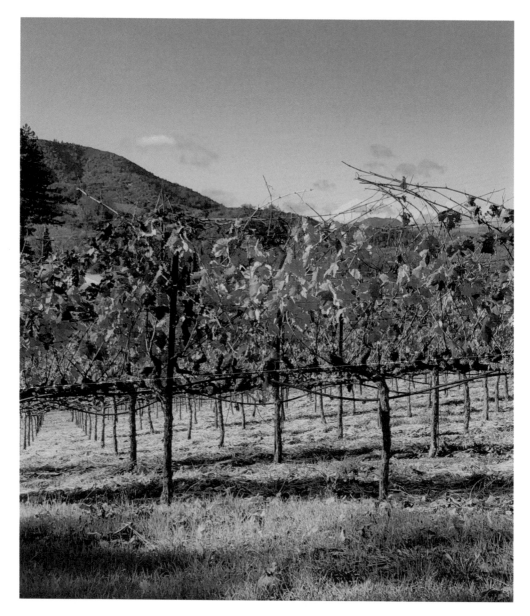

Mendocino County

Mendocino is the most underrated of the North Coast regions and the one with the most potential for long-term growth and interesting wines. Mendocino successfully grows its flagship Pinot Noir along with Chardonnay, Syrah, Zinfandel, and more.

In this green place—25 percent of the vineyards are organic—just north of Sonoma County, you won't find many wineries to visit. Most producers are relatively small and agriculture oriented—that translates to immaculate care for the vineyards and often leads to excellent wines. There are fewer AVAs than in Sonoma or Napa. POTTER VALLEY, REDWOOD VALLEY, and ANDERSON VALLEY are the biggest. Look out for cool-climate varieties like Riesling out of Potter Valley and complex, more acidic Cabernet Sauvignon, Zinfandel, Barbera, and Petite Sirah from the warmer Redwood Valley. From Anderson Valley, expect greatness!

Producers from down south, namely Sonoma, think Mendocino's Anderson

Valley Pinot Noir is grower gold. Swanky producers source from here because the grapes are fruity with a distinctive terroir tinge that you can't find elsewhere. But Anderson Valley's potential is bigger than just Pinot—its twenty or so wineries also make great Alsace varieties (Gewürztraminer, Riesling, Pinot Gris) and impressive grapes for restrained sparkling wine, too.

Not everything you taste from Mendocino will be great, but in my experience you're going to get a more consistent balance between fruit, earth, and the textural components—alcohol, acid, and tannin—than from some more well-known regions. If you don't like earthy wine, this may not be the best region for you, but if you're interested in the world of terroir, there's not a better place in California to start.

CLOSEST CITY: *Mendocino's wineries are 2 to 2.5 hours northwest of San Francisco by car.*

Central Coast of California

Spanning from San Francisco down to Santa Barbara and east to the Livermore Valley and Paso Robles, the Central Coast is gigantic. Winemaking only takes place in pockets since much of the area is reserved for suburban sprawl around San Jose and San Francisco, the coastal majesty of Big Sur running 90 miles (145 km) from Carmel to San Simeon, and the "salad bowl" of California south of Monterey, where veggies are grown to sustain the US populace. Even with nonwine features, there's still an abundance of viticulture.

The Central Coast wasn't a wine area (with the exception of a few Catholic missions that grew grapes) until the 1960s when growers from the North Coast, looking for more land to meet expanding demand, headed south and found pockets where they could grow quality grapes. Some places were great for massive production of lackluster grapes that made cheap Chardonnays, Merlots, and Cabernets. But scrappy producers scouted quality areas and struck wine gold.

Because the area is so large and variable, I'll comment below on those appellations you will see most often and what they have to offer.

Monterey

In the northern Central Coast is the Monterey AVA, which encompasses a bunch of other AVAs. This is a relatively cool area with breezes off Monterey Bay, so this is prime land for growing Chardonnay and Pinot Noir, which crave cooler weather. The flatish slope of the vineyards makes mechanical harvesting a great option. That reduces labor costs dramatically, making this area the playground of the big guys: Constellation, Gallo, Kendall-Jackson, and Delicato own much of the land here. About 70 percent of grapes grown in Monterey go into the broader Central Coast or California appellation wines, so even though the area is a grape-growing powerhouse, it's not as common to see the Monterey AVA listed on the bottle.

What may be more common is to see places like the ARROYO SECO, CARMEL VALLEY, CHALONE, and SANTA LUCIA HIGHLANDS AVAs. These small pockets are home to wineries that make excellent, often pricey Chardonnay and Pinot Noir. Santa Lucia Highlands is the most important of the sub-AVAs. The appellation is high in the Santa Lucia Mountains so it gets abundant morning sun, but then is walloped by cold air in the afternoons. The grapes have a long growing season, producing full-bodied Chardonnay and bold Pinot Noir with noticeable acidity. Earthy, acidic Syrah is also successful here.

CLOSEST CITY: *The northern part of the Central Coast is about a 2-hour drive south from San Francisco.*

San Luis Obispo County

Like most places worth their salt in the Central Coast of California, San Luis Obispo County (or SLO as it's affectionately abbreviated) makes impressive wine because of the cool marine air influence from the Pacific Ocean, without which it would be too hot to grow grapes. The county is big on wine—it's got nearly 28,000 acres (11,330 ha) planted and more than a hundred wineries.

With cool marine breezes and fog, grapes get time to mature over the course of a long growing season, giving them full fruit flavors while maintaining an acidic freshness.

Chardonnay and Pinot Noir are the stars of the region, but Rhône natives Syrah and Viognier do well in the slightly warmer spots near the coast, too. Experiments with aromatic whites like Riesling and Gewürztraminer are proving successful, so if you see one, give it a try.

There are two sub-AVAs in San Luis Obispo wine country: EDNA VALLEY and ARROYO GRANDE VALLEY, both of which you'll see on wine labels. Edna Valley is just 5 miles (8 km) from the Pacific Ocean and runs northwest to southeast, so it benefits from cool Pacific breezes that filter in from the beautiful Morro Bay (*Finding Dory* anyone?). Edna Valley makes mainly high-acid yet fruity Chardonnay and Pinot Noir, with Syrah and Viognier growing in acreage in the slightly warmer sites.

In Arroyo Grande, acidic yet fruity Chardonnay and Pinot Noir grow on hillsides close to the coast, but here the inland areas above the fog line are warm and also produce bold, fruity, higher-alcohol Zinfandel and Syrah. You'll rarely find a wine area that makes both sparkling and robust reds, but Arroyo Grande makes the paradox work.

CLOSEST CITY: *The two valleys are next to one another and are about a 3.25-hour drive north from Los Angeles and a 3.5-hour drive south from San Francisco. They're a 1.5-hour drive north from Santa Barbara.*

Paso Robles

Drive to the halfway point between San Francisco and LA and you'll hit Paso Robles, which locals pronounce with an American accent—it's PAH-so ROW-bulls. And don't think about putting on that Spanish accent and correcting them! This is a fast-growing region and it's got plenty of room to keep going: It encompasses more than 600,000 acres (24,280 ha) of land with only 32,000 acres (13,000 ha) under vine.

The boundaries of Paso Robles span from Monterey County in the north, 25 miles (40 km) south, and then from 6 miles (9.6 km) inland from the Pacific to 35 miles (56 km) east. You can imagine that the kinds of grapes that thrive in vineyards 6 miles from the coast are vastly different from those 41 miles (66 km) from the coast. Actually, you don't need to imagine: It's a fact that the warmest areas accumulate 20 percent more heat than the coolest areas, which changes the landscape for grape growing completely. Annual rainfall also varies dramatically—there's little rain in the east and often 45 inches (114 cm) or more right next to the

Pacific. Elevations range depending on the subarea. Soil types vary, and that changes what grows well in certain areas, too.

Similar to Sonoma County, Paso's wine regions are blocked from direct Pacific Ocean access by coastal mountains. And like Sonoma, the area is cooled by the grace of a large gap in these mountains through which cool marine air flows, the Templeton Gap. Wineries closest to it in the west have vastly different climates than eastern areas, which get no help from the cooling breezes of the Pacific and are just plain hot during the day, even if they do get cool at night.

Given the picture I've painted about the differences of this area, it's mind-boggling that for forty years it was under one appellation: Paso Robles. Unless you visited and saw the dichotomy, buyers of Paso came to know only one style associated with the area—jammy, high-alcohol Zinfandel and Cabernet Sauvignon from inland vineyards made by large wineries that had big distribution networks.

After years of hard work and lobbying the (often clueless) Tax and Trade Bureau of the US government, which puzzlingly regulates wine AVAs, the producers of Paso (led in large part by my favorite in the

WHAT TO EXPECT FROM
PASO ROBLES AVAS

Western, Pacific-influenced AVAs:	**Warmer, inland AVAs with moderate Pacific influence:**	**Hot, inland areas:**
Balanced Zinfandel, white and red Rhône blends, and Bordeaux styles. There are signs we may see a crop of great Pinot and Chardonnay coming in the future, given the cooler pockets.	Generally balanced but fruity and sometimes alcohol-rich Rhône varieties, Italian reds like Sangiovese and Barbera, and full-bodied Cab.	Rich, sometimes flabby, and often mass-produced wines (the traditional stereotype of Paso Robles wines). Specialties are Viognier, Petite Sirah, Zinfandel, and Cabernet Sauvignon, among other heat-tolerant grapes.
Adelaida Distrtict	El Pomar Distrtict	Paso Robles Geneseo Distrtict
Paso Robles Willow Creek District	Creston District	San Juan Creek
Templeton Gap District	Paso Robles Estrella District	Templeton Gap District
Santa Margarita Ranch (southern coastal area)	San Miguel District	Paso Robles Highlands District

area—Tablas Creek) finally made a huge breakthrough in 2014 when Paso Robles was split up into eleven separate AVAs (see sidebar, page 273). If producers make use of these appellations, we'll be able to figure out the style of the wine based on place. Although it's going to take time for producers to start labeling their wines by sub-AVA rather than just Paso Robles, the better ones are doing it, so look for that as a sign of quality.

CLOSEST CITY: *Paso Robles is a 3.25-hour drive southeast of San Francisco and a 3.25-hour drive northwest of Los Angeles. It's about a 2-hour drive north of Santa Barbara.*

Santa Barbara County

On the southern end of the Central Coast and just an hour and a half north of Los Angeles are the wine areas of Santa Barbara County. Located at latitude 34.5° north, this playground of Ronald Reagan and Oprah Winfrey has a secret geological weapon: distinctive east to west mountain ranges that cool things down and make this low-latitude spot more similar to places at latitude 45° north than 35° north.

After 12 million years of plate movement, give or take, the Santa Ynez Mountains pivoted, becoming the most distinctive east-west mountain range from Alaska to Chile. This is great for wine. Whereas north-south coastal mountains can block cooling ocean influence, making the occasional gap in the ranges essential because they allow cool air to filter into inland regions, Santa Barbara's east-west valleys serve as funnels, sucking in fog and marine air, and creating cooler temperatures farther inland than you'd expect. That means cool-climate grapes like Pinot Noir and Chardonnay thrive here.

Most of the vineyards are on mountainsides, since slopes get ample sun during the day. The light and heat allow grapes to fully mature, but the Pacific influence lets them do so in their own good time. Slow ripening means grapes get a balance of fruit flavor and acidity, and are more moderate in alcohol.

The most famed and exciting wine comes from the cool vineyards near the Pacific. These have soils full of marine sediment and limestone that impart a mineral, earthy quality that can remind you of fuller Burgundy wines. There are also warmer inland areas that make wines from Merlot, Cabernet Sauvignon, Grenache, Viognier, and Syrah, among others. For me, the real gems are the cool-climate wines, and this is what I buy from Santa Barbara. There are two important sub-AVAs of Santa Barbara.

SANTA MARIA VALLEY: In the northernmost portion of the Santa Barbara County AVA, just 15 miles (24 km) from the Pacific Ocean, temperatures in the Santa Maria Valley don't get much higher than 75°F (24°C), and it can get so cool and windy that, if not for the intensity of sun during the day, grapes couldn't grow.

Intensely flavored wine of mainly Chardonnay and Pinot Noir are the area's specialties. You'll find Chardonnay with citrus and tropical fruit flavors, and (usually) balanced oak. These wines are often sharper in acidity than wines from Sonoma and Napa. The Pinot has ripe cherry and red and black berry flavors with high acid and mild oak influence. In the east, where it's warmer, Rhône varieties (Syrah, Grenache, Roussanne, Marsanne), some Merlot, and Cabernet Sauvignon grow on sunny hills.

In the Burgundian tradition, Santa Maria Valley puts great importance on vineyard. The best example is the Bien Nacido vineyard. It's huge and varied, but widely considered the best in class, and you'll see it on the label of many top producers' wines. You'll also see Nielsen, Julia's Vineyard, Foxen Estate Vineyard, and Solomon Hills, among others.

CLOSEST CITY: *The town of Santa Maria is a little more than a 1-hour drive north of Santa Barbara and 3 hours north of Los Angeles.*

SANTA YNEZ VALLEY: Santa Barbara's biggest, most touristy appellation owes its popularity to the 2004 dark comedy that made Pinot Noir explode in the United States, *Sideways*, which was set here (the credit goes specifically to Sta. Rita Hills Pinot). Although few saw the movie, its effects on the wine industry were huge as it seeped into the wine consciousness of Americans. As a result, Pinot, the hardest grape to grow by most winegrowers' accounts, was in high demand, and liberties were taken to make it "friendlier" for American palates. Large producers relied on the Tax and Trade Bureau rule that a mere 75 percent of the grape stated on the label has to be in the bottle and chucked in 25 percent of Syrah, Merlot, and other "surplus" varieties to make the wine big and beefy (see the classification section, page 91, for more on this regulation). It's not Santa Ynez's fault that demand outstripped production or that the film wound up changing the appetite for and style of American Pinot Noir (part of what is dubbed the "Sideways Effect" in the wine biz). Producers were probably as surprised as anyone that they'd experience a boom in tourism!

The Santa Ynez Valley stretches east to west but narrows where the valley meets the ocean, so the cooling influence of the Pacific is less prevalent than in Santa Maria Valley. You'll find Chardonnay and Pinot Noir in the west, closest to the Pacific where it's cool and foggy. The wines are fruitier and fuller than those of Santa Maria Valley but balanced. The eastern end of the valley is warmer and grows Syrah, Viognier, Merlot, and Cabernet Sauvignon, all of which are often mediocre, especially when compared with the wines in other parts of the Central Coast (cooler parts of Paso Robles come to mind).

In the western flank of the Santa Ynez Valley, close to the Pacific, is the prestigious STA. RITA HILLS appellation. (I'm not being lazy by putting "Sta." for "Santa" in Sta. Rita Hills. The historic Santa Rita winery of Chile sued the appellation because of the name similarity and won.) There seem to be two types of Pinot Noir in Sta. Rita Hills. Some Pinots are huge—with high alcohol and heavy, dark fruit. These are hard to pair with food, but are a beloved style by many. Other Pinots are more restrained, lower in alcohol, and friendlier with food. There's good Chardonnay, Syrah, Sauvignon Blanc, and Viognier here as well, but in smaller quantities, since Pinot makes up 75 percent of plantings.

CLOSEST CITY: *Los Olivos and Solvang in Santa Ynez Valley are 40 to 45 minutes northwest of Santa Barbara by car and about 2.75 hours northwest from Los Angeles. Lompoc (LAHM-poke) in Sta Rita Hills is 1 hour northwest of Santa Barbara by car, and Buellton is about 45 minutes northwest of Santa Barbara. Each is about 2.75 hours northwest of Los Angeles.*

Santa Barbara has some other emerging areas.

HAPPY CANYON OF SANTA BARBARA: The warmest area of the Santa Ynez Valley, Happy Canyon is a good place to grow balanced reds—Cabernet Franc, Cabernet Sauvignon, Merlot, Petit Verdot, Syrah, and other Rhône varieties thrive here.

BALLARD CANYON: A tiny appellation above the fog line, Ballard Canyon has hot days and cold nights. It has staked its future on cooler-climate Syrah, which ranges from big and heavy to acidic and herbal when from cooler vineyards.

LOS OLIVOS: Sandwiched between Happy Canyon and Ballard Canyon in the east and west respectively. Los Olivos is the land of Rhône varieties—Syrah, Grenache, Mourvèdre, and whites Roussanne, Grenache Blanc, and Marsanne, along with others, can be found both as stand-alone wines and in blends.

CLOSEST CITY: *Happy Canyon is in Santa Barbara, which is a 2-hour drive northwest from Los Angeles. Both Ballard Canyon and Los Olivos are about a 50-minute drive north of Santa Barbara and a 2.5-hour drive from Los Angeles.*

Inland Central and Central Eastern California

The Central Valley

The giant inland Central Valley of California is hot and dry. It's another country from the laid-back, coastal California stereotype. Here is where Middle America begins—in attitude, in income, and in politics. The Central Valley, a tract of land for farming on a mass scale, is the primary source for almonds, tomatoes, cotton, apricots, asparagus, and, of course, grapes, for all of the United States. The grapes grown here are for bulk wine—mass-produced, homogenized, characterless plonk, made in huge industrial complexes and full of additives. Within the Central Valley is one small pocket of quality winemaking: Lodi. You'll see it on bottles, so it's good to know.

LODI: Lodi is 100 miles (161 km) east of the San Francisco Bay on the San Joaquin and Sacramento River Deltas. The Delta breezes and the Bay Area climate prevent Lodi from getting too hot and enable it to make something better than bulk wine. That said, Lodi is quite warm and the wines reflect that. In my experience, most Lodi reds are alcoholic and too fruity with low tannin and low acid and are overoaked, making them a mouthful. The best reds in the area are Zinfandels from vines more than a hundred years old. The best whites are Rhône varieties—Viognier, Roussanne, and even Picpoul with full fruit flavors, soft, rich body, and full aromatics.

As you can tell, the wines are not my style. But if you love that huge style, head right to the Lodi section of your wine shop!

CLOSEST CITY: *Lodi is a 45 minute drive south of Sacramento, California's state capital, by car.*

Sierra Foothills

Originally planted with vines to slake the thirst of gold miners in the 1860s, today the Sierra Foothills is a boutique area with variable wine quality.

Even though production is minuscule relative to other regions—it has just a hundred wineries that contribute less than half of a percent of California's wine production—the landmass of the appellation is 2.6 million acres (1.05 million ha)! The Sierra Foothills stretches from the Central Valley east to the Sierra Nevada. This is a hot, inland area where reds grow best, especially Zinfandel, which is about half of production. Cabernet Sauvignon, Syrah, and the northern Italian grape, Barbera, each make up a few hundred acres of vines. The mountainous terrain reaches up to 3,000 feet (900 m), and the elevation mitigates hot daytime temperatures so there is balance in these wines. That said, Sierra Foothills makes bold, high-alcohol reds.

Within this AVA are multiple others. EL DORADO is good but AMADOR COUNTY is the most promising and prominent area. Its production centers around ripe, fruity, higher-alcohol Zinfandel, but Italian grapes like Aglianico, Barbera, and Sangiovese, Portuguese grapes, and some Rhône varieties like Syrah and Viognier are on the rise. Expect fruity, jammy, smooth wines with ample oak influence but balance from a good producer.

CLOSEST CITY: *The state capital, Sacramento, is the closest city to these areas, which are between 45 minutes and 1.5 hours east, southeast, and northeast by car.*

The Wrap-Up

Are there other areas in California that make wine? Yes. The Santa Cruz Mountains appellation makes outstanding cool-climate Chardonnay, Pinot Noir, Rhône varieties, and balanced Cabernet Sauvignon. Southern California, specifically Temecula, makes drinkable Cabernet Sauvignon, Zinfandel, Rhône varieties, Chardonnay, Merlot, and Sauvignon Blanc. And Livermore and other parts of the Central Valley also make Chardonnay and bold reds like Petit Sirah, Zinfandel, and Cabernet Sauvignon. But we can't cover everything so a tip of the hat to them and others I undoubtedly missed. I've covered the majors and this should get you further than where you were with California before you read this!

The Pacific Northwest of the United States

Oregon

Oregon has a reputation that far exceeds its winemaking muscle, but when you make outstanding-quality Pinot Noir and Pinot Gris as its top producers do, it's well earned. Oregon has a unique wine culture—winemakers take their craft seriously and keep close company with each other. As a result, plonk rarely comes out of the state.

It makes sense from a cultural perspective. Oregonians are known for their pride in local food and wine (famous chef and cookbook author James Beard was from Portland) and for their dedication to the environment. I guess they attract like-minded souls because the group of California winemakers that came to the state in the 1960s found quick success when they planted Pinot Noir in cooler areas and watched magic happen. David Lett of Eyrie Vineyards, Dick Erath of Erath Winery, the Adelsheims of Adelsheim Vineyard, and others moved from California one by one and started to make Pinot Noir the likes of which the United States hadn't seen before.

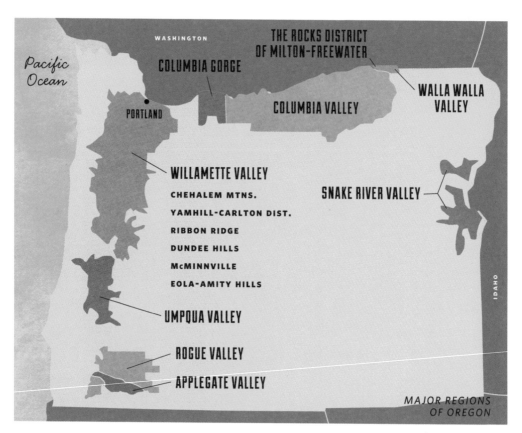

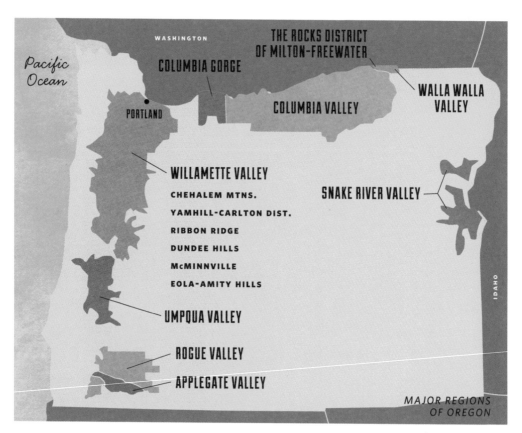

WILLAMETTE VALLEY

CHEHALEM MTNS.

YAMHILL-CARLTON DIST.

RIBBON RIDGE

DUNDEE HILLS

McMINNVILLE

EOLA-AMITY HILLS

UMPQUA VALLEY

ROGUE VALLEY

APPLEGATE VALLEY

MAJOR REGIONS OF OREGON

In an interesting twist, even though Oregon is largely Pinot Noir country, it didn't choose to grow the natural Burgundy partner—Chardonnay—as its main white counterpart. Instead, producers chose another native Burgundian grape that is the adopted daughter of Alsace and Northern Italy now: Pinot Gris. Oregon's version is a little less reliable than its Pinot Noir—Pinot Gris is sometimes more like the thin Pinot Grigio of Northern Italy than the rich Alsace style—but I find it's worth trying for the one time you get an amazing bottle. The state also makes wines of Bordeaux and Rhône grapes, but the real showstoppers are the Pinots (Noir and Gris) and that's what you should seek out.

The vineyards here are small and many are organic and biodynamic, or at least salmon safe, which means they protect wild salmon by keeping waste out of rivers. The small guys make many different styles of Pinot based on vineyard location. Appellation and terroir matter here—you won't taste the same Pinot from Dundee Hills that you taste from McMinnville. It's a fascinating place for a Pinotphile.

There are many other appellations around southern Oregon and in the Columbia Valley/Columbia Gorge area on the Washington border, as well as on the Idaho border, but the fine wine mainly comes from the Willamette Valley and its sub-AVAs.

Willamette Valley (will-AM-it)

Willamette is Oregon's big region for Pinot Noir grapes. In a hilly area sheltered by the Coast Range in the west and the Cascade Mountains in the east, Willamette is cool, dry, and sunny during the growing season. The area has a cool climate and vastly different terroir from town to town, which allows picky Pinot to thrive and pick up different flavors, depending on where it's grown. Most Oregon wineries once fell into this large appellation, but with time, producers carved up Willamette into discreet sub-AVAs to help us differentiate what we were getting.

The majority of wine is still from the larger Willamette AVA, so it may help to describe the general profile of its Pinot Noir.

- High in acid, which makes them good with food
- Fruity (lots of cherry and red berry flavor)
- Moderate to high in alcohol (more than 13 percent)
- Variable when it comes to secondary flavors and aromas (like dirt, dust, or cola)

Because flavors can vary drastically from place to place, following I give you broad generalizations of what to expect from top Pinots from the subappellations of Willamette Valley so you can better take a chance on one you may like. This is especially important because Oregon is *not* usually a good value. It's expensive to grow grapes here, and prices reflect that—the wine is good but rarely overdelivers for the price.

DUNDEE HILLS: Red berry and cherry smells and flavors but with prominent herbal, spice (like Asian spice), and earth qualities. The distinguishing factor is that there are low notes in the wine like a dark forest—damp soil or tea leaves.

EOLA-AMITY HILLS: Fresh black and red fruit but floral and herbal with strong acidity.

MCMINNVILLE: Abundant black fruit flavors with spice and earth. These brawny Pinot Noirs are loaded with tannin and acid.

RIBBON RIDGE: The smallest but most prestigious of the sub-AVAs. You'll find fruit flavors, but with its strong tannins and acid, this wine is for aging. With time the wines develop spicy, floral, and mild red berry flavors, with softer acid and tannin.

YAMHILL-CARLTON: Soft tannins, lots of black fruit flavors often with floral and smoky notes, too. These wines can be heavy, but they range depending on site and clone. For me, they tend to have flavors like a cherry Coke.

CHEHALEM MOUNTAINS: With dusty, lighter soils, this area produces Pinots that can be lighter in style with bright red berry and cherry notes and a peppery, earthy flavor.

CLOSEST CITY: *Willamette Valley is a 1 hour-drive south from Portland.*

Washington State

Washington is the second-largest wine-producing state in the United States, and in many cases the quality of its juice is as good, if not better, than that of the number one wine producer down the coast. Washington has crazy quirks in its geography and geology that make it prime for winegrowing, and it seems like each year growers find new and better ways to make the most of them. The warm, sunny climate during the growing season means that this is mainly red wine country, but there are pockets where whites thrive as well. Cabernet Sauvignon, Merlot, and Syrah dominate but warm-weather whites like Semillon and Viognier make stunning wines. Chardonnay, Riesling, and Sauvignon Blanc are here too, but with a few key exceptions I

MAJOR REGIONS OF WASHINGTON

CANADA

PUGET SOUND

COLUMBIA VALLEY

• SEATTLE

WAHLUKE SLOPE

RED MOUNTAIN

YAKIMA VALLEY
RATTLESNAKE HILLS
SNIPES MOUNTAIN

Pacific Ocean

WALLA WALLA VALLEY

COLUMBIA GORGE

OREGON

HORSE HEAVEN HILLS

find most of this stuff to be only OK and often overpriced for the quality.

Even with the state's number two billing in the US wine world, Washington wines aren't as popular as they should be and don't seem to make it into the consciousness of wine drinkers when they think about American wine. But I think that in the next few decades Washington may get its due. Between climate change in California and our desire to explore different flavors in wine, it's Washington's time. Leading the charge for highly differentiated wines are two big areas: Yakima and Walla Walla, both of which are in the desert, far to the east of the cool, rainy city of Seattle. I discuss those as well as the giant valley that encompasses most of the state, Columbia Valley, in the following sections.

Columbia Valley

Covering a third of Washington, the Columbia Valley appellation is a catchall for nearly every grape grown in the state. With the exception of the less prolific areas of Columbia Gorge to the south and Puget Sound to the west, all Washington winemaking takes place in Columbia Valley. Because it is so vast, this appellation of 43,000 acres (16,207 ha) is sort of like the California appellation farther south, in that you never know what you're going to get from a wine marked "Columbia Valley" unless you know the producer. Fifty-eight percent of vineyards are planted to reds and 42 percent to whites, with Cabernet Sauvignon, Merlot, Riesling, and Chardonnay being the most widely planted grapes. You'll find more than thirty other grape varieties growing here, too.

Diversity is a strong suit for Columbia Valley, as is purity of the fruit flavors in the best wines. You can easily pick out the dark fruit and bright herbal notes in the Cabernet or the red fruit and mint in the Merlot. The whites are more erratic, and flavors depend on the warmth of the vineyard—hot areas create fuller, fruitier, lower-acid whites (sometimes flabby and lacking distinction) and cooler vineyards churn out citrusy, acidic, minerally wines.

You'll also find what I think are some of the best Syrahs in the United States, but this grape's flavors also depend on site. In hotter places, jammy, alcoholic, black fruit–flavored wines abound. In cooler ones, peppery, earthy wines with red and black fruit and a great balance of tannin, acid, and alcohol create Washington's signature wines.

Columbia Valley temperatures are consistently warm during the day and cool at night, providing a long growing season for vines. At latitudes between 46° and 48° north, which is where the Columbia Valley sits, the grapes must be planted on south-facing slopes to catch every bit of sun. This latitude also means that Washington gets more hours of sunlight than parts farther south in the summertime, which aids ripening. The best vineyards in Columbia Valley lie at elevation and have nutrient-poor soils, making grapes struggle and intensifying their flavors. Winds in many of the top vineyards are common, which makes skins thicker, again creating more intense flavors, especially in reds.

The Cascade Range in the east provides a rain shadow, making everything east of it bone-dry: Irrigation from the Columbia River and its tributaries means it's not always Mother Nature that determines how vigorous a vine is—the grower plays a huge role. Given the high daytime heat and controlled irrigation, some wines are high in alcohol, so you need to check the bottles if you're looking to drink them with food (see the pairing chapter, page 296, for more on this). From a great producer, the balance against the fruit and the often mineral and earth notes make Columbia Valley wine a tasty treat.

Following are a few subappellations you should seek out.

THE WASHINGTON WINE MALL

Thirty minutes northeast of Seattle, dozens of wineries have tasting rooms set up to get locals and tourists to taste their wares. This wine outlet mall of sorts is in a town called Woodinville. Most all of the wineries grow their grapes in south-central/eastern Washington's Columbia Valley and its subregions, where the hot days, cool nights, and soil variations make a perfect environment for vines. But instead of having their crush and winemaking facilities close to the vineyards so the grapes can be processed with minimal risk of damage, many wineries in Woodinville truck their grapes from vineyards in the Columbia Valley (and its subregions) one to two hours north to winemaking facilities in Woodinville. I love Washington wine, but this is a bizarre quirk of the Washington wine industry that I just don't understand no matter how many times it's explained to me. Why would they chance it? And isn't it operationally inefficient? I don't get it. Never will.

WAHLUKE (WAH-LOUK) SLOPE AVA is an isolated, hot area that accounts for 15 percent of grape acreage in Washington. The gentle slopes, uniform soils, reliable winds, and lack of rain make the area a great place for larger wineries to source grapes if they want a consistent product year after year (i.e., lower-tier wines where vintage variation is unacceptable). If you see Wahluke Slope on the bottle, expect ripe, full, fruity reds of Cabernet, Merlot, and Syrah and full bodied whites.

HORSE HEAVEN HILLS is in the southeast portion of the state and produces 25 percent of Washington's grapes. It's the workhorse region (pun intended) of Columbia Valley. Here, thirty-seven varieties grow—66 percent red and 34 percent white, with Cabernet Sauvignon, Merlot, Chardonnay, Riesling, and Syrah leading the pack. The best vineyards can make balanced yet fruity, albeit heavy, wines. Look for special sites like Alder Ridge, Andrews-Horse Heaven Vineyard, Canoe Ridge, and Champoux Vineyards, which are marked on some of the top bottles of Washington wine and are must-tries.

YAKIMA VALLEY (YAK-EH-MAH—THINK OF THE COWLIKE ANIMAL): The oldest appellation in Washington, Yakima is big and the quality of its wines ranges dramatically. What to look for from the good guys? The cooler pockets make wines with great acidity and often have an earthy, dusty quality behind the ripe fruit. Chardonnay is grown here, but Cabernet, Merlot, and particularly Syrah are the most interesting wines and the stars of the future. Nested within Yakima are two big AVAs. Both are at elevation and have poor soils, big temperature diurnals, and strong winds. From the RED MOUNTAIN AVA, named for the

WHAT MAKES WASHINGTON SO DIFFERENT?

I'm going to get dorky now because I want to explain a cool, unique thing about Washington's lay of the land. This is a place where you can actually see the results of geological machinations of time, especially the effects of the mighty Missoula Floods of the last Ice Age, 10,000 to 15,000 years ago. This is when a huge glacial lake in eastern Washington, which contained more water than the Great Lakes Erie and Ontario combined, decided to seek greener pastures in the west. Pressure from the glacier's weight caused little cracks in the ice dams that contained the lake, and they wound up bursting more than forty times, shooting out water at what the US Geological Survey estimates was a "rate ten times the combined flow of all the rivers of the world." These floods formed the current course of the Columbia River, which has an effect today on Columbia Valley vineyards.

As you drive along the valley, you can see that the rocks and mountains have clearly marked striations that are essentially time markers of how the land changed from these floods. Another result of the floods: A lot of the vineyards contain glacial loess—windblown deposits of sand and silt over gravel from glaciers. This is rare in wine regions. All this is cool stuff, and I bring it up because it's a reason that Washington wines taste different.

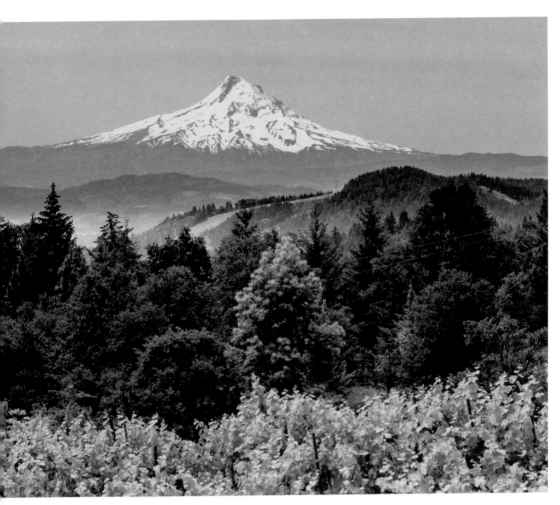

red grass that grows on its slopes, expect full-flavored yet acidic reds: Cabernet Sauvignon, Merlot, Syrah, Cabernet Franc, Malbec, and Petit Verdot are star players.

RATTLESNAKE HILLS, named for the reptile that inhabits its grounds, makes slightly more red than white wine. Blackcurrant- and herbal-flavored Cabernet Sauvignon dominates, with variable Merlot and Riesling, impressive Malbec and Syrah, and sometimes restrained Chardonnay.

CLOSEST CITY: *Union Gap, the beginning of Yakima Valley, is a 2-hour drive southeast from Seattle. Prosser, a more tourist-friendly town with some of the top wineries, is 3 hours from Seattle.*

WALLA WALLA: The popular kid of the Washington wine world, Walla Walla gets courted by all the critics, and with good reason. The standard of excellence in Walla Walla (and the dedication of the winemakers) is as consistent as the high quality of the wines. As one producer told me when I visited, "This is an area that developed around a quality standard, not around a growing region." These wines have a distinct dirty flavor (I mean that in a fabulous way) and a true sense of place—there's no doubt these wines are a product of the earth. They're consistently fruity, spicy, and earthy, with fresh acidity and mild tannin. Although the alcohol is high because the hot days raise sugar levels in the grapes, the cool nights ensure the wines have bright acid and strong tannins to balance things out. The diurnals (page 46) and a long, sunny growing season give the wines dimension and complex flavors.

Cabernet Sauvignon and Merlot (they make up nearly 70 percent of plantings) can be delicious with bold, black fruit and strong tannin, but the true gem of Walla Walla for me is the Syrah, which is spicy, earthy, acidic, and tannic, with black fruit, olive, and bacon notes. Whites are only about 4 percent of production, and the honeyed, acidic Viognier, the star of the northern Rhône, is the standout.

Although critics blather about it, Walla Walla remains a well-kept secret in the US wine world. It doesn't get the credit it deserves, maybe because the wines are pricier than those from the wider Columbia Valley ($30 on up)—but they are worth it for a splurge. Seek out top Walla Walla wines and see if you agree!

CLOSEST CITY: *Walla Walla is a 5-hour drive southeast from Seattle and a 5-hour drive northeast from Portland. It's a haul, but worth the effort if you have time and are in the area.*

The East Coast of the United States

For most of its history, the East Coast has been out of the quality winemaking game. Disease, humidity, pests, and erratic weather have made growing *Vitis vinifera* an impossibility despite 250 years of earnest effort. But technology, know-how, and, frankly, the right people came along about three or four decades ago, and East Coast areas of Virginia, the Finger Lakes of New York State, and Long Island started

making wines that have transformed the right coast into a winemaking force that wine lovers shouldn't ignore. (Yes, that includes you, my friends in California, who are laughing at the idea that the right coast makes good wine!)

With cooler climates, weather that's closer to Bordeaux than Napa, and an East Coast sensibility possessed by the winemakers (I'm told we tend to have slightly less sunny dispositions and more innate stubbornness than our West Coast counterparts), wine styles from the East Coast represent a middle ground between New World and Old World. Although some wines are god-awful, many are great with food and lovely for sipping, and range from pleasant to world-class. Moreover, these three regions have their own identities that could represent a new future for American wine, if they can boost production, widen distribution, and convince skeptics that flavor, not track record, matters most in wine.

Virginia

The state's residents have been trying, maybe harder than anyone on the East Coast, for more than two centuries to make internationally recognized wine. Thomas Jefferson, the third president of the United States, was an impassioned wine lover and tried for decades to cultivate vineyards in Central Virginia near his Charlottesville home before he resigned himself to exclusively importing French wine. Many tenacious farmers followed in his footsteps, but for most of Virginia's history, winemaking has been an exercise in futility. Until now!

Unlike the consistently sunny West Coast of the United States, the East Coast is temperamental (insert East Coast people vs. West Coast people joke here).

The weather in Virginia is unpredictable, and winemakers have to be ready for nearly anything each year. Humidity, pests (including bears eating the grapes!), and excessive rain, and the rot and disease that often result, are yearly challenges for winemakers. Then there's the constant learning curve. Even with twenty or thirty years of experience, Virginia's producers discover new things about their regions and vineyards each year. Winemakers constantly adjust—replanting vineyards, choosing new varieties that may do better in their microclimate, and adjusting picking regimens. It's a region of adaptation.

Despite these challenges, in the last thirty or so years, the threads have come together for Virginia. Production is tiny—only about 6,400 acres (2,590 ha) of *Vitis vinifera* grow here—but some of it is outstanding. Virginia wines have a distinct character: In the best, you'll find a fusion of earthy, terroir-driven flavor and a lovely lightness. The wines generally have moderate alcohol, high acidity, and mouth-drying tannins. They're flavorful, but also mild and elegant—not as earthy as European wines, nor as bold as those from California or Argentina.

The biggest success stories are Viognier and Chardonnay for white, and Cabernet Franc, Petit Verdot, and Bordeaux-style blends for reds. Cab Franc is the lead red in these blends because it does well in the moderate temperatures of Virginia's foothills. The temperature in most winegrowing areas of Virginia is too cool for Cabernet Sauvignon, which needs heat to ripen fully, and often too warm for flavorful, nuanced Merlot, which likes it a tad cooler.

Although many areas are making wine in Virginia, Charlottesville/Monticello and areas around Front Royal/Linden are best.

Charlottesville/Monticello Area:

Charlottesville and the surrounding areas are in the rolling foothills of the Blue Ridge Mountains, a subsection of the great Appalachian Mountains. The elevation makes the area cool enough for vineyards, but the sunny, hot days of summer allow grapes to fully ripen. Look for Cabernet Franc and Bordeaux blends and snappy Viognier. You'll find interesting varietals here, too—influenced by the many Europeans who call Charlottesville home. From Gros Manseng to Nebbiolo, you won't be bored in the MONTICELLO AVA.

CLOSEST CITY: *Charlottesville is a 1-hour drive northwest from Richmond and a 2.5-hour drive southwest from Washington, DC.*

Areas around Front Royal/Linden

The wineries hiding in small enclaves in the foothills of the Blue Ridge Mountains have excellent soils, cool nights from the elevation, a warm growing season, and some of the top wineries in Virginia. If you trek out this way, seek out Linden, run for thirty years by Jim Law. His wines are in a class of their own, as are the wines of others who have worked with him—especially Jeff White of Glen Manor Vineyards in the Front Royal area. Bordeaux blends, varietals, and Chardonnays are most common here.

CLOSEST CITY: *Delaplane, Front Royal, and Linden are a little more than a 1-hour drive west of Washington, DC.*

New York

Picture it: It's Manhattan. It's 1667. The Dutch are pining for the Bordeaux that they so loved while back in the homeland. They cook up a scheme to plant grapes and make wine in their new home. They import *Vitis vinifera*, stick it in the ground on their newly conquered land, and expect they will have wine in no time. But it doesn't quite work out that way. Because try as they might, *Vitis vinifera* really didn't like New York. But all wasn't lost. Scrounging around for other options, they looked to native grapes, especially Concord and Delaware, which flowed into the market. New Yorkers loved the sweet, gloppy, syrupy wine these grapes produced. As a result, New York became home to the first bonded winery in the United States, Pleasant Valley Wine Company in the Hudson River Region.

Today, New York is number three in US grape production and has more than four hundred wineries, most of which are in the Finger Lakes AVA. So why isn't more wine from New York in the market? Well, more than 80 percent of the wine is still made of *Vitis labrusca*, namely Concord grapes (hello, Manischewitz, the nasty sweet kosher wine made in the state), and that's not a very appealing sipper for most wine lovers. But things are changing fast in New York. The Finger Lakes produces world-class Riesling, and the Chardonnay is improving yearly. Long Island, where I grew up, has some lovely red blends using Merlot and Cabernet Franc. My old homeland is even growing tasty Pinot Noir and Chenin Blanc in some spots! Other regions like Lake Erie, Niagara Escarpment, and Hudson River Region are trying to improve their *Vitis vinifera* too, which may mean we'll see more of New York on store shelves soon. For today, however, I'll focus on the two top winegrowing regions of New York: the Finger Lakes and Long Island.

Finger Lakes

Even though producers have tried to make wine in this region for more than a century, it's only in the last fifty or sixty years that *Vitis vinifera* has thrived here. And "thrive" is a relative term: The Finger Lakes is the biggest winegrowing region in New York State, but around 75 percent is *Vitis labrusca* (native grapes) and French-American hybrids. *Vitis vinifera* (Riesling, Chardonnay, Cabernet Franc, etc.) is just 25 percent of the pie but growing.

The Finger Lakes owes its *"vinifera revolution"* to a guy named Dr. Konstantin Frank, a Ukrainian immigrant who held a PhD in winegrowing. He arrived at the viticulture station of Cornell University in the Finger Lakes in the 1950s, and although others had failed, he used his experience to prove that *vinifera* could succeed. He helped growers correlate wine quality with vineyard location and soil. That meant vines were replanted on gentle slopes slightly above the lakes, where they received the benefits of the lake effect (this works well for everyone, since lakeside vacation homes don't take up prime vineyard space!). An industry blossomed from his work, and today the area, including the winery named after him—Dr. Konstantin Frank Winery—makes world-class wine, specifically Riesling, with beautiful lime, peach, or apple fruit, a steel-like acidity, and a finish as clean as the flavor of mineral water. Other whites are glorious too—aromatic grapes like Gewürztraminer, Pinot Gris, and Grüner Veltliner. Although lots of folks push their Cab Franc or red blends, I remain unimpressed. Trust me—when you visit this region, you do it for the whites.

CLOSEST CITY: *The Finger Lakes region is a 4.5-hour drive northwest of New York City, so your best bet is to fly into Rochester or Syracuse, each of which is about a 1.5-hour drive from the region, or into Ithaca, 1 hour east by car.*

Long Island

For all the haters of my homeland—the ones who make fun of my accent, call it "Strong Island" (something I never heard until I left the place), and back in the day asked if I was related to Amy Fisher (who shot her much-older boyfriend's wife in the face, created a career for herself as the Long Island Lolita, and lived very far from me)—I've got a news flash for you: Long Island may have its cultural quirks but it's making great wines. And for those who have no idea where or what Long Island is, forget all that and let me explain a few things about the area.

Long Island is in the southern part of the state of New York. It's shaped like a fish. The head is made up of the New York City boroughs of Queens and Brooklyn (from where half of my family hails, the other half being from Manhattan). The east end splits into a fish tail with two peninsulas. The north fork, which abuts Long Island Sound in the north and Peconic Bay in the south, was once home to unending potato farms and sod fields, with an occasional pumpkin patch (which I visited every year in my youth). It's now home to

grape growers and wineries. The south fork, between Peconic Bay in the north and the Atlantic Ocean in the south, has only four wineries, since most of the available real estate is occupied by mansions and businesses that cater to the wealthy and wannabe (and because the Atlantic influence means whipping storms are more of a risk to vines).

Q+A

How can grapes can grow in the Finger Lakes? Don't they freeze and die off?

The key to Finger Lakes viticulture is in the name: The wine story is the lakes. Lake Ontario, the huge lake to the north, warms southerly currents in the freezing winter and helps cool down temps in the summer. The eleven Finger Lakes that run north-south are among the deepest lakes in North America, and they do the same thing Lake Ontario does on a local level—they warm the vineyards in the winter so the vines aren't destroyed by cold, and they cool down the heat in the summer to allow the grapes to gather acidity. The depth of the lakes means they retain heat and radiate it in the cold weather, keeping the Finger Lakes vineyards alive and viable in the freezing temps of winter. The three main lakes for premium viticulture are Keuka (QUEUE-ka), Seneca (SEN-eh-ka), and Cayuga (KAY-oo-ga).

This is a tiny area: More than fifty producers make wine from about 3,000 acres (1,214 ha). The flagship red grapes are bright, acidic Cabernet Franc and spicy, juicy, fruity Merlot, and the main whites are grassy, herbal Sauvignon Blanc and lemony, acidic Chardonnay. As with a lot of emerging regions, only a handful of producers are making impressive wine, but these wines are worth finding.

There aren't dramatic diurnals (page 46) and the Long Island Sound and Peconic Bay keep daytime temperatures warm through the fall so grapes get time to fully ripen. But the threat of heavy rain always looms, and it can destroy a vineyard in the summer or early fall. Fortunately, the soils are well drained and sandy, which means the land absorbs torrential rains quickly.

Although constrained in growth by being on an island and the not so minor issue that local politicians make it hard to start any new winery, Long Island wineries are and will continue to be producers of boutique, small-production, delicious wines that are great to try if you can find one.

CLOSEST CITY: *The Long Island wine area is about 75 miles (121 km) east of New York City. With no traffic, that's about 2.5 hours by car. In the summer, it's more like 5 hours (the region sees more than a million visitors a year, most in the summertime). It seems weird but there aren't too many roads that can get you from New York to the east end—it's called* Long Island, not Wide *Island.*

Q+A

Maybe the most important question in the book: Did you have huge, hair-sprayed hair and a perm when you were a teenager on Long Island?

Somehow I had the foresight not to go there. In fairness, I also had thick, pin-straight hair as a kid and couldn't get it to feather or stay in a bang "claw" no matter how much hair spray I used. I had all one length, long hair that forced me to hold my head to one side because it was too heavy for me to hold straight. My sister on the other hand . . . bang claw city. Her volume was impressive and the envy of many!

Grape to New World Region Mapping

To wrap up the New World, on the pages that follow is a chart of the places that do an excellent job with a specific grape and have a reputation for top wines of that grape.

The Wrap-Up

After years of being an elitist beverage in the United States, wine has entered the mainstream. Consumption overall and per capita grows each year, and the American market is one of the most influential for wine producers around the world. Still, Americans love domestic wares, and why wouldn't we? As more styles become available from all over the United States, our appetite and interest in wine seem to grow by the day. With wineries in all fifty states and access to pretty good ones on both coasts and even in the Midwest (Michigan, in particular for Riesling), visiting and learning more about wine are fast becoming a national obsession for Americans. A worthy pursuit!

NEW WORLD REGION MAPPING

Reds

GRAPE	COUNTRY	SUBREGION
CABERNET SAUVIGNON/ BORDEAUX BLENDS	AUSTRALIA	**South Australia** Coonawarra **Western Australia** Margaret River
	NEW ZEALAND	Hawkes Bay
	SOUTH AFRICA	Stellenbosch Paarl Franschhoek
	CHILE	Maipo Valley Rapel Valley Maule Valley
	UNITED STATES	**California** Napa Valley and subregions Alexander and Dry Creek Valleys of Sonoma Paso Robles in the Central Coast Santa Cruz Mountains **Washington** Yakima Walla Walla Columbia Valley **New York** Long Island **Virginia** West of DC—Front Royal, Linden, West Loudon County
PINOT NOIR	AUSTRALIA	**Victoria** Yarra Valley
	NEW ZEALAND	Marlborough Central Otago Martinborough
	SOUTH AFRICA	Walker Bay
	CHILE	Bío Bío Itata Malleco Casablanca
	UNITED STATES	**California** Los Carneros in southern Napa and Sonoma Russian River Valley of Sonoma Sonoma Coast of Sonoma Monterey in the Central Coast Eden Valley in the Central Coast Santa Barbara County, Santa Maria Valley, Santa Ynez Valley, Sta. Rita Hills in the Central Coast

Reds

GRAPE	COUNTRY	SUBREGION
PINOT NOIR (continued)	**UNITED STATES** (continued)	*California (continued)* Arroyo Seco, Carmel Valley, Santa Lucia Highlands in the Central Coast Anderson Valley in Mendocino *Oregon* Willamette Valley and subregions
	CANADA	*Ontaria* Niagra Peninsula and subregions
SHIRAZ/SYRAH	**AUSTRALIA**	*Southeast Australia* Barossa McLaren Vale *Western Australia* Margaret River
	SOUTH AFRICA	Paarl Franschhoek Swartland
	CHILE	Limarí and Elquí Valleys (Coquimbo) Rapel Valley
	UNITED STATES	*California* Dry Creek Valley in Sonoma Paso Robles in the Central Coast Mendocino Santa Barbara County (emerging) *Washington* Yakima Walla Walla
	CANADA	Okanagan (especially from Oliver and Osyoos)
MERLOT	**AUSTRALIA**	*Western Australia* Margaret River
	NEW ZEALAND	Hawkes Bay
	UNITED STATES	*California* Napa *Washington* Yakima Walla Walla *New York* Long Island

Reds

GRAPE	COUNTRY	SUBREGION
ZINFANDEL	UNITED STATES	*California* Dry Creek Valley of Sonoma Paso Robles in the Central Coast Mendocino Sierra Foothills Amador County
CABERNET FRANC	UNITED STATES	*California* Varies based on producer—most in Sonoma *New York* Long Island *Virginia* Monticello Western Virginia
	CANADA	Niagara Peninsula Okanagan
GSM BLENDS (GRENACHE/ SYRAH/ MOURVÈDRE)	AUSTRALIA	*South Australia* Barossa Valley
	UNITED STATES	*California* Paso Robles in the Central Coast
MALBEC	ARGENTINA	Mendoza
CARMÉNÈRE	CHILE	Colchagua/Rapel Valley

Whites

GRAPE	COUNTRY	SUBREGION
CHARDONNAY	AUSTRALIA	***Victoria*** Yarra Valley ***Western Australia*** Margaret River
	SOUTH AFRICA	Stellenbosch Paarl Constantia Walker Bay Elgin
	CHILE	Casablanca/San Antonio Valleys Maipo Valley Bío Bío Itata Malleco
	UNITED STATES	***California*** Most parts of Napa Valley Los Carneros in southern Napa and Sonoma Russian River Valley in Sonoma Sonoma Coast of Sonoma Monterey in the Central Coast Santa Barbara County in the Central Coast Eden Valley in the Central Coast Arroyo Seco, Carmel Valley, Santa Lucia Highlands in the Central Coast ***Washington*** Yakima Valley ***New York*** Long Island ***Virginia*** Front Royal Linden
	CANADA	Niagara Escarpment—Twenty Mile Bench, Beamsville Bench
SAUVIGNON BLANC	AUSTRALIA	***Western Australia*** Margaret River
	NEW ZEALAND	Marlborough Martinborough
	SOUTH AFRICA	Constantia Walker Bay

Whites

GRAPE	COUNTRY	SUBREGION
SAUVIGNON BLANC (continued)	**CHILE**	Casablanca San Antonio Valleys Maipo Valley Limarí and Elquí Valleys (Coquimbo)
	UNITED STATES	*California* Napa Valley
RIESLING	**AUSTRALIA**	*South Australia* Eden Valley Clare Valley *Tasmania*
	NEW ZEALAND	Central Otago
	UNITED STATES	*California* Mendocino *Washington* Columbia Valley *New York* Finger Lakes
	CANADA	Niagara Peninsula Okanagan Valley
PINOT GRIS	**UNITED STATES**	*California* Mendocino Sonoma *Oregon* Willamette Valley and sub-AVAs
SEMILLON	**AUSTRALIA**	*New South Wales* Hunter Valley *Western Australia* Margaret River
	SOUTH AFRICA	Stellenbosch
VIOGNIER	**UNITED STATES**	*Washington* Walla Walla *Virginia* Monticello
CHENIN BLANC	**SOUTH AFRICA**	Stellenbosch Paarl
TORRONTÉS	**ARGENTINA**	Salta

Other Kinds of Wine

GRAPE	COUNTRY	SUBREGION
SPARKLING WINE	AUSTRALIA	*Victoria* Yarra Valley *Tasmania*
	SOUTH AFRICA (CALLED CAP CLASSIQUE)	Franschhoek
	UNITED STATES	*California* Los Carneros in southern Napa and Sonoma Mendocino
SWEET WINES	AUSTRALIA	*Victoria* Rutherglen (from the Muscat grape)
	SOUTH AFRICA	Constantia
	UNITED STATES	*New York* Finger Lakes
	CANADA	Ontario (ice wine of Riesling, Cabernet Franc, Vidal Blanc)

FOOD AN
PAIR
fo
NORMAL

ID WINE
INGS

r

PEOPLE

Food and wine pairing is a much-discussed subject, and it should be—wine is at its best when it's partnered with food! The issue most of us face when tackling this subject is that there are two main schools of thought on pairings and both seem flawed. On the one hand, experts write guides that prescribe pairings in a formulaic manner. These remind me of using the fortune telling kids' toy the Magic 8 Ball. Ask your question, shake it up, and the answer appears. Done.

If you don't like that prescriptive model, then there are people who say that those pairing suggestions are condescending and antiquated. These people go with the "drink what you like" philosophy and encourage you to drink any wine you enjoy with any food you enjoy.

What's the verdict on these methods? I say they're both wrong. But each camp is right in its own way, too.

On the free-for-all side, wine *is* about enjoying what you drink, but I find it unhelpful that these "gurus" leave you with very little guidance. This method can leave you making some abominable pairings (I have experience with this, trust me).

On the traditionalist side, not everyone has the same taste, so not all pairings are going to work for everyone. Add to that the fact that food has changed dramatically—fusion cuisine with internationally influenced spices and flavors are commonplace now—and there is a monkey wrench in old pairings. Also, if you alter a recipe just a bit, it can completely change the wine that will work. Without understanding why flavors work together, you won't be able to make that adjustment.

Finally, if you just look something up, Magic 8 Ball style, you aren't learning how

to pair. In this chapter, I want to teach you the basics so you can do it anytime, anywhere. Let me offer a cliché: *Give a man fish, and he eats for the night. Teach a man to fish, and he eats for a lifetime.* Cheesy? Yes, but it's fitting here.

In the end, I side with the traditionalist more because there is certain stuff that goes with certain other stuff, and not just because it's always been that way. Biology plays a part, as do key principles of how certain sensations, textures, and tastes interact with most people's mouths. The traditionalists use these ideas, but they do it without explaining why things work together and that makes us dependent on them for any future pairings (not a bad business model but not helpful for us DIY pairers). The downside is that we are left wondering if it's their opinion or based on something more substantial.

As a final note, I don't want to be a drama queen here: Most wine and food go well together, and it's hard to find extremes—really nasty pairings or really phenomenal ones. But I think I can help increase your hit rate and your chances for the latter using a nuts and bolts how-to to help you in this quest for the Holy Pairing Grail. Using exercises and ideas about food flavors and wine flavors, you'll be a thoughtful and skilled pairer in no time!

Before I get into it, I'll add another friendly reminder. I mention this in great detail later in the chapter on choosing wine (see page 314): In seeking a good pairing in a restaurant or even at home where there are multiple dishes, never be shy about skipping a bottle in favor of going by the glass to do what's right for the food and for the wine. A one-bottle-fits-all solution rarely works.

BIOLOGY BASICS OF PAIRING

Let's jump right back to high school biology. Remember this? We don't *taste* lemons, leather, tobacco, peaches, meat, or bread. Our olfactory epithelium senses those things and sends the info to our brain, which then ID's it as a plum or an apricot or whatever. And to layer on

PAIRING VOCABULARY 101

I'd be remiss in not putting these key pairing terms here before we take off into detail on pairing. We need to talk about three concepts that you probably are familiar with.

COMPLEMENTS: Wine can complement a food. That does not mean it tells the food it looks pretty in that sauce (that would be "compliment," of course). It means wine can have flavors, textures, and structures similar to the food. That trait creates a harmonious feeling in your mouth. Everything just works together—no push and pull, no fanfare, just smooth sailing.

CONTRASTS: On the other side, opposites attract. Here you take two totally different taste sensations and pit them against each other. Interesting things can occur as your brain reconciles what your mouth is feeling. Then you're excited for the next bite. Contrasts take more mental energy but are well worth the attempt.

WEIGHT: You've probably heard about matching food and wine weight. Heavy foods, heavy wines. This concept is important because it addresses step #1 in the pairing process: It puts you in the right ballpark for pairing. The concept of heavy is pretty intuitive when it comes to food—hearty, robust flavors that stick to your mouth and ribs. When we think light food, we think vegetables, white fish, and citrus flavors—things that don't hang around your mouth or stomach for too long. Wine is similar, although weight often has to do with body, which is driven by alcohol and sugar. More on that to follow.

complexity, texture, temperature, and the perception of "cool" (think menthol) or "hot" (tequila shot) are part of our experience of flavor, too. Funny enough, as discussed in Chapter 1, the things that we think of when we describe flavor have very little to do with what our mouths actually are capable of. It's all about our noses.

So what does this have to do with wine? Well, pairing magic begins when we start paying attention to things other than "apple" or "plum" or "spice" and start thinking what our mouths experience.

A while back, I found a few great exercises from Bruce Zoecklein, PhD, a food scientist at Virginia Tech in the United States, to clearly illustrate how your mouth reacts to certain wines. I've adapted them for normal wine people and used them in my classes. The following exercises really work, and the reactions will stick in your head if you take the time to do them. They truly give you a sense of why certain foods and wines are natural friends.

EXERCISE #1

ACIDIC WINE AND ACIDIC FOOD

YOU NEED

A super acidic white wine (examples are in the charts that follow this section)

•

A lemon wedge

Try the lemon and then the wine. The wine will seem *sweeter or smoother*. Acid piled on top of acid cancels itself out.

What does this mean for pairing?
High-acid foods are going to taste even better with the addition of acidic wine. So if you're having asparagus, lettuce, artichoke, and other green veggies that people say are hard to pair with, bring the acid.

EXERCISE #2

ACIDIC WINE AND SWEET FOOD

YOU NEED

That same super acidic wine from Exercise #1

•

A packet of sugar

Try the sugar and then the wine. The wine will seem horribly bitter or tart.

What does this mean for pairing?
Watch for foods with sweet glazes, dried fruit, or other sweet sauces. If sugar is a main component in a dish, you're best off with a slightly sweet wine (like an off-dry Vouvray, a Chenin Blanc from the Loire Valley in France), not a dry, acidic one.

TANNIN AND FAT

YOU NEED

A very tannic, astringent red wine. One of the four most tannic wines on earth should do the trick: Cabernet Sauvignon, Nebbiolo (Barolo, Barbaresco, Nebbiolo d'Alba, Langhe Nebbiolo), Syrah, or Tannat are the short list. Cabernet and Syrah from more moderate (not hot) climates will show more tannin, so France may be a better bet than California or Australia, for instance. (examples are in the charts that follow this section)

•

A pat of butter
(the real stuff, not margarine)

Try the wine first to experience the tannin in all its mouth-puckering glory. Then try the butter and sip the wine again. Different wine, no? The wine should seem less bitter and even a little fruitier. There is a chemical reaction going on here, so this is less about perception (like with the acid excercise) and more about reality.

What does this mean for pairing?
If you ever wondered why Cabernet Sauvignon is recommended with red meat or rich cheeses, this should explain it. When tannins bind with fat, it's heaven for your mouth. Although this may not be news to you, it's nice to isolate the exercise so you know why it works.

THE WILD CARD . . . SALT

YOU NEED

The two wines from the previous exercises: a high-acid white and a tannic red

•

Table salt

Lick the salt and then try the white wine. The wine may seem salty, even though wine has no salt in it. If you throw salt on something and then have an acidic wine, the combo magnifies the salt sensation.

Now try the salt and then the tannic red. Ouch. The tannins may seem out of control. That's rough—literally rough feeling, and rough for your brain to process.

What does this mean for pairing?
With salt, we're not only talking about main dishes. Salt can change your perfectly planned pairing. You better figure out how salty something is before you decide on the pairing. Oysters and Chablis are a classic pairing because the salt is augmented. If you hate it, now you know why! For reds, people usually recommend the gentler, less tannic Pinot Noir to accompany salty, cured meats. Salt magnifies tannins, and for most people that's not a pleasurable sensation. For you, as it has been in some people in my food and wine pairing seminars, it may be awesome so try the exercise and see what you think.

MY THREE-STEP PAIRING PROCESS

I hope you tried at least one or two of those exercises to ensure I wasn't completely snowing you. They are helpful in internalizing how your body reacts to certain combinations. There are scientific principles at work here. Although we will get into nuance below, this is a good grounding for you to experience what happens to your perception when certain common food and wine components come together.

Acid, sugar, and salt are essential in food preparation. Now you can look for the components in stuff you are cooking or ordering and understand how wines may or may not pair. That goes a long way in making you a fantastic pairer.

And now let's pull this all together into my big methodology—my Three-Step Pairing process. Here are the steps:

STEP #1: Consider food weight and texture to get into the ballpark of what color and type of wine may go with the food you're eating.

STEP #2: Based on what you learned from the exercises above, pay attention to a wine's structure and how it will pair with food.

STEP #3: Think about the dominant flavors in your mouth after you eat a bite of food (usually it's not the main course but the sauce on top or even the preparation of the sides, e.g., garlic mashed potatoes, that dominates the plate).

Do these rules seem overly simplistic? Maybe. But they work. Now let's break down how to use these three ideas and we'll launch you into the world to try them out for yourself. Then you can send me love letters or hate mail depending on what you find.

The Three-Step Pairing Process in Action

STEP #1: DETERMINING FOOD WEIGHT This is intuitive for many of us on the food side, but on the wine side you may be less sure about what is heavy and what is light. Although vintages and producers can change this, I've provided a general list of wines that range from light to heavy and the foods they often go well with on page 304.

STEP #2: FIGURING OUT WINE STRUCTURE I'm never one to be too theoretical. But per my earlier point about Magic 8 Ball pairing, I also don't want to get too specific.

I think the most helpful thing for understanding structure in food and wine pairing is to talk about the main components of a wine—from a structure, texture, or flavor point of view—and then list possible matches in food type. Use the tables for direction (not prescription) when pairing.

STEP #3: DECIPHERING DOMINANT FLAVORS If you follow the first two steps, chances are you're not going to get a bad pairing. You may even consistently get a great one. But if you combine those rules with this step of pairing by flavor, you're going to increase your odds for greatness even more.

How do you do this? Pay attention to the two all-important words on the menu, in your recipe, or in your head as you're throwing spices into a dish like a magician waving a wand: "with" or "in."

Food gets its flavor from a few places—the raw materials and the seasonings and sauces, which can change the game completely. If you're having strongly flavored side dishes, they can easily hijack the show. So when you're thinking about a pairing, make sure you take into account the final flavor that's going to hang around after you swallow the food.

When you start to do that, you'll realize that the generic "steak and Cabernet" may not be the right pairing. While the idea of bold red and steak may be right, the flavoring of that steak matters. Is it prepared with peppercorn? If so, Syrah or Malbec, with their spicy profiles, are better matches. Is it steak tartare? If so, a bold white (yes, a *white*) Rhône wine like a Châteauneuf-du-Pape blanc or white Crozes-Hermitage or St-Joseph, or Chenin

Blanc may be the best pairing of all. The tartare is rich and a little spicy but still delicate and could benefit from these fruity, yet soft and spicy wines. Another example: think about a halibut with a miso sauce vs. with a mango salsa—different flavors require different pairings even though the fish is the same.

It's essential that you don't get lost in the meat, the pasta, or the vegetable; instead, become obsessed with your sauce and the flavors of your sides. The lasting flavors in your mouth are the ones that dominate your pairing experience.

Success or failure in pairing has a lot to do with personal preference. For example, do you like contrasting flavors, like lemon and cream, or do you prefer things that are complementary, like mushroom and an earthy Pinot Noir? As long as you get the

FOOD AND WINE BY WEIGHT

FOOD *(listed light to heavy)*	WINE DESCRIPTION *(listed light to heavy)*	EXAMPLES OF WINE *(listed light to heavy)*
Salads, light vegetarian dishes, soft cheeses	Light, unoffensive whites	Unoaked Chardonnay/Chablis, Sancerre, Muscadet, Pinot Grigio
Heavier cheeses (not blue), spicy appetizers, white fish, scallops, lighter seafood	Medium-bodied, less aromatic whites	Oaked Chardonnay, Chenin Blanc, Soave, Pinot Gris, New World Sauvignon Blanc
Poultry, salmon, lobster, pastas with cream- or oil-based sauces	Heavier, aromatic whites or lighter-style reds	***Whites:*** Côtes du Rhône Blanc, Fiano, Viognier ***Reds:*** Pinot Noir (Burgundy), Barbera, Dolcetto, Rosé
Italian food/tomato-based dishes, pizza	Italian reds	Chianti, Barbera, Nebbiolo, Southern Italian reds (Taurasi/Aglianico, Nero d'Avola, Primitivo)
Pork, veal, game (like venison)	Light to medium reds (sometimes big whites)	***Reds:*** Some Zinfandel, Merlot/Right Bank Bordeaux, Pinot Noir (California), Syrah, Chianti, Nebbiolo-based reds (Barolo, Barbaresco), Austrian reds ***White:*** Oaked Chardonnay
Bbq, fried food, grilled vegetables and meats	Medium to heavy reds with a spicy note	High-alcohol, heavy Zinfandel; New World Merlot and Cabernet Sauvignon; some Shiraz; Rioja; Malbec
Beef, lamb, some mushroom dishes	Heavy reds with a kick (tannin, spice, high alcohol, etc.)	New World Cabernet Sauvignon, Syrah from Rhône, Left Bank Bordeaux, Châteauneuf-du-Pape
Dessert of any kind	Sweet white or red—must be sweeter than the dessert	***Whites:*** Sauternes, late harvest Semillon, Champagne (doux) ***Reds:*** Port, Banyuls

elements in Steps #1 and #2 in sync, this step is about the details. But your ability to nail this step is where you could have a wine experience that will transform your idea about food and wine together and open a world of amazing flavor for you. To help, the following charts are a general guide of common wine flavors so when you're thinking about nuance you can pinpoint some bottles that will work.

Although the charts are all great for generating ideas, this stuff takes time to learn. Much of it is trial and error and paying attention to the combinations that work best for you. The more you experiment (hopefully in a more methodical fashion using the tools in this chapter) the better you'll do.

WINE'S STRUCTURE: ALCOHOLIC

TYPES OF FOOD THAT WORK WITH THIS COMPONENT	WHY?	EXAMPLE OF WINES
Simple food	High-alcohol wines can ruin any nuance in your delicately seasoned food. Keep it simple, with few seasonings, and you'll be better off. Fortunately, you can still use salt, since alcohol will make wine seem sweeter and less salty (good tip if you oversalt a dish!).	**Reds:** Zinfandel/Primitivo from Puglia, Italy Aglianico from Southern Italy Grenache/Garnacha from Spain, southern France, or Australia Monastrell/Mourvèdre from southern Spain or from Bandol, France
Slightly sweet foods (not desserts) where brown sugar or fruit is a component, for example	The alcohol can be complementary, as our mouths read alcohol as sugar. This can be a great match.	**Whites:** Gewurztraminer from Alsace, France Some New World Chardonnay or Viognier
Huge caveat: No spice with high-alcohol wines!	Why no spice? The hot, vodka shot-like sensation will make the spice in the food even hotter, causing a five-alarm fire in your mouth.	

Finding alcoholic wines: We luck out here. In most winemaking countries, alcohol content is required to be listed on the label for a winery to export or import. It's listed on the bottle as % ABV, or alcohol by volume. For more detail and definition around alcohol levels, see page 34.

WINE'S STRUCTURE: TANNIC

TYPES OF FOOD THAT WORK WITH THIS COMPONENT	WHY?	EXAMPLE OF WINES
Protein-rich foods with strong flavors: hard, aged, pungent cheese and red meat with lower salt preparations	Tannins are at their best when they can bind with protein and fat. They mellow out, and the food seems more velvety and flavorful (and can take on the fruit attributes of the wine).	The four most tannic grapes in the world: • Cabernet Sauvignon • Nebbiolo (found in Barolo and Barbaresco of Italy) • Syrah • Tannat, made as a stand-alone in Southwest France and Uruguay
Things that mimic meat but have a "meaty" texture, like mushrooms	This is probably more a flavor thing than a texture thing, but the "meaty" feeling of grilled or baked mushrooms mimics the effect of tannin and meat, although the wine will still seem a little sharp.	Any wine with these grapes as a significant portion of the blend

Finding tannic wines: Tannins are influenced by a number of factors, mainly the skins and seeds of the grape (page 32). But barrel aging, oak selection, and winemaker magic (infusing oxygen with a pump mitigates tannins, for instance) are important, too.

Age is essential as well: Tannins are a natural preservative in wine, helping it age, but with time they fade. An older wine will be mellower than a younger one (another reason vintage is important to note).

WINE'S STRUCTURE: SWEET

TYPES OF FOOD THAT WORK WITH THIS COMPONENT	WHY?	EXAMPLE OF WINES
Sweet food—the wine should always be sweeter than the food.	You have to align the flavors, but sweet and sweet is the only way to go. That way nothing overpowers anything else.	Sweet wines come from all over the world and from so many different grapes. ***The most famous:*** • Sauternes from Bordeaux • Port from Portugal (only sweet versions) • Vin Santo from Italy • Sweet Muscat from various places in southern France • Sweet wines of Germany—look for Spätlese or Auslese with alcohol levels below 11% ABV, and for Eiswein, and Beerenauslese • Tokaji from Hungary • Late harvest and ice wines from the US and Canada
Spicy or salty foods (pay attention, Asian food lovers!)	Sweet wines can help with spice and saltiness, taming these components. Spice is mellowed but not overshadowed by a lightly sweet wine.	Look for "off-dry" on the labels of wines around the world. For example, Vouvray from the Loire Valley in France in an off-dry style. Kabinett, Spätlese, and Auslese with alcohol levels of less than 11% ABV from Germany

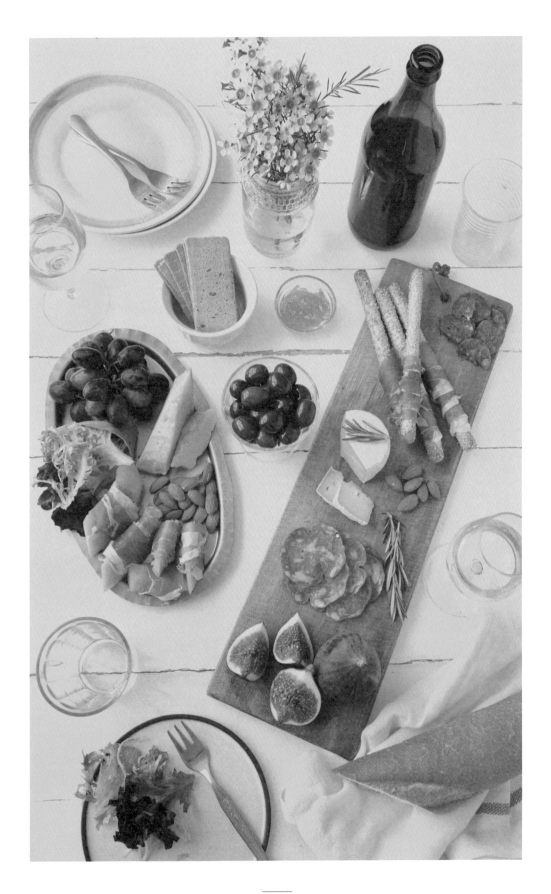

WINE'S STRUCTURE: ACIDIC

TYPES OF FOOD THAT WORK WITH THIS COMPONENT	WHY?	EXAMPLE OF WINES
Creamy or buttery, or protein-rich foods, egg-based dishes	The acid cleans out your mouth and refreshes it after the heavier food—it's a contrast	**Sauvignon Blanc:** Sancerre from France, or wine from Chile, South Africa, or New Zealand **Chardonnay:** Chablis or white Burgundy from France **Champagne,** for eggs especially, since the bubbles lighten the flavors
Other acidic foods like asparagus, spinach, tomatoes, or artichokes, foods with citrus-based sauces	Tough to pair with, but if you put the acid in the food up against the acid in the wine, the reaction makes the food softer and less sharp.	**Champagne** **Grüner Veltliner** from Austria **Whites from Northern Italy** (the light bitterness complements the veggies): Roero Arneis, Soave, Verdicchio **Acidic reds:** *French:* Beaujolais and red Burgundy (Pinot Noir); *Italian:* Barbera, Dolcetto, and Nebbiolo from Piedmont; Chianti, Vino Nobile di Montepulciano, and Brunello di Montalcino from Tuscany
Salty foods like shellfish, fish, salty cheese, or soy sauce–based sauces	High acid and salt can create amazing pairings, even though the salt is magnified. If this is tasty for you, look for wines that have a briny (think pickle juice), salty quality even if they aren't actually salty. If this is a bad pairing for you, try off-dry wines instead.	**French:** *Loire Valley:* Muscadet, Pouilly Fumé; *Burgundy:* Chablis; *Provence:* Rosé **Spanish:** Albariño from northwest Spain **Especially for dishes with soy sauce:** *German:* dry or off-dry Riesling; *French:* off-dry Chenin Blanc from the Loire Valley (Vouvray)

Finding acidic wines: Look for wines from cool places. If they're from northern or mountain climates, generally they're acidic. Vintage matters, too: cooler years = more acidic wines.

Examples of winegrowing regions that produce acidic wines: Loire Valley and Burgundy in France, Germany and Austria, and often New Zealand.

Serving temperature: Although not a structure element, serving temperature is vital to your perception of wine. It can appear to change a wine's flavors and structure. For instance, when wine is cold, it seems less sweet and less flavorful (which is great when you have cheap wine that has nasty aromas and flavors). If a red wine is cold, it seems infinitely more tannic and frankly undrinkable. Serving Temperatures (page 335) has a detailed chart to help you figure out the right temps for each kind of wine.

TWO OTHER RULES OF THUMB TO SUPPLEMENT THE PAIRING PROCESS

The traditional pairings that old-school Magic 8 Ball sommeliers recommend came about for a reason: Wines from specific regions were tailor-made, over the course of time, to go with the local food of the region. This is particularly true in Europe.

If you are at a loss to pair, ask yourself: Is this mainly an Italian dish? Is it Spanish influenced? Does it have a German flair? The answers will help you find a nuanced wine. When you're in a pinch, just think about the sauces and the spices that are going into a dish or being served.

Rule 1

Look at the flavors in the food, trace their origins, and pick a wine from that area. "What grows together goes together."

For example, a meaty dark broth or sauce would be an excellent match with red Bordeaux or the stuff that goes into a Bordeaux blend (Cabernet Sauvignon, Merlot, Cabernet Franc, Petit Verdot, Malbec, Carménère). Nothing is better with risotto than an Italian white like Gavi or Soave or, if it's mushroom based, a Barbera

or Dolcetto. Pork-based tapas? Go for Rioja. Seafood? Wines made seaside are best: Albariño from Spain, rosé from Provence, and Muscadet from France make excellent pairings with white fish and shellfish. And nothing goes better with pizza than Chianti, or Nero d'Avola from Southern Italy. You get the idea.

The derivative spices and flavors (oregano, thyme, pepper) will help you figure out the origin of the cuisine, and you should be able to find a great wine to match. Rarely do a food and wine from the same place clash. It's the harmony of being consumed together for centuries—winemakers figured out which grapes suited the cuisine and which winemaking techniques would work best to highlight the food.

Since New World wines derive from Old World regions, the pairing logic still applies—think about where the grape is originally from and that should help inform you about what flavors and foods go best.

The "No Tradition Issue"

What about cuisine that comes from a place without a wine tradition? The most obvious example is Asian food, which has varied flavors. You don't have much choice but to retreat to the three-step process. Asian food is about sauces and spice—it can't be lumped into one category. Although most off-dry white wines will pair, specifics count.

For example, a lot of Chinese dishes feature things like steamed pork, shrimp, eggs, and spicy chicken. Consider the weight of the dish and then the seasonings. We're following all the rules we discussed: We still want to stay away from tannic or high-alcohol wines that can make the

Q+A

I've heard that Old World wines are better food wines. Why is that?

For their high acidity, moderate tannin, and subtlety, it's true that European wines are often better with food. But there's potentially a reason and that has to do with how they developed. In ancient times, water was undrinkable, and often the only way to get liquid in one's diet was to drink wine (or beer). As a result, wine became a drink that was always on the table. Because of its presence for basic survival, it evolved alongside the local cuisine and became a food-friendly beverage. Likely, wines that clashed with the food fell out of favor, and those that blended well are what we have today.

spice seem exaggerated. Here are a few examples of things that work.

SWEET-AND-SOUR CHICKEN: Rosé, with its fruity, strawberry profile, lower alcohol, and bright acidity, will lighten the sweet in the sauce and neutralize the sour (acid/acid combo smooths everything).

SHRIMP DUMPLINGS: Something with great acid and made near the sea (the rule still applies, even though it's a different sea), as mentioned above—Albariño or Muscadet would do the trick.

PORK FRIED RICE OR DISHES WITH HEAVIER MEAT OR INCLUDE LOTS OF EGG OR GARLIC: Sparkling wines, or fuller whites like California Chardonnay or Viognier will let the egg and garlic shine without overpowering the flavor or textures.

In a world where our food choices have multiplied and people have moved beyond Chinese food, a few different cuisines bear consideration.

Thai food is bold, and the addition of things like tamarind, lemongrass, and curry change the pairing. As a general rule, what I mention about off-dry wines in the chart (page 306) is true here—but if you want something different, here are some ideas.

DISHES WITH A STRONG LEMONGRASS FLAVOR: Pair with something complementary, such as Alsace Gewurztraminer or South African, Chilean, or New Zealand Sauvignon Blanc.

RED MEAT WITH MOST CURRIES: Cabernet Franc's softer tannins and earthiness go well with the heat of the curry. Its tannins bind with the meat to make the dish seem velvety.

MASSAMAN CURRY (WHICH IS RICH IN TAMARIND), SWEETER GREEN CURRY, AND RED CURRY: Off-dry Vourvray/Chenin Blanc, off-dry Riesling, Provence rosé, or Beaujolais will work.

PAD THAI: Sparkling wine helps offset the saltiness.

You can apply these rules to many Indian foods too, which use spices in different combinations, but have the same sort of complexity as Thai dishes

AROMA/FLAVOR IN THE WINE	WHITE EXAMPLES	RED EXAMPLES
Citrus (lemon, lime, grapefruit)	Sauvignon Blanc, unoaked Chardonnay	Sangiovese (orange)
Tropical (pineapple, kiwi, melon)	New World Chardonnay, New World Sauvignon Blanc, Chenin Blanc	N/A
Fruits from trees (peach, apple, plums)	Chardonnay, Riesling, Albariño	Zinfandel, New World Cabernet Sauvignon, Malbec
Dried fruit (raisins, prunes)	Aged Chenin Blanc or Muscat	Amarone, Port, Muscat, Grenache, some ripe, higher-alcohol Cabernet Sauvignon, Merlot, or Zinfandel, Mourvèdre/Monastrell
Flowers (jasmine, gardenias, lilies for whites/rosés, violets, dried flowers for reds)	Riesling, Chenin Blanc, Verdejo, Fiano di Avellino, Chablis, California Sauvignon Blanc	Beaujolais, Cabernet Franc, Nebbiolo, Bordeaux, Sangiovese
Green or dried herbs (oregano, thyme, sage)	Bordeaux Blanc, New World Sauvignon Blanc	Red Bordeaux, Cabernet Franc, Carménère, Chilean Cabernet Sauvignon
Vegetables (green pepper, asparagus)	Sauvignon Blanc, Grüner Veltliner	Cabernet Franc, Cabernet Sauvignon (cooler/rainy vintages can create these flavors)
Nutty (almonds, hazelnuts)	Amontillado or fino Sherry, Italian whites, older white Burgundy	Tawny Port, Sangiovese, Tempranillo
Berry (strawberry, raspberry, blackberry, cranberry)	Sauvignon Blanc (gooseberry), some Riesling (blackberry)	Pinot Noir, rosé, Grenache/Garnacha, Cabernet Sauvignon (blackberry), a lot of other reds
Savory sautéed herbs (thyme, sage)	White Bordeaux or Grenache blanc (thyme)	Bordeaux, Cabernet Franc, Merlot, Malbec (thyme, sage)
Black or white pepper	Grüner Veltliner (white), Gewürztraminer (black)	Zinfandel (black), Syrah (black), Blaufränkisch, Zweigelt from Austria (black)
Wines that spend time in oak often have these flavors: caramel, butterscotch, vanilla for whites and mocha, wood/oak, pencil, cedar, cigar box, baking spices (cinnamon, nutmeg, clove) for reds	Chardonnay, Sauvignon Blanc, Chenin Blanc, California Viognier, any wines that have spent time in oak	Syrah/Shiraz, Cabernet Sauvignon, Malbec, Merlot, Rioja, Zinfandel

and a warm spice component similar to Thai food.

Finally, with sushi, look at high-acid white wines like Pinot Grigio, Champagne, Muscadet, and Chablis. Some of the best pairings are off-dry German Rieslings and the rich, fuller-feeling wines of Alsace—Riesling, Gewurztraminer, or Pinot Gris or even something like an Austrian white like Grüner Veltliner, which will make the fish feel soft, impart a bit of fruit flavor, and harmonize the textures and flavors.

Let's say that you have been saving a red Burgundy—a grand cru—for fifteen years, and that this vintage is ready to be opened and enjoyed. You decide to

Rule 2

Especially when dealing with old or complex wines, decide who is the star of the meal: the food or the wine. Food and wine shouldn't have to duke it out. When there's a clear star, let it shine.

cook up a big feast at your house. You get excited and make a spicy, savory Moroccan beef dish, which comes out perfectly.

You have wine-loving friends over. You open the bottle and everyone savors the wine—it has softened with time, is like Indian spices, and has a velvety, delicious texture. You can't wait to have it with your food masterpiece, so you do . . . and you can't taste the wine at all because all you taste is cumin from the food.

The lesson: There is no costarring when you're dealing with an older wine or one that has a bold profile. Give it a trophy. A big one. Put it on the mantel. Don't make it fight for the starring role with your food. Complex or strongly flavored food will kill the nuance and complexity that the wine took time to develop in the bottle.

Remember that older wine becomes more complex and much mellower with time. Its flavors will be subtle, so don't kill it with really flavorful food.

And if you're wondering, the opposite situation occurs with bold, young wine. The wine can overshadow the food if it's too strong for the dish.

The Wrap-Up

Food and wine pairing is complex and there is a lot to digest (bad pun intended) but now you have some idea of why and how wine can go with certain foods. The ideas set forth here can really be applied to any dish. How will you know if it works? Get out there and start experimenting.

tip

**Old or complex wine =
simple food
AND
complex food = simple wine**

8 | PICKI
WIN
at i
WINE S
RESTA

NG A

NER

the

HOP OR

URANT

Here's a question for you. Do you know any other product besides wine that has hundreds of brands of virtually the same thing from which to choose presented side by side on the shelf? Cookies? No. Cereal? Not *hundreds*. Clothes or shoes, maybe (which, incidentally, I worked in at the beginning of my career so I guess I'm a sucker for crazy products), but not much else.

How did wine turn into this ridiculous collection of bottle after bottle of indistinguishable blur? And how do you even *begin* to make sense of the dozens of personality-less names on a restaurant wine list? Printer ink doesn't do much to make something appetizing, and the descriptions offered on lists are often comical in their complete lack of useful information.

This industry is cluttered with brands. Today's wine shops are a far cry from the ones of years ago that had a section of jug wines, a section of French, Italian, and Spanish wines, and a memorable stink of broken jug "Chablis" on the floor. Fancy wine racks, private temperature-controlled rooms, wooden floors, and undistinguished wines are the order of the day now. Most times the only info you have to go on are those tags that say some dude gave the wine an arbitrary score from 1 to 100 (such a fake-out because I've never seen a score published for a wine with less than a 75, have you?).

At the risk of sounding like a communist, I gotta ask: Is there such thing as too much choice? I would argue that in wine, the answer is yes. It's to our detriment that the market is able to bear so many different wines. It leaves us with too many unanswered questions: What's the difference between the fifteen Pinot Noirs from

California, apart from price? What's the difference between the Australian Chardonnay and the California Chardonnay for exactly the *same* price? And what is the deal with all the European wines? You go to the store, the Wall of Wine snickers at you, and all you can do is stand there in utter defeat.

When I entered the wine industry as a marketer, I thought I would be able to do something to help normal people figure out the differences between wines—a system or a sticker or something that would explain the flavors or proper occasion on which to drink the wine. But once I was in the mix, I realized that was never going to happen. Instead I was part of a team that spent our time coming up with marketing stories about bottles that were just going to sit on the shelf until they went on sale or got a review from some guy with bad hair. We kept introducing more and more brands to the market (sometimes putting a different label on the same wine with a very minor tweak, if any at all), causing more clutter and confusion.

The bad news is that the industry isn't changing. So now the question is *what* do you do with the Wall of Wine? You've got options. You could do what my husband and co-podcaster, M.C. Ice, does. He narrows the wine world by price. His favorite thing to do in a big wine store is to find the wine with the biggest difference between the alleged real price (always inflated) and the sale price and get the best deal. You may be in his camp, or if you don't like his method, you could choose from pretty labels. Or you can go off recommendations from people who blindly tell you something is a great wine without ever asking you what kind of wine you like to drink. You could get those magazines and buy what *they* say is good. Occasionally you recognize a specific place you may have visited or like and you can buy off that.

The restaurant is a whole other monster. There's a lot more on the line there. First of all, the price is three to four times as expensive so there is more risk in making a decision. Second, you may have to rely on the server or sommelier to help you. You've got to hope that she knows enough *to* help you. It's a crapshoot. And piling on to the stress, if you don't know how to communicate with the sommelier, you may wind up with something nasty.

Stressful? Yes. But if we get logical about the process of selecting a wine, we can pare down the overwhelming selections and figure out how to approach a store and a wine list. With structure and what you've learned in this book, you're going to shop smarter, get what you like more often, and be able to experiment within a set of parameters rather than blindly.

Take what you want from this chapter and chuck the rest, but my hope is that it at least gets you thinking about the things that are important in choosing a wine so you feel empowered to make good decisions.

WINE SHOPPING IN A STORE

Although every place that sells wine, apart from a gas station or convenience store (poor quality, but limited selection), is a cluster, you can reduce your stress by figuring out where to shop. The good thing: You usually have a choice. The really good thing: If you don't have a choice, in a lot of places you can order wine online and have it shipped to you, so the possibilities multiply.

Picking the Right Shop

What makes a good wine shop? This is so subjective but we can narrow the field and get you thinking about what's important to you. It's not going to be the same for everyone.

The First Cut . . . Is It in Good Shape?

Like any other store, it's safe to say that wine shops that are dirty, that smell (even like wine, an indication that spilled bottles haven't been cleaned up), that have rude staff, and that are not conveniently located are off the list. If the shop is clean, and it looks like people care about the place (notice I am not saying it has gorgeous wooden storage and fancy signs), then you can surmise that the wine is probably stored properly (so it doesn't spoil), the staff actually care about the product, and, hence, the store has passed the first hurdle.

On the subject of store location, one of the essential things in picking a shop is that it's like your *Cheers* (in case you aren't old enough to know, it was a show about a bar where "everybody knows your name"). Most people who work there need to know you if you're going to buy wine a lot. If the place you really like is a pain to get to, you're not going to get to know the staff. That's bad. The more the staff know you and what you like, the easier it will be for them to recommend bottles for you. When you come in, they may have something ready for you based on what they've learned about your preferences. So pick a convenient shop, even if it's not perfect. Save the inconvenient shop for big shopping trips when you want to buy a case or so for the next couple of weeks and you have a good idea of what you want to get.

The Next Cut . . . What Kind of Shopping Experience Do You Like to Have?

Now, here's where personal preference comes in. You've got to decide what kind of shopper you are.

Remove wine from the equation. When you shop for clothes, for example, do you like to go to stores where someone offers help but allows you to browse on your own? Or do you like when the salesperson gives you personal attention and directs you to things you may like? The kind of shopping experience you prefer comes into play in wine big time.

For example, I dislike when salespeople follow me around and offer to help, unless I specifically ask. I'm an independent shopper for everything. That means a few things for me.

- First, I like places with a big, well-organized selection. That allows me to look around before honing in on something specific.

If I'm shoe shopping and I need a pair of black boots, I want to be able to find them all in one place right away.

- Second, I like to make preliminary decisions and then get specific help. I'm big into self-filtering. If there are four pairs of black boots, I'll get it down to two and I don't need help with that.
- Third, when I finally ask for help, my expectation is that the salesperson will be able to give me pointed information about what I've narrowed down. So if I ask for a size in one pair of black boots and the store is out of them, I don't want the person trying to sell me the zebra-striped pumps with a neon pink bottom. I've already narrowed the field—let's not get crazy.

A lot of people prefer to have guidance from the get-go. If you like personal attention, you need to choose a place that will offer advice and hang out with you while you shop. A lot of times this means that the store will be smaller (and hence have a smaller selection), but you may also have the opportunity to learn more by forming a personal relationship.

Think about the kind of shopper you are and it will help you with your next step.

Wine Shop Dating

You're going to have to jump into the wine store dating pool after you figure out how you like to shop for wine. Just as everyone's taste in partners varies, we all have different preferences in wine shops. You've got to tune in to what you want in a shopping experience and then decide the types of places you want to woo.

Much like dating, you'll know if a shop has what you want within minutes after walking in. A quick walk around the store will tell you if it has the kind of selection and layout for you. But what makes the real difference of whether or not you're willing to commit to a long-term relationship is the staff.

A Committed, Loving Relationship

Even if you're not a real people person, as a wine lover you've got to find someone you trust at a wine shop. That person is your key to getting the best wine you can get. This person can turn you on to all sorts of things you may not know about and help you make decisions because, in a good place, the staff has tried most everything in the store.

Find someone who speaks your language (I've given you some help on language in Chapter 1). A receptive, cool wine salesperson will get it when you tell her what you like or what you unequivocally don't like, which is often easier to communicate. The more you visit the shop and report to the salesperson on what you liked or didn't like from previous purchases, the more she will be able to direct you to wines for you. A good wine person will also understand that what *she* likes may not be what *you* like and not judge you for it. I can tell you how important this is from personal experience.

I used to have a shop that I frequented. One of the guys who worked there got this point so well. He and I share some preferences, but after talking to me and seeing what I chose for myself and the sections that I looked at most, he knew the kinds of wines I looked for and was able to direct me to the best wines for me. Even though he didn't like very acidic Chablis from France, for instance, he knew that I loved that wine, and he gave me the one that fit my budget. That's a good wine person and one to whom I have committed for the long haul.

In contrast, in the same shop, there was a guy who drove me nuts. He directed me to wines that were outside my price point and wines that he loved but that were not at all my style. I always needed to politely decline his recommendations, but then I got to the point where I tried to go when he wasn't working so I could avoid this uncomfortable situation. If he was the only dude in this store, I wouldn't go back.

In my story, the second guy is perfectly nice but doesn't "get it." There are plenty of other experiences I've had where I walk into a store and the person is a schmuck. Some are like members of the walking dead and have no clue; others make me feel dumb, insecure, or pressured. This is when I flee. I personally choose the "glance at my phone and bail" ploy, but you can choose your escape method. Regardless of how you bail, let's face it: Next! You're not going on a second date with that jerk. Move on to greener pastures.

Polygamy Is Important

This is where the dating analogy breaks down for me (although it may still hold for some of you—no judgment): *Monogamy isn't encouraged.* You have to play the field. I wouldn't stop at the first wine shop you like. Be a swinger when it comes to courting these shops. You'll probably find a level of comfort at one that you don't have at another. You've got to have at least two wine shops to which you are faithful. I have one for its great New World selection and one for its fantastic Old World selection. It creates a good balance. Because I like larger stores where I can roam, both have that feature, but when I need help,

the staff is ready to jump in and help me decide between the two Côtes du Rhônes I want or to find the earthiest California Pinot Noir.

OK now, step one is complete. Now we've got you a store that's a great fit for you. But we've done absolutely nothing to help you learn how to shop for wine better. Let's fix it and show you how. If you can narrow down your selection criteria, you'll make better use of the staff at the shop and be empowered to help yourself.

HOW TO PICK A WINNER

When I lived with my sister in Boston and was just getting into wine, I used to meander into wine stores knowing this: I wanted some. That was pretty much it. What did that mean? I spent a lot of time staring down the Wall of Wine trying to figure out what to buy.

For lack of a better method, I wandered in, looked at price, looked at label, and then just grabbed something, usually feeling very lame as I walked to the cashier. I remember looking around at other people in line, insecurely thinking that they thought I was a dolt for making a stupid decision on a bad bottle of wine. If the store was empty, I'd sometimes ask for help, but as soon as the person started asking me questions about what I wanted, it went downhill quickly. I often left empty-handed.

When I started to learn more about wine, I looked at the process of buying in a different light. I tried to track my wine shopping, blow by blow. I realized that I had become much more methodical than I thought.

For example, as I was driving my beat-up Nissan Sentra (named Barry) into the parking lot of my favorite store, I started to think about why I was going in there. Having a sense of purpose kept me on track. Knowing *what* I was shopping for allowed me to focus on an area of the store, rather than feeling overwhelmed by the endless choices. So I devised a shopping methodology, which is pretty simple. This isn't rote, so adapt it as you like; the goal is for you to pick up something that will help you shop for wine more efficiently, making it less onerous.

Get Yourself up to Speed

If you don't continually learn about yourself and what you like, it's going to be a beast to go shopping. You're reading this book, and, I hope, learning from it, but don't stop here. Seek out wine classes, blogs, videos, podcasts, and tastings so you can learn more about the topic of wine (shameless plug, winefornormalpeople.com has a pretty good selection of podcasts, classes, and videos!). Take note of places that make wine you like, so you can shop by region and not by labels. Knowing you like white vs. red wine or sweet wines vs. dry wines will reduce your choices to something more manageable. Learn a little and keep going. It will make the shopping process fun, not scary.

Go with Purpose

Regardless of how much you know about wine, a great thing to do is to ask yourself as you're heading to the store: *Why am I here today?* Some possible answers:

- To drink wine with dinner tonight

- To get wine to sip this week
- To get wine for a dinner party
- To get wine for a gift

After you clarify your purpose for shopping, it will be easier to figure out the next few things.

For instance, let's say the wine is for you to drink for tonight. Since that's kind of an instant gratification scenario, you can start to think about what you're in the mood for. Let's use this as an example and go through the shopping process.

Give the Store a Haircut

No matter what the occasion, it's easiest to make your first cut on wine color/type. Decide on the kind of wine you want—bubbly, rosé, white, or red? Then ask yourself—do I want a sweet wine or a dry wine or something in between (off dry)?

If you answer those two questions, you've cut down the selection in the store by at least 40 percent and sometimes more. To make the process more concrete, if you decide you want a dry white wine, for example, you've now cut all nonwhite wines and all sweet or sort of sweet white wines out of the list. With the precision of a canine tracker, you can now sniff out your mark: You'll only look at dry whites.

The Devil's in the Details

Next in our example, you've got to think about what you're in the mood for and what you like in a dry white.

- Do you want a light, low-alcohol, lower-acid wine that you can just sip?
- Do you want something with a little more mouth-filling, juicy fruit or more mouth-watering acidity?

- Or do you want a high-alcohol, oaky, rich-tasting wine?

Once you get the vocabulary down, you can use Chapter 1 and pages 332–33 to help you layer on other considerations. For example, for a white, do you want a wine that's . . .

- Fragrant—like flowers
- Fruity—like citrus fruit; like ripe apples; like tropical fruit
- Grassy—or like green herbs
- Creamy—like butter
- Oaky—tastes like licking a 2 by 4
- Acidic/tart—something that makes you think of sucking a lemon
- Mineral-like—something that reminds you of a waterfall or chalk
- Something to have without food?

For a red wine . . .

- Fruity—like cherries or fresh berries; like plums or blackberries or blackcurrants; like dried fruit
- Earthy—like dried leaves or potting soil or dirt kicked up on a dusty country road
- Floral—like roses or violets
- Tannic—mouth drying or bitter
- Acidic—mouthwatering or tart
- Lighter style
- Heavy and high in alcohol
- Medium-bodied

With a few descriptions of what you like or even just the rough cuts of color, sweet vs. dry, and light vs. full, it's going to be much easier to go into a good wine shop, explain what you like to your favorite wine person, and reduce your options to a number you can decide among.

Your Appetite for Adventure

The first "cuts" for determining what you like and what you want are essential to shopping. But with time, and as you learn more, you may start asking yourself if you want something you usually have or if you want something new that fits your criteria. For instance, you may like fruity, acidic Sauvignon Blanc from New Zealand, but you may want to see what else is "out there." With a little research or the help from a good wine consultant in a shop, you could be directed to a steely Albariño from Spain or a Grüner Veltliner from Austria. When you have an open mind, the world is your oyster.

Speaking of the world, although we've covered much of this in Chapter 4 (page 78), there's another cut you may consider while going through your decision-making process. In very general terms, fruitier, more sippable wines often come from the New World (everywhere that isn't Europe). More subtle-tasting, earthy, and often more food-friendly wines come from the Old World. Use that heuristic to pare the selection even more!

The Golden Coin Rules All

Just think how far this process has taken you! It gets you in the ballpark of wines you want, and we haven't even asked the question that's important to us all: *What do I want to spend?* This is going to cut down the selection criteria to a handful of bottles. I know it's tempting to go here first, but I encourage you to figure out what you want before you think about price. If you do that, you can go for the best value among the handful of wines that fit what you want. Wouldn't you rather get the best thing you can afford than something that's great for the money but not what you really want?

One other caveat on budget. If a salesperson is helping you, take my friendly advice: Pick an upper limit for what you're willing to spend and don't let the person sway you. Stand firm. There's plenty of choice out there. If you're reasonable, you'll be able to get something you want for the price you're willing to pay. If that store doesn't have it, there are others. Trust me.

Pulling It Together and Filling in the Blanks

So with all this, you're ready to pick a winner! Now you're ready to ask for help. You pared down your choices, so now use the shop to cast the deciding vote. Give the staff as much information as possible. The more detailed your description of what you want, the more likely they are to be able to recommend something. Be open to suggestions but make sure that you use your own judgment when making a selection—don't get pressured into something if it doesn't sound like exactly what you need.

Do a little research on your own. If there's no one around or you don't like or trust the person in the store, use your phone or go on the Internet before you get to the store to ensure you're armed with a few ideas of what you want. And once you're in there, don't rely on those little tags. Just because someone else rates a wine well doesn't mean it's a great wine. Look up a wine if you're considering it and try to figure out what it may taste like and if that works for you.

Now you can do a Mad Libs–esque exercise to choose among the ten or fewer wines that fit the bill for what you want.

WINE 🍎 LIBS

I want a _____ wine that is
dry/sweet

_____ .
bubbly/rosé/white/red/dessert

The wine should be

_____ flavored.
light/medium/full

I like wines that are

_____ .
*fruity/floral/earthy/oaky/alcoholic/grassy/
creamy/tart/mouth drying/tannic*

I refuse to spend more

than $_____ .

FLIPPING THE SCRIPT . . . SLIGHTLY

Getting a wine for immediate gratification is only one type of shopping. You may have other needs too, and that will require a slight modification to the process above. Let me run through three big occasions where you'll need to make changes.

For a Dinner Party

The game changes here. If you're buying a wine to serve with dinner or for the host of a dinner party, you've got to consider what's being served to make sure the wine doesn't clash with the food. Chapter 7 on food and wine pairing (page 296) has got you covered on this, but here's a quick summary. Lots of Old World wines go better with food, so you may want to bring one of these for your host or hostess. If

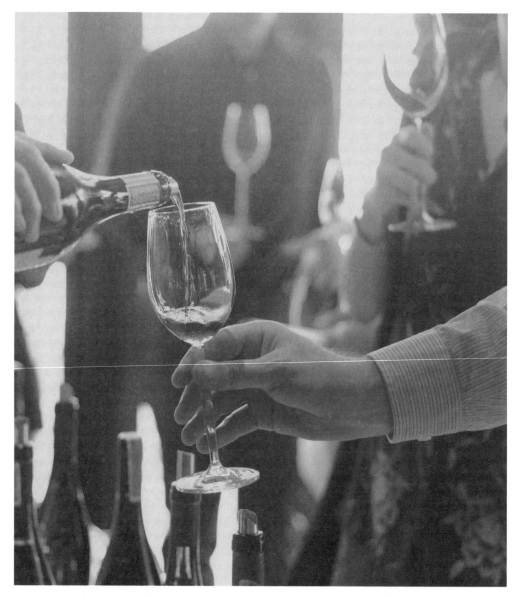

you want to bring a predinner sipper, New World wines or those from warmer regions of the Old World (think southern Europe) will be solid bets. Generally more fruit = more sippable. And you can never go wrong with bringing someone bubbles or dessert wine.

For a Gift

You can go through the shopping process outlined previously, but you have to substitute your own preferences for those of the gift recipient. Everyone has a different sense of taste.What you think is awesome, the recipient may think is donkey. So if you're going to buy a present for someone, it helps to ask around ahead of time to find out what the person likes to drink. Some additional questions to the ones listed previously may help you get a great bottle.

- **Does the person drink red, white, sparkling, or all?** What brands? You can get something similar if you know this.

- **Do you want to introduce the person to something new,** or go with a standby he or she usually purchases?
- **Do you know what the person likes to eat?** There's all sorts of research that says people who like spicy foods like flavorful wines (they have more insensitive palates). If he or she likes bland food, you may want to go very basic (oaked Chardonnay). Taste in food could be a clue as to what to buy.

Here, especially, stand firm on price. You can get great wine in every price point, so don't be tempted to overspend because you're stressed about impressing someone. Doing research on the Internet, taking note of what the person likes, going to a good wine shop, and being patient will get you far.

To Have and to Hold: Aging

If you're buying wine to stick in your cellar for a while, considerations are different, again. Remember that 95 percent of wines on the market should be chugged within three to five years of bottling. If you're planning to hold on to a bottle for longer, make sure it's the kind of wine that ages well (see page 74). Wines with higher tannin and acid content and lower alcohol (13 percent or less) that grow in cooler climates tend to age better than wines that grow in warmer places and are really fruity and bolder in flavor. Watch the vintage when you buy wines to age, too. You don't want to get a something from a less than stellar year, then wait fifteen years, only to find out that the wine would have been better if you'd popped it ten years before!

HOW TO USE A SOMMELIER AND HOW TO GIVE THE WINE LIST PERSONALITY

Although the wine shop and its Wall of Wine aren't always fun experiences, at least you've got options. If you get stressed out, you can bail easily. You walk out the door and your long national nightmare is over.

Not so at a restaurant.

You're kind of in a hostage situation, and if you want wine, you're going to need to deal with the wine list, the ceremonial BS that goes along with approving a bottle of wine, and the person standing there smiling or grimacing at you, waiting for you to choose among the little black words with either nonexistent or generally meaningless descriptions.

Well, similar to shopping for wine, you'll go through a process of elimination, but this time you'll place more emphasis on the food and wine pairing. Then—especially in a nice restaurant—you'll have to contend with someone who isn't optional, as the person in the wine shop is. At minimum, this person in the restaurant takes your wine order; at maximum, he could transform your dining experience into something memorable and fabulous.

Rather than review the wine-shop process, which will work for the wine list, too (although you have to know more about wine types before you cut down the selection . . . *hello*, smartphone or looking at the wine list before you go to the restaurant to get some ideas!), let's talk about your new BFF—the sommelier and how to use her.

I AM NEITHER A SOMALIAN OR A SAILOR

I'm not going to tell you that you have to speak French to like wine. If that's true, then I'm out of luck. But I also don't think you have to completely ignore the right pronunciation of a word in another language because it's unfamiliar.

I know it's not an easy word to say, but folks who serve wine, know about food and wine pairings, and have some knowledge of how to help you pick wines are sommeliers. They are not:

Sailors, or Seamen-NAYS

•

From East Africa or Somalia

•

Part of the four-syllable word set: so-MAHL-eee-yay

•

They are: summ-uhl-YAYs

What's the Job of a Sommelier?

Sommelier is defined by Merriam-Webster's as "a waiter in a restaurant who has charge of wines and their service: a wine steward." The dictionary also says that the word derives from old French, specifically the word *soumelier*, an official charged with transportation of supplies or, more specifically, a pack animal driver.

This derivation explains a lot. We can't deny that some sommeliers are, in fact, pack-asses. And now we know that their bad attitude isn't their fault. It's in their blood to act like that way—they're just living up to their heritage.

For another view, the certifying body for wine service professionals (wine waiters) is The Court of Master Sommeliers. I'm certified through this organization, and according to the main book it uses for its course, the job of a sommelier includes:

• Ensuring all beverages are in good condition when served
• Ensuring that the customer receives the best possible service
• Communication with the guest—including the ability to describe all flavors of every drink served, the ability to describe every word on a wine bottle, and the ability to describe all foods and preparations on the list
• Upselling wine to the guest

We need to take this book with a grain of salt, because it also has a section on how to address the Queen of England, since she'll, of course, be coming to most restaurants in Great Britain and around the world. (As a point of trivia, you should never begin a conversation with her, and if she asks you something, you use "Your Majesty" preceding your answer, followed by "Ma'am" for any subsequent communication.)

The point is, the responsibilities of a sommelier are to make you happy and to know everything about the restaurant's drinks, food, and how they go together. However, keep in mind the last point on the above list. The job (and it does depend on the person and the restaurant) is also to sell you more and more expensive wine. To get the best wine, you need to figure out if you can trust the sommelier or if you need to go it alone with a wing and a prayer, and a smartphone, of course.

Sommeliers or wine stewards come in all types. Some are really cool, service oriented, and helpful. Others are information-hoarding, nasty, little people you want to smack because they ruin your dinner with their supercilious attitude. Regardless of personality or lack thereof, the true problem is that until you feel it out, you can't tell if the sommelier has advanced knowledge or, more commonly, if he just knows more than most of the other people in the restaurant and that's why he's in charge of the wine program and service. Remember—just because someone is telling you about wine doesn't mean he knows about it.

How to Use a Sommelier

You have no idea when you walk into a restaurant for the first time what you're going to get out of the sommelier or server.

Well, it's *your* dinner and you are paying for the wine and the service, so you need to steer the conversation to get the wine you want. For the wine portion of the meal, you've got to lay down some parameters.

Sommelier Showtime

Even if you know a thing or two about wine, or if you're going to use the shopping process of elimination we laid out earlier in the chapter to go it alone (which is really fun and something I think you should try occasionally), a sommelier is a great resource. If you communicate the choices you're stuck between, the sommelier should help you get a great result.

That said, we are dealing with people, not computers, so there's a big X factor. Your job is to figure out how big an X factor.

If you feel out your sommelier and ask some key questions, you can easily decide if it's worthwhile to take the person's advice or go with your instinct.

When the sommelier comes to the table and asks you if you have questions about the wine list, this is your chance to suss him out. Not in a jerky way, but in a nice, conversational one. The best way is to ask a few softballs to see if he knows what he's talking about. One idea is to have a general conversation about what wines he thinks pair best with the restaurant's cuisine. If it seems logical, that's a green light. Or you can ask him what he likes to drink. This seems simple, but you'd be surprised at some of the answers you'll get even in nicer restaurants. I've had people say things like, "I don't know because I really don't like wine" (from a server) or "I really love to drink (*fill in the most expensive wine on the menu here*)."

As an aside, I don't think it's ever appropriate for someone who is working with wine to admit that she doesn't drink, even if it's true. I've found this often to be the case with servers, and it's maddening.

I hope you won't get into one of these situations and instead you find that the person can dork out a little bit with you on wine. When the sommelier is describing wines to you, use the powers of translation you learned in Chapters 1 and 2 to figure out if this is a kind of wine you're going to like. If the sommelier knows what she's doing, she will have an opinion, be able to give you great information because she knows what wine and food on the list pair best, and be thorough about her descriptions. If that happens, you're in good shape. She may introduce you to something you didn't know about but makes the meal even better than you had anticipated.

Maximizing Your Communication with the Sommelier

FOOD FIRST: In a restaurant, you'll want to select your food before you find the right wine. Most likely, you're going to the restaurant for the good eats. The wine needs to match what you're chowing on, so food rules all here. Your sommelier needs parameters in helping pick wine for you and your food choices are a great starting place.

DO A LITTLE LEGWORK: Try to narrow the field by thinking through a few things—wine color, the sauces or lasting flavors of each dish's main components. Use the details on food and wine pairing in Chapter 7 (page 296) to figure out a ballpark of the best pairings for the food you're ordering. If you have a few ideas before the sommelier comes to the table, it may be easier to assess if you're on the same page with her.

BE OPEN TO BY-THE-GLASS: People feel weird about this because they want to share the experience of wine with one another. But if everyone at the table is ordering a different weight or style food, one bottle of wine isn't going to suit everyone. There's going to be a loser in the bunch. To avoid that and make sure everyone has a delicious experience, go by the glass. There's no reason you should have a heavy Cab with your perfectly pre-pared white fish in a miso glaze because your spouse is ordering a prime rib. You should never buy a bottle if someone is going to lose out on good food because of the order. By-the-glass always seems more expensive, but it may be about the same price because you'll drink less, and it will definitely make everyone a lot happier.

CHOOSE A PRICE RANGE: Stick to your guns on this point before the sommelier comes to the table. Don't budge if you're on a budget.

Some Watch-Outs

Here's a big one: A great way to turn a good sommelier bad? Get into a pissing match over who knows more. If you don't agree with what she says or think she's full of it, don't challenge her. Fighting the sommelier's jerkery with your own brand of schmuck-dom is not going to enhance your experience, and it's likely to diminish your enjoyment of the meal. Zen it out.

Even with a good sommelier, don't forget that it's her job is to sell you wine. Be on guard—even if the person is knowledge-able, if she starts wandering far afield of your price point, *abort!* Figure it out your-self. Respecting your budget parameters is part of good service.

A Final Word on Sorting Out the Wine List, Especially in a Business Situation

There are times, especially in a business situation, where you feel you have to tackle the wine list on your own with little guidance from the sommelier. If you're charged with this task, what do you do to cut down the forty-page list to find the right bottle? Here are three tips.

1. Use the shopping process (page 321) to give the list a haircut.

2. Don't forget the other people at the table. If you're out for business, make sure you take into account peo-ple's preferences for certain wines. Don't just order because you want to

show them you can. Remember the by-the-glass option if you come to an impasse on wine types that everyone will enjoy.

3. Don't feel the need to show how much you know about wine to anyone. You will always seem smarter if you admit that you don't know everything about the subject and if you let others who have an opinion chime in. It's just wine, and the relationships you have with colleagues and friends are far more important than proving to anyone that you are wine savvy.

Insider Tips on Wine Lists

I did restaurant marketing for the big hulking winery, and I've been a server and bartender, so let me share a few little secrets you should know about price and quality in the restaurant setting.

- The cheapest bottles have the highest markup, sometimes as much as four or five times what the restaurant paid for the bottle. The most expensive bottles have the lowest markup. Although you probably won't want to spend that much on wine, they are the best deals on the list.
- The by-the-glass price is generally the price the restaurant paid for the bottle. The restaurant just needs one sale to break even. So don't feel bad about asking for a taste of wine before you buy it. If the bottle is open, someone else has already paid for it, essentially. Make sure the wine is what you want, and that it's not flat, which is often the case especially in hotel bars and chain restaurants where the staff usually isn't trained to tell when a wine has gone bad. The bartender is

happy to give you a taste—no skin off his nose.

- Especially in independent restaurants (something that's not a chain), there is often a hidden gem in the lower or middle pack of the list. It's something that's not a very popular wine but that the wine buyer really likes. So you may see an Australian Shiraz, which is out of fashion right now, or a Vouvray from the Loire Valley. Because the wine buyer likes it, it's on the list and the markup isn't that bad. Look for it, or if your sommelier or server is cool, ask about it. Sometimes it's easy to spot right away (told you this could be fun—it's like *Where's Waldo?*).
- Sometimes (not always) wines in flights or on special are there because the restaurant needs to get rid of the vintage. This doesn't mean the wine is bad (we're not talking day-old bread here), and it may be a great deal. Don't be shy about asking why a wine is on special. It could be a great value, as the restaurant tries to make space on the list for other stuff it wants to carry.

The Wrap-Up

Now you are fully equipped to go out and buy or order wine. Be your normal self, ask questions, and approach it all in good fun with a touch of method to your choosing, and you are great to go.

WINE TRAVEL TIPS

Advance Planning

1. Pick the Right Time of Year

SPRING: The winemakers and winegrowers are well rested after the hard work of harvest in the fall, and they aren't too busy to hang around the winery and talk to you. Vines are in bloom, wine release parties may be happening.

SUMMER: This is the season that brings the crowds, especially where the New World system of open cellar doors and wineries is the order of the day. And summer weekends? It's when everyone—interested in wine or not—goes to taste wine. It can be a real bust if you're looking to learn.

FALL: You'll see pickers in the vineyards, watch trucks transporting tons (literally) of grapes on the roadways, and get a view into the crush pad. The staff will be able to give you a sense for how the harvest is shaping up, and you may even be able to sneak by a vineyard and get a taste or two of ripe grapes fresh off the vines. Weekends are still a total cluster in busy regions, but if you can go during the week, this is an ideal time to see how things get done in a winery.

WINTER: Yeah, it's cold and the vines don't look pretty but if you want to spend unencumbered time with staff and winemakers, go in winter.

2. Research

Look into the wine specialties of an area (check in this book for those!) so you know what to expect. Figure out who the notable producers are or the "must-visits" in the area. Even if you normally eschew large producers, if it's your first time in a wine region, know that sometimes the big properties have amazing hospitality experiences and are on the list of places that every wine lover should hit.

If you want to visit small wineries, call ahead to make sure someone can taste with you. During your fact-finding, jot down all the places you may want to visit that require reservations, along with their phone numbers, physical addresses, and email addresses.

Another option is to use a tour company. In regions where access to wineries is limited, like Burgundy, France, or Piedmont, Italy, local guides can help provide transportation, translation, and access to wineries that may be difficult to get into on your own. The downside is that the properties they visit are usually not the top of the heap in terms of quality or reputation, but if you're looking for a more cultural experience and don't want to deal with planning, go this way.

3. Get a Map!

Plot your winery list on Google Maps, drive to the one farthest from the hotel or Airbnb, and work your way back over the course of the day. It's much lower stress this way, and you won't be scrambling to make it to places before they close.

4. Book a Room and a Car

Accommodations can fill up fast, and touring wineries is exhausting (day drinking will wipe you out!). Use the map to figure out what towns are closest to the areas you want to explore. Make sure you tank up on gas, since there aren't a lot of gas stations in vineyard areas!

On-the-Ground Guerilla Tactics

1. Pack and Ship

Get a box with shipping material and fill it as you go. Check the box as luggage or ship it when it's full. Alternately, buy and bring a wine suitcase and use that.

2. Stock Up on Provisions

Make sure to buy bottled water and non-perishable snacks to keep in the car. Water can keep you from feeling tired and from getting a massive hangover. Buy the stuff ahead of time, because once you head into wine country, you won't easily find stores that have snacks and nonwine drinks.

3. Important Etiquette Reminders

Be nice to the tasting room staff. Also, I know it's tempting to drink everything put in front of you, but don't get wasted. Pace yourself, spit, share tastings with your friend or spouse or family member—whatever the strategy, please avoid getting trashed. It's disrespectful to the winery.

4. Take Pictures of the Labels from Wines You Like

Especially if you aren't going to buy them at the winery but plan to seek them out at home or order them direct later, take pictures. You can upload them into a wine app and enter your notes so you remember what you liked.

5. Save Your Palate for Wines You Love

If you don't love something you taste, don't drink it—spill it out. The staff won't be offended and you'll save your palate for something tastier.

6. No Guilt Buying!

If the wines are a total letdown, you don't have to buy anything. Taste the stuff, cut it short if it's really bad, and thank the staff with a quick goodbye. Guilt buying is a waste of money and it takes up the space you could use for better bottles.

Special Things about European Wine Travel

When going to Europe, don't just hop in a car and go looking for wineries unless you're in a place that has a wine route, like Alsace in France. On the Continent, you have to make inquiries via email or phone. Driving distances are always farther than they look at first glance. And if you don't speak the language of the country, hire a tour guide who does.

If you are buying wine in Europe, you may need to pay a tariff to bring it home. You can check a box of wine as luggage, and when you get to customs in your home country, you'll need to declare your wine. For anything more than a liter of wine per person, Canadian and US travelers pay about $1 to $3 per bottle or less. Just be sure to declare everything and to bring in twelve bottles or fewer.

WHITE WINE VOCABULARY

Put Words to Your Thoughts

1. Sight
What does the wine look like?

COLORS:
Clear
Light/pale
Greenish
Straw colored
Yellow
Golden
Amber

OTHER VISUAL CUES:
Hazy/stuff floating in it
Bubbles—if the wine is sparkling, how small and long lasting? If not sparkling, can you taste them in the wine?
Thick legs (alcohol)
What else?

2. Smell and Taste
What are the main and secondary notes that you taste and smell?
Citrus (lemon, lime, grapefruit)
Tropical (pineapple, kiwi, melon)
Fruits from trees (nectarine, apricot, peach, apple)
Grapes or berries
Dried fruit
Flowers (or dried flowers)
Honey
Green or dried herbs (oregano, thyme, sage)
Vegetables (green pepper, asparagus)
Nutty (almonds, hazelnuts, nuts)
Gasoline, rubber, sulfur
Butter
Stream, wet rocks, earth, dirt, chalk, talc
Caramel, butterscotch, vanilla
Exotic spices
Wood/oak

What else? If these words don't work for you, think about why you feel the wine is great or nasty.

3. Texture
What does the wine feel like in your mouth?
Acidic/tart
Sweet/cloying
Dry
Alcoholic/hot
Tannic/rough or astringent/chewy/puckering
Bitter or sour
Watery
Salty (like saltwater or brine)
Creamy/round
Metallic (like eating aluminum foil)
Soapy
Heavy/full flavor and mouth coating
Medium/less full feeling
Light/not much happening

4. Finish
Finish: What final impression does the wine leave?
Washed out your mouth then went away
Stuck around a moderate amount
Will last for the next three days on your tongue

5. Final Conclusion
☐ Yum—I love it!
☐ It's just OK.
☐ That is *horrible.*

Think about why.

RED WINE VOCABULARY

Put Words to Your Thoughts

1. Sight
What does the wine look like?

COLORS:
Brown
Ruby
Garnet
Brick red
Crimson/blood red
Orange
Purple/black

OTHER VISUAL CUES:
Reflective
Watery rim
Opaque
Hazy/stuff floating in it
Bubbles
Thick legs (high alcohol)
What else?

2. Smell and Taste
What are the main and secondary notes that you taste and smell?
Berry (strawberry, raspberry, blackberry, grape)
Fruits from trees (plums, figs, banana, orange)
Dried fruit (raisins, prunes)
Flowers (roses, violets, potpourri)
Vegetables (green pepper, green beans)
Savory herbs or spice (thyme, sage)
Dirt, wet soil, dusty road, farm, horse stable, chalk
Pepper
Unripe/green/like plant stems
Baking spices (cinnamon, nutmeg, clove)
Exotic spices (chai tea, curry)
Vanilla, chocolate, mocha
Caramel, butterscotch, vanilla
Dark caffeinated beverages (coffee, tea, Coke)
Pencil, cedar, cigar box
Wood/oak
Weird stuff (tobacco, chickens, leather, horse
   sweat, cough syrup, Band-Aid bandage

What else? If these words don't work for you, think about why you feel the wine is great or nasty.

3. Texture
What does the wine feel like in your mouth?
Acidic/tart
Sweet/cloying
Dry
Alcoholic/hot
Tannic/rough or astringent/chewy/puckering
Bitter or sour
Watery
Salty (like saltwater or brine)
Creamy/round
Metallic/like eating aluminum foil
Velvety
Soapy
Heavy/full flavor and mouth coating
Medium/less full feeling
Light/not much happening

4. Finish
What final impression does the wine leave?
Was light and went away fast
Stuck around a moderate amount
Am still chewing on it and the flavor will last
   for the next ten days in my mouth

5. Final Conclusion
☐ Yum—I love it!
☐ It's just OK.
☐ That is horrible.

Think about why.

1855 CLASSIFICATION of
BORDEAUX CHÂTEAUX

PREMIERS CRUS (FIRST GROWTHS)

Château Lafite Rothschild	Pauillac
Château Margaux	Margaux
Château Latour	Pauillac
Château Haut-Brion	Pessac
Château Mouton Rothschild	Pauillac

DEUXIÈMESCRUS (SECOND GROWTHS)

Château Rauzan-Segla	Margaux
Château Rauzan-Gassies	Margaux
Château Léoville-Las Cases	St-Julien
Château Léoville Poyferré	St-Julien
Chateau Léoville Barton	St-Julien
Château Durfort-Vivens	Margaux
Château Gruaud-Larose	St-Julien
Château Lascombes	Margaux
Château Brane-Cantenac	Margaux
Château Pichon-Longueville-Baron	Margaux
Château Pichon-Longueville Comtesse de Lalande	Pauillac
Château Ducru-Beaucaillou	St-Julien
Château Montrose	St-Estèphe
Château Cos-d'Estournel	St-Estèphe

TROISIÈMES CRUS (THIRD GROWTHS)

Château Kirwan	Margaux
Château d'Issan	Margaux
Château Lagrange	St-Julien
Château Langoa Barton	St-Julien
Château Giscours	Margaux
Château Malescot St-Exupéry	Margaux
Château Boyd-Cantenac	Margaux
Château Cantenac-Brown	Margaux
Château Palmer	Margaux
Château La Lagune	Haut-Médoc
Château Desmirail	Margaux
Château Calon-Ségur	St-Estèphe

TROISIÈMES CRUS (THIRD GROWTHS) cont.

Château Ferrière	Margaux
Château Marquis d'Alesme-Becker	Margaux

QUATRIÈMES CRUS (FOURTH GROWTHS)

Château Saint-Pierre	St-Julien
Château Talbot	St-Julien
Château Branaire-Ducru	St-Julien
Chateau Duhart-Milon-Rothschild	Pauillac
Château Pouget	Margaux
Château La Tour Carnet	Haut-Médoc
Château Lafon-Rochet	St-Estèphe
Château Beychevelle	St-Julien
Château Prieuré-Lichine	Margaux
Château Marquis de Terme	Margaux

CINQUIÈMES CRUS (FIFTH GROWTHS)

Château Pontet-Canet	Pauillac
Château Batailley	Pauillac
Château Haut-Batailley	Pauillac
Château Grand-Puy-Lacoste	Pauillac
Château Grand-Puy Ducasse	Pauillac
Château Lynch-Bages	Pauillac
Château Lynch-Moussas	Pauillac
Château Dauzac	Margaux
Château d'Armailhac	Pauillac
Château du Tertre	Margaux
Château Haut-Bages Libéral	Pauillac
Château Pédesclaux	Pauillac
Château Belgrave	Haut-Médoc
Château de Camensac	Haut-Médoc
Château Cos Labory	St-Estèphe
Château Clerc-Milon	Pauillac
Château Croizet-Bages	Pauillac Château Cantermerle
Château Cantermerle	Haut-Médoc

SERVING TEMPERATURES

Basic Overview

DRY WHITES, SPARKLING
40–50°F (4–10°C)—Quick chill with ice water, not in the freezer!

ROSÉS
45–55°F (7–13°C)

FULL-BODIED WHITES, LIGHTER REDS
50–60°F (10–16°C)

FULL-BODIED REDS
60–65°F (16–18°C)

40-45°F (4-7°C)
- Ice Wine
- Muscadet
- Vinho Verde
- White Rioja (cheap)

45-50°F (7-10°C)

Alsace whites/ varieties	Chenin Blanc-based wines (Savennières, Vouvray)	Sauvignon Blanc-based wines (Pouilly Fumé, Sancerre)
Chablis and white Burgundy	Fino Sherry	Sweet wines (Tokaji, Sauternes) White Bordeaux
Champagne and sparkling (keep a little colder)	Riesling	White and tawny Port
	Rosé	White Rhône

50-55°F (10-13°C)
- Better white Burgundy
- Chardonnay
- Viognier

55-60°F (13-16°C)

Aged tawny Port, ruby Port	Madeira	Valpolicella
Chianti	Pinot Noir (Burgundy)	
	Rioja	

60-65°F (16-18°C)

Barolo	Merlot	Shiraz
Brunello	New World Pinot Noir	Vintage Port
Cabernet Sauvignon	Northern and southern Rhône wines	Zinfandel
Fuller sherries: amontillado, oloroso	Red Bordeaux	

335

BIBLIOGRAPHY

Pearlman, Jonathan. "Million bottles of Australian wine to be poured down the drain." *Telegraph*, July 16, 2013, https://www.telegraph.co.uk/news /worldnews/australiaandthepacific/australia /10183213/Million-bottles-of-Australian-wine-to -be-poured-down-the-drain.html.

"Planning Your Visit to California's Wine Country." *Wall Street Journal*. http://guides.wsj.com/wine /going-wine-tasting/planning-your-visit-to -californias-wine-country.

Stromberg, Joseph. "The Human Nose Can Distinguish Between One Trillion Different Smells." *Smithsonian Magazine*, March 20, 2014. https://www.smithsonianmag.com/science -nature/human-nose-can-distinguish-between -one-trillion-different-smells-180950175/?no-ist.

Vine Health Australia. "Phylloxera." http://www .vinehealth.com.au/bio-security/phylloxera.

Zoecklein, Bruce. "Matching Table Wines with Food." *Virginia Polytechnic Institute and State University*, November 2007. https://www.apps.fst.vt.edu /extension/enology/extonline/foodwine.html.

Wine Websites

Austrian Wine Marketing GmbH:
www.austrianwine.com

Bourgogne Wine Board (BIVB):
www.bourgogne-wines.com

CIVP–Conseil Interprofessionnel des Vins de Provence: http://provencewineusa.com

Coonawarra Grape and Wine Incorporated (CGWI):
https://coonawarra.org

Deutsches Weininstitut (German Wine Institute):
www.germanwineusa.com

Finger Lakes Wine Alliance:
www.fingerlakeswinealliance.com

Inter Rhône Association: www.vins-rhone.com

Italian Wine Central: https://italianwinecentral.com

Jancis Robinson: https://www.jancisrobinson.com

Margaret River Wine Association:
www.margaretriverwine.org.au

McLaren Vale Grape Wine & Tourism Industry Association Incorporated: https://mclarenvale.info

Napa Valley Vintners (NVV):
https://napavintners.com

New Zealand Winegrowers: www.nzwine.com

Paso Robles Wine Country Association:
https://pasowine.com

Sonoma County Tourism Bureau:
www.sonomacounty.com

Sonoma County Winegrowers:
https://sonomawinegrape.org

Virginia Wine: www.virginiawine.org

VQA: Ontario's Wine Appellation Authority:
www.vqaontario.ca/AboutVQA

Washington State Wine Commission:
www.washingtonwine.org

Wine Australia: www.wineaustralia.com

Wine Institute: www.wineinstitute.org

Wine Marlborough: www.wine-marlborough.co.nz

Wines from Spain: Trade Commission of Spain:
https://winesfromspainusa.com

Wines of Chile: www.winesofchile.org

Wines of Great Britain: www.winegb.co.uk

Wines of Portugal: www.winesofportugal.info

SERVING TEMPERATURES

Basic Overview

DRY WHITES, SPARKLING
40–50°F (4–10°C)—Quick chill with ice water, not in the freezer!

ROSÉS
45–55°F (7–13°C)

FULL-BODIED WHITES, LIGHTER REDS
50–60°F (10–16°C)

FULL-BODIED REDS
60–65°F (16–18°C)

40–45°F (4–7°C)	Ice Wine Muscadet Vinho Verde White Rioja (cheap)		

45–50°F (7–10°C)	Alsace whites/
	  varieties
	Chablis and white
	  Burgundy
	Champagne and
	  sparkling (keep a
	  little colder)
		Chenin Blanc-based
		  wines (Savennières,
		  Vouvray)
		Fino Sherry
		Riesling
		Rosé
			Sauvignon Blanc-
			  based wines
			  (Pouilly Fumé,
			  Sancerre)
			Sweet wines (Tokaji,
			  Sauternes) White
			  Bordeaux
			White and tawny Port
			White Rhône

50–55°F (10–13°C)	Better white Burgundy Chardonnay Viognier		
55–60°F (13–16°C)	Aged tawny Port, ruby Port Chianti	Madeira Pinot Noir (Burgundy) Rioja	Valpolicella

60–65°F (16–18°C)	Barolo
	Brunello
	Cabernet Sauvignon
	Fuller sherries:
	  amontillado,
	  oloroso
		Merlot
		New World Pinot Noir
		Northern and
		  southern Rhône
		  wines
		Red Bordeaux
			Shiraz
			Vintage Port
			Zinfandel

BURGUNDY GRAND CRU

by

COMMUNE

Chablis
All Chardonnay

BOLD STYLES: Les Clos, Valmur, and Vaudésir

MEDIUM STYLES: Bougros and Blanchots.

LIGHTER, FLORAL STYLES: Les Preuses and Les Grenouilles

UNOAKED VERSIONS: Maison Regnard, Jean Durup, J. Moreau, and Jean-Marc Brocard

OAK USERS: René et Vincent Dauvissat and Domaine Francois Raveneau

Gevrey-Chambertin
All Pinot Noir

BOLD STYLES: Le Chambertin, Chambertin-Clos de Bèze, Griotte-Chambertin, and Mazis-Chambertin, plus Clos Saint-Jacques, a premier cru considered as good as a grand cru

MEDIUM STYLES: Ruchottes-Chambertin, Charmes-Chambertin, and Mazoyères-Chambertin

LIGHTER STYLES: Chapelle-Chambertin and Latricières-Chambertin

NOTABLE PRODUCERS: Domaine Armand Rousseau, Dugat-Py, Domaine Leroy, and Denis Bachelet

Morey-Saint-Denis
All Pinot Noir

BOLD STYLES: Clos de la Roche, Clos de Tart, and Clos Saint-Denis

LIGHTER STYLES: Clos des Lambrays and Bonnes Mares

NOTABLE PRODUCERS: Domaine de Dujac, Domaine Ponsot, and Domaine de les Lambrays

Chambolle-Musigny
Pinot Noir and Chardonnay

BOLD STYLE: Bonnes Mares (Pinot Noir)

LIGHT BUT COMPLEX STYLE: Le Musigny (mostly Pinot Noir with some Chardonnay). Les Amoureuses is a premier cru Pinot Noir considered to equal a grand cru. It's similar to Musigny.

NOTABLE PRODUCERS: Domaine Georges Roumier, Jacques-Frédéric Mugnier, and Domaine Comte Georges de Vogüé

Vougeot
All Pinot Noir

BOLD STYLE: Clos de Vougeot

NOTABLE PRODUCERS: Domaine Leroy, Mugneret-Gibourg, Méo-Camuzet, and Anne Gros

Flagey-Échezeaux
All Pinot Noir

BOLD STYLE: Grands-Échezeaux

MEDIUM-WEIGHT STYLE: Échezeaux

NOTABLE PRODUCERS: Domaine de la Romanée-Conti, Lamarche, and Dujac

Vosne-Romanée

BOLD STYLES: Romanée-Conti, La Grand Rue, La Romanée, and Richebourg

MEDIUM STYLES: La Tâche and Romanée-Saint-Vivant

NOTABLE PRODUCERS: Domaine Romanee-Conti, Domaine Leroy, Dugat-Py, and Méo-Camuzet

Pernand-Vergelesses, Ladoix, Aloxe-Corton
Pinot Noir and Chardonnay

BOLD STYLES: Le Corton (95% Pinot Noir with 5% Chardonnay)

MEDIUM STYLES: Corton-Charlemagne (Chardonnay)

NOTABLE PRODUCERS: Louis Latour, Domaine Leroy, Joseph Faiveley Puligny-Montrachet

Chassagne-Montrachet
All Chardonnay

BOLD STYLES: Le Montrachet, Chevalier Montrachet, and Bâtard-Montrachet

MEDIUM STYLES: Bienvenues-Bâtard-Montrachet and Criots-Bâtard-Montrachet

NOTABLE PRODUCERS: Louis Latour, Domaine Leroy, and Joseph Faiveley

BIBLIOGRAPHY

Books

Coates, Clive. *The Wines of Burgundy*. Berkeley: University of California Press, 2008.

Johnson, Hugh and Jancis Robinson. *The World Atlas of Wine*. 7th ed. London: Mitchell Beazley, 2013.

Lazarakis, Konstantinos. *The Wines of Greece (Classic Wine Library)*. Oxford: Infinite Ideas, 2006.

MacNeil, Karen. *The Wine Bible*. 2nd ed. New York: Workman Publishing Company, 2015.

Robinson, Jancis, ed., and Julia Harding, ed. *The Oxford Companion to Wine (Oxford Companions)*. 4th ed. Oxford: Oxford University Press; 2015.

Robinson, Jancis, Julia Harding, and José Vouillamoz. *Wine Grapes: A Complete Guide to 1,368 Vine Varieties, Including Their Origins and Flavours*. New York: Ecco Press, 2012.

Stevenson, Tom. *Sotheby's Wine Encyclopedia*. London, DK Publishing, 2011.

Articles

Asimov, Eric. "Taming of the Bestial Bandol." *New York Times*, March 18, 2014. https://www.nytimes.com/2014/03/19/dining /taming-of-the-bestial-bandol.html.

Beltrami, Alexis. "Sushi and Wine." *StarChefs*. http://www.starchefs.com/wine/features/html /sushi_wine.shtml.

Brook, Stephen. "The Two Montrachets." *Decanter*, October 7, 2005. https://www.decanter.com /premium/the-two-montrachets-247896 /#p63b0ZEYRXqI52RD.99.

Buzzeo, Lauren and Joe Czerwinski. "Learn Every-thing You Need to Know About Vins Doux Naturels." *Wine Enthusiast Magazine*, December 20, 2012. http://www.winemag.com/Web-2012 /Naturally-Sweet.

Byron, Ellen. "Uncork the Nose's Secret Powers." *Wall Street Journal*, February 20, 2013. https://www.wsj.com/articles/SB1000142412788 7323696404578300182010199640.

Cork Quality Council. "Incoming Natural Corks—Average TCA Score." December 2018. https://www.corkqc.com/products/incoming -natural-corks-average-tca-score.

Dobie, Karen. "Wine Industry Over a Barrel." *Smart Company*, February 14, 2012. https://www.smartcompany.com.au/finance /economy/crushing-issues.

Edgar, Crystal. "D-Harmony: Dim Sum and Wine Pairings." *Inside Italian Wine Merchants*, March 16, 2012. http://www.insideiwm.com /2012/03/16/d-harmony-dim-sum-and-wine -pairings.

For the Love of Port. "FAQs." http://www.fortheloveofport.com/faqs.

Goode, Jamie. "Spotlight on Portugal's Dão Region." *Wine Anorak*. http://www.wineanorak.com /dao1_overview.htm.

Goode, Jamie. "Tannins." *Wine Anorak*. www.wineanorak.com/tannins.htm.

Hancock, Elise. "A Primer on Smell." *Johns Hopkins Magazine*, September 1996. http://www.jhu.edu/jhumag/996web/smell.html.

Heeger, Jack. "Building a Perfect Wine Barrel." *Napa Valley Register*, January 28, 2008. http://napavalleyregister.com/news/local /article_7aa4f8a2-bef1-5df7-ad76-6a191b2b8f2f .html.

Journo, Laurent J. "Wine Annual Report and Statistics, France." *USDA Foreign Agricultural Service, Global Agricultural Information Network*, July 7, 2015. https://gain.fas.usda.gov /Recent%20GAIN%20Publications/Wine%20 Annual%20Report%20and%20Statistics_Paris _France_7-7-2015.pdf.

Lacey, Stephen. "Factors and Trends Affecting the Bordeaux Wine Market." *Wine and Spirits Educa-tion Trust White Paper*, February 2012.

O'Keefe, Kerin. "Soave's quiet revolution." *Decanter. com*, July 3, 2009. https://www.decanter.com /features/soaves-quiet-revolution-246665.

BIBLIOGRAPHY

Pearlman, Jonathan. "Million bottles of Australian wine to be poured down the drain." *Telegraph*, July 16, 2013, https://www.telegraph.co.uk/news /worldnews/australiaandthepacific/australia /10183213/Million-bottles-of-Australian-wine-to -be-poured-down-the-drain.html.

"Planning Your Visit to California's Wine Country." *Wall Street Journal*. http://guides.wsj.com/wine /going-wine-tasting/planning-your-visit-to -californias-wine-country.

Stromberg, Joseph. "The Human Nose Can Distinguish Between One Trillion Different Smells." *Smithsonian Magazine*, March 20, 2014. https://www.smithsonianmag.com/science -nature/human-nose-can-distinguish-between -one-trillion-different-smells-180950175/?no-ist.

Vine Health Australia. "Phylloxera." http://www .vinehealth.com.au/bio-security/phylloxera.

Zoecklein, Bruce. "Matching Table Wines with Food." *Virginia Polytechnic Institute and State University*, November 2007. https://www.apps.fst.vt.edu /extension/enology/extonline/foodwine.html.

Wine Websites

Austrian Wine Marketing GmbH: www.austrianwine.com

Bourgogne Wine Board (BIVB): www.bourgogne-wines.com

CIVP–Conseil Interprofessionnel des Vins de Provence: http://provencewineusa.com

Coonawarra Grape and Wine Incorporated (CGWI): https://coonawarra.org

Deutsches Weininstitut (German Wine Institute): www.germanwineusa.com

Finger Lakes Wine Alliance: www.fingerlakeswinealliance.com

Inter Rhône Association: www.vins-rhone.com

Italian Wine Central: https://italianwinecentral.com

Jancis Robinson: https://www.jancisrobinson.com

Margaret River Wine Association: www.margaretriverwine.org.au

McLaren Vale Grape Wine & Tourism Industry Association Incorporated: https://mclarenvale.info

Napa Valley Vintners (NVV): https://napavintners.com

New Zealand Winegrowers: www.nzwine.com

Paso Robles Wine Country Association: https://pasowine.com

Sonoma County Tourism Bureau: www.sonomacounty.com

Sonoma County Winegrowers: https://sonomawinegrape.org

Virginia Wine: www.virginiawine.org

VQA: Ontario's Wine Appellation Authority: www.vqaontario.ca/AboutVQA

Washington State Wine Commission: www.washingtonwine.org

Wine Australia: www.wineaustralia.com

Wine Institute: www.wineinstitute.org

Wine Marlborough: www.wine-marlborough.co.nz

Wines from Spain: Trade Commission of Spain: https://winesfromspainusa.com

Wines of Chile: www.winesofchile.org

Wines of Great Britain: www.winegb.co.uk

Wines of Portugal: www.winesofportugal.info

With Gratitude

This book has been an incredible and long journey. So many people have supported me, and propped me up when I was ready to throw in the towel. To reiterate the dedication, no one has been more important to me than my wonderful, supportive, kind, smart, funny, loving husband and co-host, M.C. Ice. Any success I have is largely due to him. I love the guy.

An equal amount of thanks to my dad, Mark Schneider, who read and edited every word of this book, has supported all my educational and career pursuits, and has been a source of sanity, humor, and pep talks through the years. This book couldn't exist without him and my life would be boring without our chats.

Greatest of thanks to my best friend and sister Johanna Schneider. I took my first wine course with her and no one could ask for a funnier, kinder, more generous sister.

Thanks to my mother and stepdad, Margaret and Dan Dykhuizen, who have supported and never questioned any of the crazy stuff I've decided to do. And to my in-laws—Mimi and Bob Eisenbeis and my sister in-law Jill, for supporting my first wine tasting, and all the ventures that have come afterward.

A big heaping of thanks to the people who taught me so much in my professional life: George Colony, CEO and Founder of Forrester Research my first and best exposure to an amazing entrepreneur, Mitch Davis for saving my self-esteem while I was at the big hulking winery, Rick Breslin, original co-host of *Wine for Normal People*, and Jim Morris, Oded Shakked, and Laura Perret-Fontana who have been the best champions and friends in this crazy industry.

To my dear friends, book readers, life cheerleaders, and wine buds: Anna Sandler, Sadaf Roshan, Eugenia Harvey, Gigi Miller, Darrah Brustein, Magda Kotek, Catie Griggs, Melissa Hemmingway, Ryan Mullins, Matt Olson, and Eric Crane, and the folks at my alma mater, Kenan-Flagler Business School at University of North Carolina, especially Carrie Dobbins. Also, my podcast co-hosts, friends, and advisers—Ian Renwick (also a book editor) of Jaded Palates Wine Shop in the UK and Simone Madden-Grey, the Happy Wine Woman in Melbourne, Australia. Huge thanks to the staff of San Francisco Coffee in Atlanta, Georgia where most of this book was written—especially Leo Hollen Jr. (my video editor, too!), Jason, Rob, and Jan.

A heap of credit to Crystal Cox, my designer, and Peter Hoppe, my web developer, at Garetii Media, and Iris Blasi, my book publicist, for making my life easier and inspiring me.

Huge thanks to Leigh Saffold of Blue Pen Agency, my editor—if there were ever a project anywhere, on any topic, that I had to work with someone on, I'd want it to be with you. Your ideas are genius, you're an amazing listener, and I can only hope I get to work on more books with you in the future. And to Lizzie Vaughan, who took on the huge task of bringing these words to life through design—your flexibility, aesthetic, and raw talent made this book what it is. Also, thanks to Sarah Billingsley at Chronicle for believing in the book and seeing it through to the end and Vanessa Dina for putting the design on the right track!

Finally, but definitely NOT least, to my literary agent Myrsini Stephanides, who took a chance on an unknown kid—she has been my rock in this process and I love her like a sister.

INDEX

C

Cabernet Franc, 67, 108, 109, 110, 153, 154–55, 285, 292
Cabernet Sauvignon, 40, 67, 85, 108, 109, 110, 114–15, 240, 243, 247, 248, 249, 263, 290
Cachapoal Valley, 249
Cahors, 171
Cairanne, 166
California
  Central Valley, 276
  history of wine in, 261–62
  Mendocino County, 270–71
  Monterey, 271–72
  Napa, 263–65, 266
  Paso Robles, 272–74
  San Luis Obispo County, 272
  Santa Barbara County, 274–76
  Sierra Foothills, 276–77
  Sonoma, 263, 265–69
Calistoga, 264–65
Campania, 204–6
Campi Flegrei, 205
Canada, 90, 258–60
Canon-Fronsac, 113, 117
Carmel Valley, 271
Carménère, 247, 248, 292
Carricante, 208
Casablanca, 247–48
Cassis, 159
Catarratto, 208
Cava, 220–21
cement eggs, 53
Central Otago, 252–53
Central Valley (California), 276
Cerasuolo di Vittoria, 208
Chablis, 119, 120, 126–27, 337
Chalk Hill, 268
Chalone, 271
Chambolle-Musigny, 129, 337
Champagne
  grand and premier cru, 139
  history of, 143–46
  production of, 54, 140–42
  styles of, 146
  sugar levels of, 141
  terroir and, 137–39
  types of, 142–43
chaptalization, 50
Chardonnay, 68, 85, 120, 140, 240, 247, 263, 293
Charlottesville, 285
Chassagne-Montrachet, 132, 336
Château d'Yquem, 113
Château Grillet, 162

Châteauneuf-du-Pape, 164–65
Chaume, 154
Chehalem Mountains, 279
Chenin Blanc, 68, 85, 154, 155–56, 294
Chianti, 199–200
Chignin-Bergeron, 174
Chile, 90, 245–50
Chinon, 155–56
Clare Valley, 242
classification systems, 89–93
climate, 47, 85–86
climats, 123
clones, 45–46
Coda di Volpe Bianca, 206
Colchagua Valley, 249
Columbia Valley, 280–84
Condrieu, 161–62
Conegliano, 197
Constantia, 256
Coombsville, 265
Coonawarra, 242–43
Corbières, 149
Cornas, 162
Corsica, 173
Costières de Nîmes, 167–68
Coteaux du Layon, 154
Coteaux Varois en Provence, 158
Côte Chalonnaise, 120, 133–34
Côte de Beaune, 120, 130–33
Côte de Nuits, 120, 128–30
Côte d'Or, 120, 127–28
Côte Rôtie, 161
Côtes d'Aix-en-Provence, 158
Côtes de Provence, 158
Côtes du Rhône, 162, 167
Crémant d'Alsace, 105, 107
Crémant de Jura, 173
Crémant de Loire, 155
Croatia, 227–28
Crozes-Hermitage, 162
Cru Bourgeois, 112, 113, 114

D

Dão, 211, 216
Debit, 228
descriptive words
  acidic, 30–31
  astringent, 33–34
  attack, 29
  austere, 31
  balance, 38
  barnyard, 26
  big, 36
  bitter, 34

Viognier, 68, 85, 161, 294
Virginia, 284–85
volatile acidity, 24
Volnay, 132
Vosne-Romanée, 129, 337
Vougeot, 129, 337
Vouvray, 156

W

Wachau, 99
Wahluke Slope, 282
Wairau Valley, 252
Walker Bay, 256–57
Walla Walla, 283–84
Washington State, 279–84
Welschriesling, 227
Wild Horse Valley, 265
Willamette Valley, 278–79
wine. *See also* flavor; tasting; *individual locations and wines*
    acidic, 30–31, 300, 308
    aging, 21, 71, 74–76, 87, 111, 221, 325
    alcohol content of, 34–36, 305
    clarity of, 18–19
    classification systems for, 89–93
    climate and, 85–86
    color of, 19–21
    corked, 23
    geography and, 63, 80
    as gift, 324–25
    naming, 81–84
    in Old World vs. New World, 80–84, 89–93, 236–37
    pairing food and, 298–306, 308–13
    secret to understanding, 13
    skunked, 18–19
    structure of, 30–38
    sugar in, 20–21, 36–37, 141
    technology and, 87
    temperature of, 302, 335
    terroir and, 44–45, 64–65
    weather and, 88
    weight of, 299
wineglasses, 17
wine lists, choosing from, 317, 325–29
winemaker, role of, 57–59
winemaking
    fortified wine, 55
    late harvest/botrytized wine, 55, 57
    red wine, 52–54
    rosé wine, 51–52
    sparkling wine, 54–55

    terminology of, 44–48
    white wine, 49–51
wine stores
    choosing, 318–20
    shopping at, 320–25
Woodinville, 281
Württemberg, 185

X

Xinomavro, 188–89

Y

Yakima Valley, 282–83
Yamhill-Carlton, 279
Yarra Valley, 243
yeast, 20, 50, 69–70, 87
Yecla, 224
Yountville, 265

Z

Zinfandel, 67, 85, 292
Žlahtina, 228
Zweigelt, 98